O N E

There are more and more food delivery services, which is really convenient. You could live indoors forever, but going outside is important.

—ONE

Manga creator ONE began *One-Punch Man* as a webcomic, which quickly went viral, garnering over 10 million hits. In addition to *One-Punch Man*, ONE writes and draws the series *Mob Psycho 100* and *Makai no Ossan*.

Y U S U K E M U R A T A

With the right training, you can bear twice as much weight after only one month.

—Yusuke Murata

A highly decorated and skilled artist best known for his work on *Eyeshield 21*, Yusuke Murata won the 122nd Hop Step Award (1995) for *Partner* and placed second in the 51st Akatsuka Award (1998) for *Samui Hanashi*.

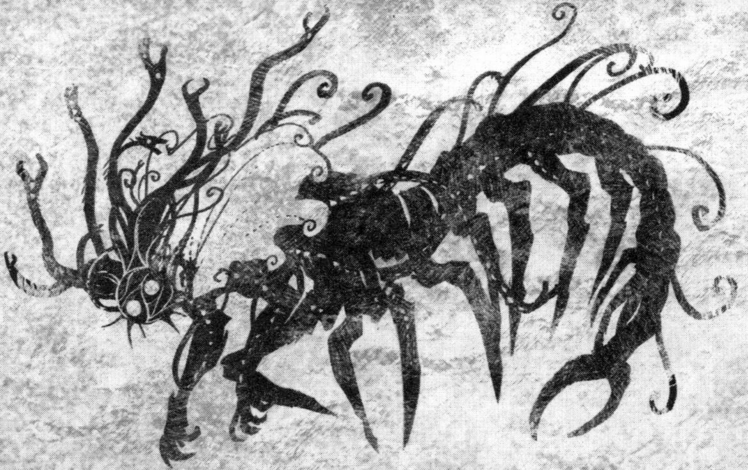

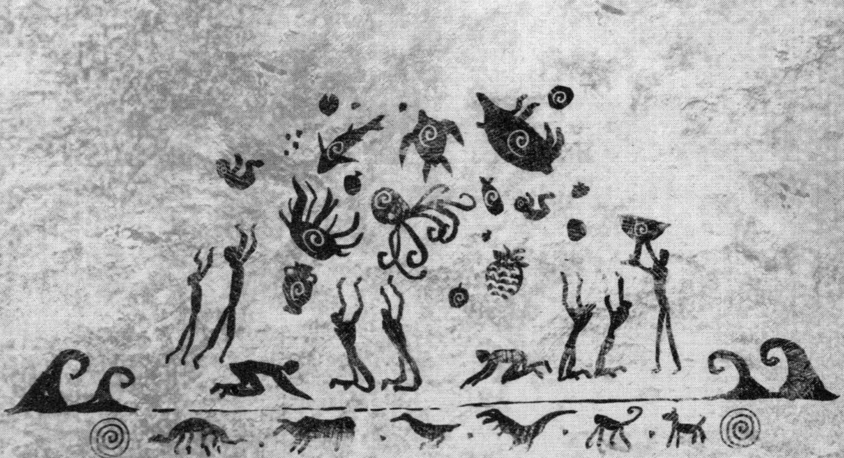

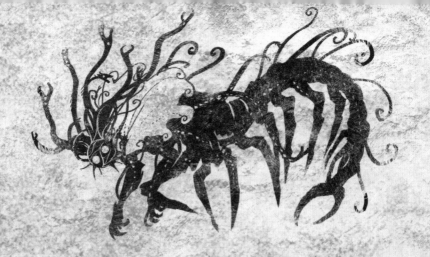

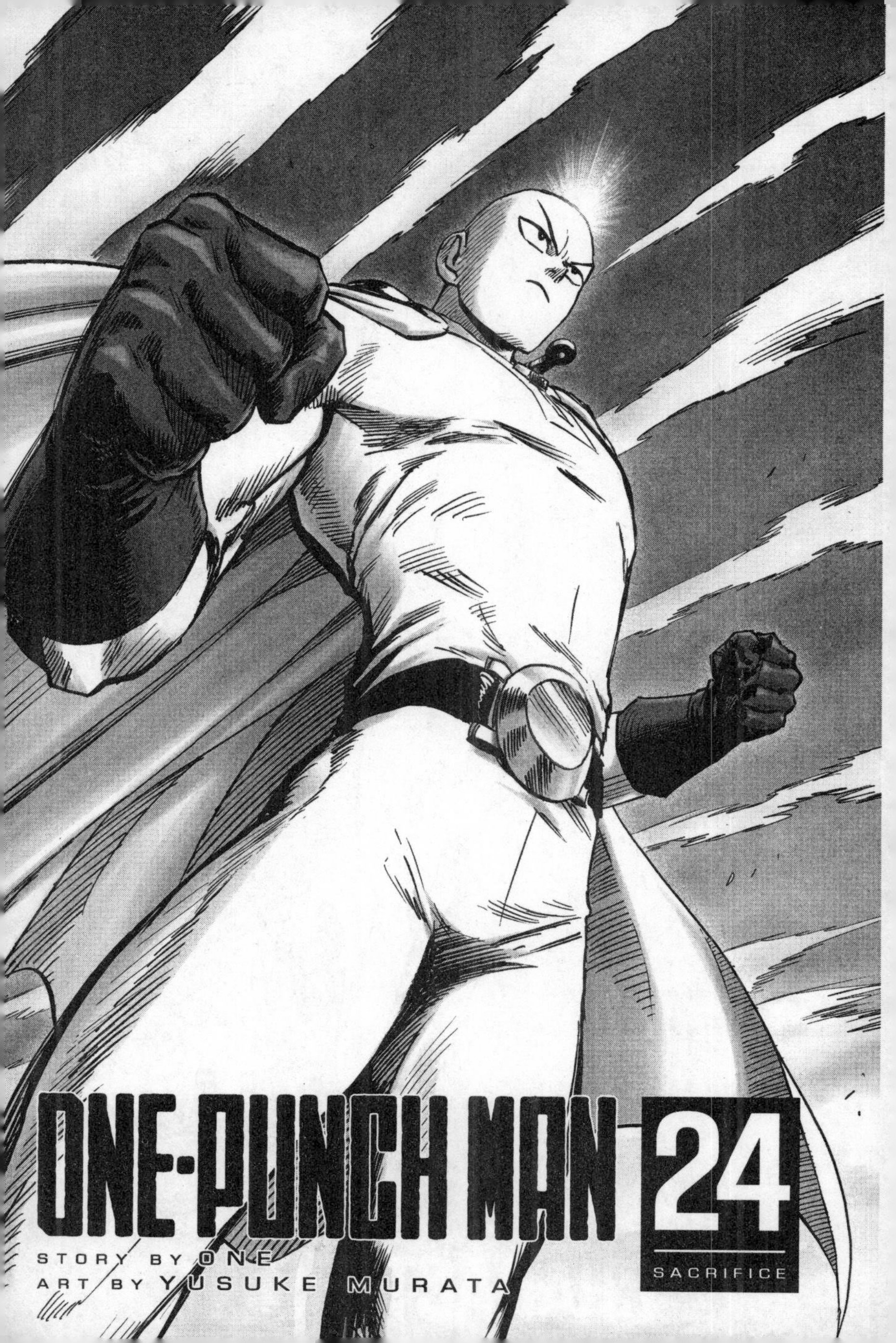

ONE-PUNCH MAN 24

SACRIFICE

STORY BY ONE
ART BY YUSUKE MURATA

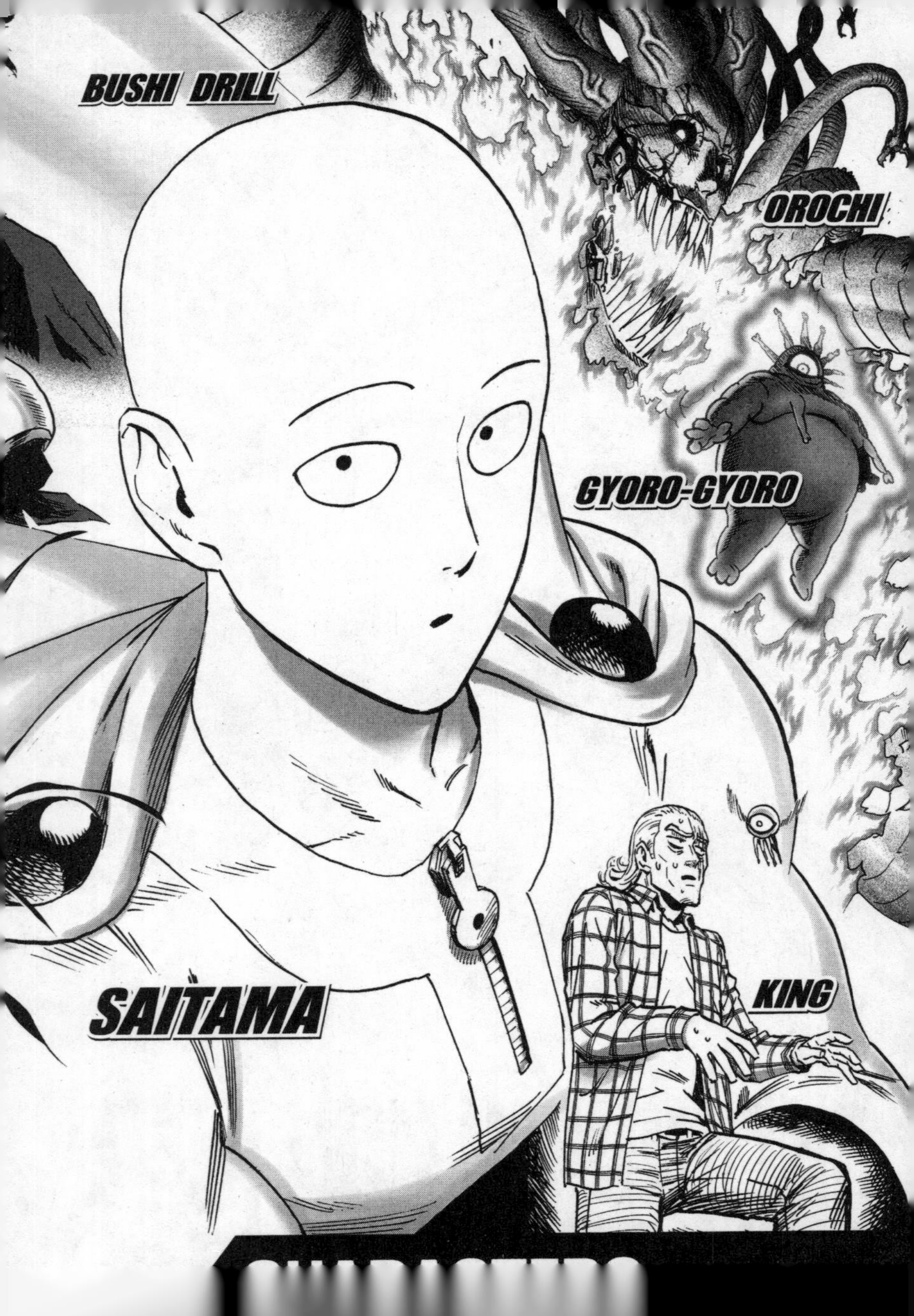
BUSHI DRILL
OROCHI
GYORO-GYORO
KING
SAITAMA

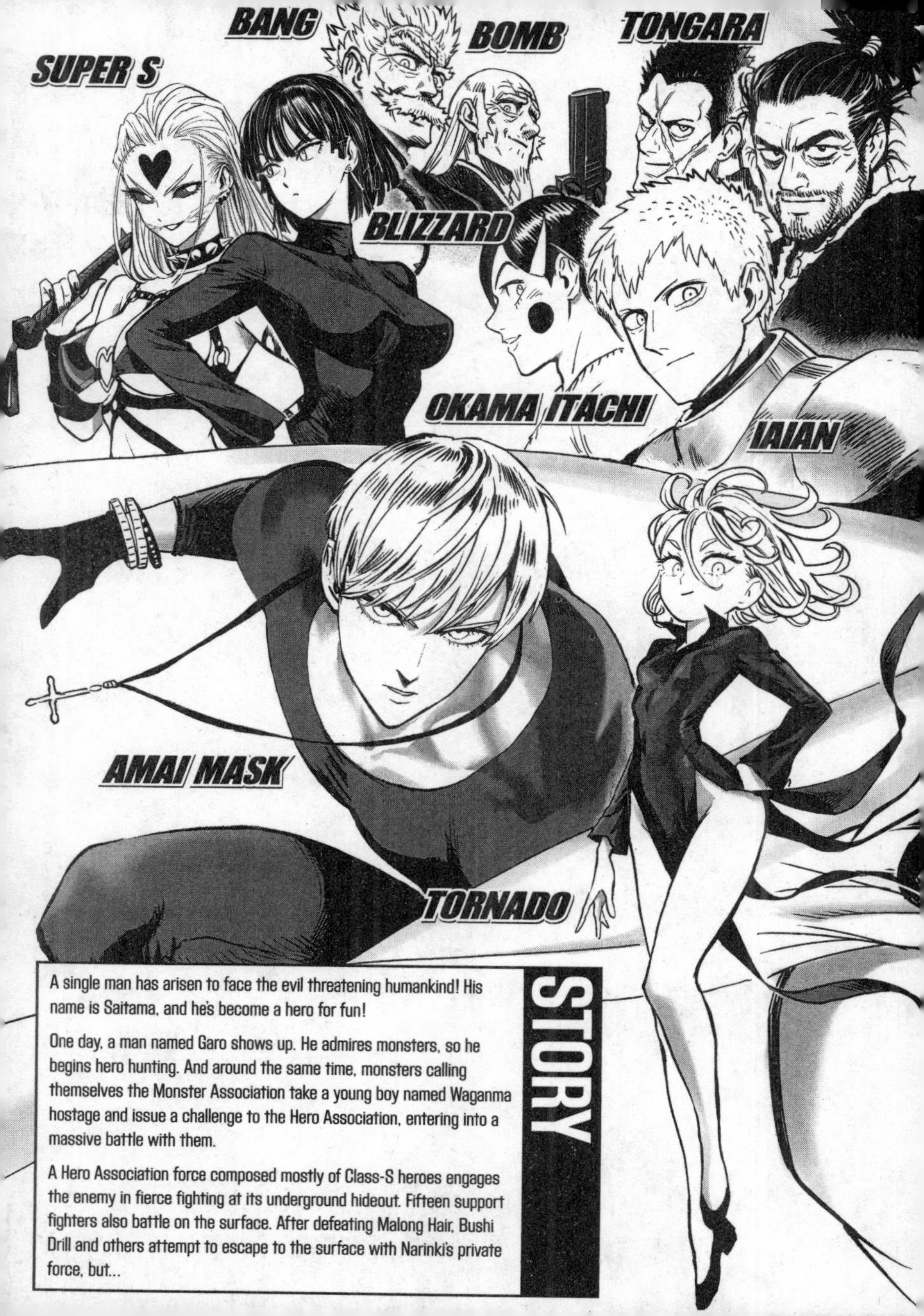
TONGARA
BOMB
BANG
SUPER S
BLIZZARD
OKAMA ITACHI
IAIAN
AMAI MASK
TORNADO

STORY

A single man has arisen to face the evil threatening humankind! His name is Saitama, and he's become a hero for fun!

One day, a man named Garo shows up. He admires monsters, so he begins hero hunting. And around the same time, monsters calling themselves the Monster Association take a young boy named Waganma hostage and issue a challenge to the Hero Association, entering into a massive battle with them.

A Hero Association force composed mostly of Class-S heroes engages the enemy in fierce fighting at its underground hideout. Fifteen support fighters also battle on the surface. After defeating Malong Hair, Bushi Drill and others attempt to escape to the surface with Narinki's private force, but...

CONTENTS

24

[SACRIFICE]

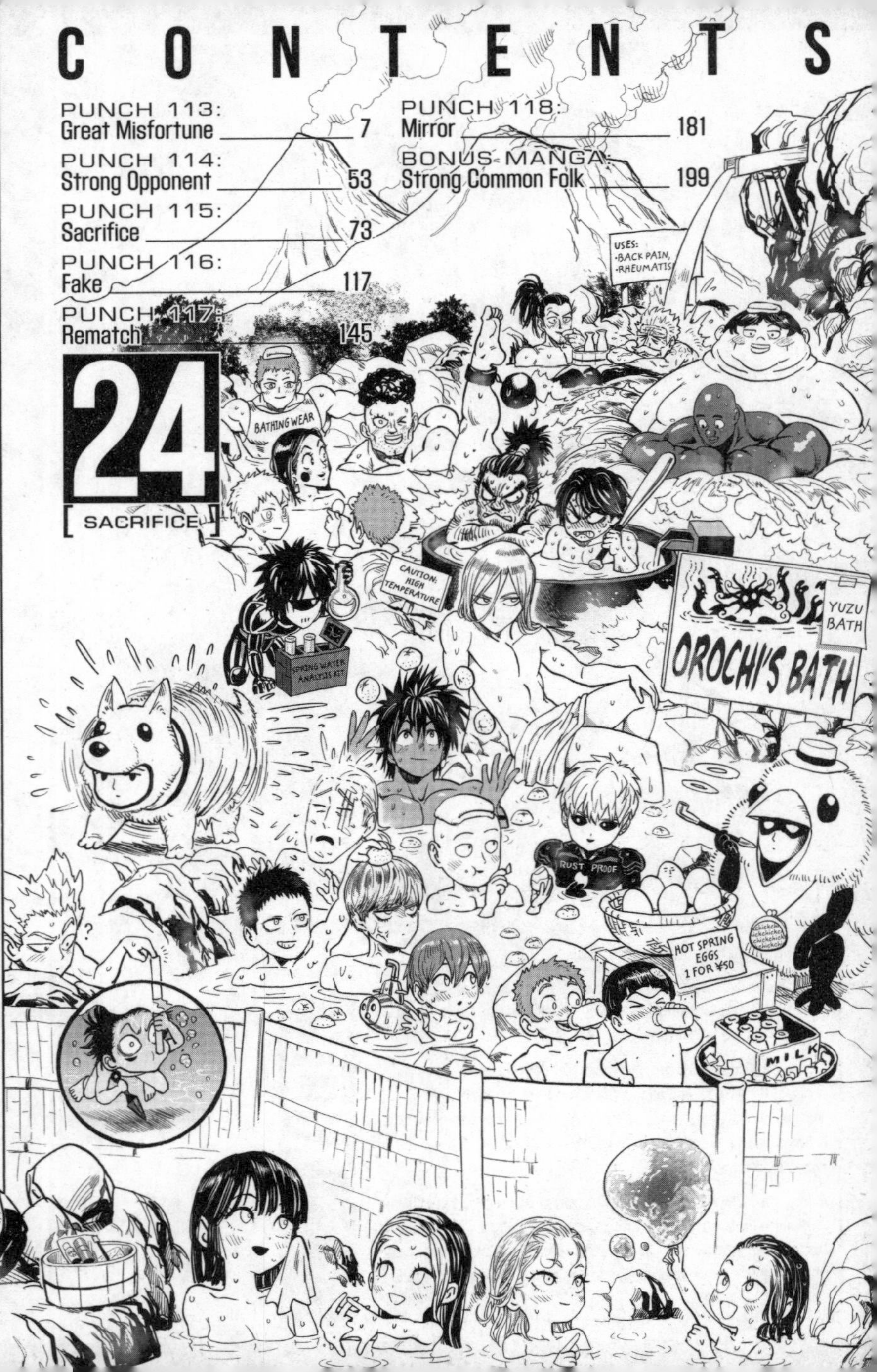

USES:
·BACK PAIN,
·RHEUMATIS
BATHING WEAR
CAUTION: HIGH TEMPERATURE
SPRING WATER ANALYSIS KIT
YUZU BATH
OROCHI'S BATH
RUST PROOF
HOT SPRING EGGS 1 FOR ¥50
MILK

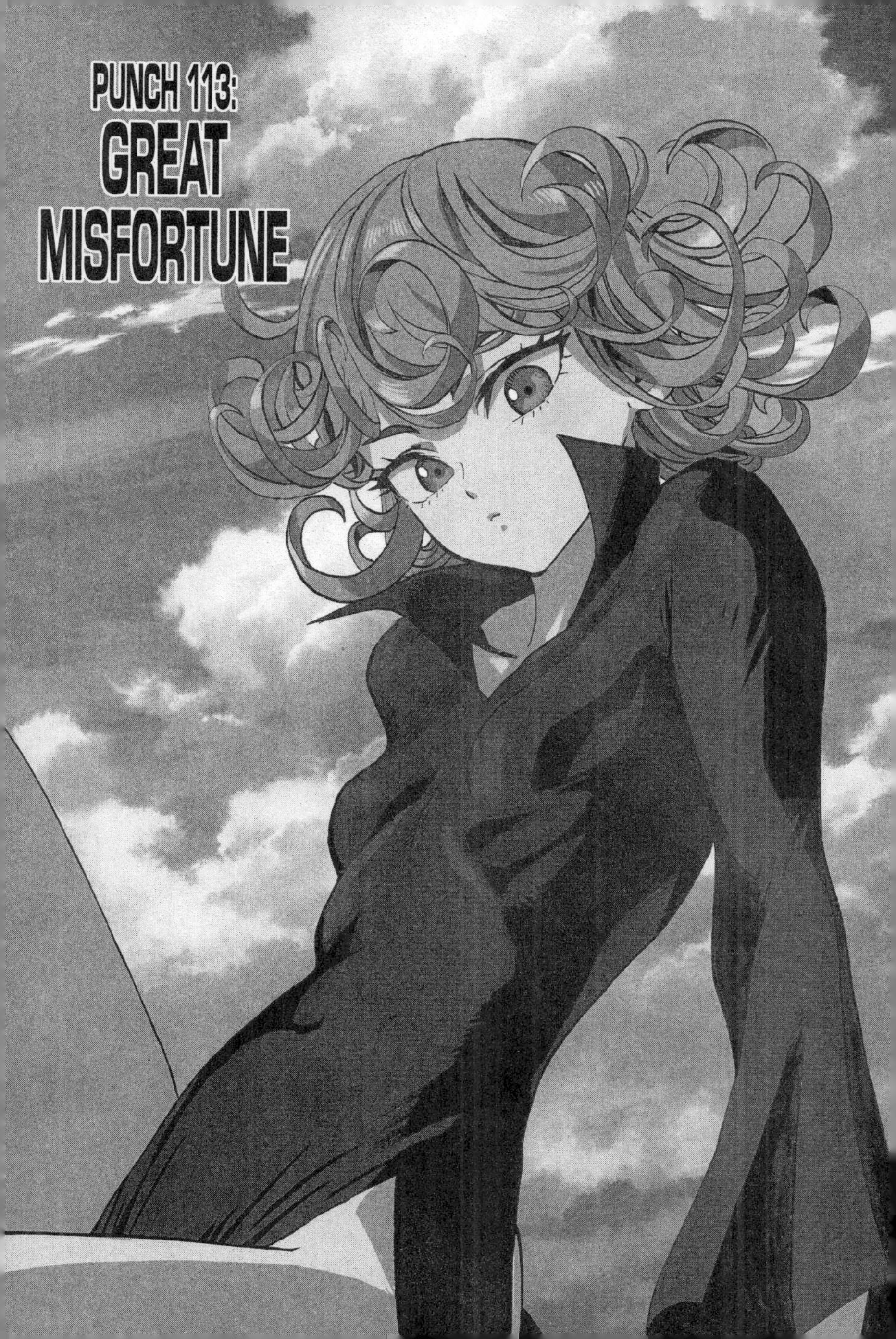
PUNCH 113:
GREAT MISFORTUNE

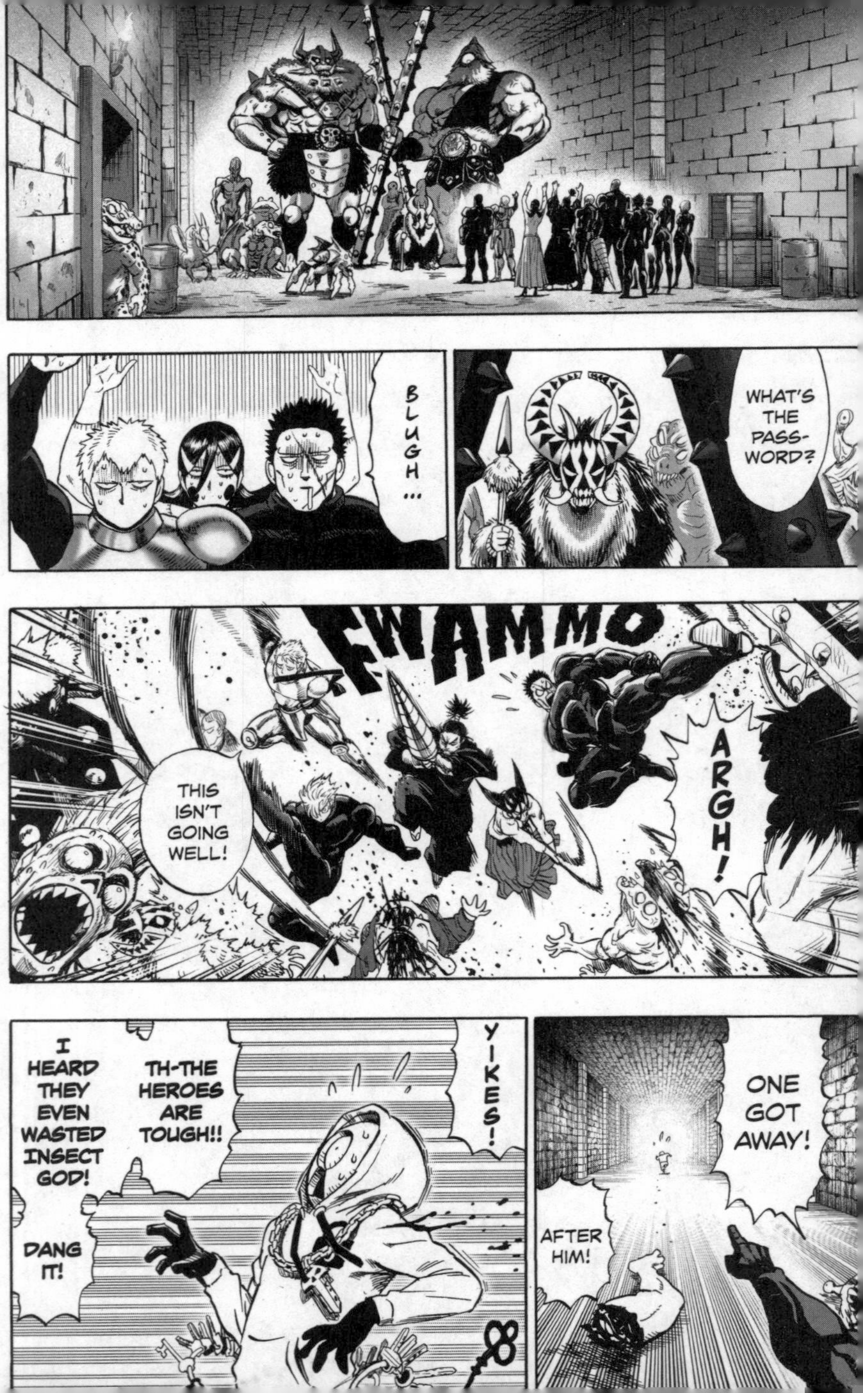
WHAT'S THE PASS-WORD?
BLUGH...
FWAMMO
ARGH!
THIS ISN'T GOING WELL!
ONE GOT AWAY!
AFTER HIM!
YIKES!
TH-THE HEROES ARE TOUGH!!
I HEARD THEY EVEN WASTED INSECT GOD!
DANG IT!

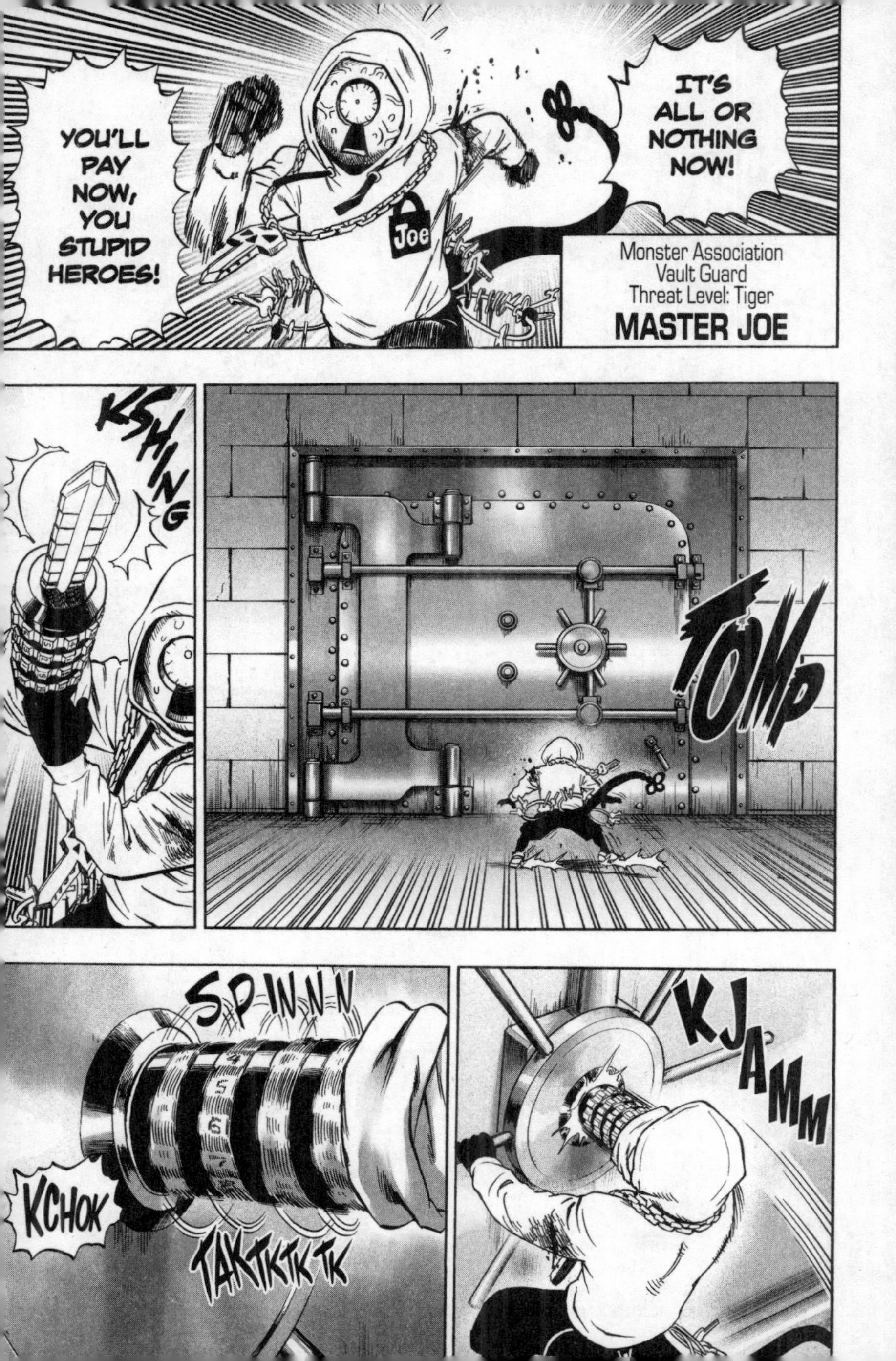
IT'S ALL OR NOTHING NOW!
Monster Association
Vault Guard
Threat Level: Tiger
MASTER JOE
YOU'LL PAY NOW, YOU STUPID HEROES!
TOMP
KSHING
KJAMM
SPINNN
KCHOK
TAKTIKTIK TK

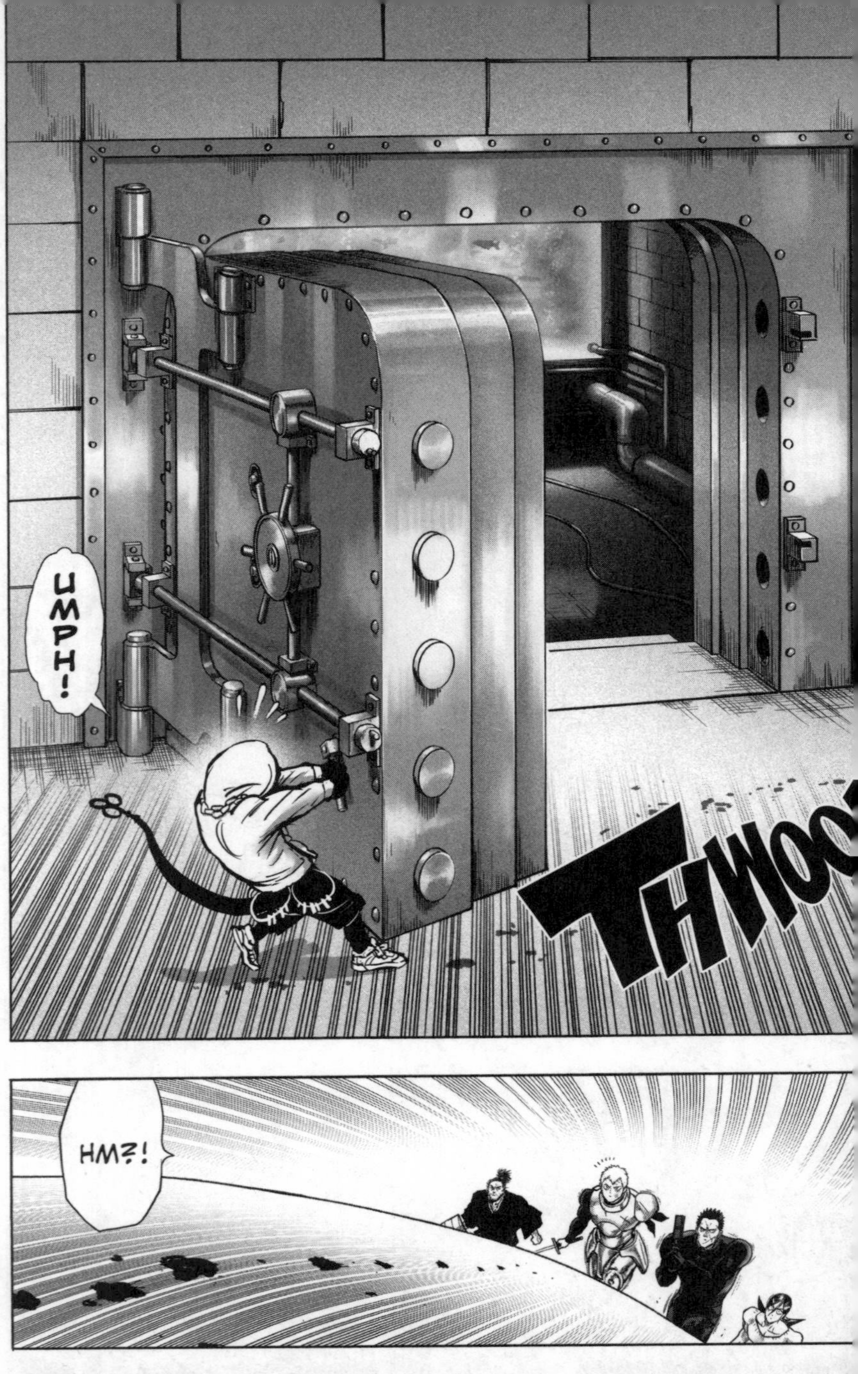
UMPH!
THWOO
HM?!

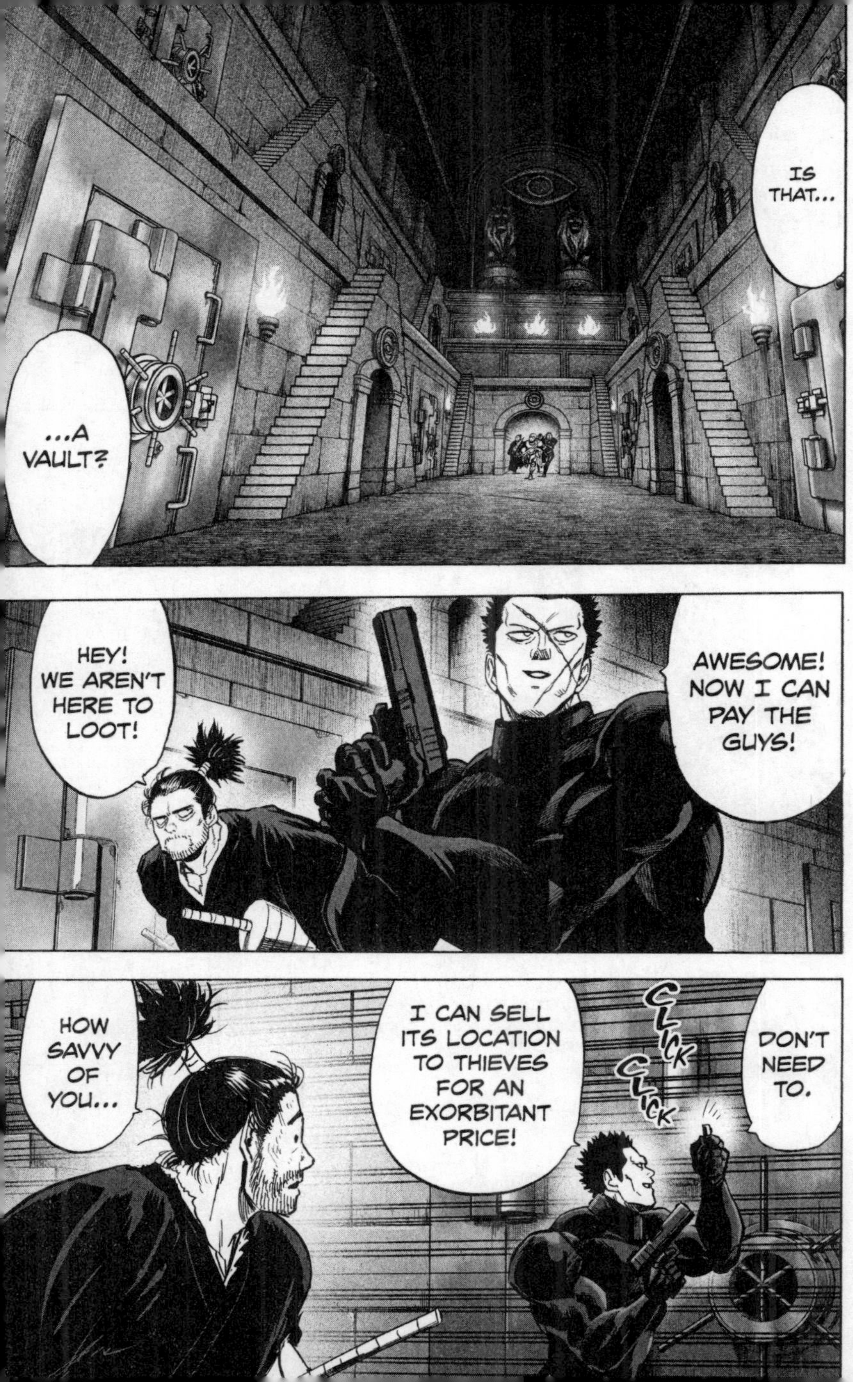
IS THAT...
...A VAULT?
AWESOME! NOW I CAN PAY THE GUYS!
HEY! WE AREN'T HERE TO LOOT!
DON'T NEED TO.
CLICK CLICK
I CAN SELL ITS LOCATION TO THIEVES FOR AN EXORBITANT PRICE!
HOW SAVVY OF YOU...

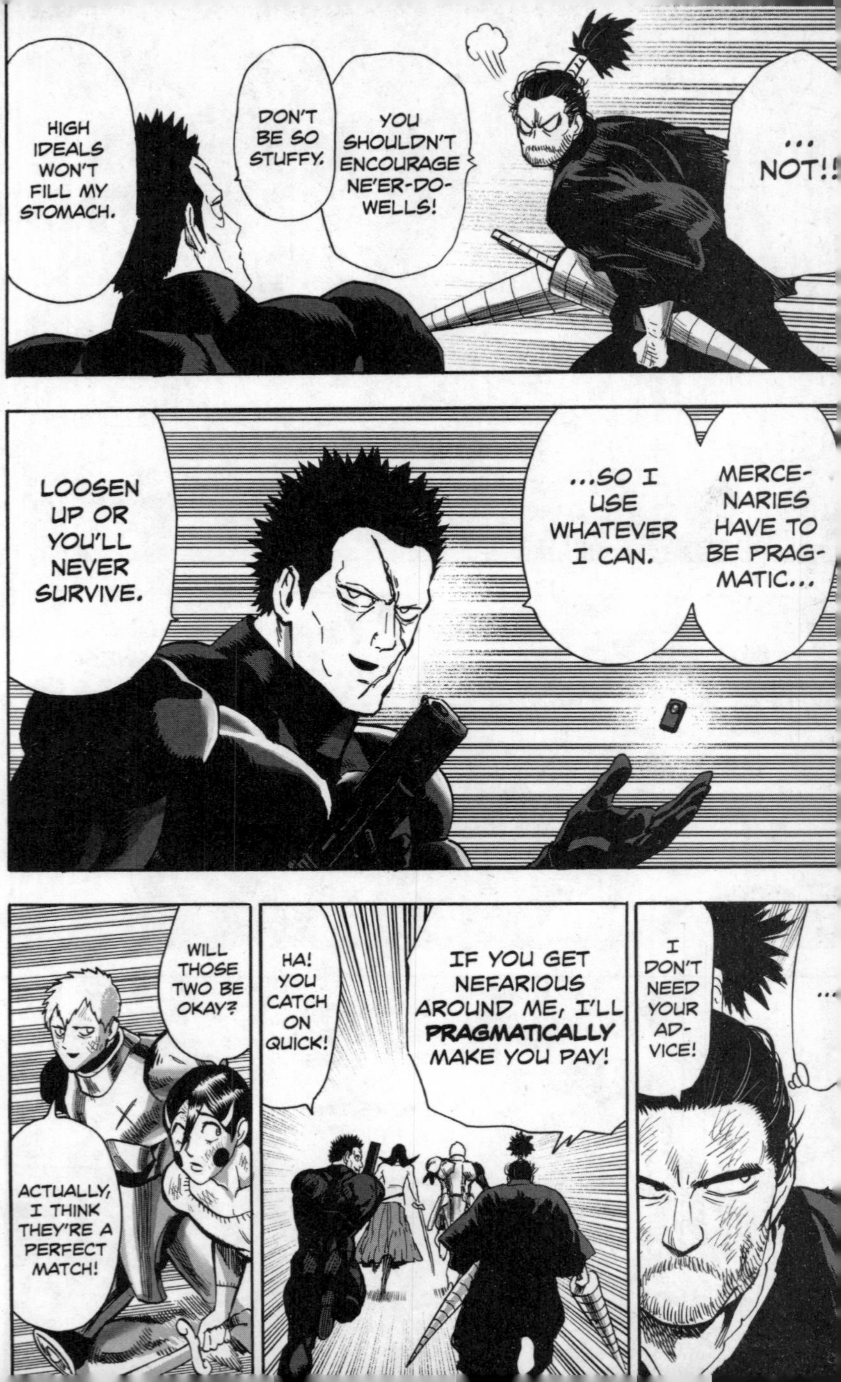
...NOT!!
YOU SHOULDN'T ENCOURAGE NE'ER-DO-WELLS!
DON'T BE SO STUFFY.
HIGH IDEALS WON'T FILL MY STOMACH.
MERCENARIES HAVE TO BE PRAGMATIC...
...SO I USE WHATEVER I CAN.
LOOSEN UP OR YOU'LL NEVER SURVIVE.
...
I DON'T NEED YOUR ADVICE!
IF YOU GET NEFARIOUS AROUND ME, I'LL **PRAGMATICALLY** MAKE YOU PAY!
HA! YOU CATCH ON QUICK!
WILL THOSE TWO BE OKAY?
ACTUALLY, I THINK THEY'RE A PERFECT MATCH!

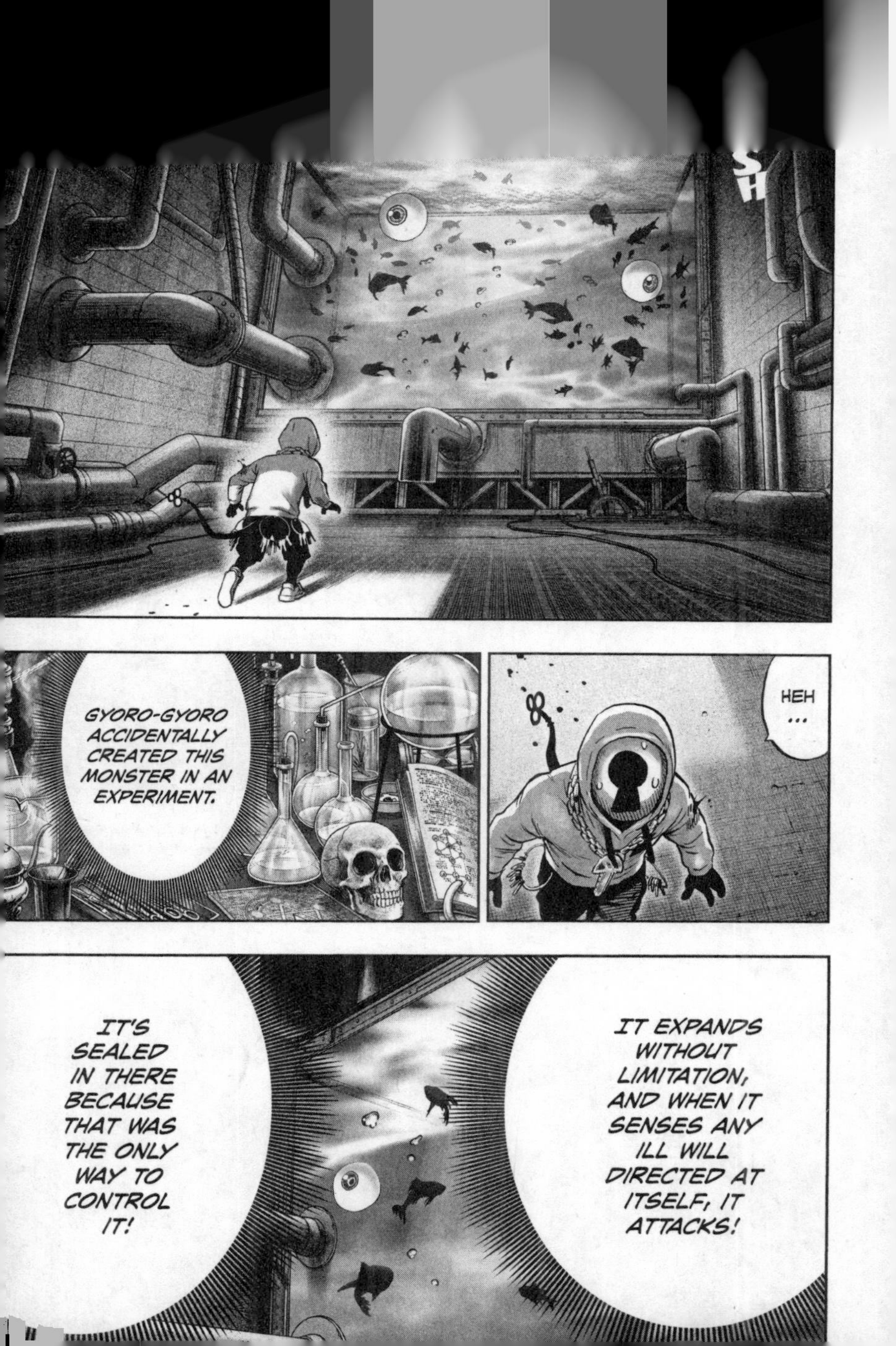
HEH ...
GYORO-GYORO ACCIDENTALLY CREATED THIS MONSTER IN AN EXPERIMENT.
IT EXPANDS WITHOUT LIMITATION, AND WHEN IT SENSES ANY ILL WILL DIRECTED AT ITSELF, IT ATTACKS!
IT'S SEALED IN THERE BECAUSE THAT WAS THE ONLY WAY TO CONTROL IT!

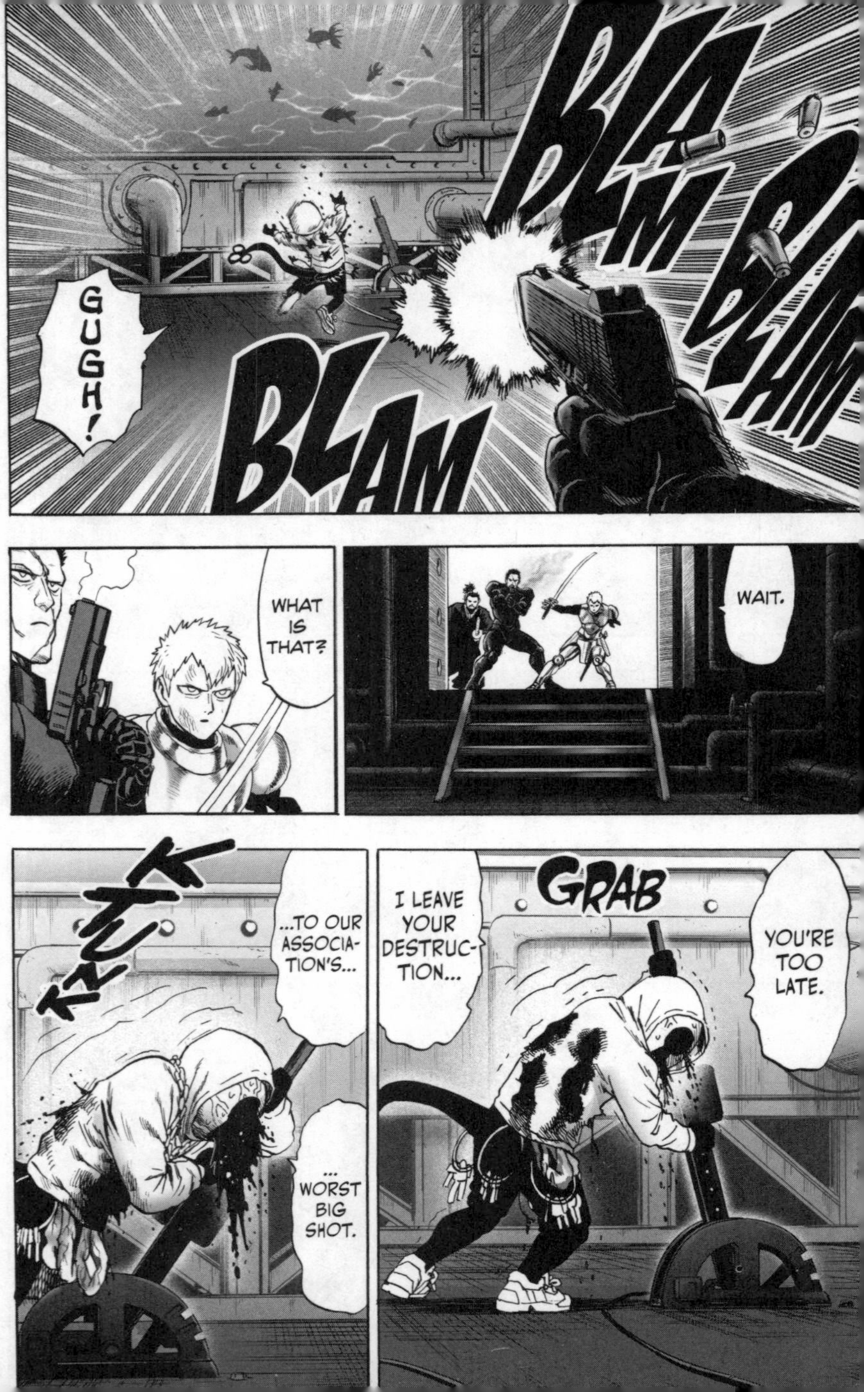
BLAM BLAM
BLAM
GUGH!
WAIT.
WHAT IS THAT?
YOU'RE TOO LATE.
GRAB
I LEAVE YOUR DESTRUCTION...
...TO OUR ASSOCIATION'S...
KTUNK
...WORST BIG SHOT.

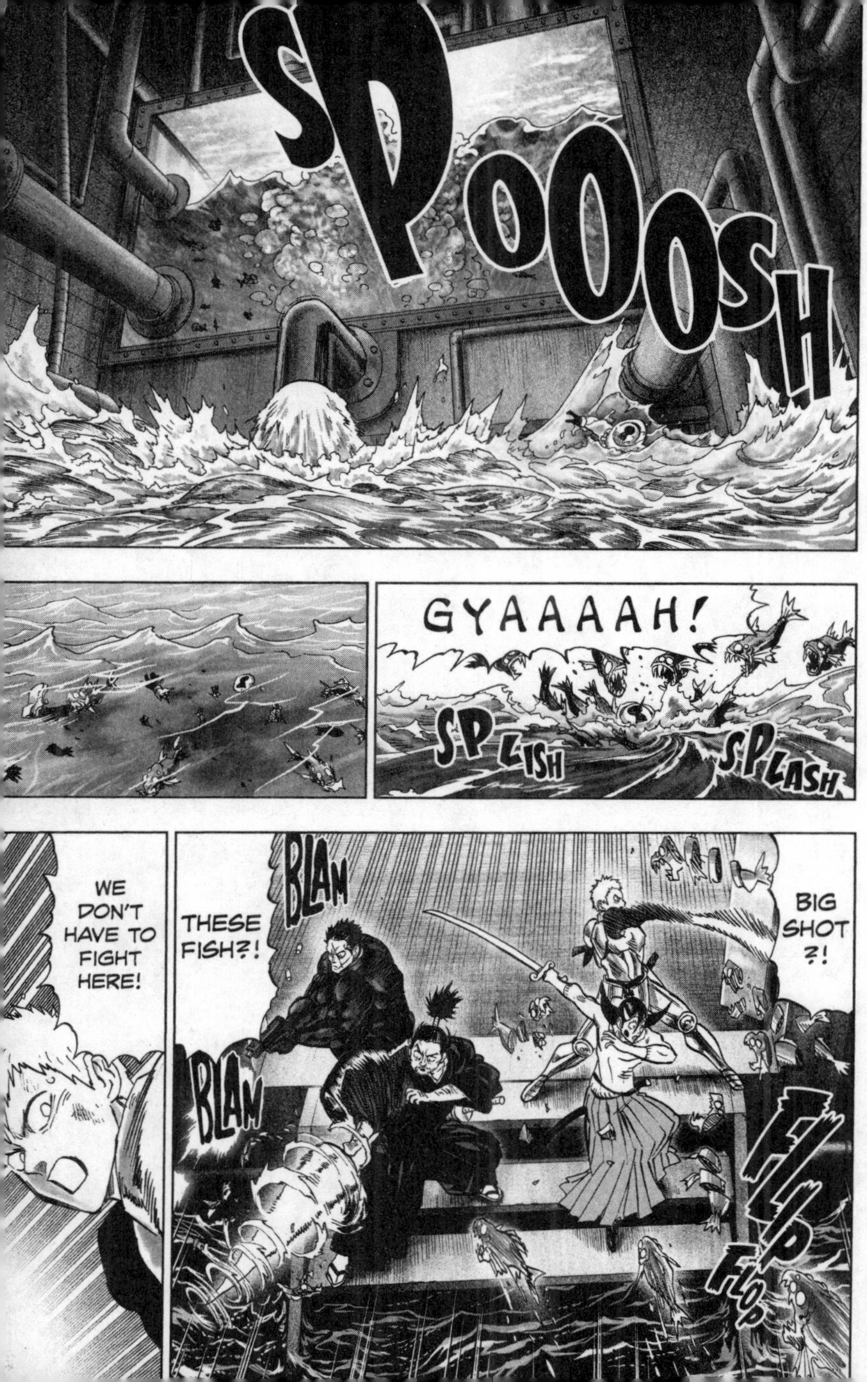
SPOOOSH
GYAAAAH!
SPLISH
SPLASH
BIG SHOT?!
BLAM
THESE FISH?!
BLAM
FLIP FLOP
WE DON'T HAVE TO FIGHT HERE!

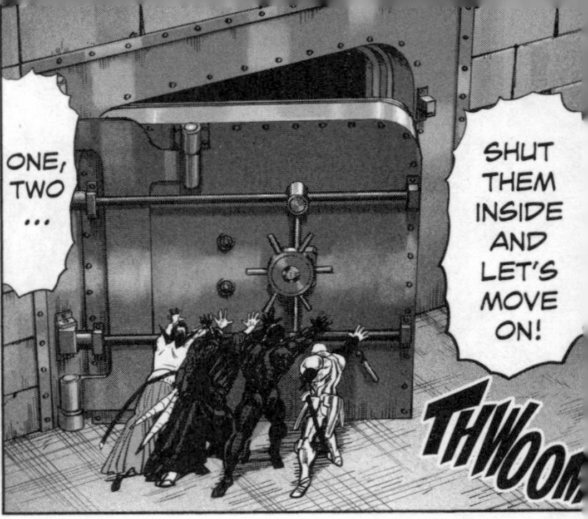
SHUT THEM INSIDE AND LET'S MOVE ON!
ONE, TWO ...
THWOOM
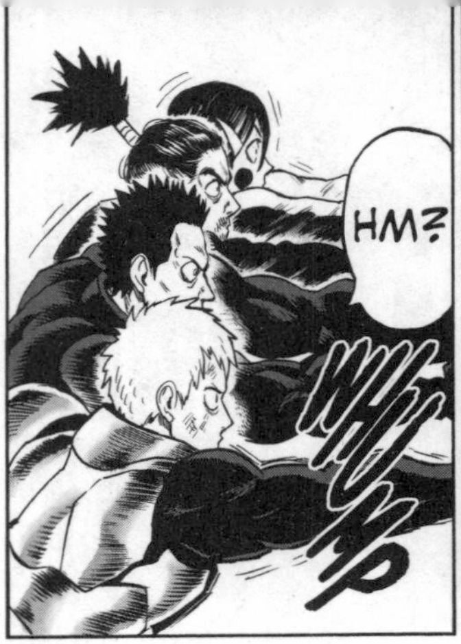
HM?
WHUMP
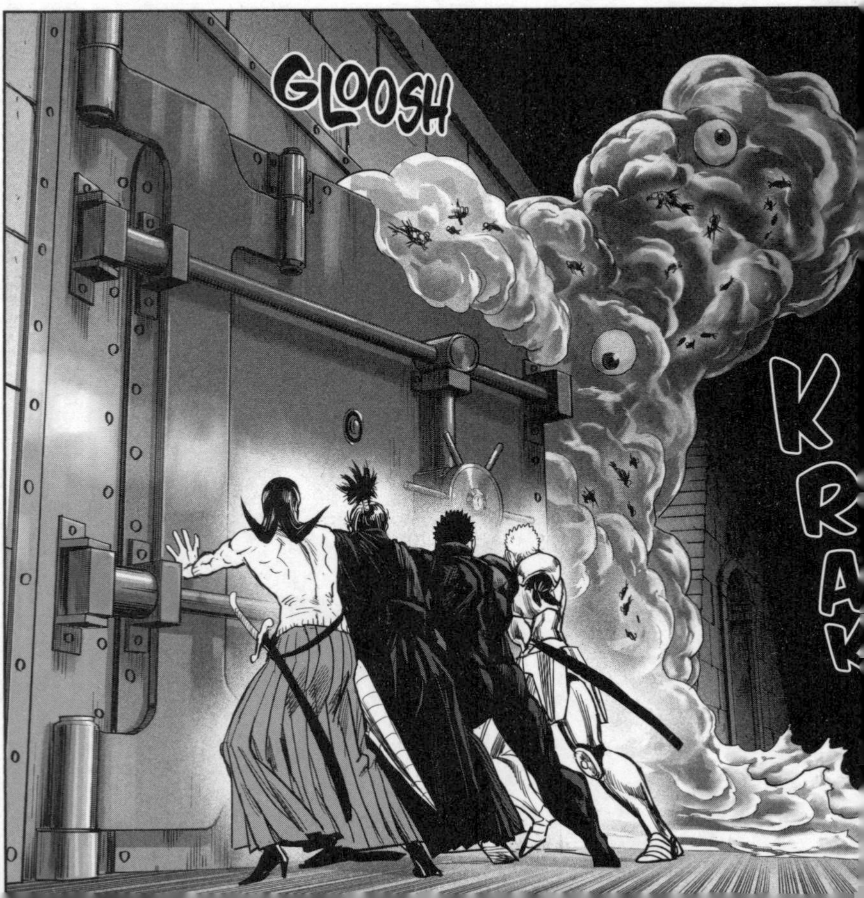
KRAK
GLOOSH

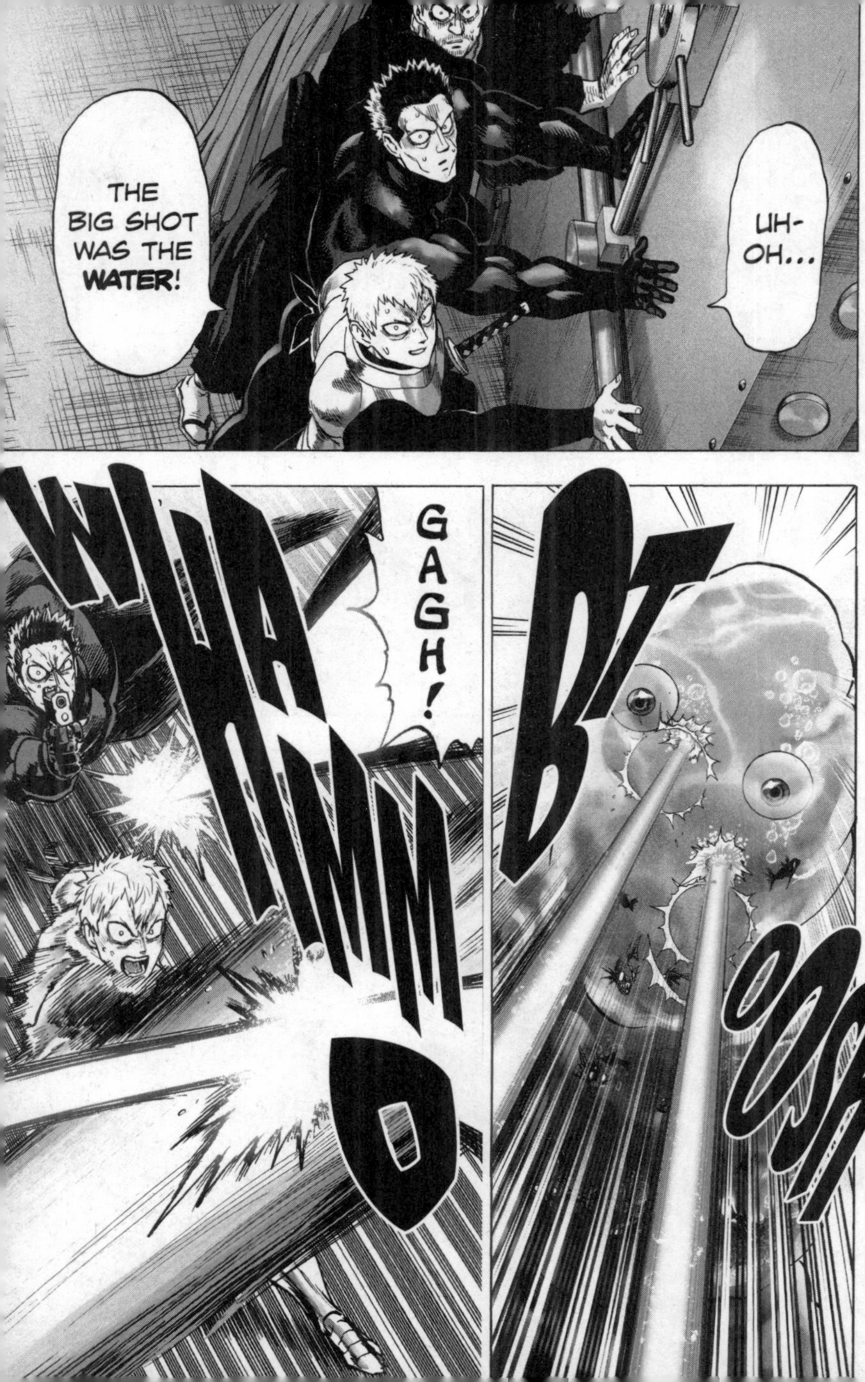
UH-OH...
THE BIG SHOT WAS THE WATER!
BOOSH
GAGH!
WHAMMM!

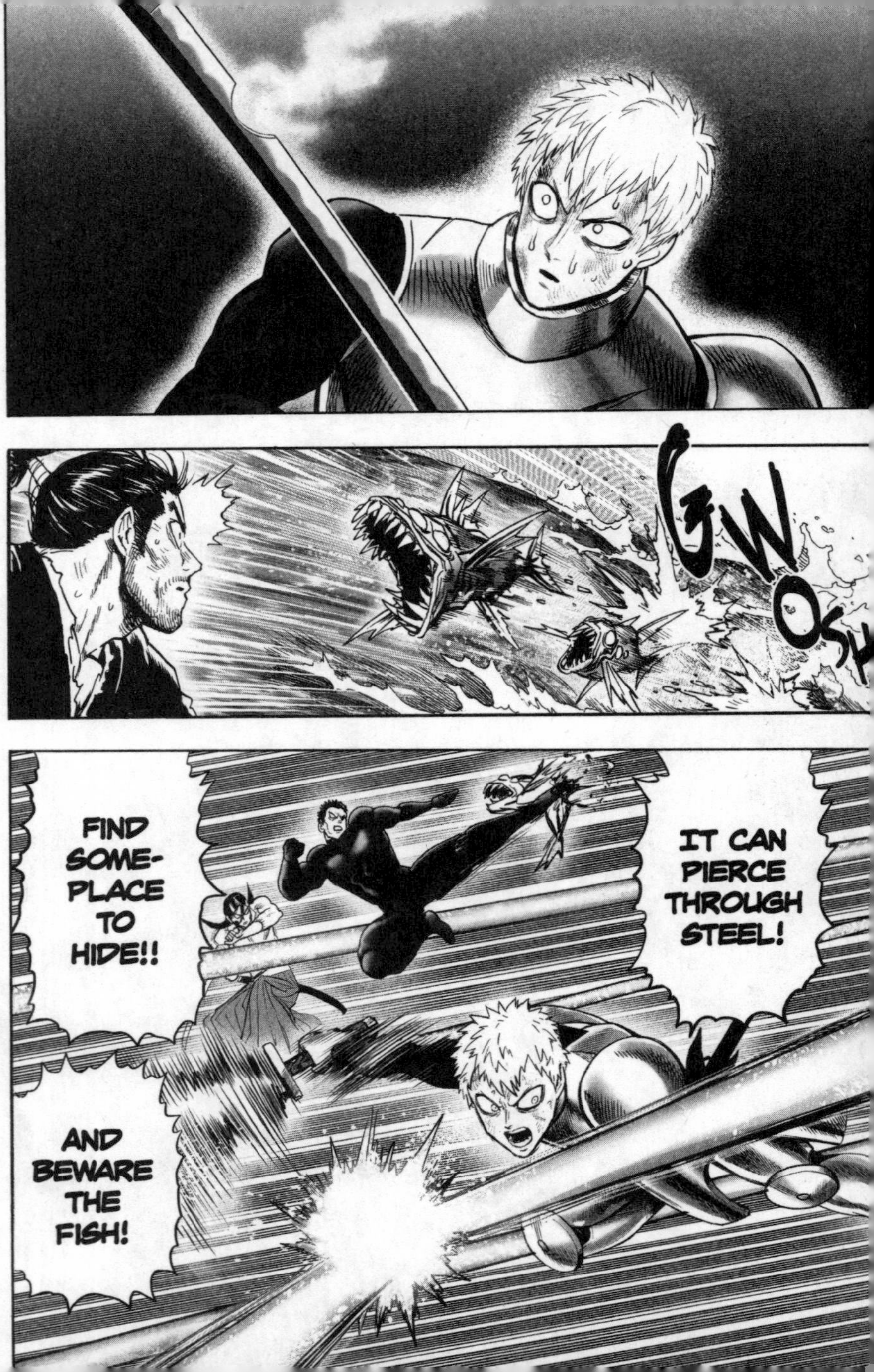
GWOSH
IT CAN PIERCE THROUGH STEEL!
FIND SOME-PLACE TO HIDE!!
AND BEWARE THE FISH!

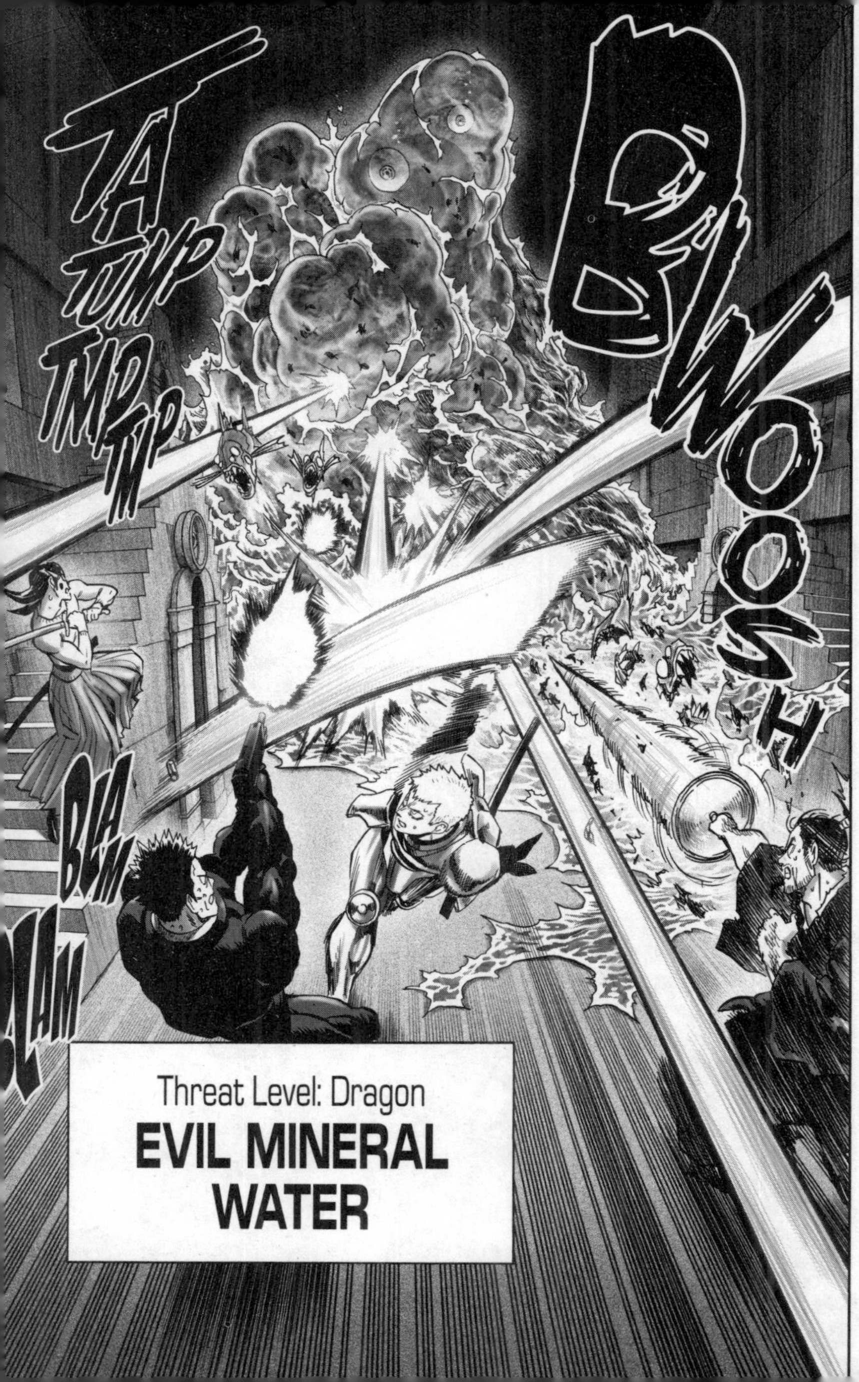
BWOOSH
TA TUMP TMP TMP
BLA
BLAM
BLAM
Threat Level: Dragon
EVIL MINERAL WATER

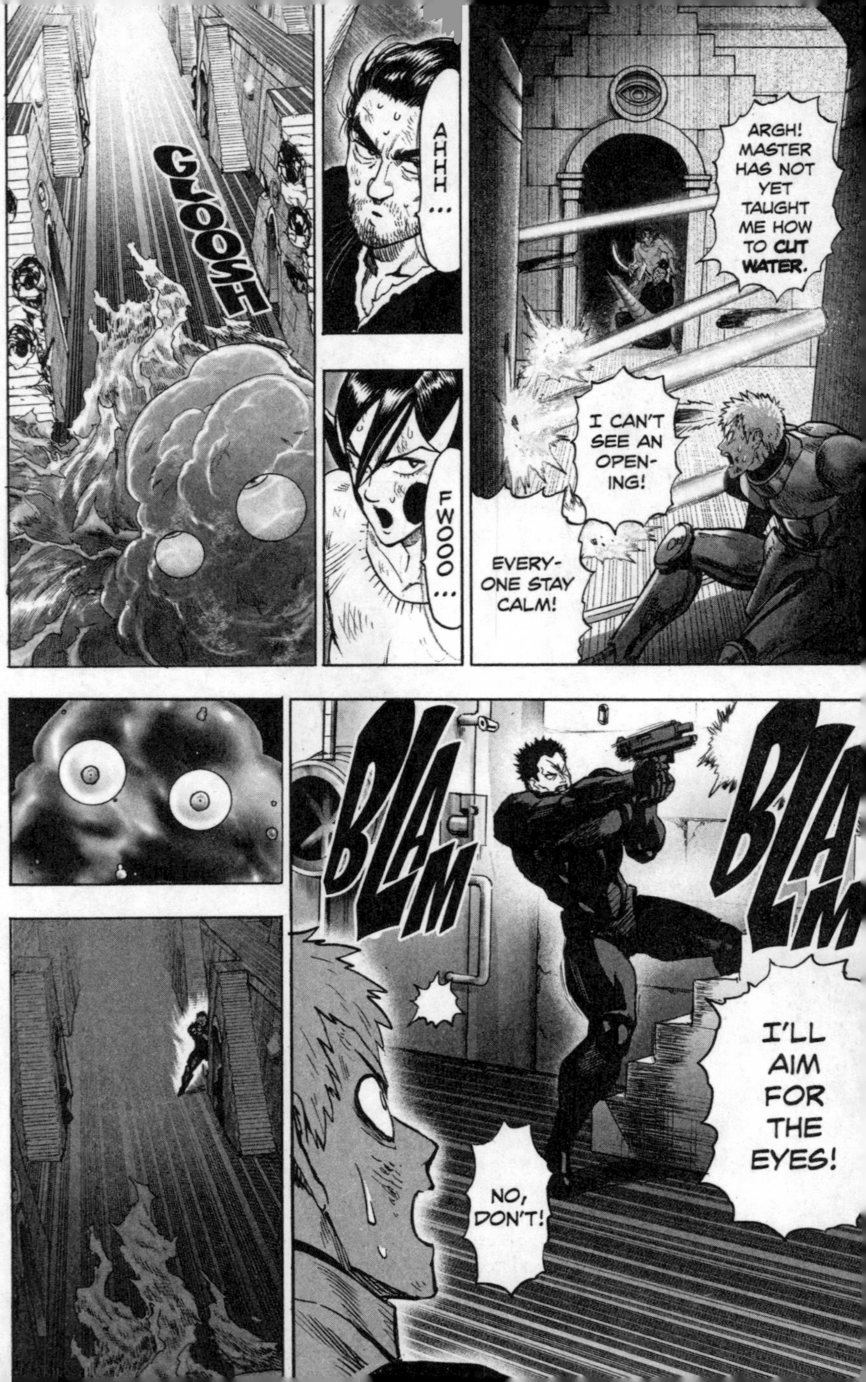
ARGH! MASTER HAS NOT YET TAUGHT ME HOW TO CUT WATER.
I CAN'T SEE AN OPENING!
EVERYONE STAY CALM!
AHHH...
FWOOO...
GLOOSH
BLAM
BLAM
I'LL AIM FOR THE EYES!
NO, DON'T!

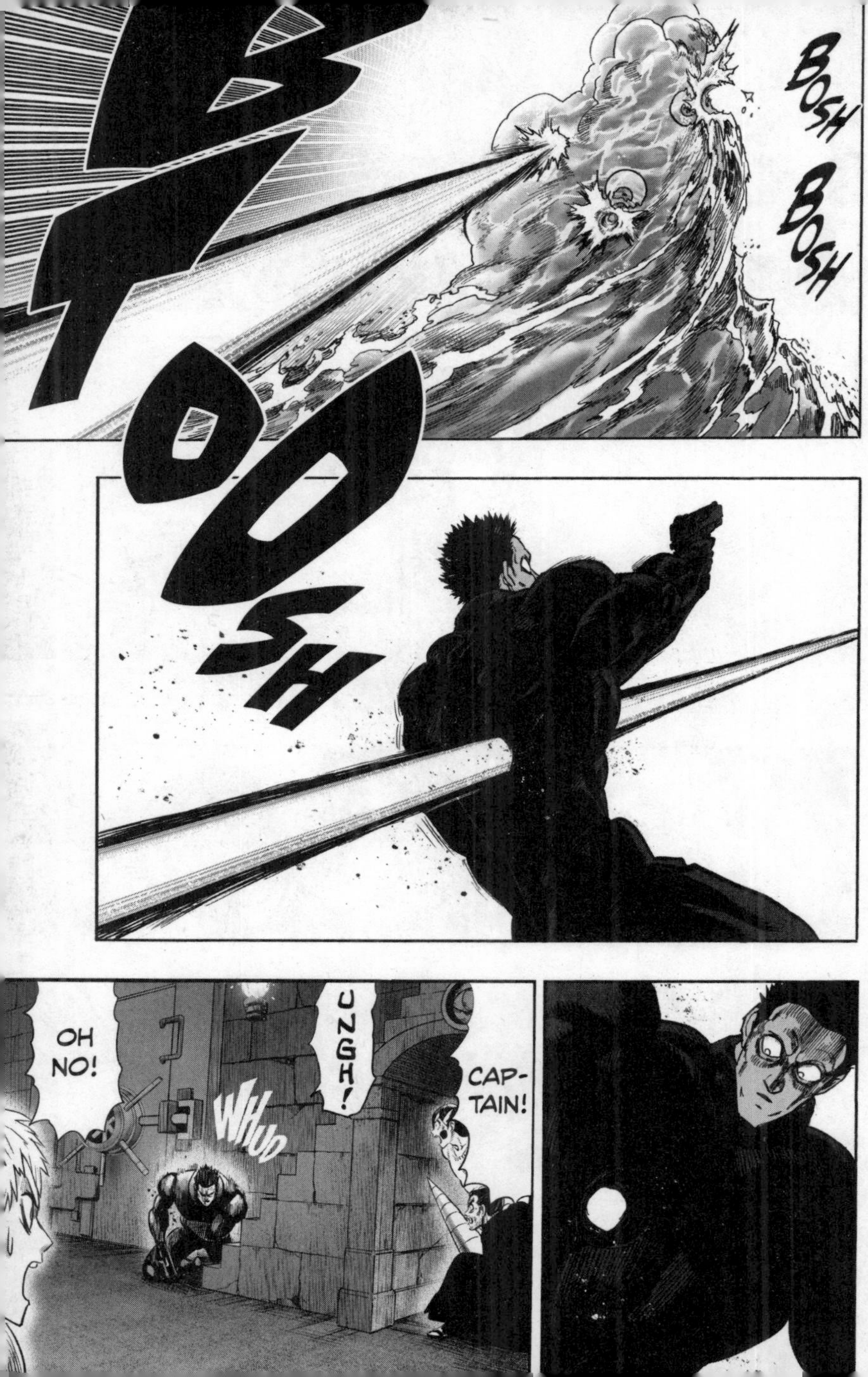
BOSH BOSH
CAP-TAIN!
UNGH!
WHUD
OH NO!

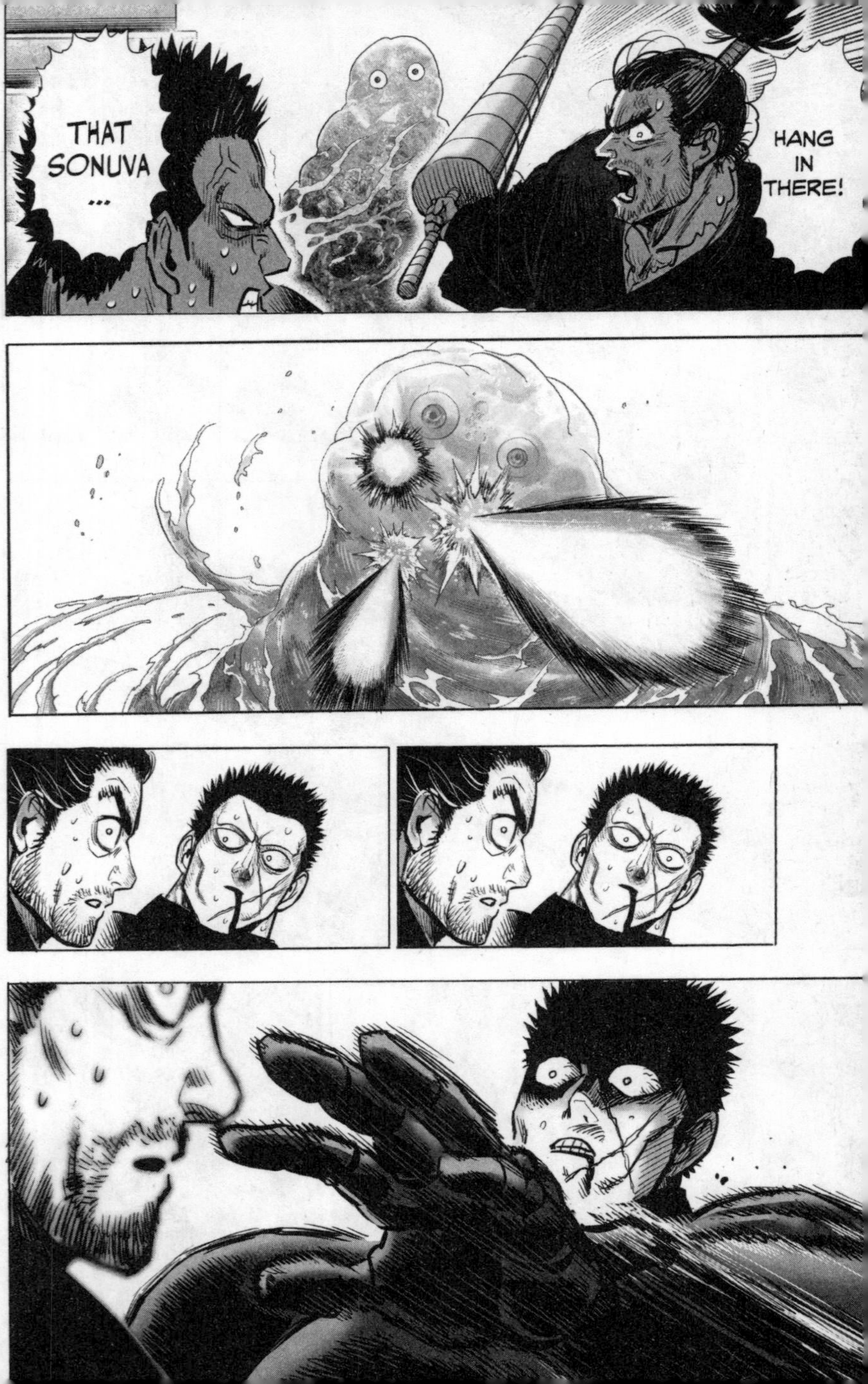
HANG IN THERE!
THAT SONUVA ...

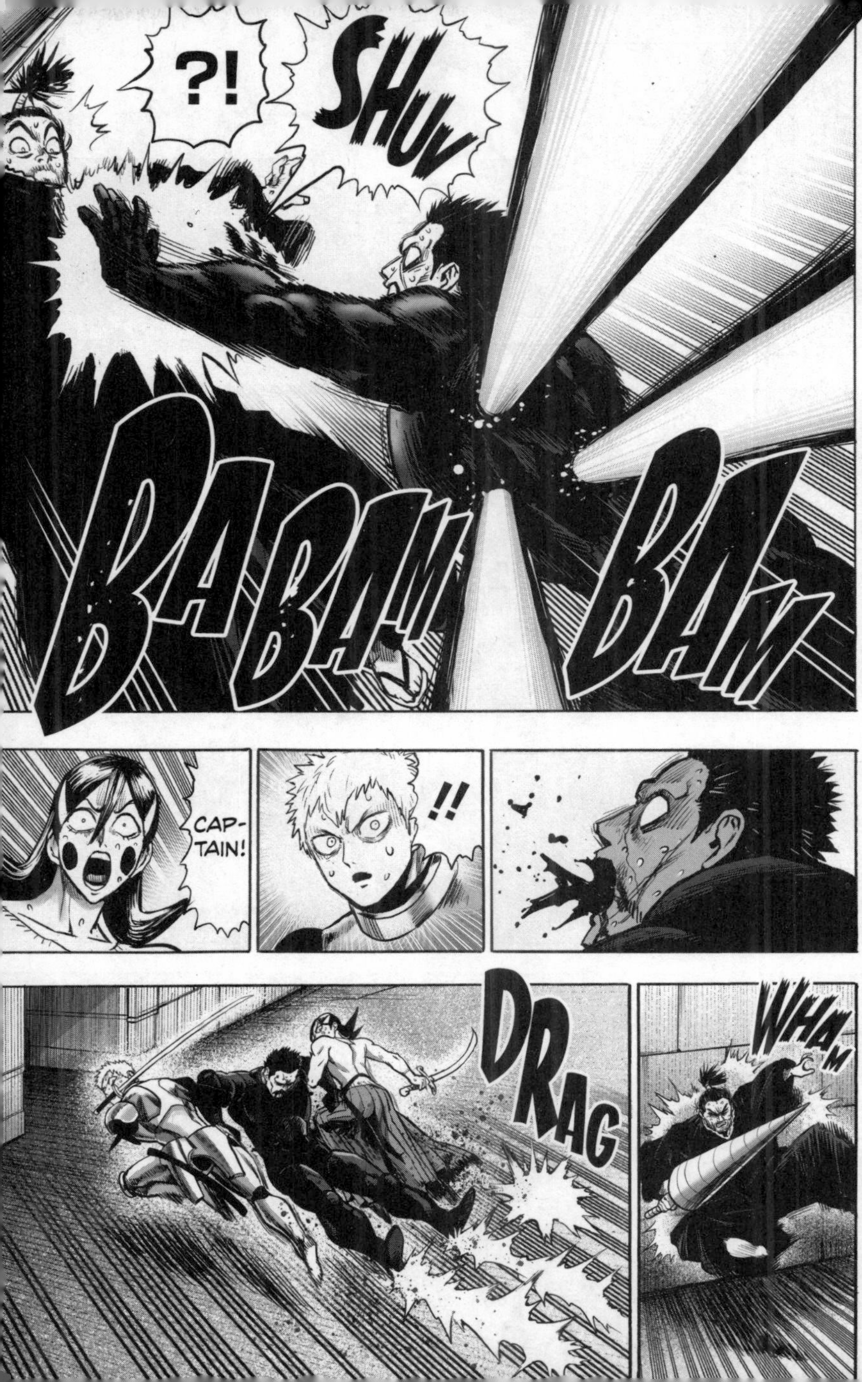
SHUV
?!
BABAM BAM
!!
CAP-TAIN!
WHAM
DRAG

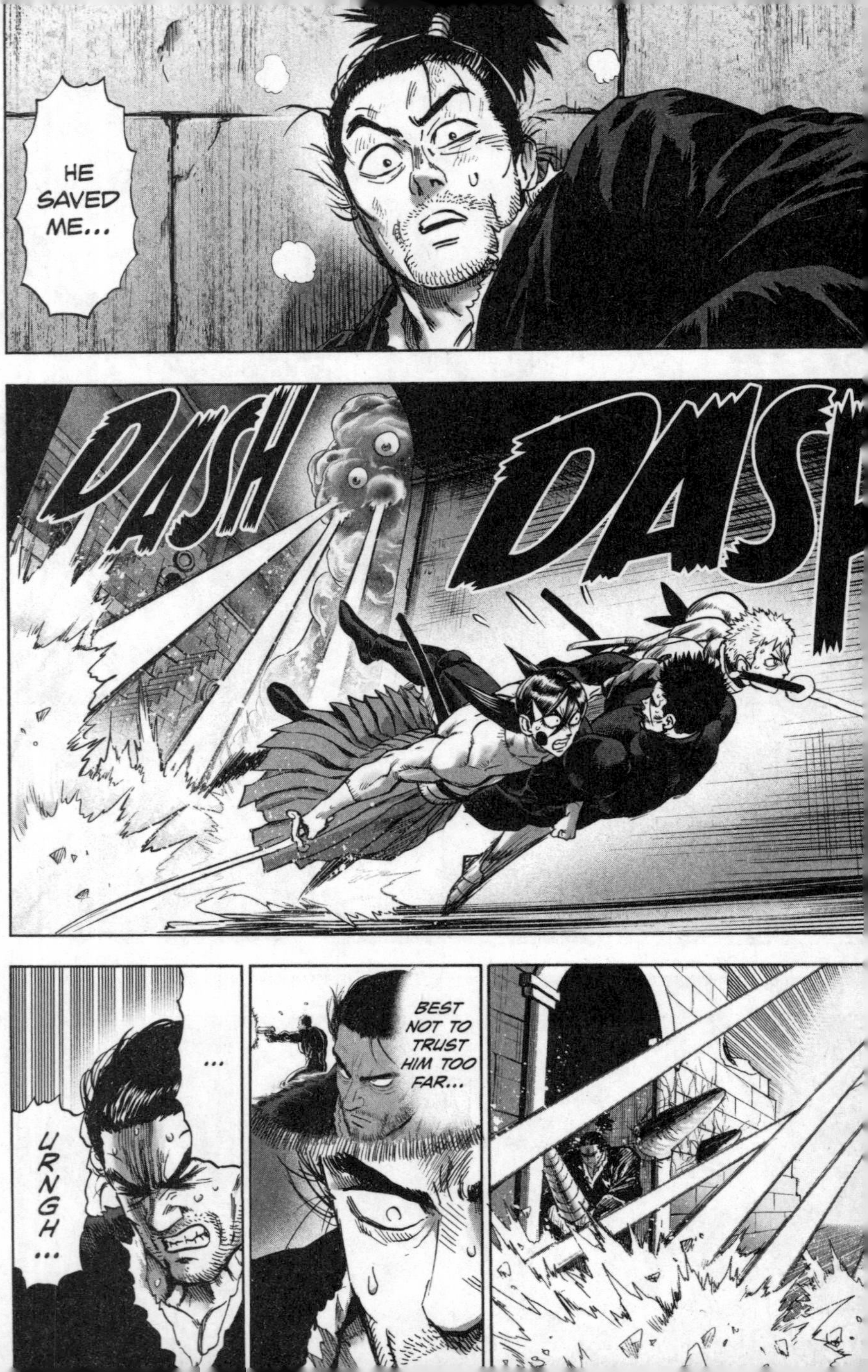
HE SAVED ME...
DASH
DASH
BEST NOT TO TRUST HIM TOO FAR...
...
URNGH...

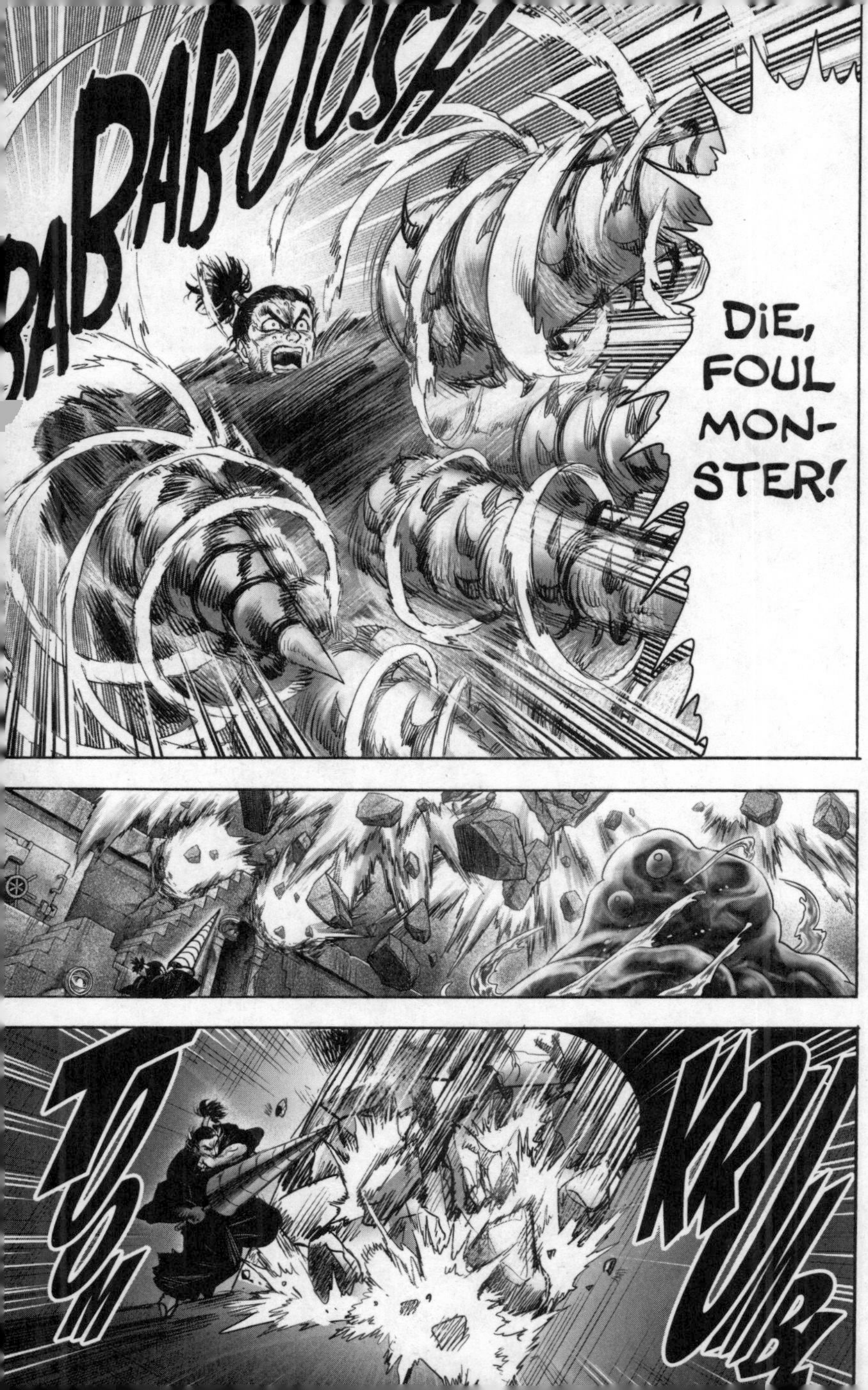
DIE, FOUL MONSTER!

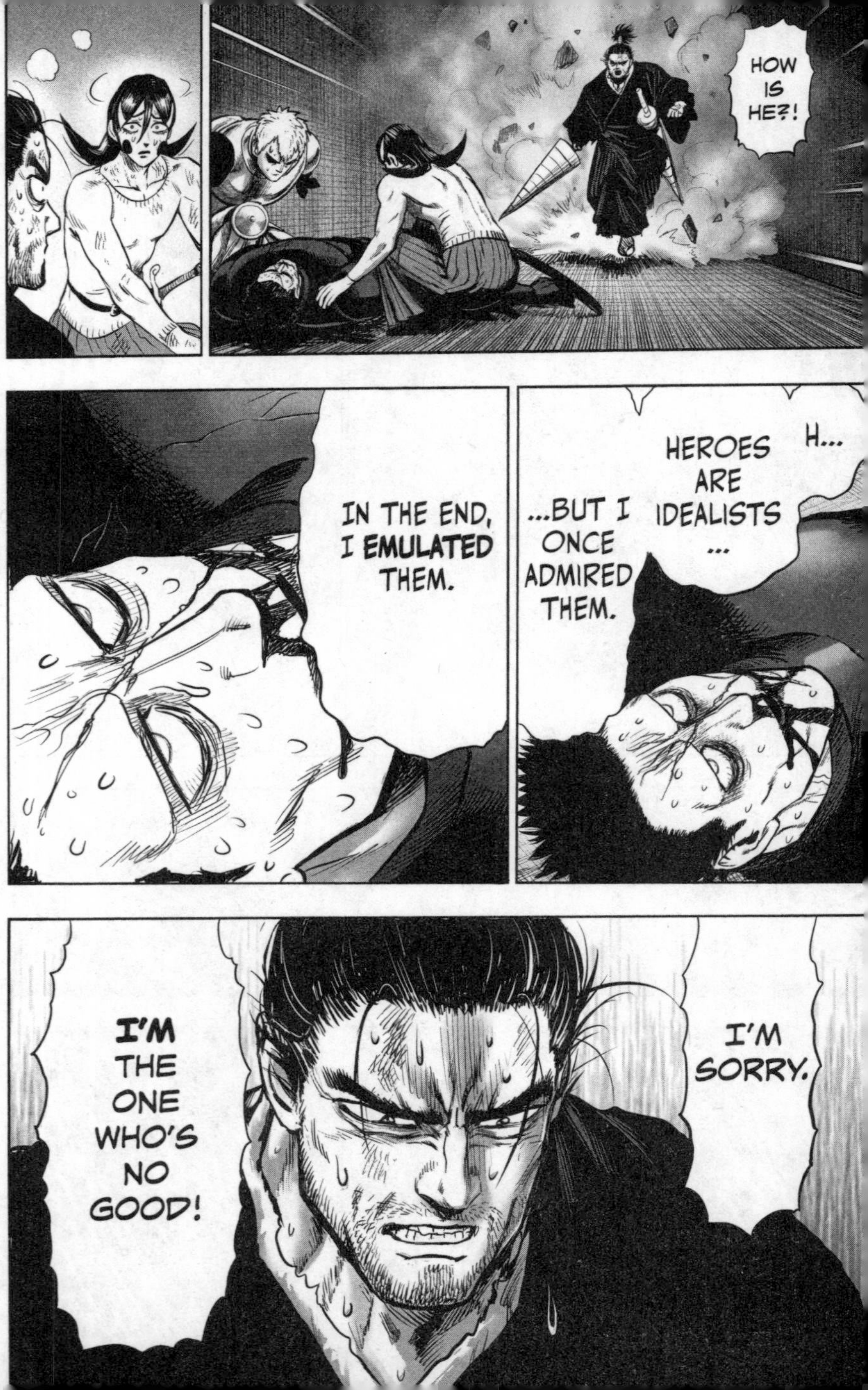
HOW IS HE?!
H...
HEROES ARE IDEALISTS ...
...BUT I ONCE ADMIRED THEM.
IN THE END, I EMULATED THEM.
I'M SORRY.
I'M THE ONE WHO'S NO GOOD!

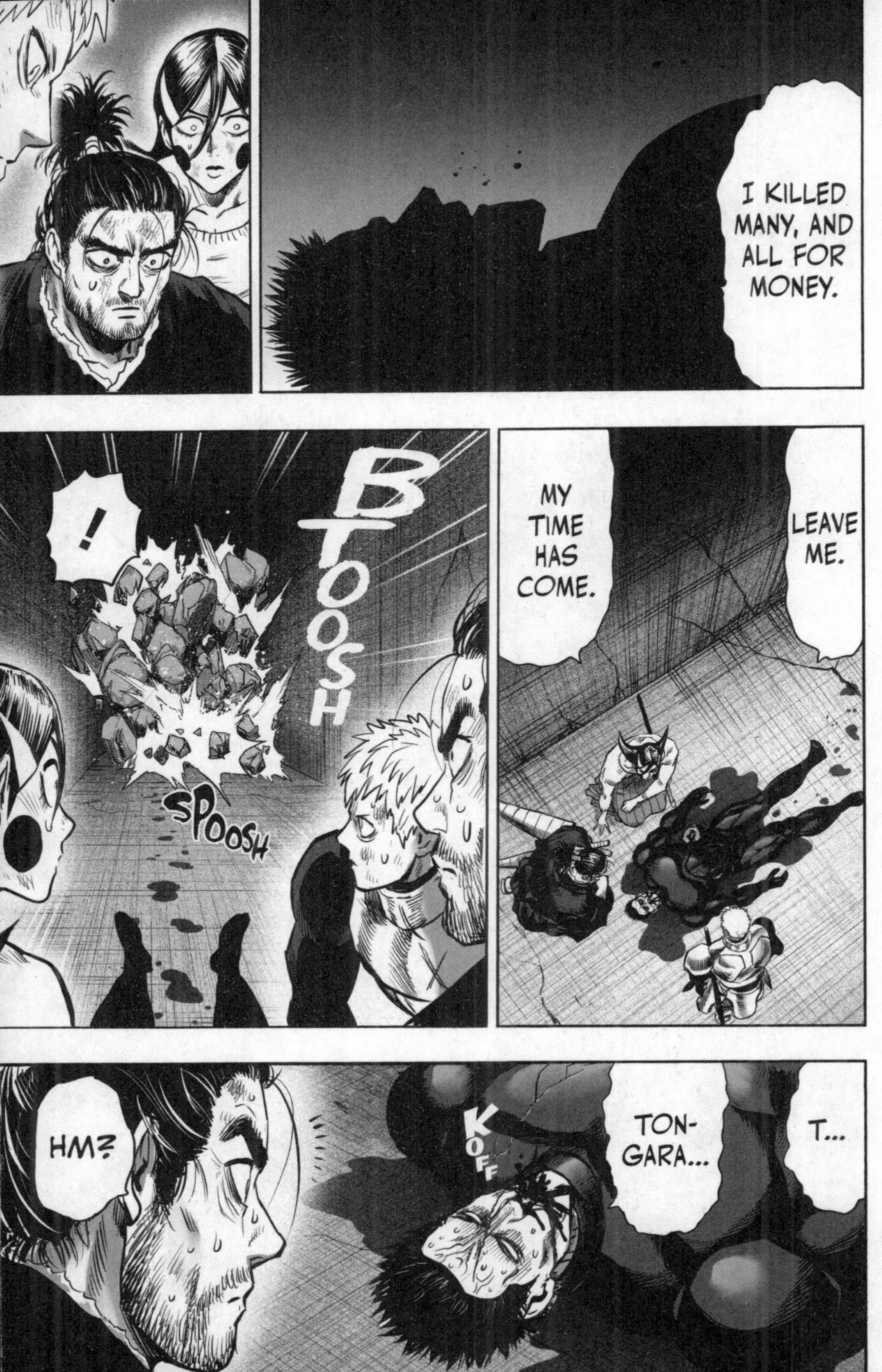
I KILLED MANY, AND ALL FOR MONEY.
LEAVE ME.
MY TIME HAS COME.
BTOOSH
!
SPOOSH
T...
TON-GARA...
KOFF
HM?

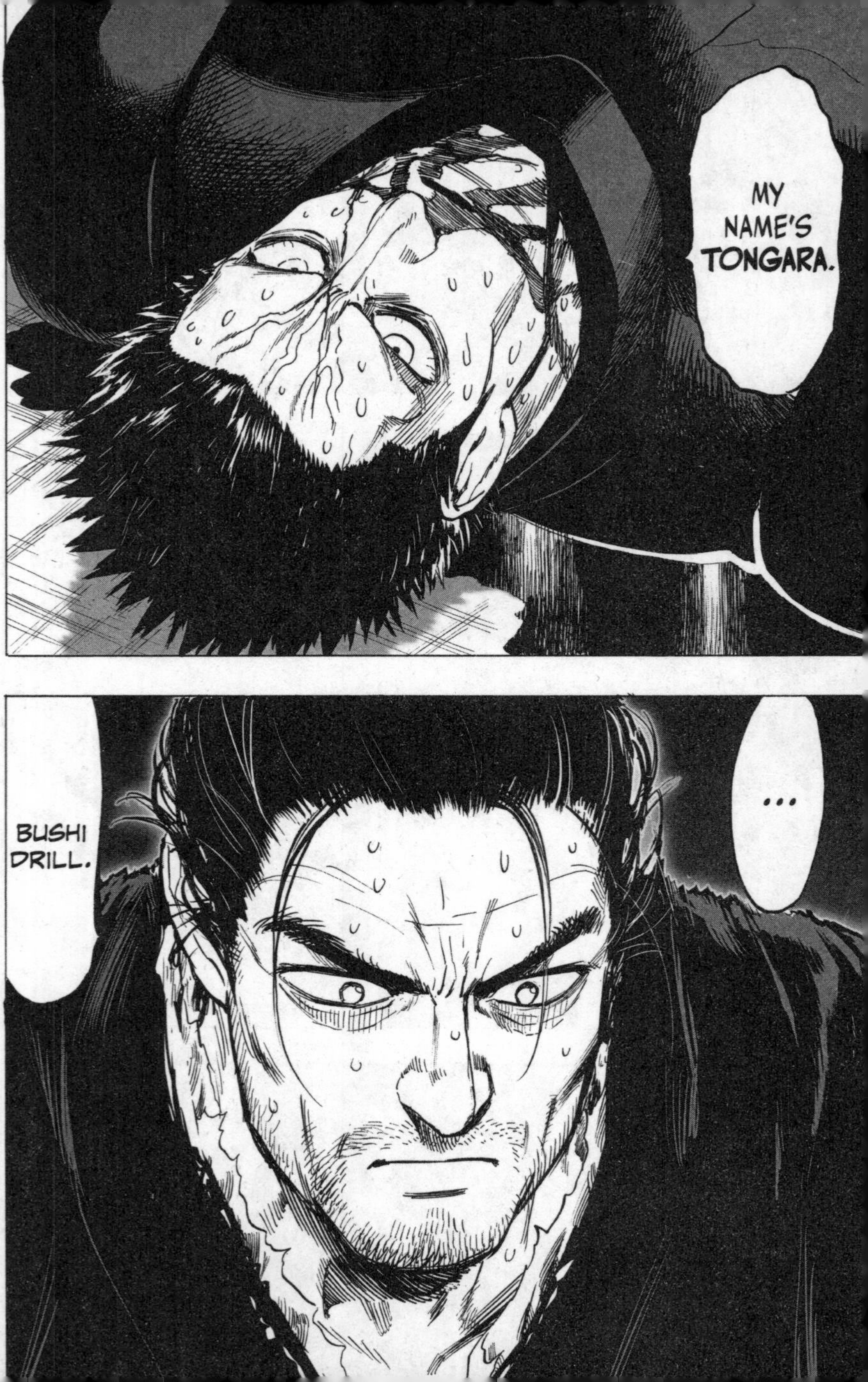
MY NAME'S TONGARA.
...
BUSHI DRILL.

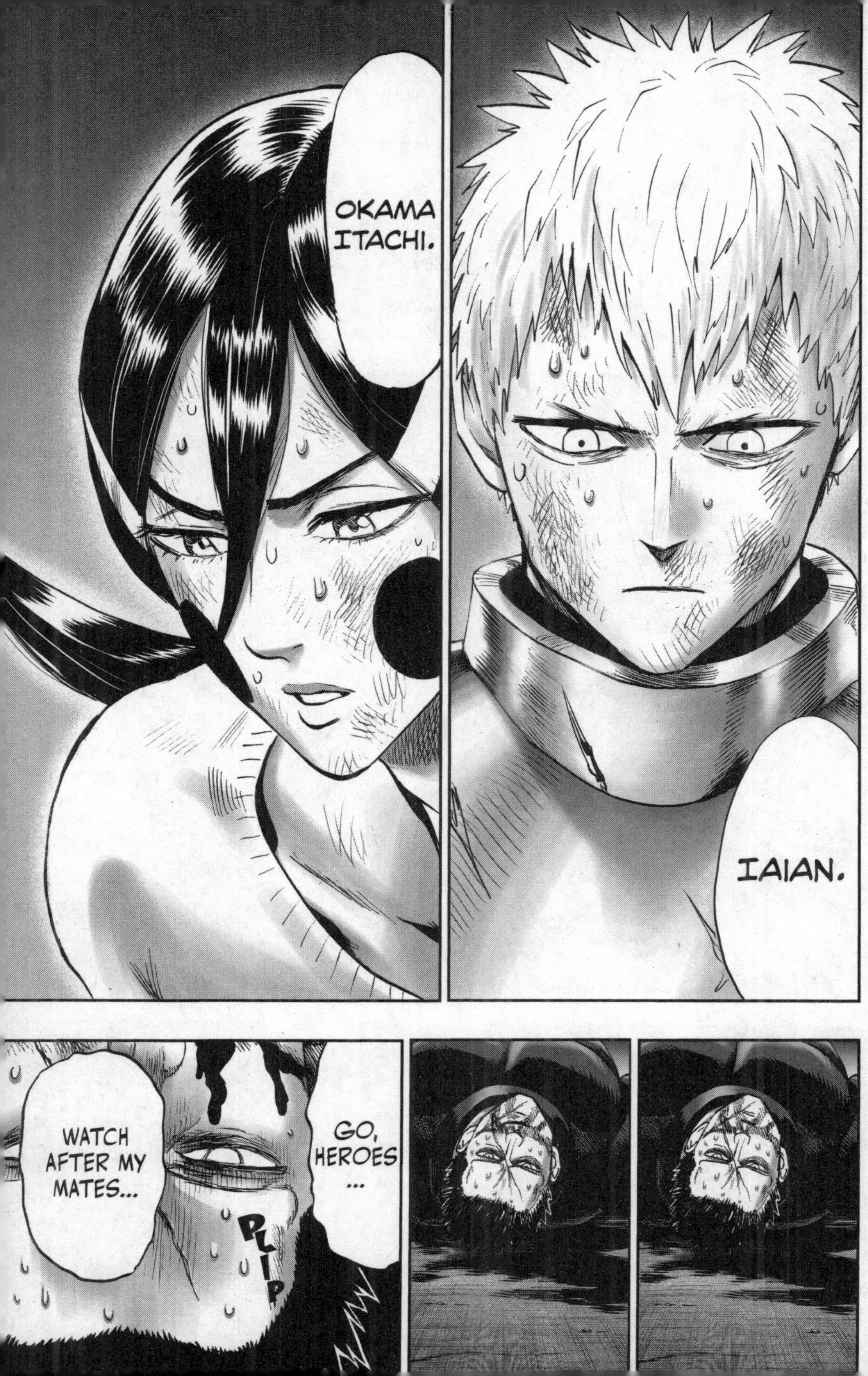
IAIAN.
OKAMA ITACHI.
GO, HEROES ...
WATCH AFTER MY MATES...
PLIP

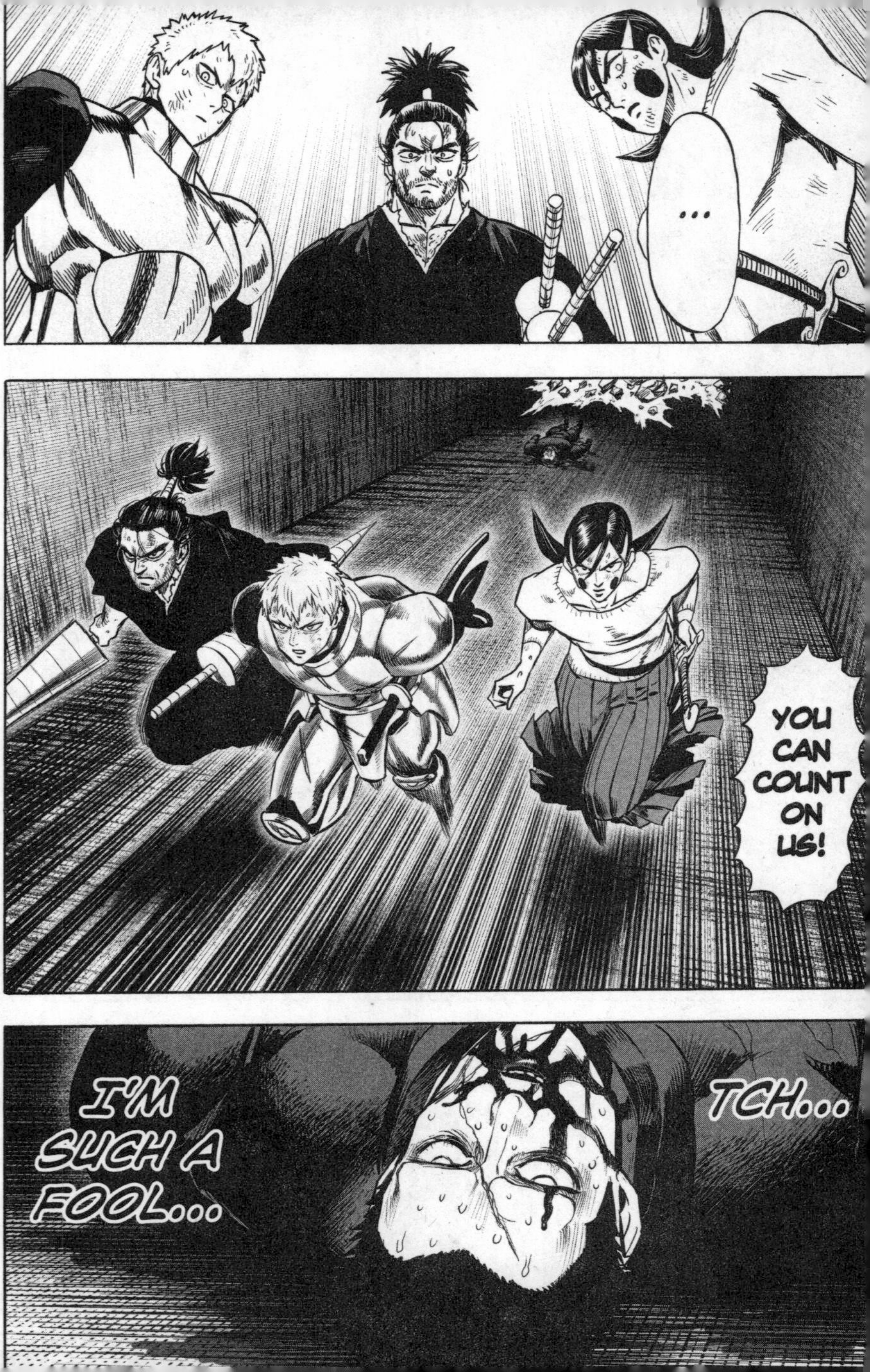
...
YOU CAN COUNT ON US!
TCH...
I'M SUCH A FOOL...

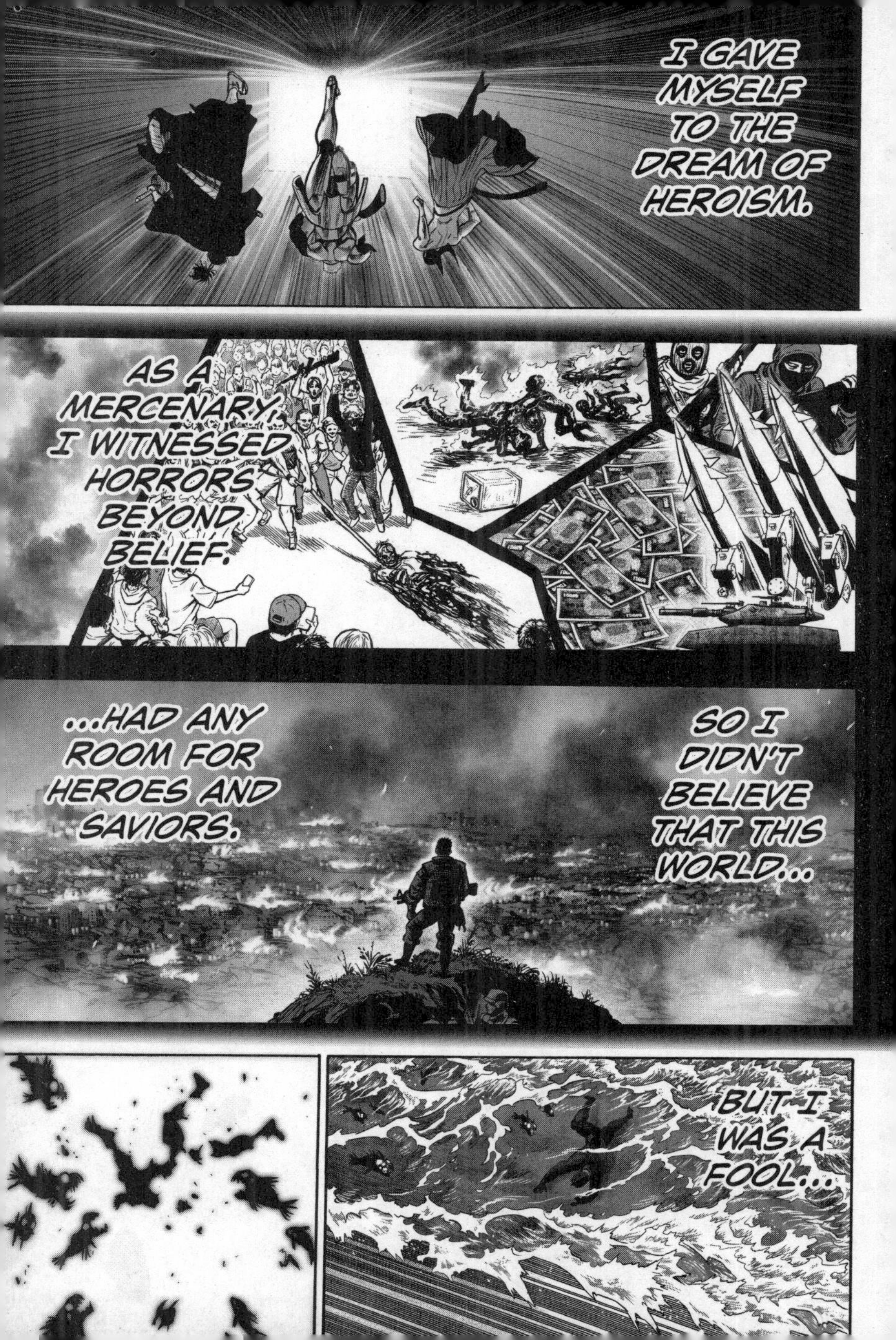
I GAVE MYSELF TO THE DREAM OF HEROISM.
AS A MERCENARY, I WITNESSED HORRORS BEYOND BELIEF.
SO I DIDN'T BELIEVE THAT THIS WORLD...
...HAD ANY ROOM FOR HEROES AND SAVIORS.
BUT I WAS A FOOL...

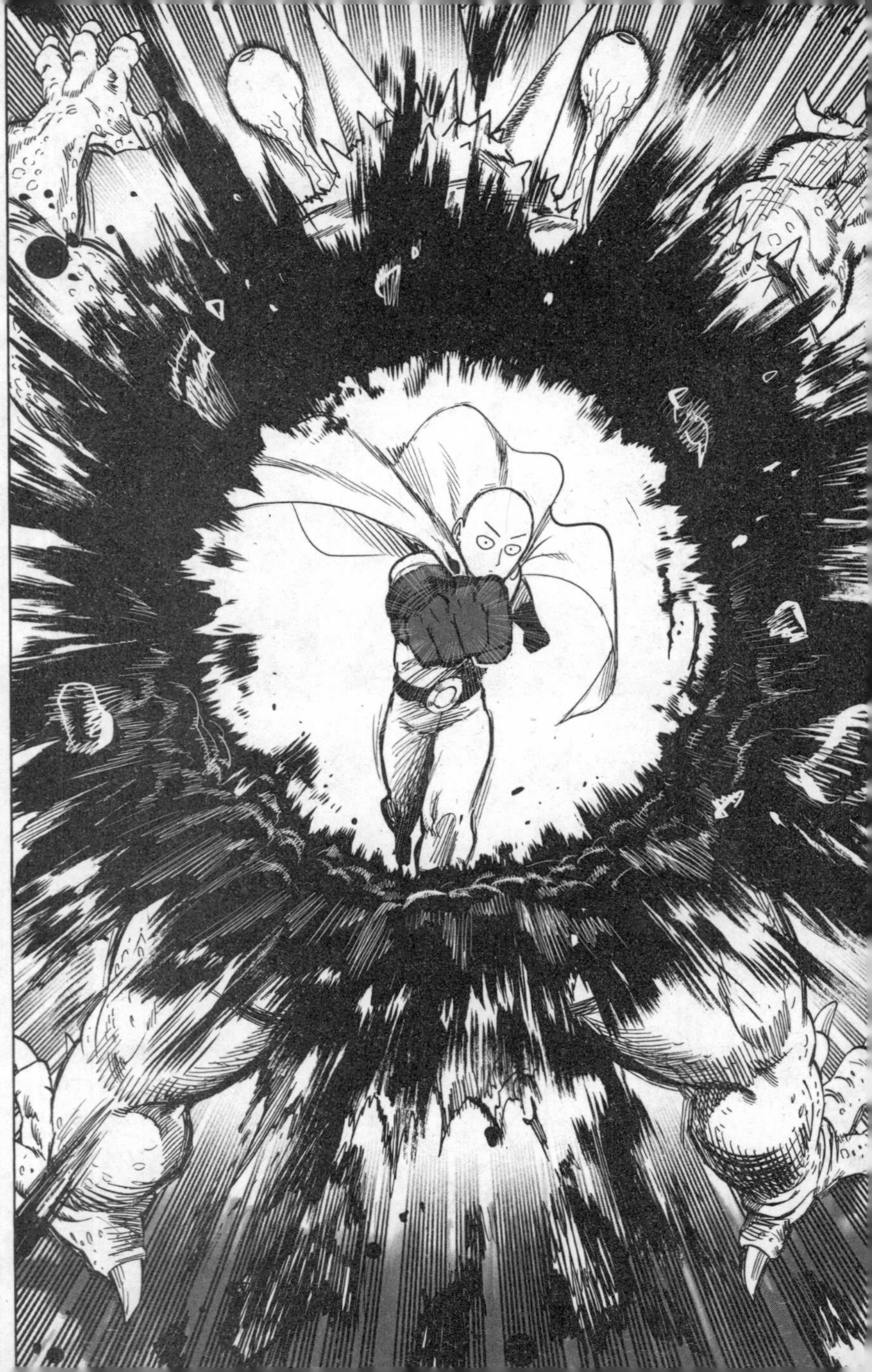

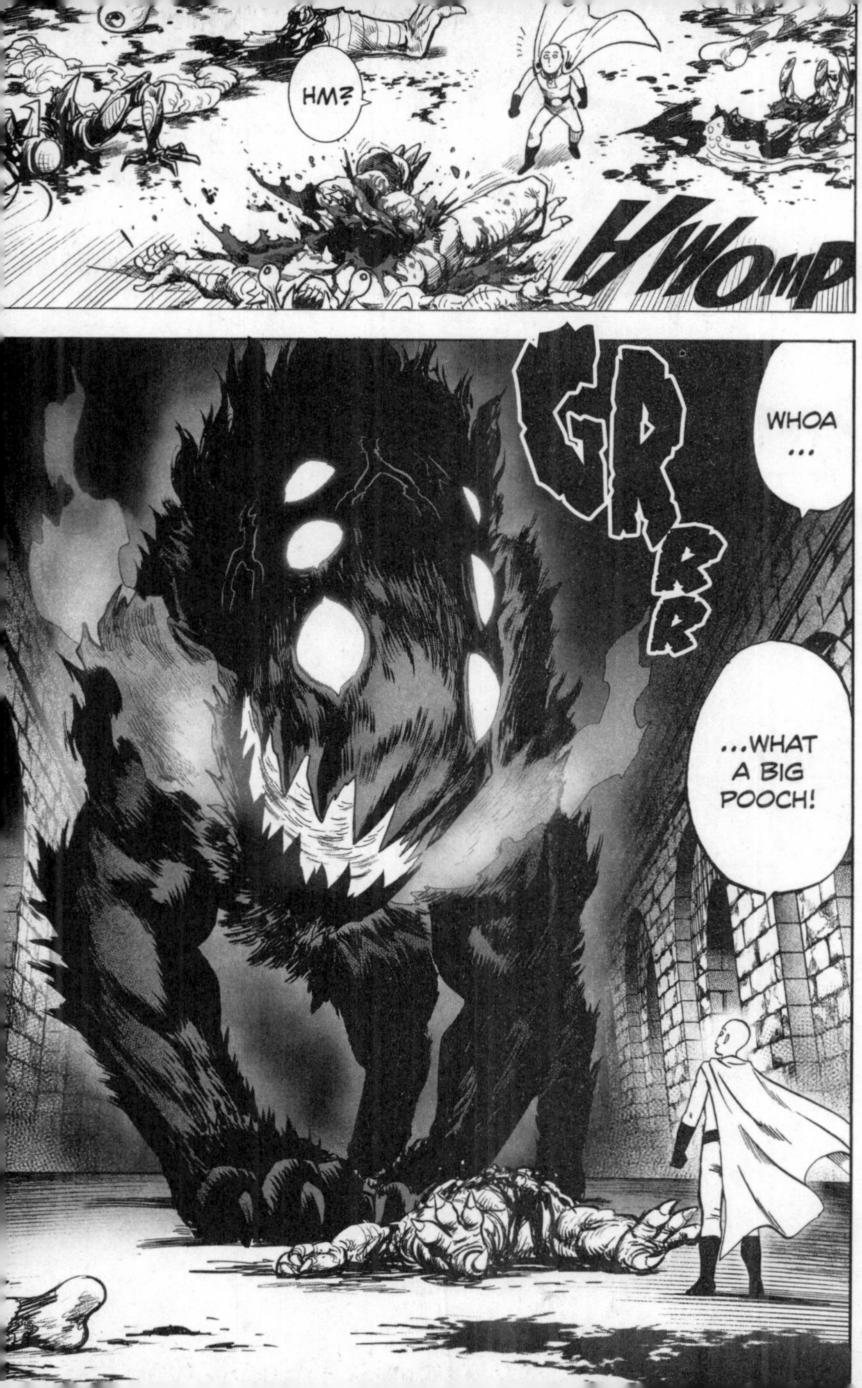
HM?
HWOMP
WHOA ...
...WHAT A BIG POOCH!
GRRRR

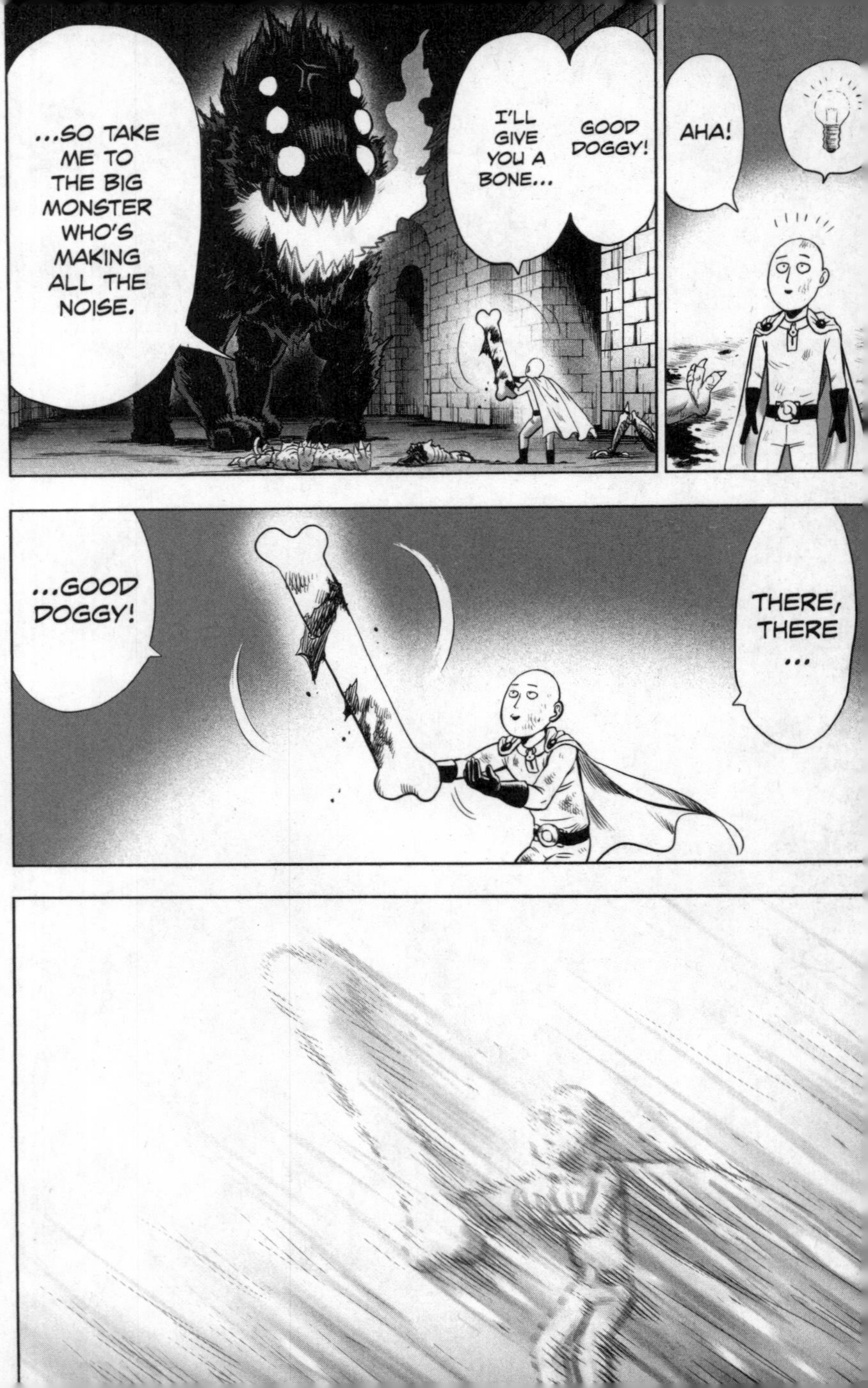
AHA!
GOOD DOGGY!
I'LL GIVE YOU A BONE...
...SO TAKE ME TO THE BIG MONSTER WHO'S MAKING ALL THE NOISE.
THERE, THERE ...
...GOOD DOGGY!

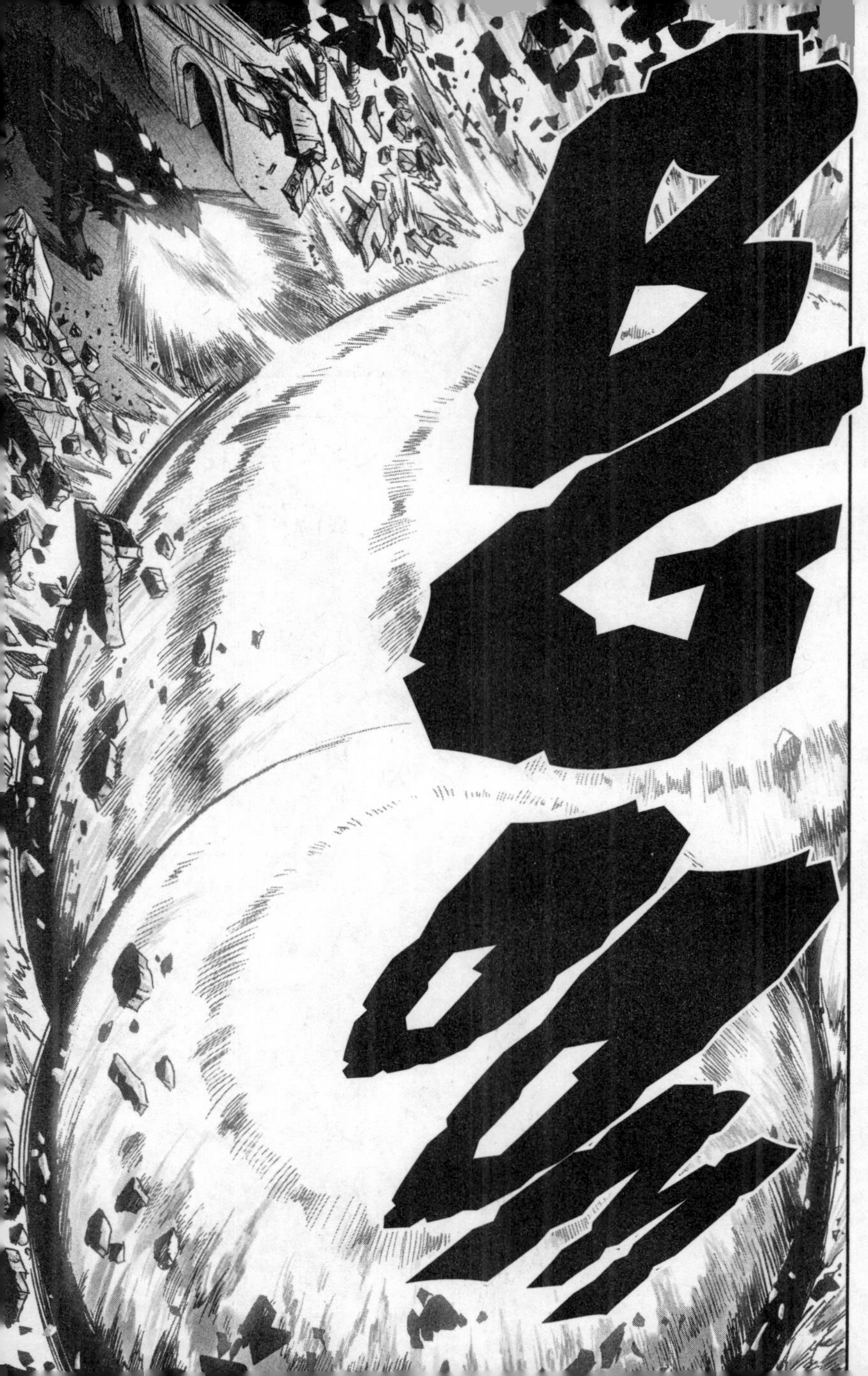
DOOM

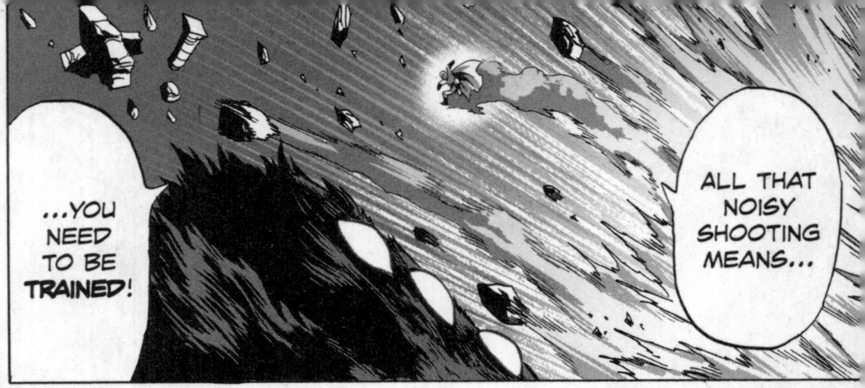
ALL THAT NOISY SHOOTING MEANS...
...YOU NEED TO BE TRAINED!

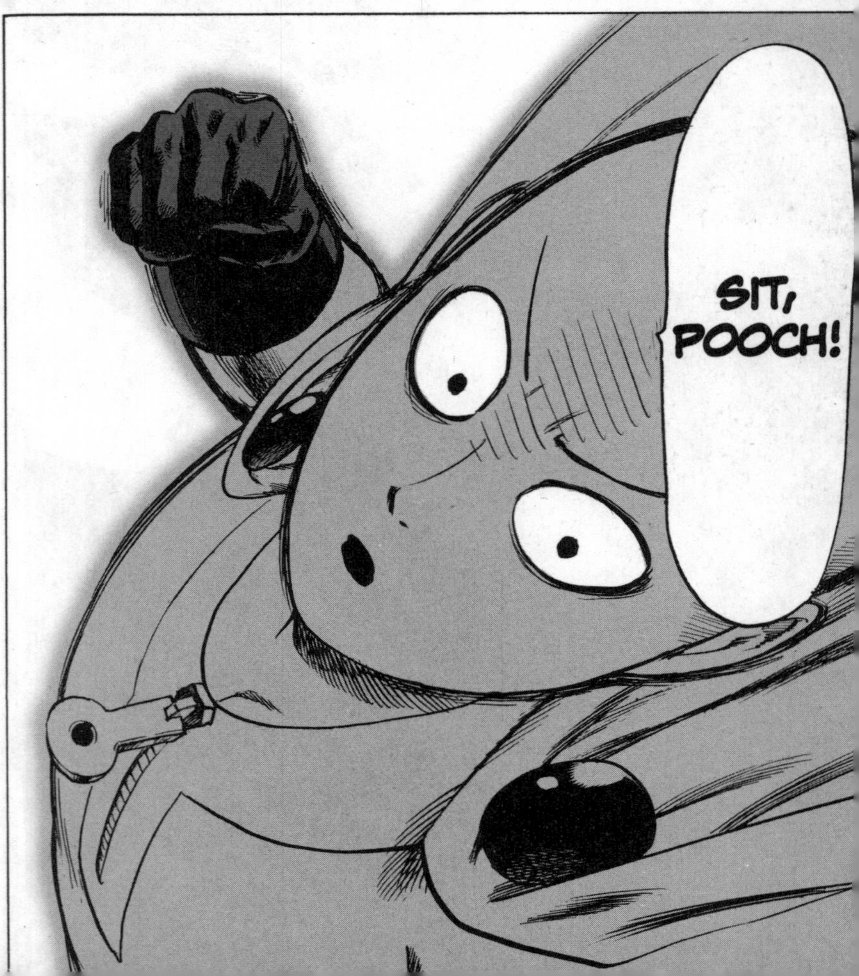
SIT, POOCH!

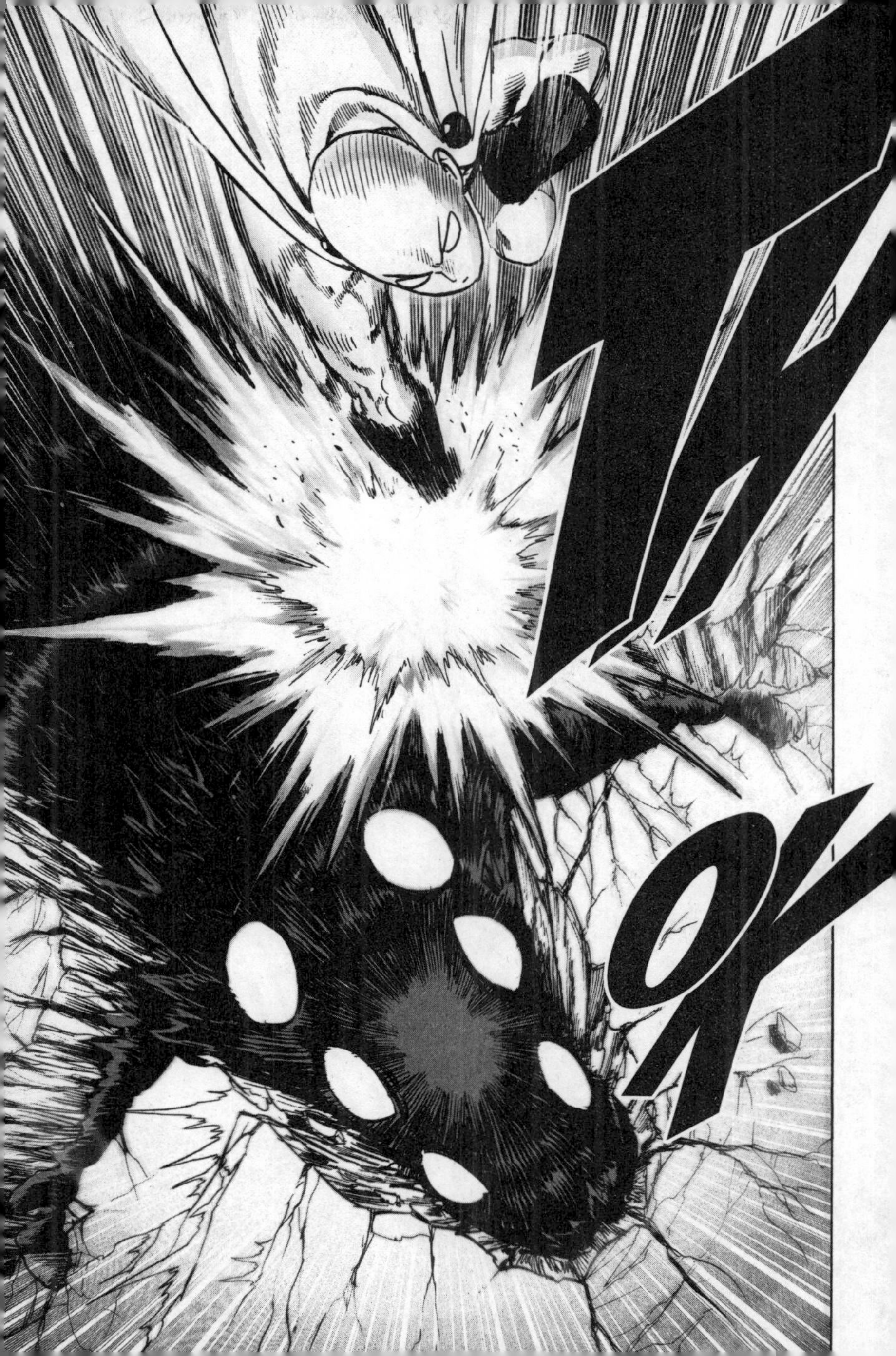

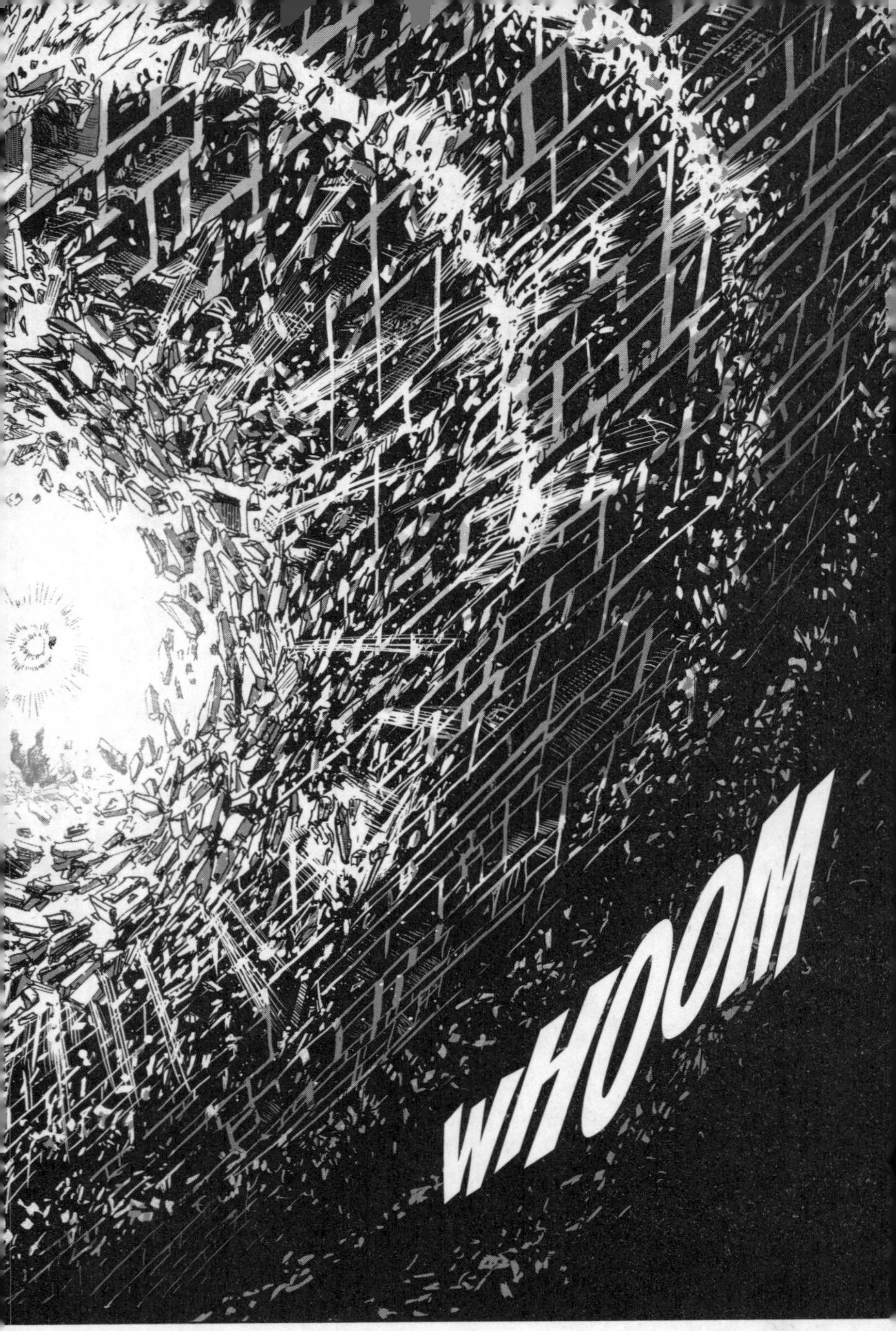
WHOOM

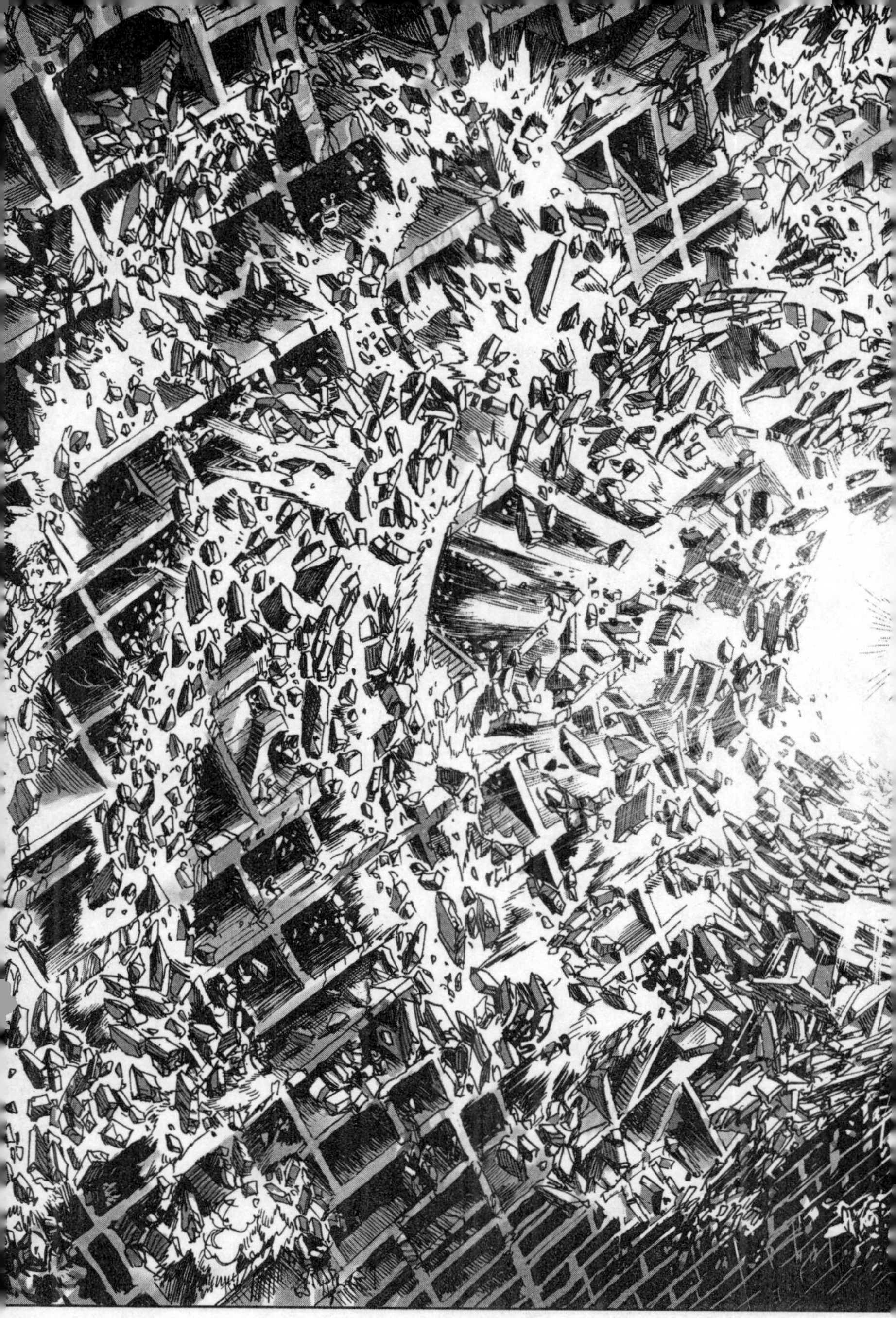

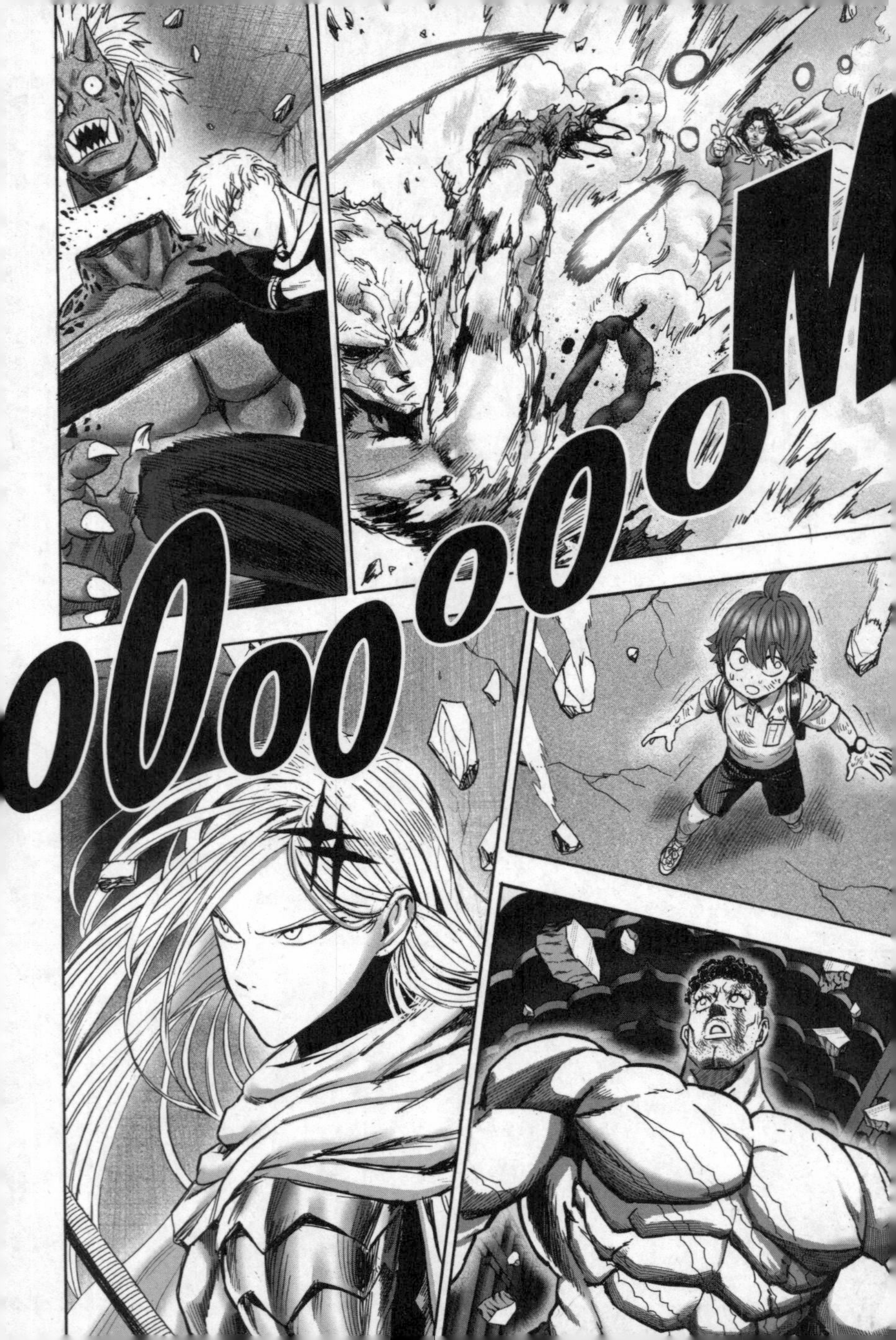

OOOOOOOOM

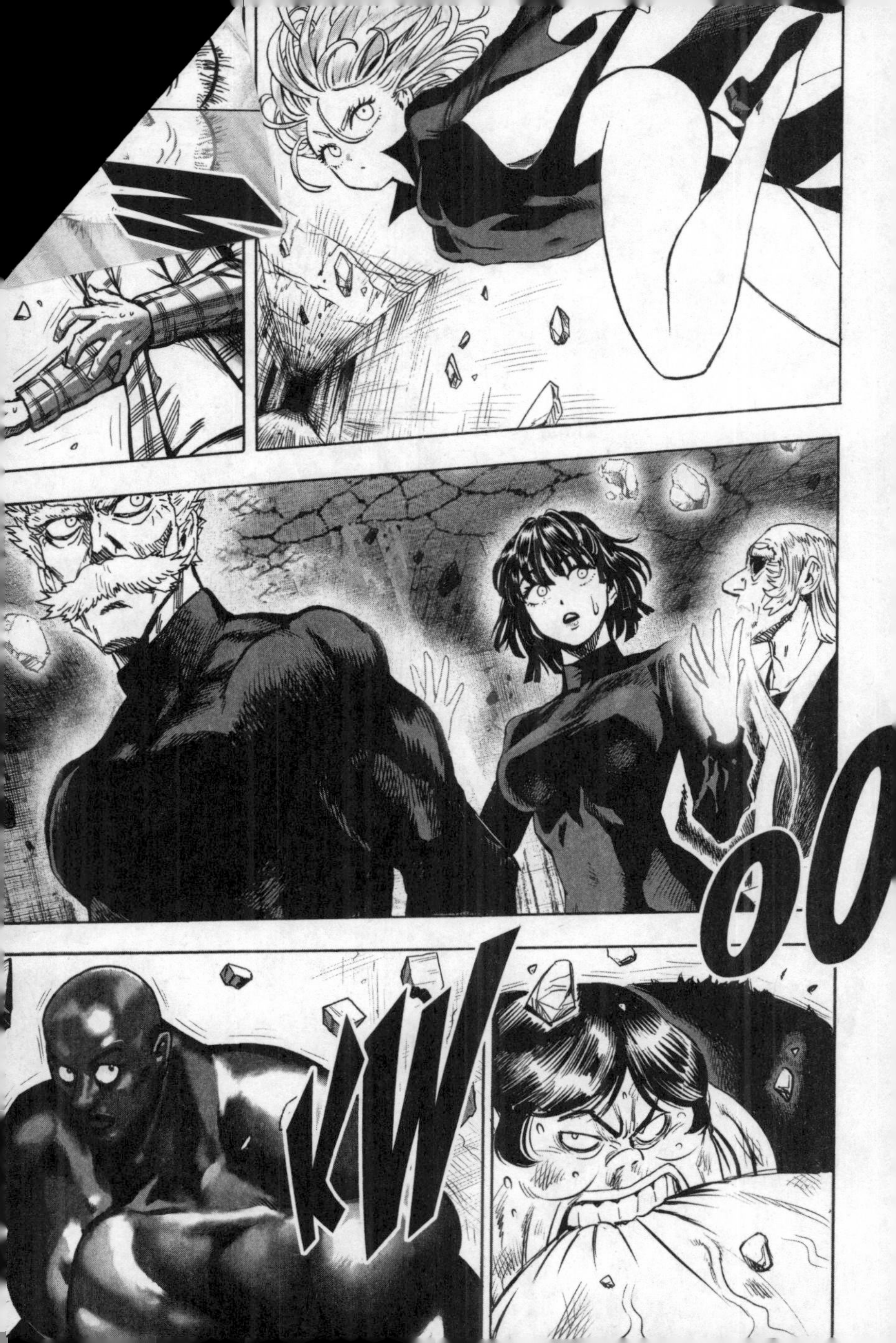
KW
OO

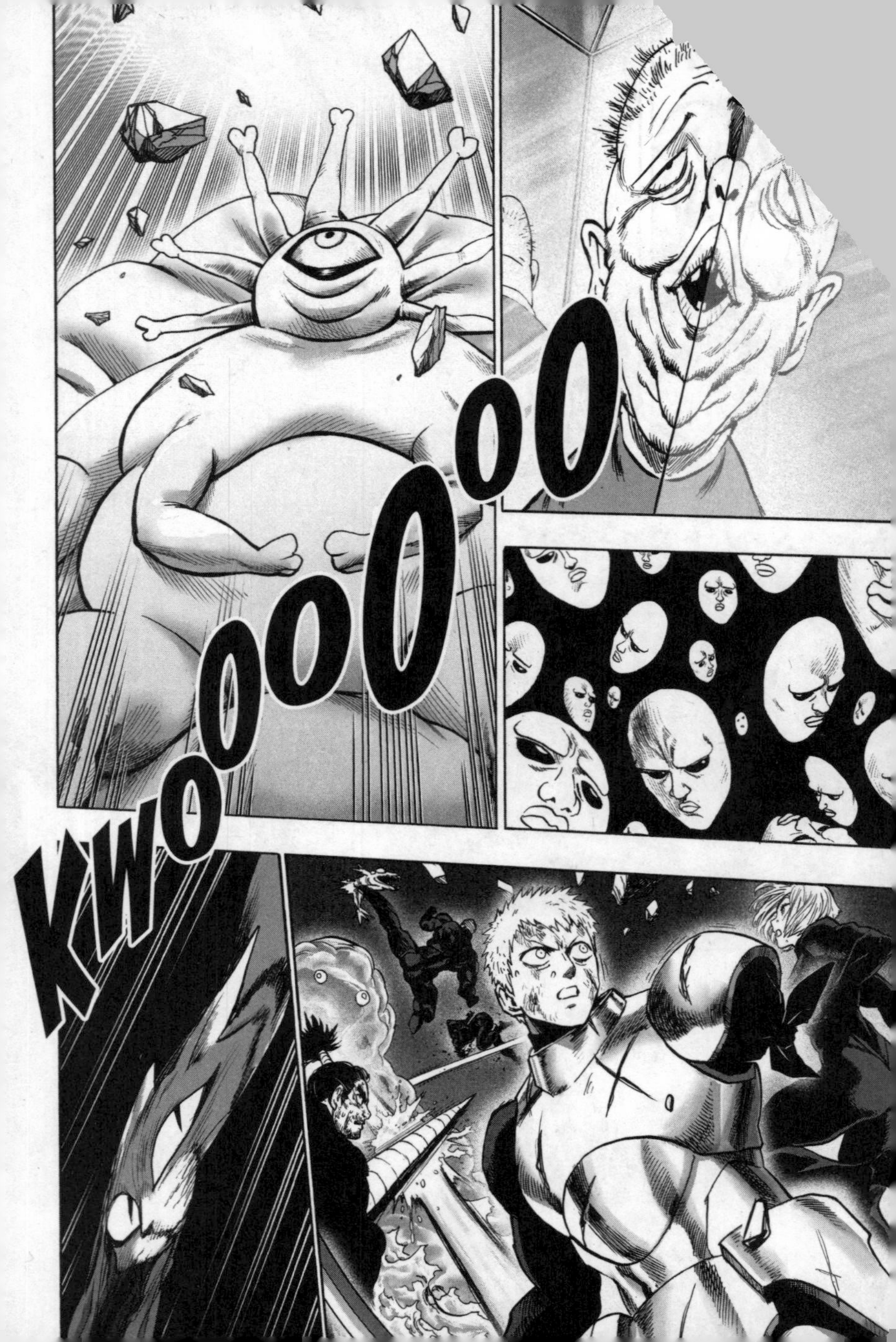
KWOOOOOOOOO

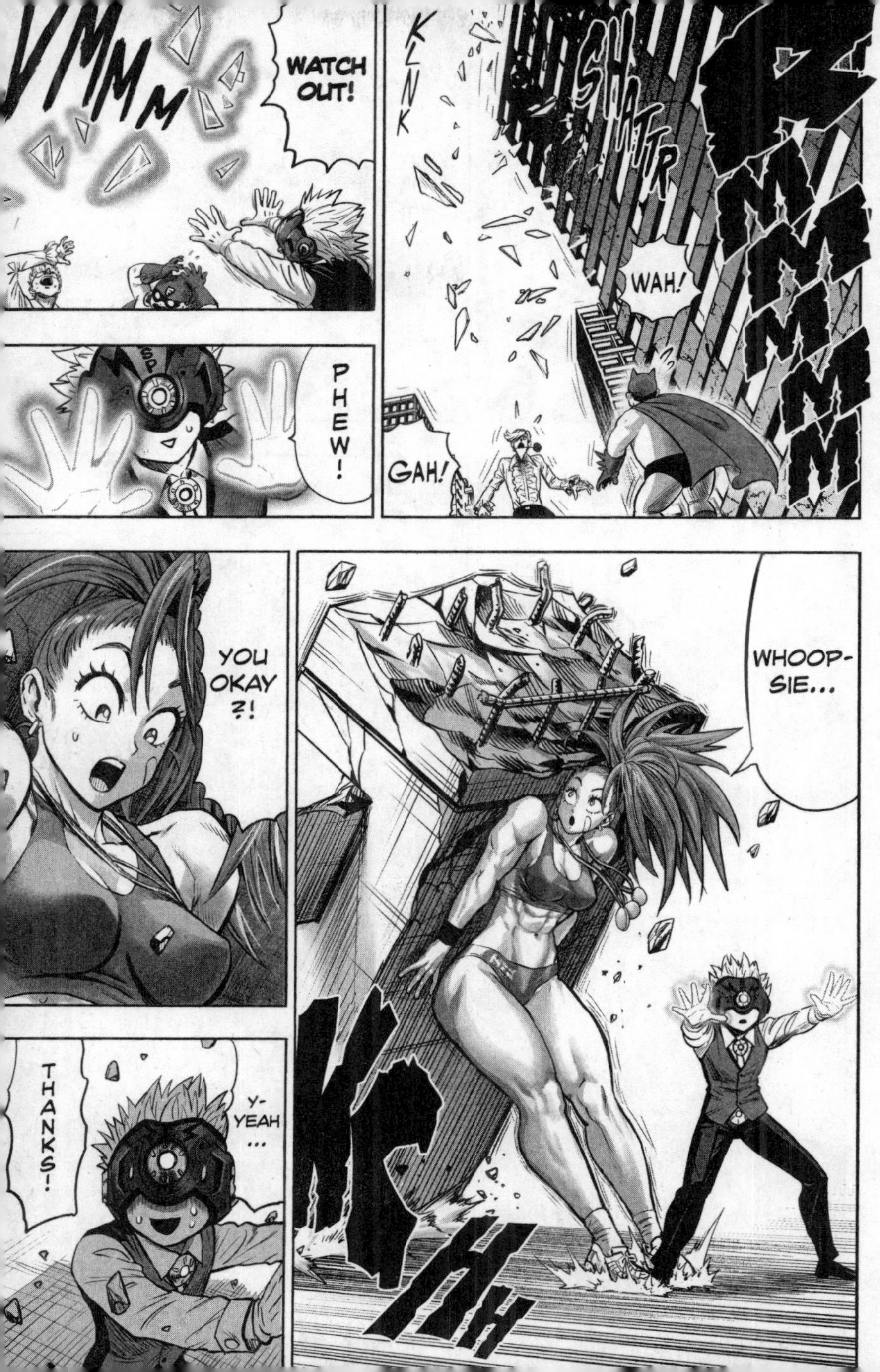
SHATTR
KLNK
WAH!
GAH!
VMMMM
WATCH OUT!
PHEW!
WHOOP-SIE...
YOU OKAY?!
Y-YEAH...
THANKS!

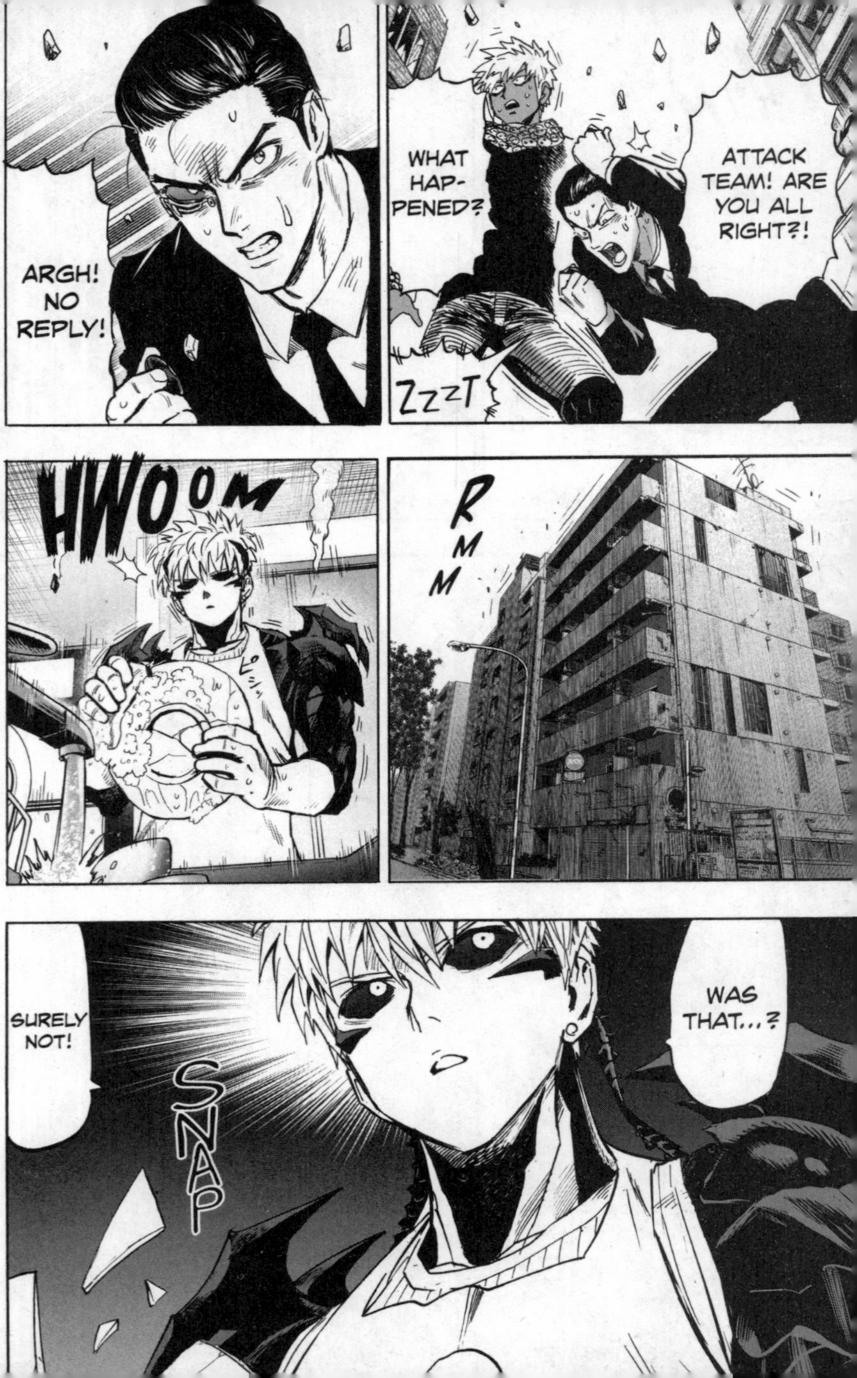
ATTACK TEAM! ARE YOU ALL RIGHT?!
WHAT HAP-PENED?
ZZZT
ARGH! NO REPLY!
RMMM
HWOOM
WAS THAT...?
SNAP
SURELY NOT!

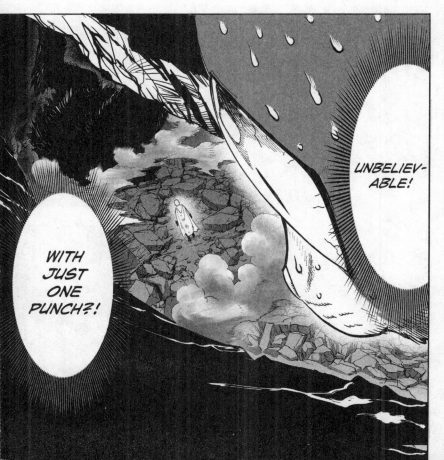

UNBELIEV-
ABLE!

WITH
JUST
ONE
PUNCH?!

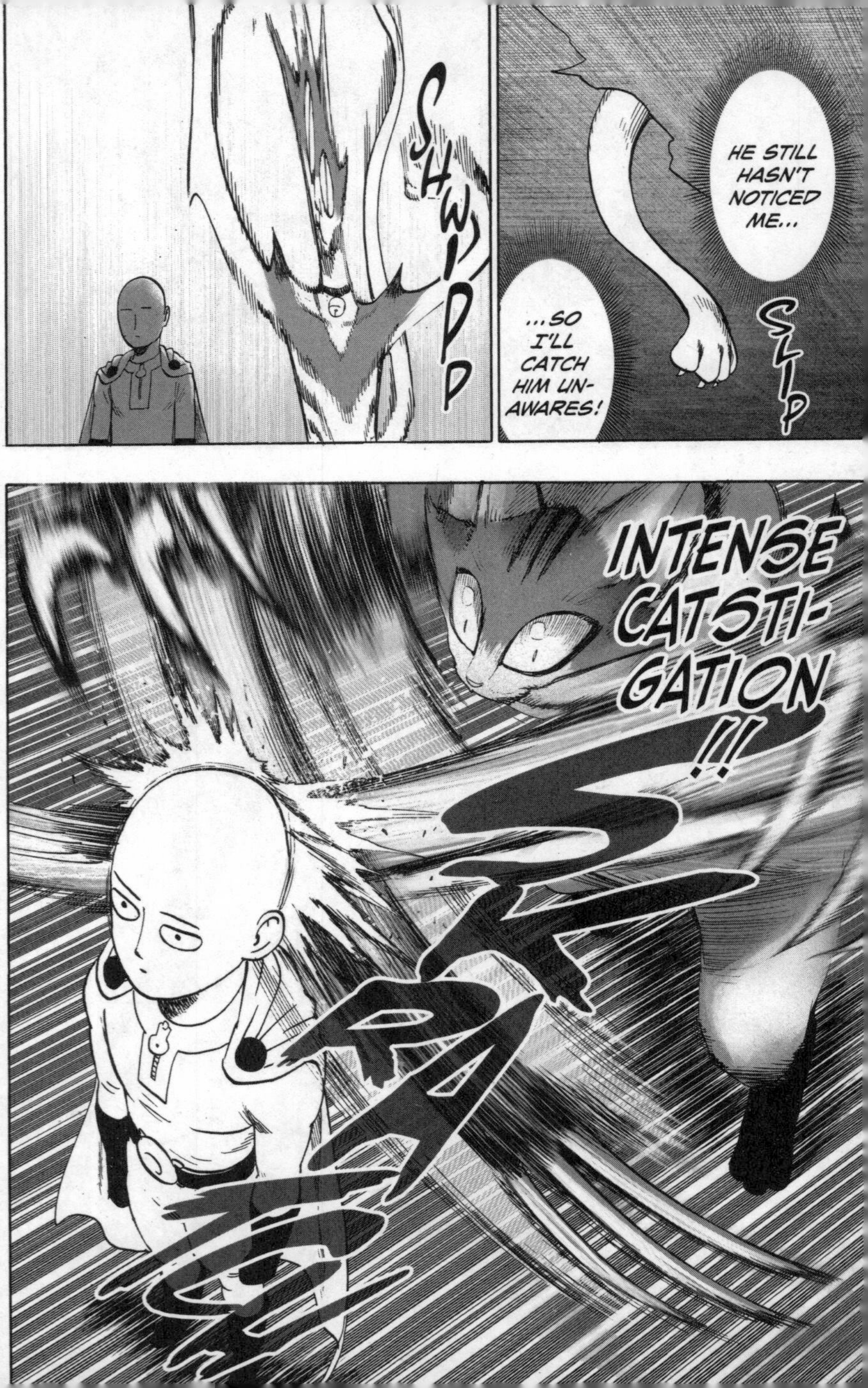
HE STILL HASN'T NOTICED ME...
...SO I'LL CATCH HIM UN-AWARES!
SLIP
SHWIPP
INTENSE CATSTI-GATION!!

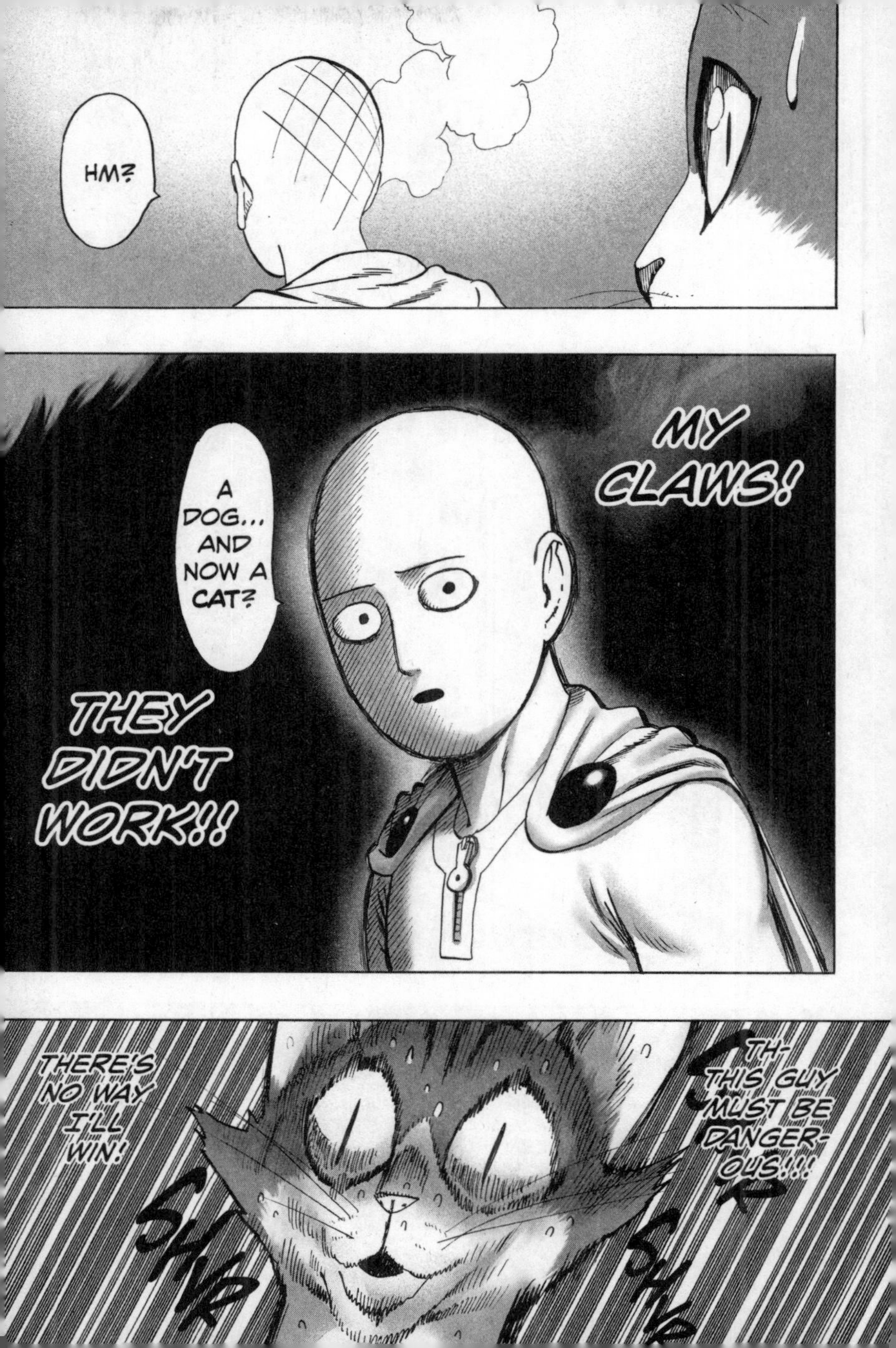
HM?
MY CLAWS!
A DOG... AND NOW A CAT?
THEY DIDN'T WORK!!
TH- THIS GUY MUST BE DANGER-OUS!!!
THERE'S NO WAY I'LL WIN!
SHVR
SHVR

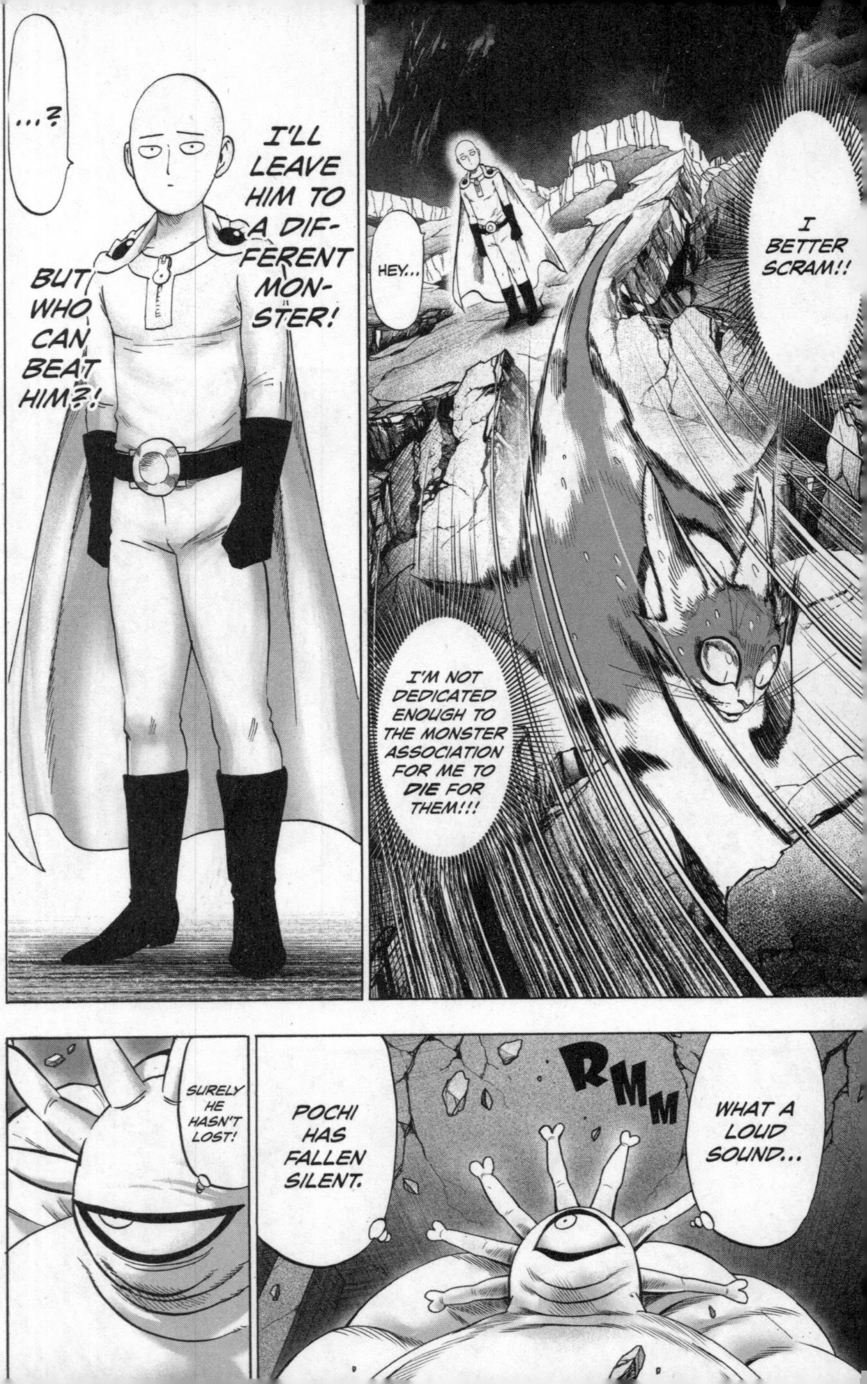
I BETTER SCRAM!!
HEY...
I'M NOT DEDICATED ENOUGH TO THE MONSTER ASSOCIATION FOR ME TO DIE FOR THEM!!!
I'LL LEAVE HIM TO A DIF-FERENT MON-STER!
BUT WHO CAN BEAT HIM?!
...?
WHAT A LOUD SOUND...
RMM
POCHI HAS FALLEN SILENT.
SURELY HE HASN'T LOST!

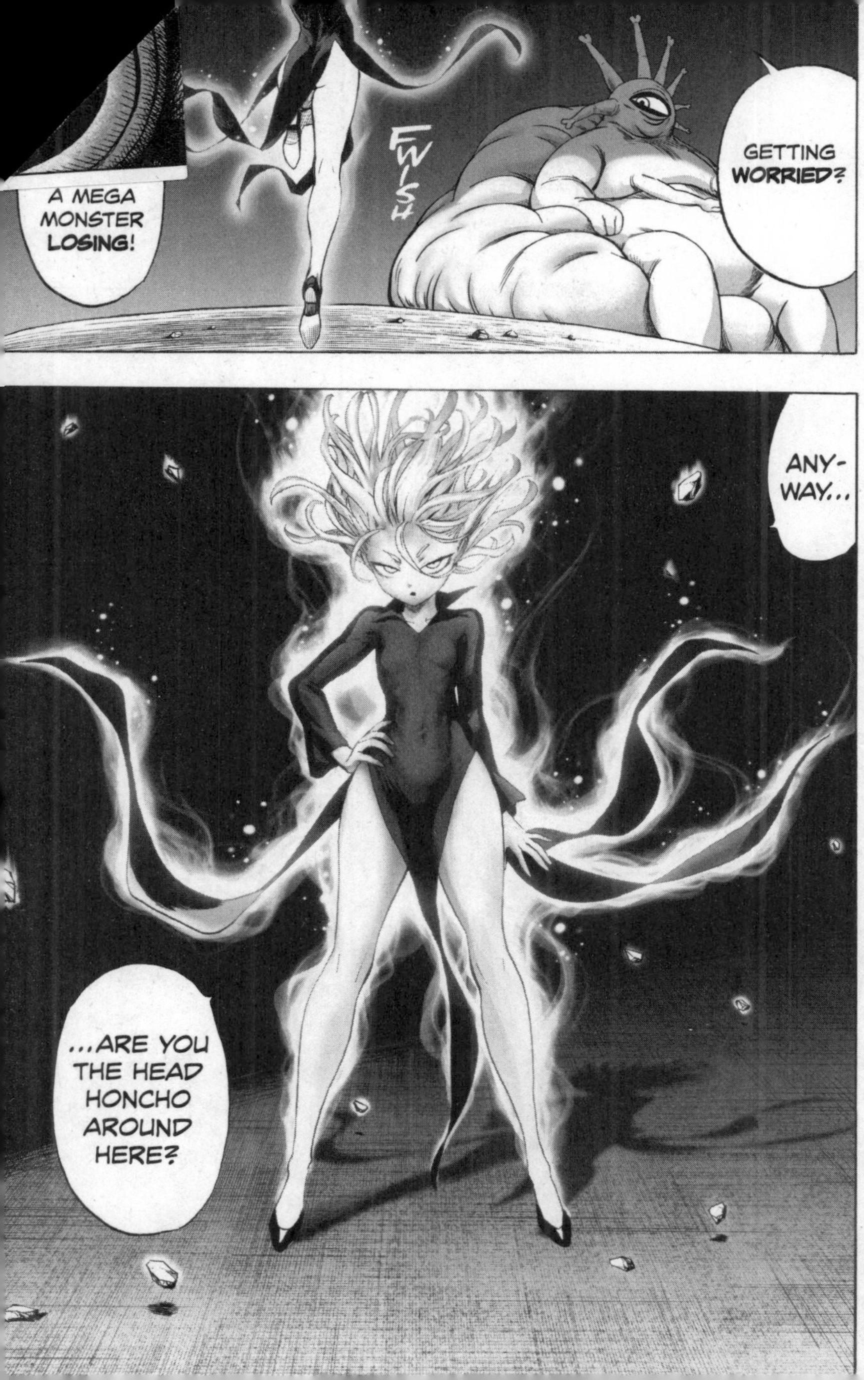
GETTING WORRIED?
FWISH
A MEGA MONSTER LOSING!
ANY-WAY...
...ARE YOU THE HEAD HONCHO AROUND HERE?

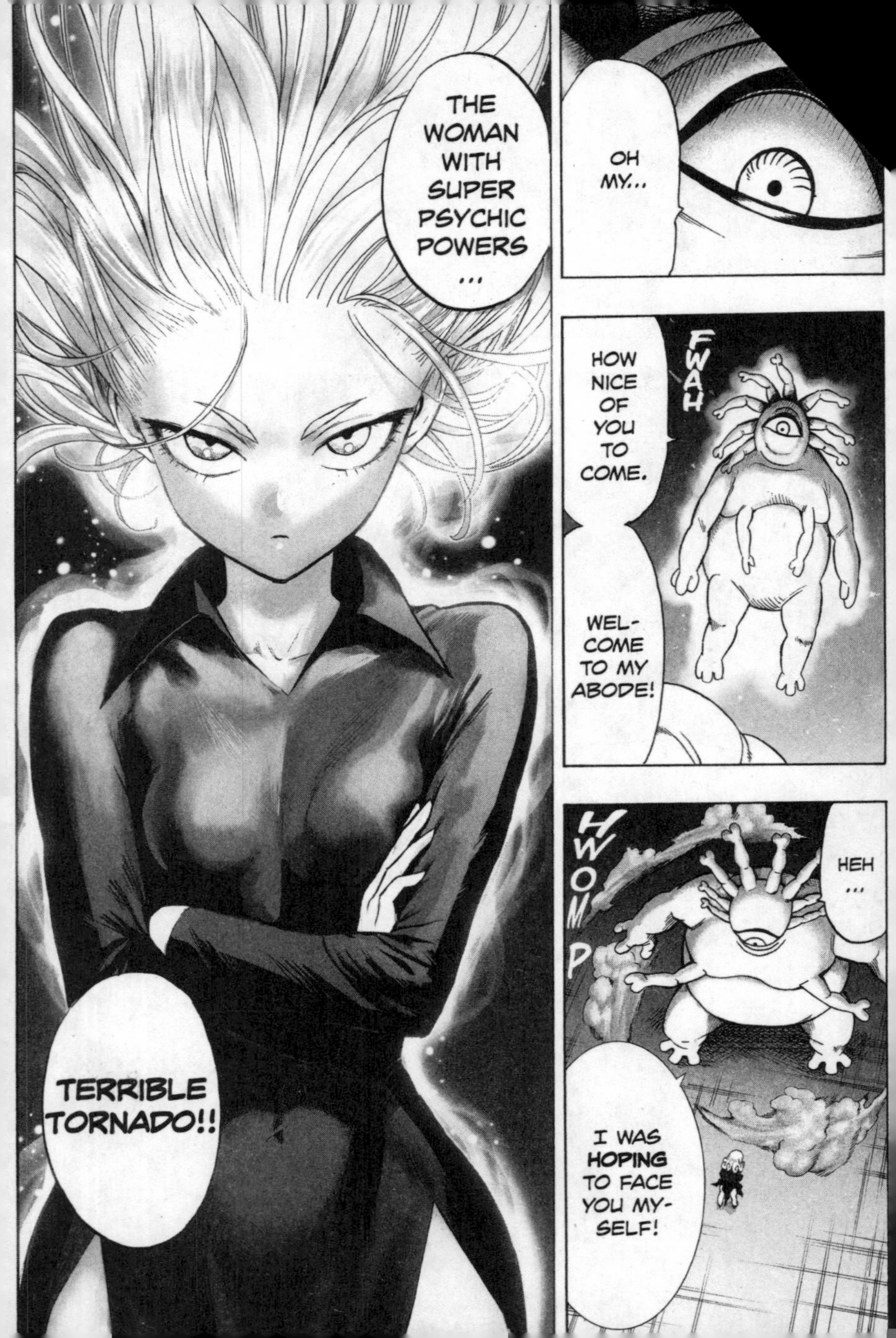
OH MY...
FWAH
HOW NICE OF YOU TO COME.
WEL-COME TO MY ABODE!
HEH ...
HWOMP
I WAS **HOPING** TO FACE YOU MY-SELF!
THE WOMAN WITH SUPER PSYCHIC POWERS ...
TERRIBLE TORNADO!!

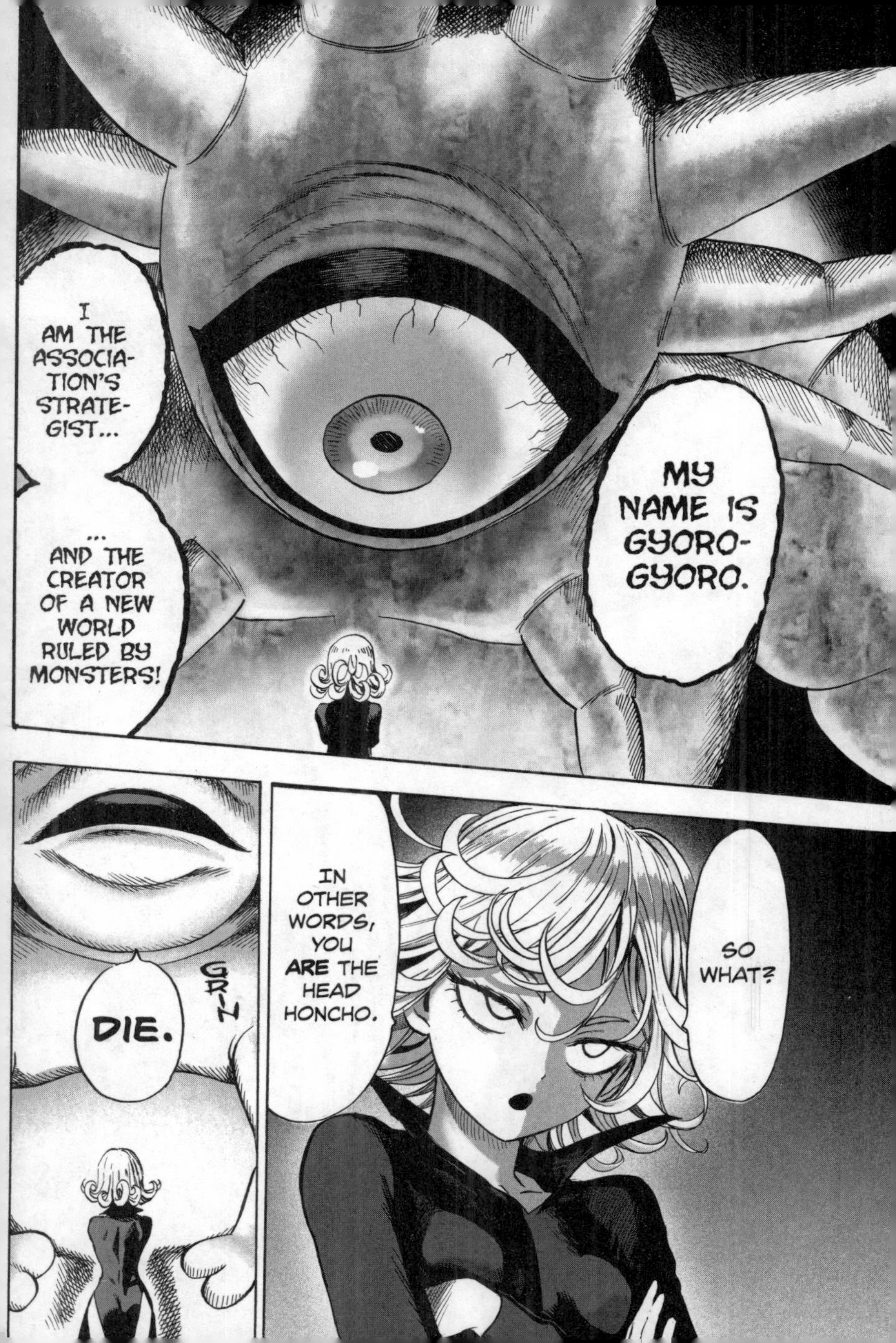
MY NAME IS GYORO-GYORO.
I AM THE ASSOCIATION'S STRATEGIST...
...AND THE CREATOR OF A NEW WORLD RULED BY MONSTERS!
SO WHAT?
IN OTHER WORDS, YOU **ARE** THE HEAD HONCHO.
GRIN
DIE.

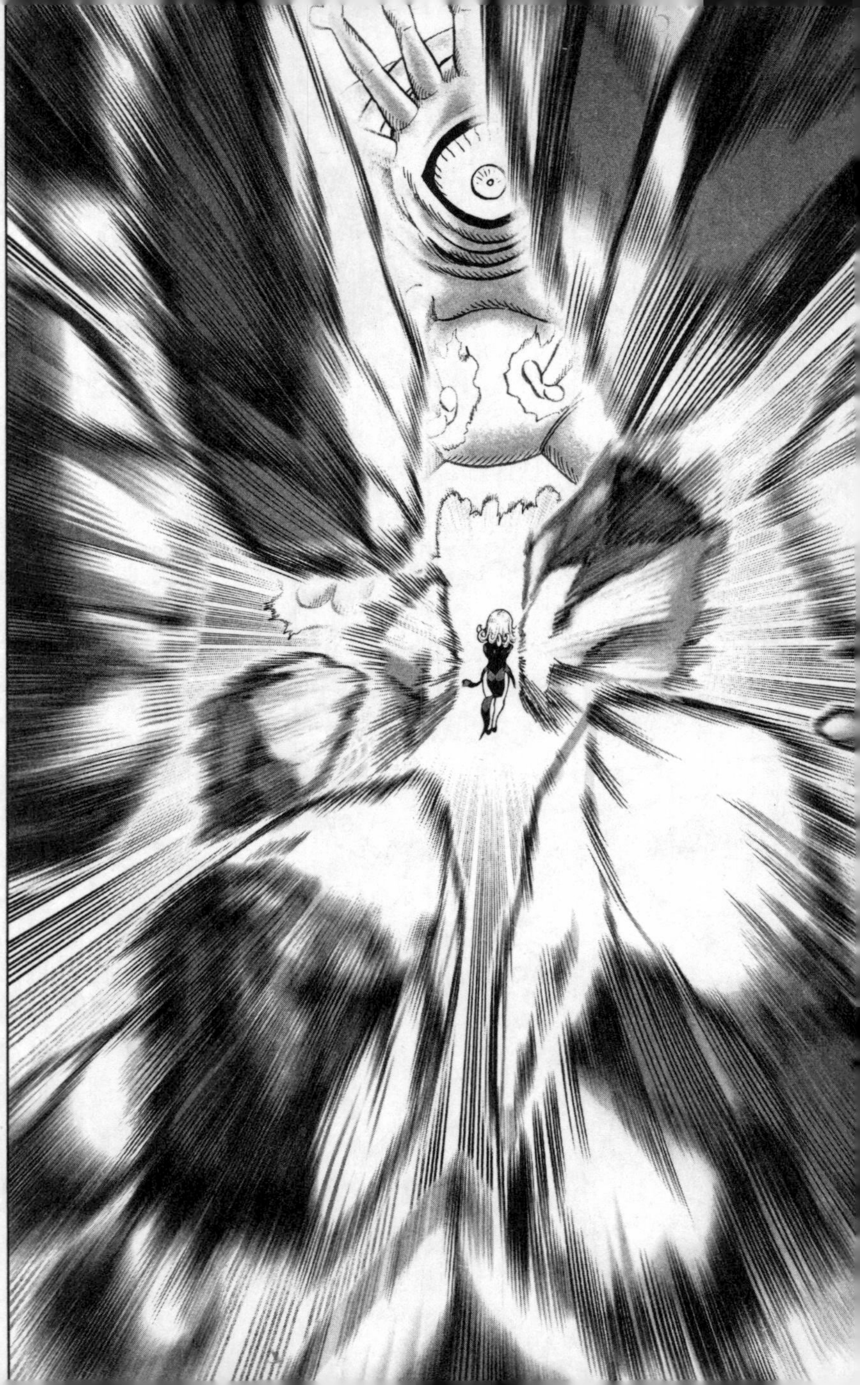

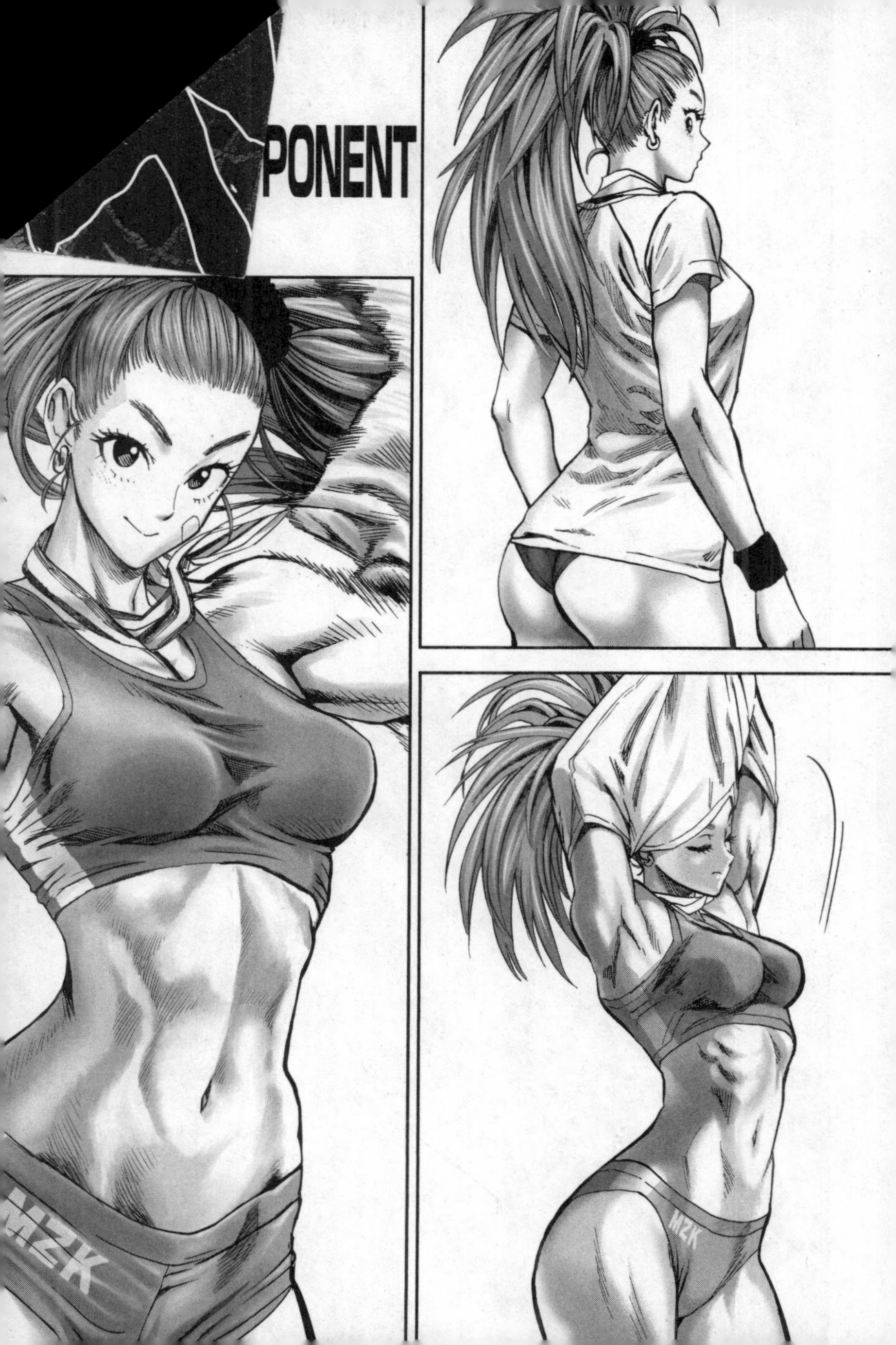
M2K
PONENT
M2K

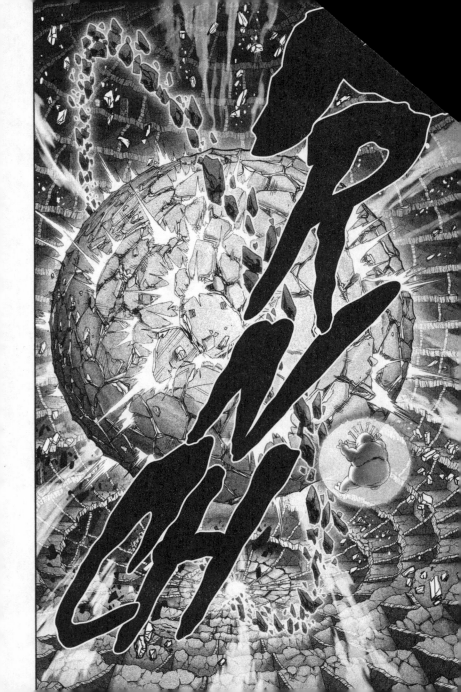

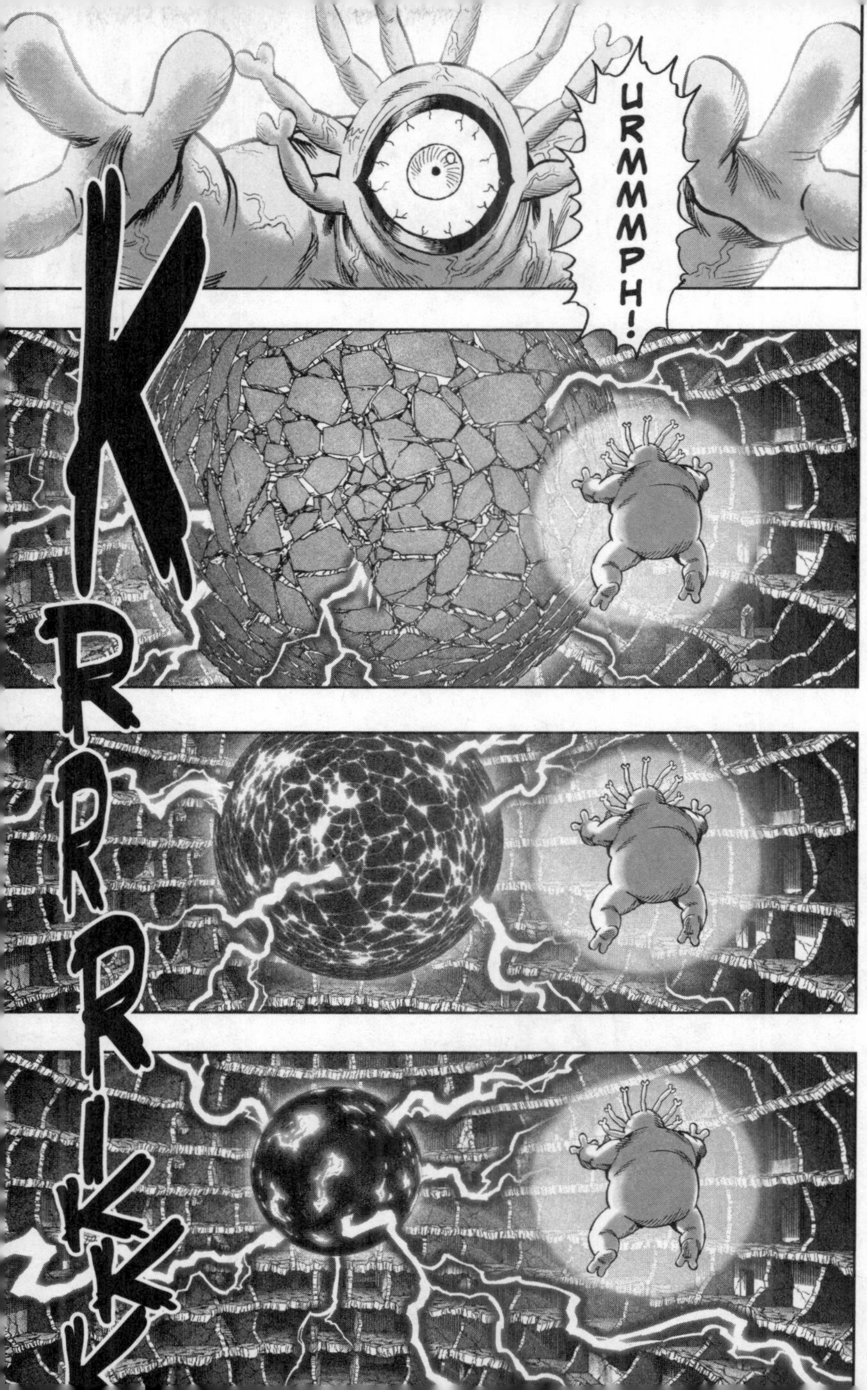
URMMMMPH!
KRRRRKK

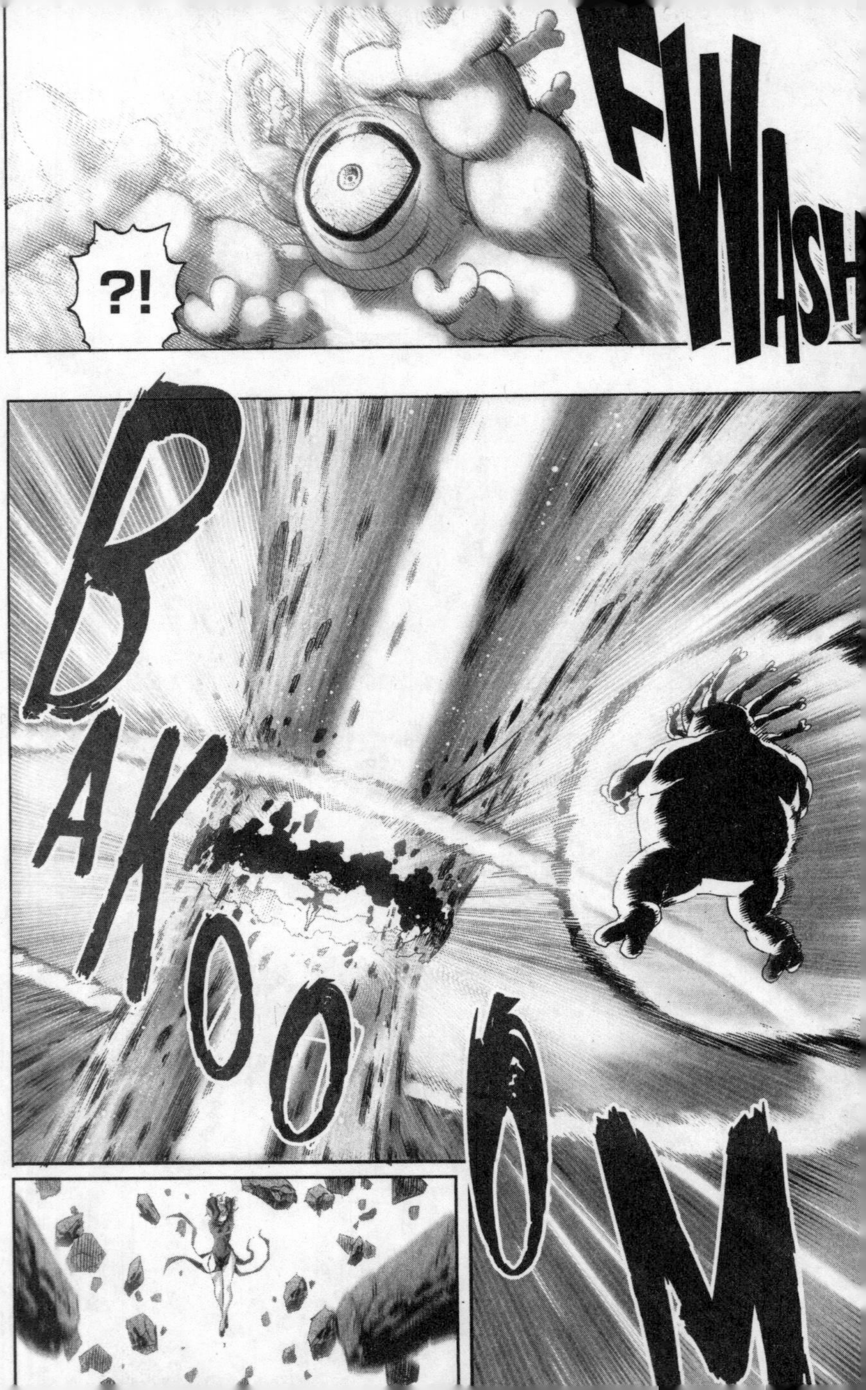
FWASH
?!
BAKOOOOOM

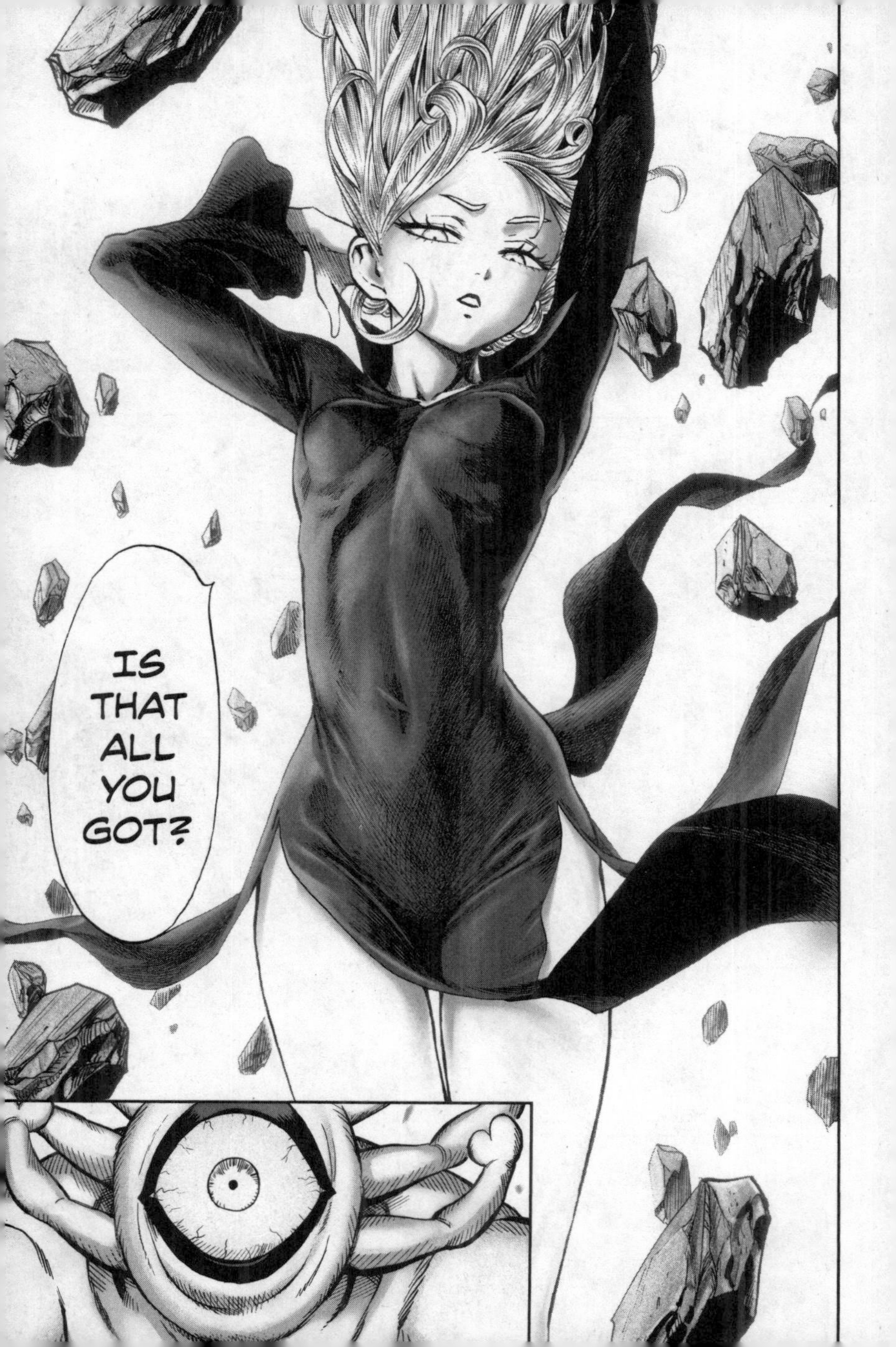
IS THAT ALL YOU GOT?

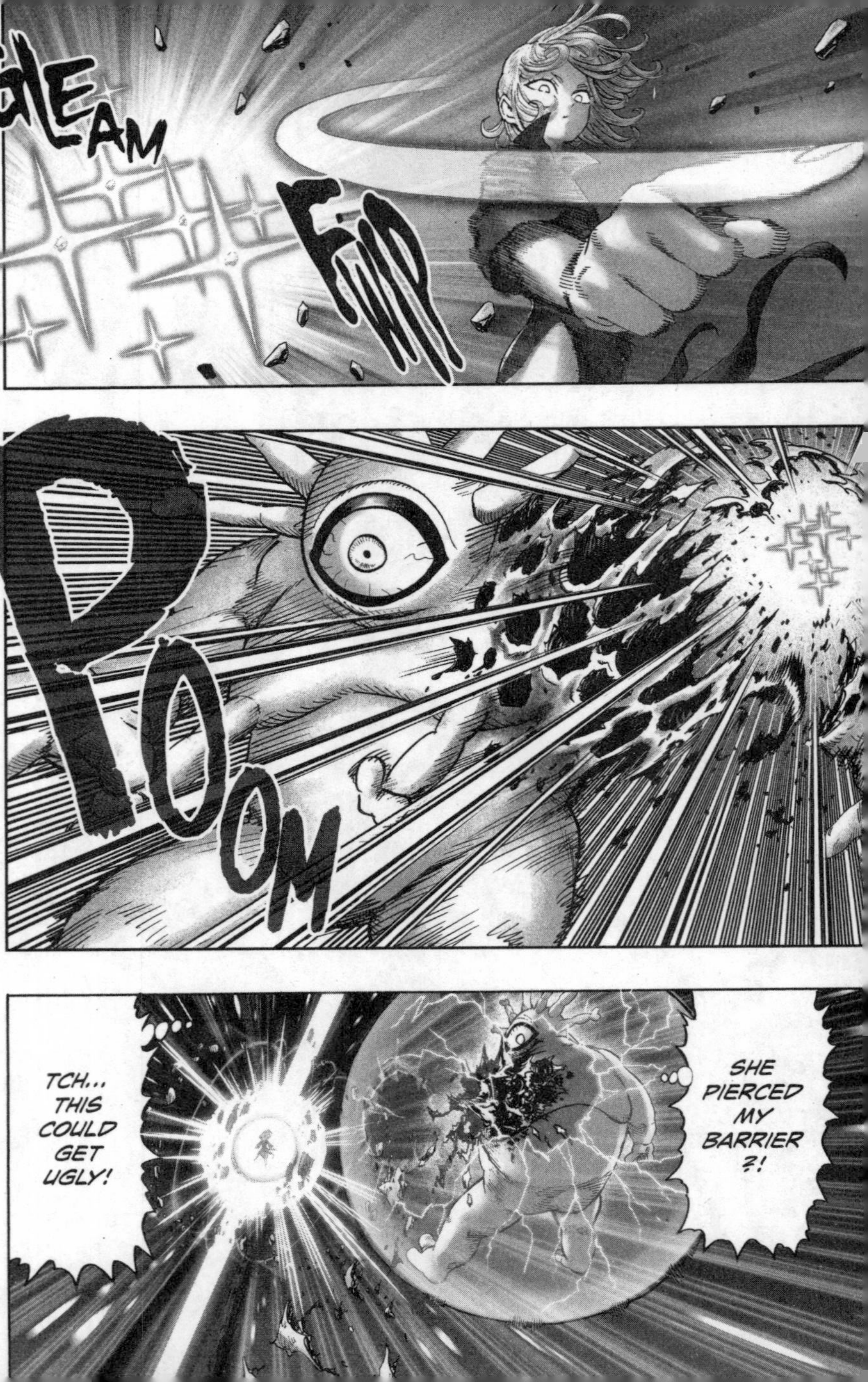
FWIP
GLEAM
POOM
SHE PIERCED MY BARRIER?!
TCH... THIS COULD GET UGLY!

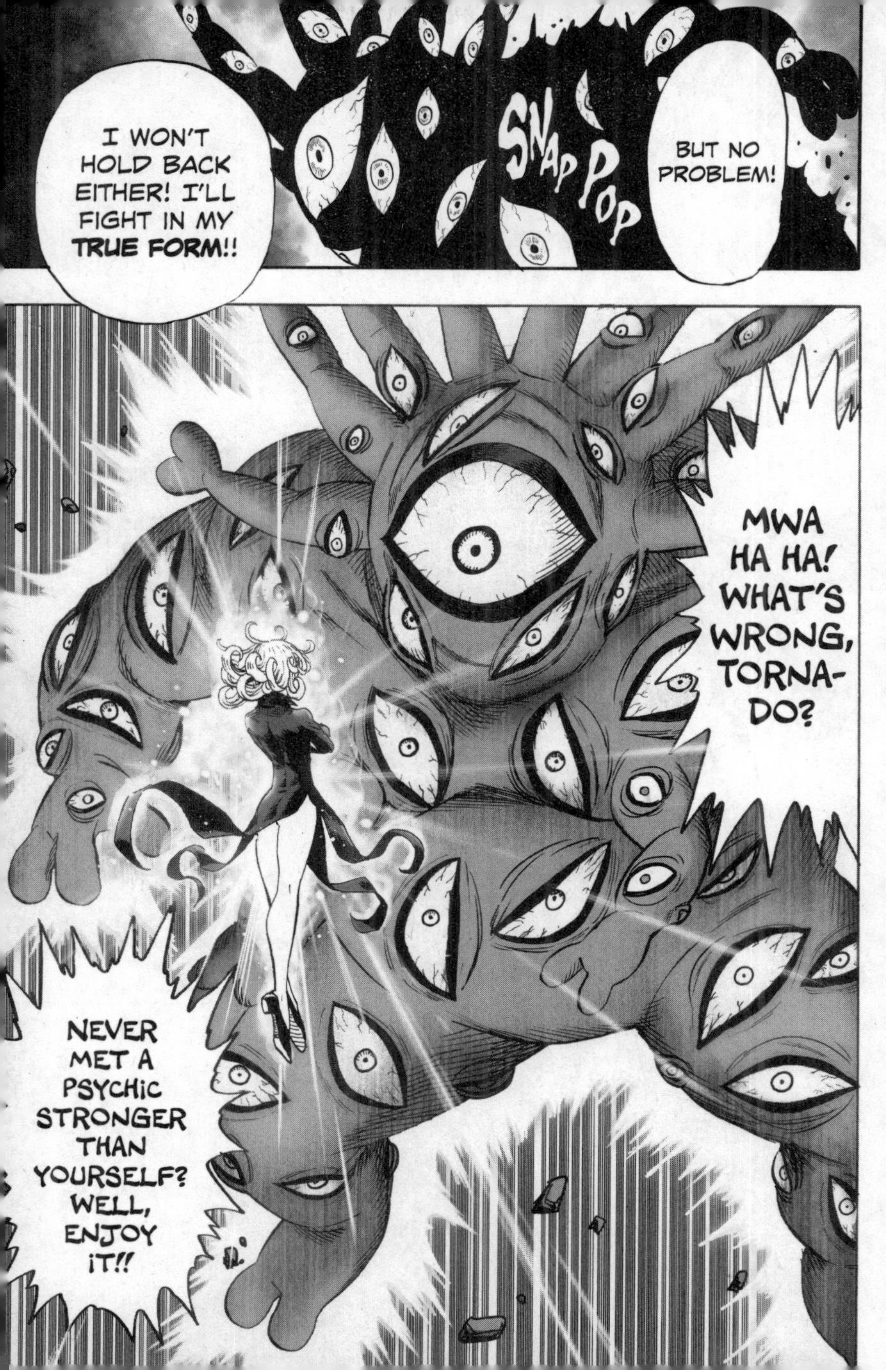
BUT NO PROBLEM!
SNAP POP
I WON'T HOLD BACK EITHER! I'LL FIGHT IN MY **TRUE FORM**!!
MWA HA HA! WHAT'S WRONG, TORNA-DO?
NEVER MET A PSYCHIC STRONGER THAN YOURSELF? WELL, ENJOY IT!!

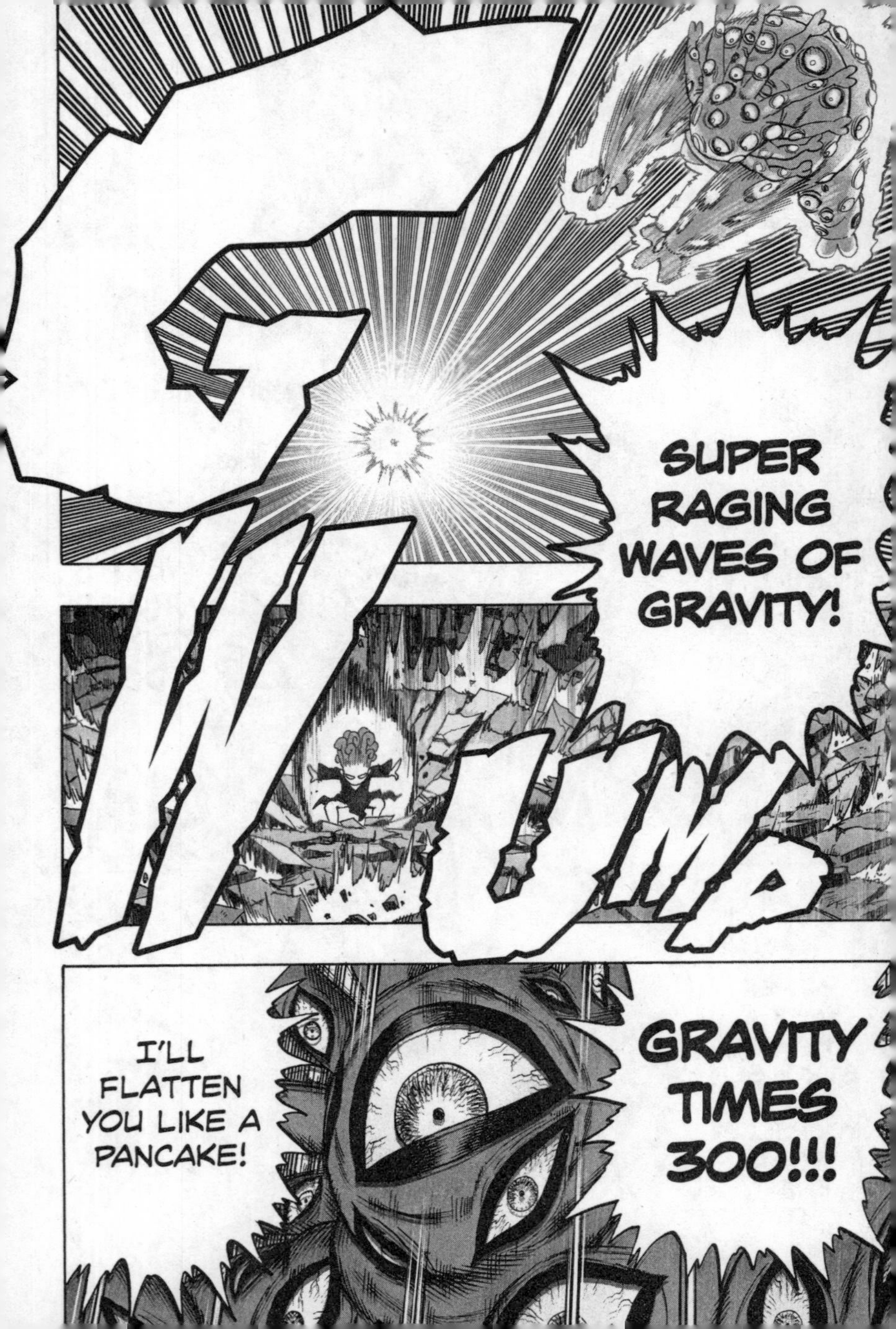
SUPER RAGING WAVES OF GRAVITY!
GRAVITY TIMES 300!!!
I'LL FLATTEN YOU LIKE A PANCAKE!

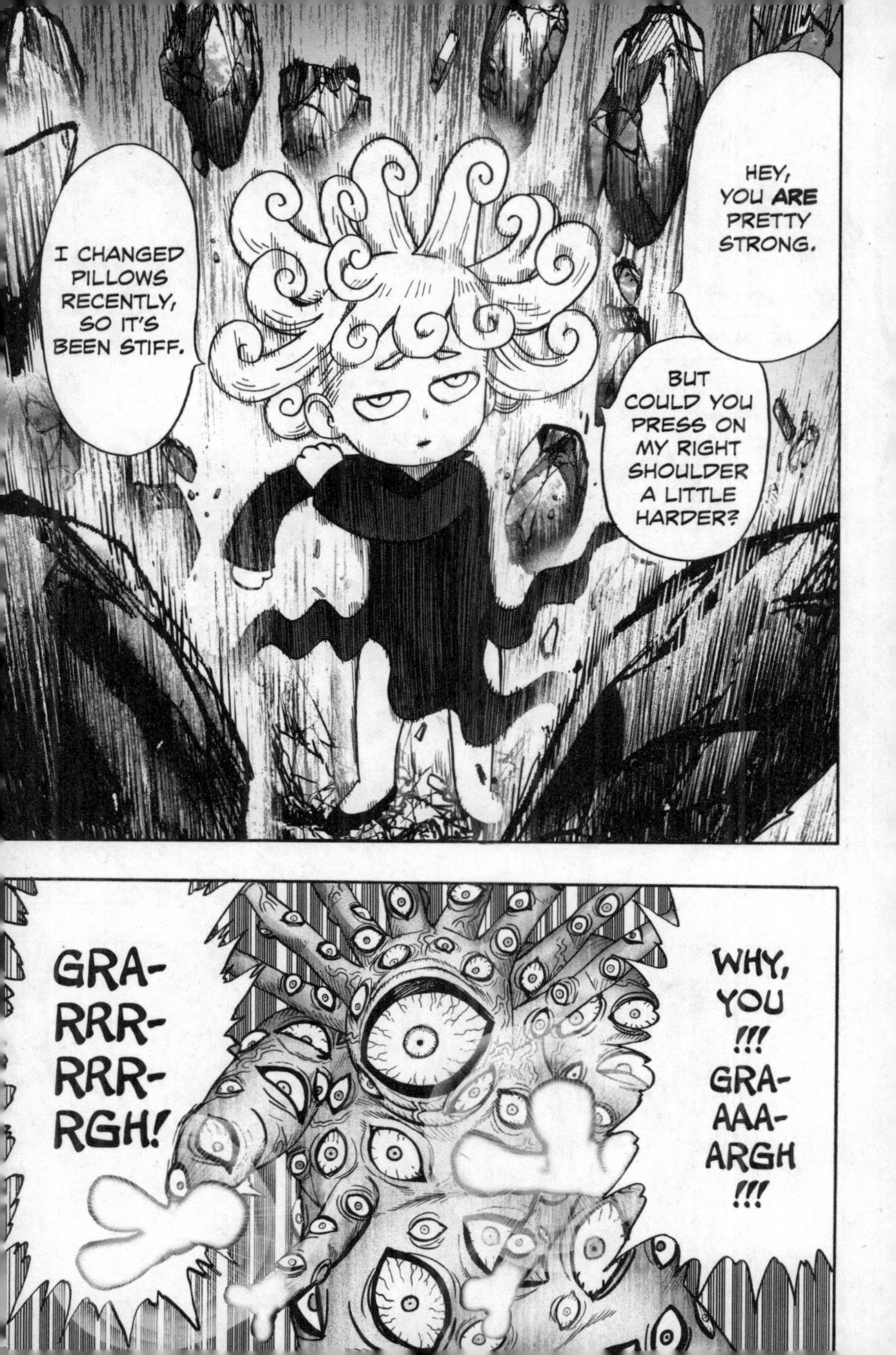
HEY, YOU **ARE** PRETTY STRONG.
BUT COULD YOU PRESS ON MY RIGHT SHOULDER A LITTLE HARDER?
I CHANGED PILLOWS RECENTLY, SO IT'S BEEN STIFF.
WHY, YOU!!! GRA-AAA-ARGH!!!
GRA-RRR-RRR-RGH!

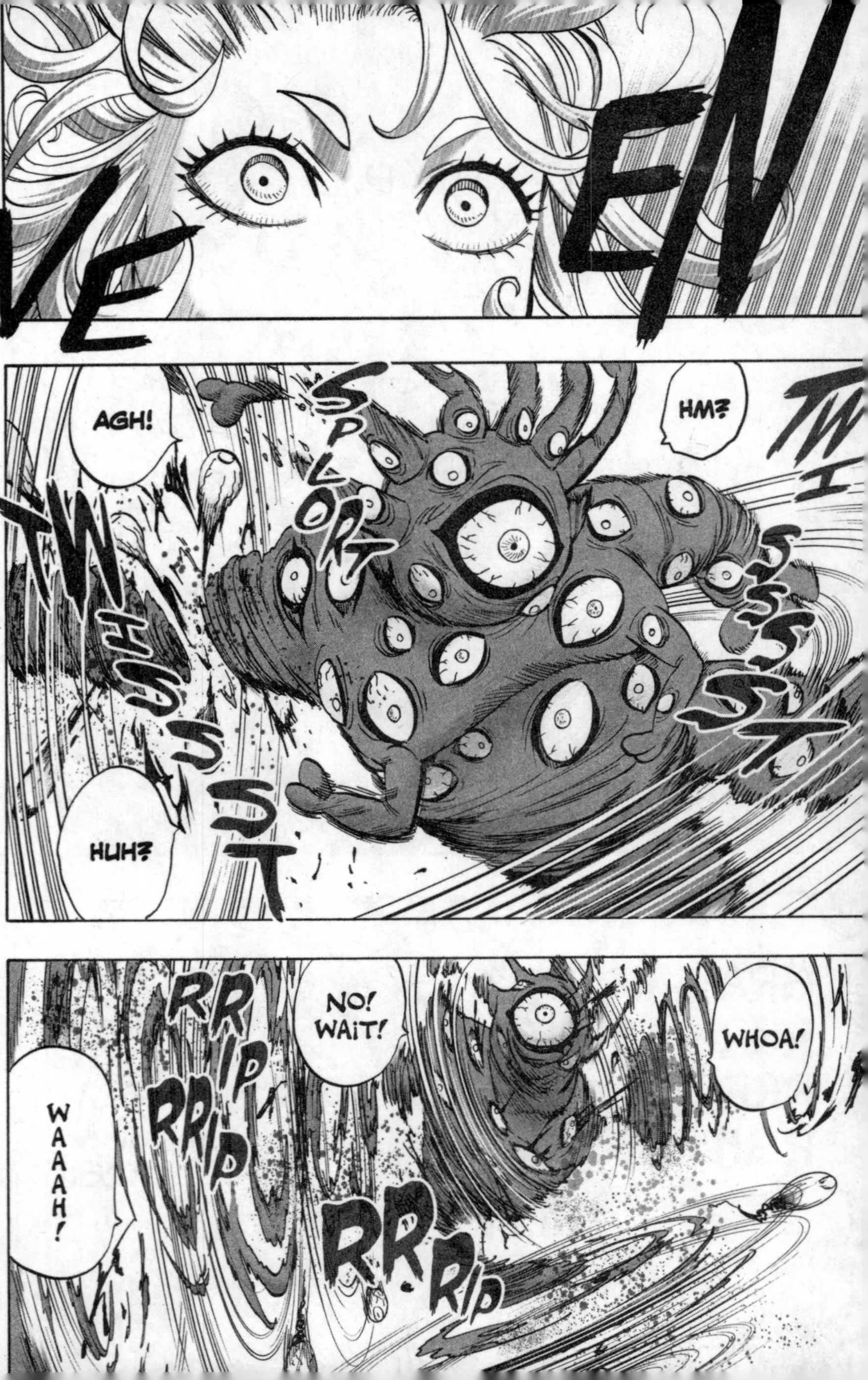
VEEN
HM?
TWISSST
SPLORT
AGH!
TWHISSST
HUH?
WHOA!
NO! WAIT!
RRIP RRIP
RRRIP
WAAAAH!

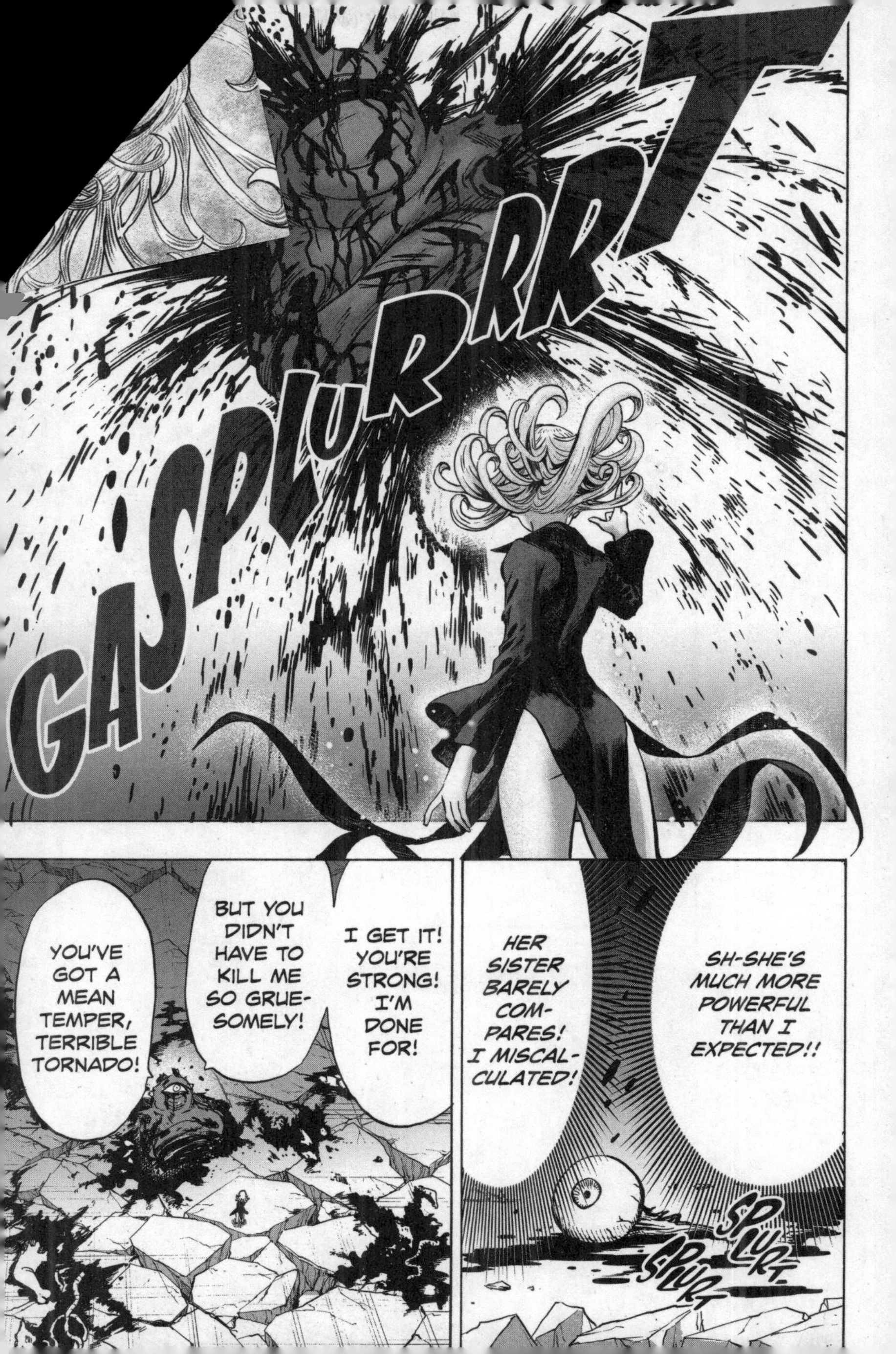
GASPLURRRT
SH-SHE'S MUCH MORE POWERFUL THAN I EXPECTED!!
HER SISTER BARELY COMPARES! I MISCALCULATED!
SPLURT
SPLURT
I GET IT! YOU'RE STRONG! I'M DONE FOR!
BUT YOU DIDN'T HAVE TO KILL ME SO GRUESOMELY!
YOU'VE GOT A MEAN TEMPER, TERRIBLE TORNADO!

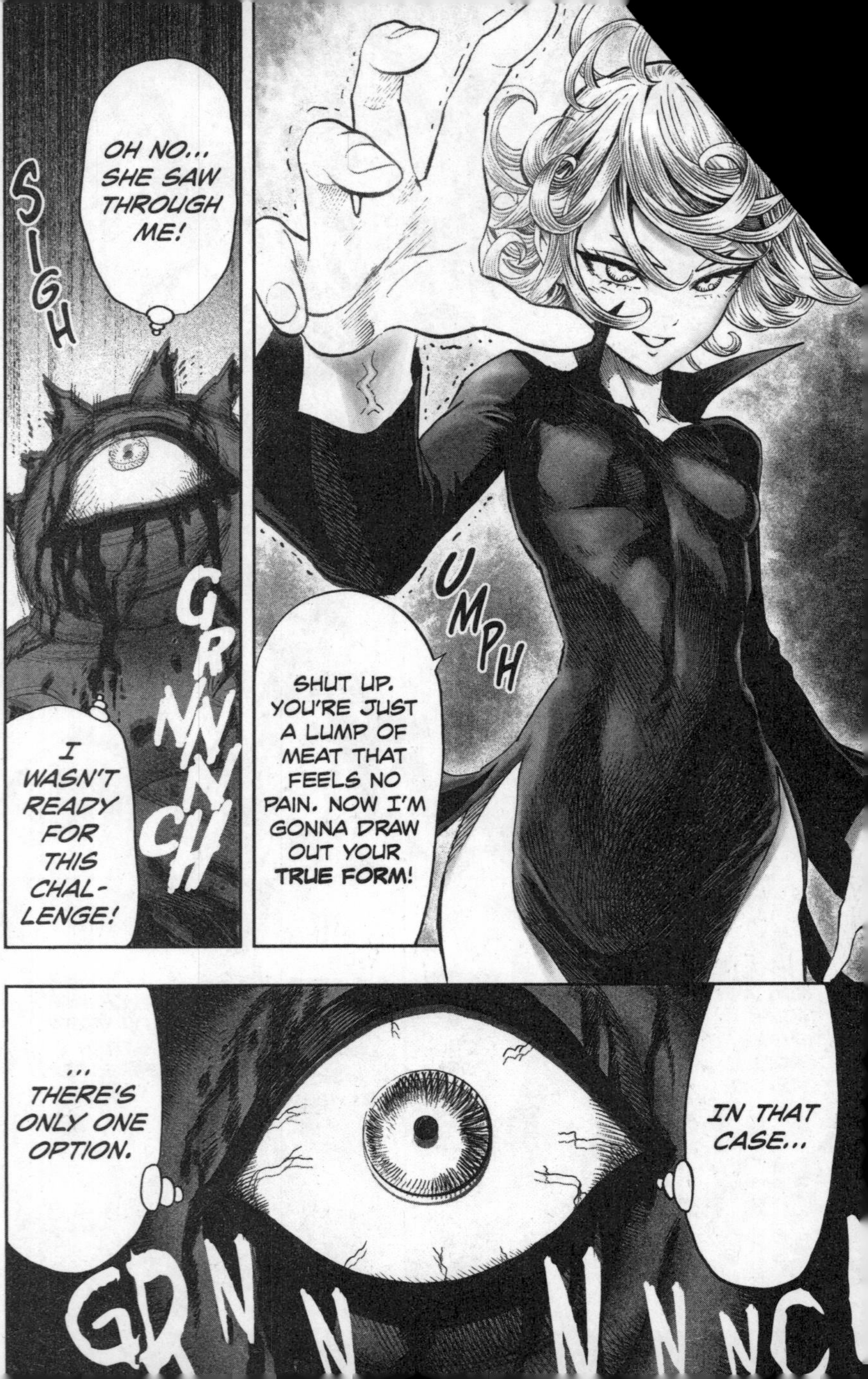

UMPH
SHUT UP. YOU'RE JUST A LUMP OF MEAT THAT FEELS NO PAIN. NOW I'M GONNA DRAW OUT YOUR TRUE FORM!
OH NO... SHE SAW THROUGH ME!
SIGH
I WASN'T READY FOR THIS CHAL-LENGE!
GRNNNNCH
IN THAT CASE...
... THERE'S ONLY ONE OPTION.
GRNNNNNNC

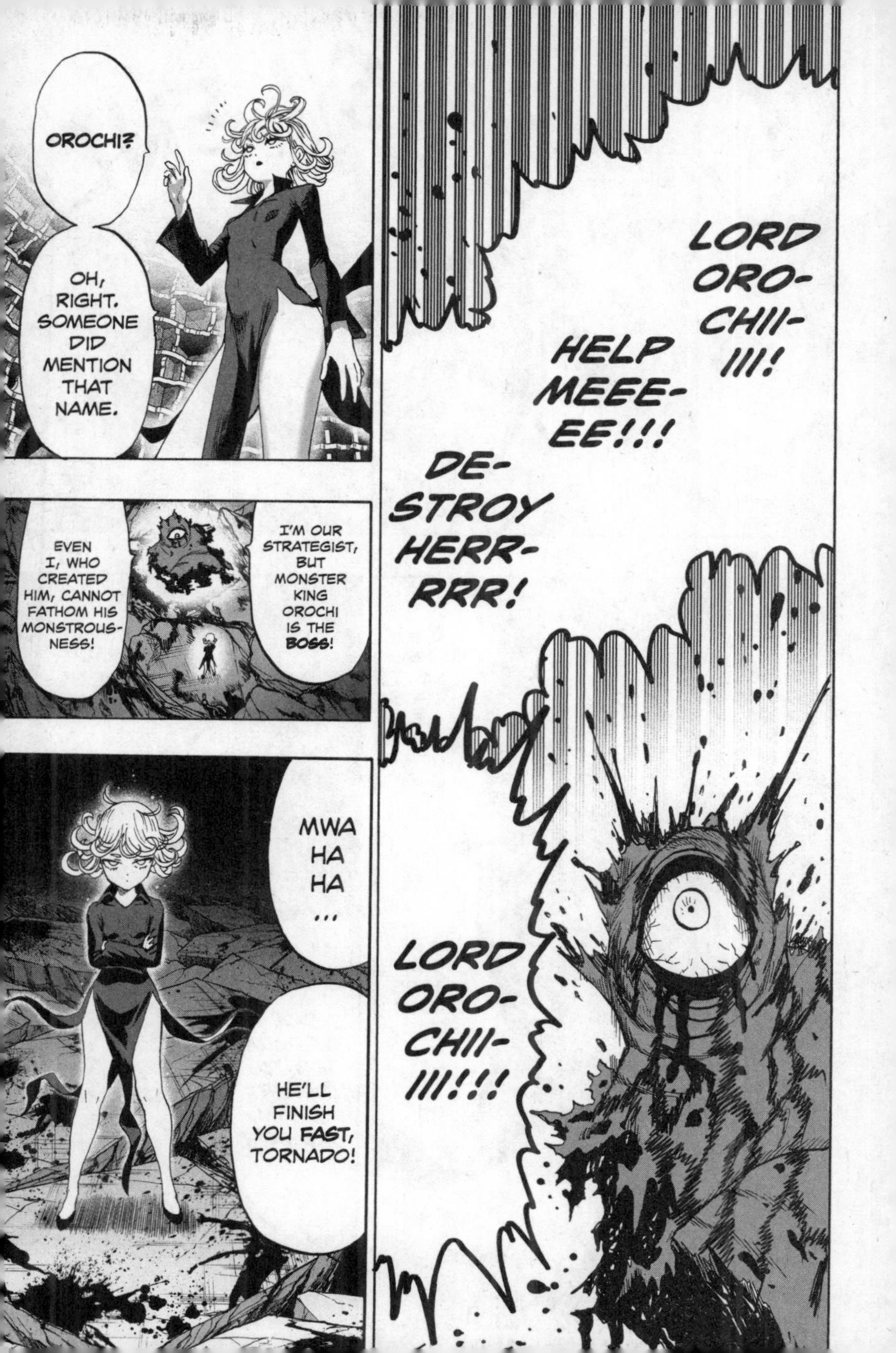
LORD ORO-CHII-III!
HELP MEEEE-EE!!!
DE-STROY HERR-RRR!
LORD ORO-CHII-III!!!
OROCHI?
OH, RIGHT. SOMEONE DID MENTION THAT NAME.
I'M OUR STRATEGIST, BUT MONSTER KING OROCHI IS THE BOSS!
EVEN I, WHO CREATED HIM, CANNOT FATHOM HIS MONSTROUS-NESS!
MWA HA HA ...
HE'LL FINISH YOU FAST, TORNADO!

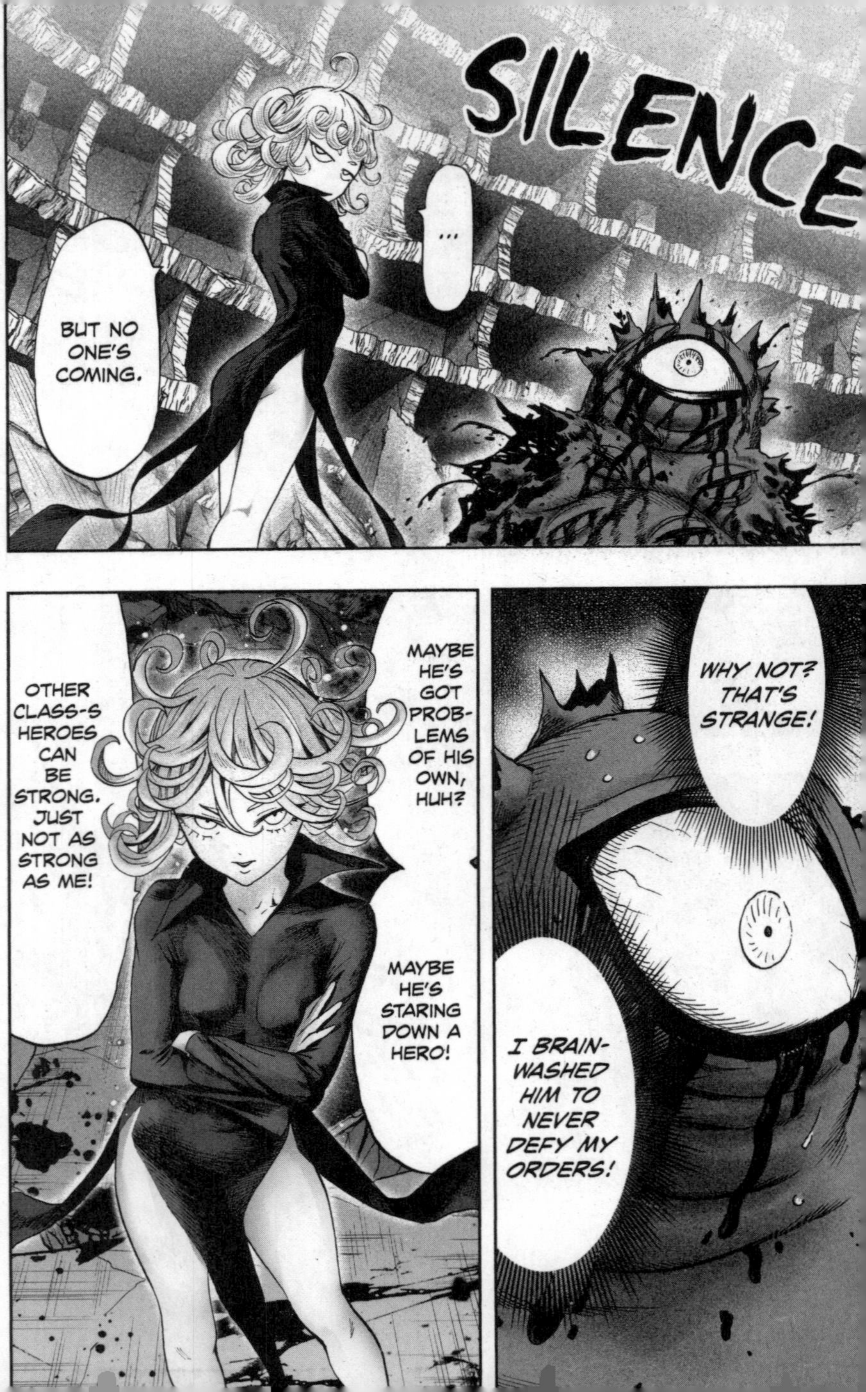
SILENCE
...
BUT NO ONE'S COMING.
WHY NOT? THAT'S STRANGE!
I BRAIN-WASHED HIM TO NEVER DEFY MY ORDERS!
MAYBE HE'S GOT PROB-LEMS OF HIS OWN, HUH?
OTHER CLASS-S HEROES CAN BE STRONG. JUST NOT AS STRONG AS ME!
MAYBE HE'S STARING DOWN A HERO!

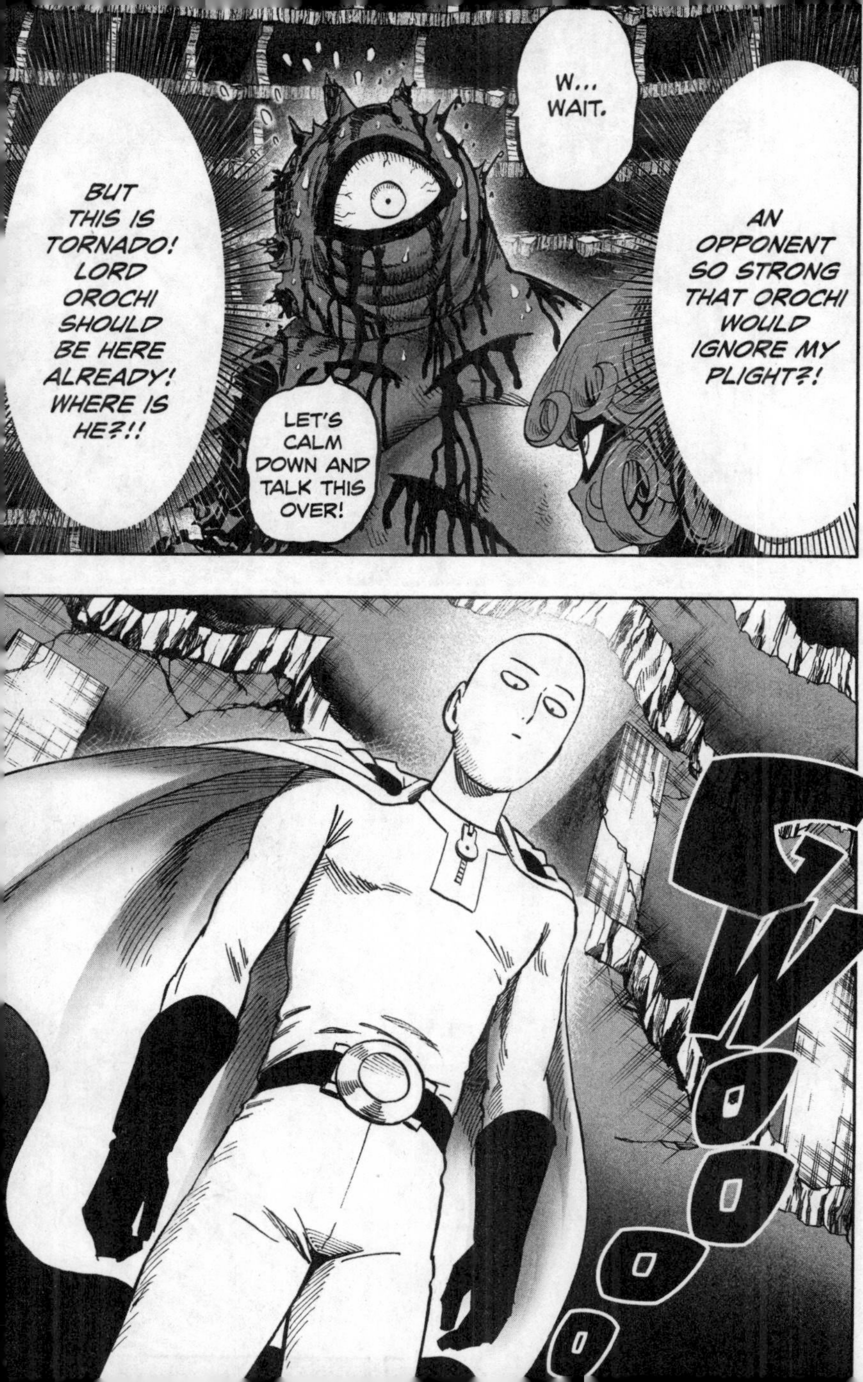
W... WAIT.
AN OPPONENT SO STRONG THAT OROCHI WOULD IGNORE MY PLIGHT?!
BUT THIS IS TORNADO! LORD OROCHI SHOULD BE HERE ALREADY! WHERE IS HE?!!
LET'S CALM DOWN AND TALK THIS OVER!
GWOOOO

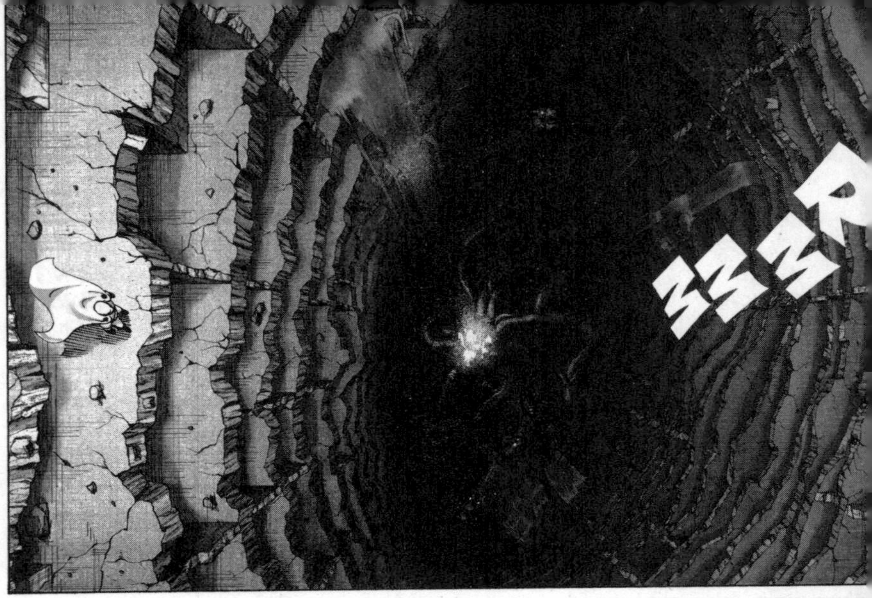
RMMM
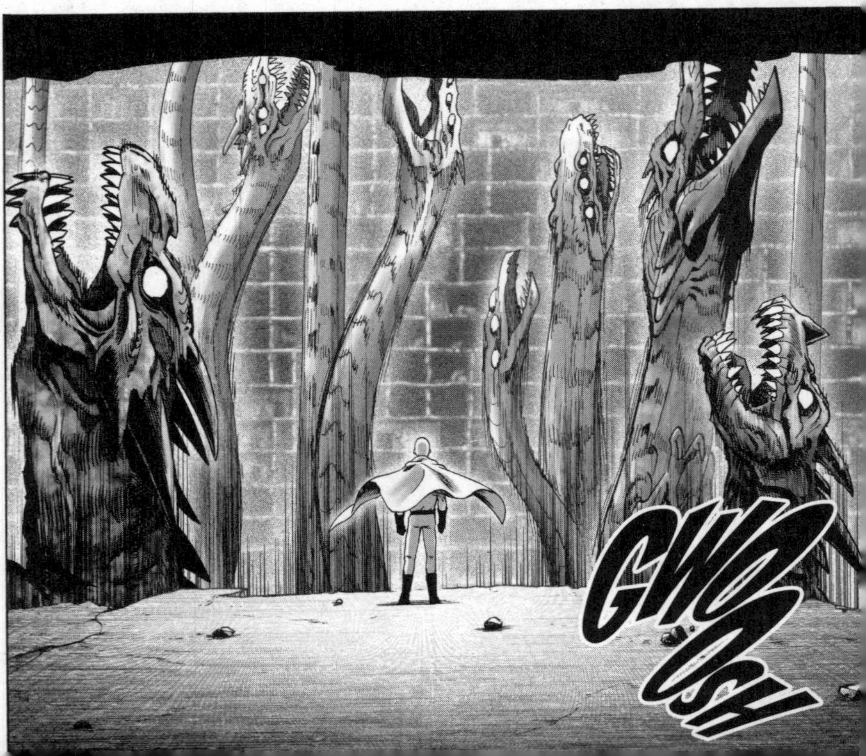
GWOOSH!

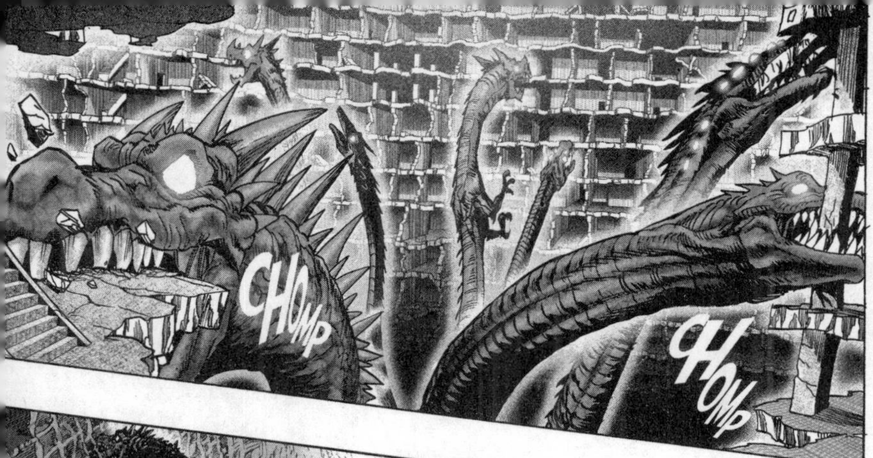
CHOMP
CHOMP
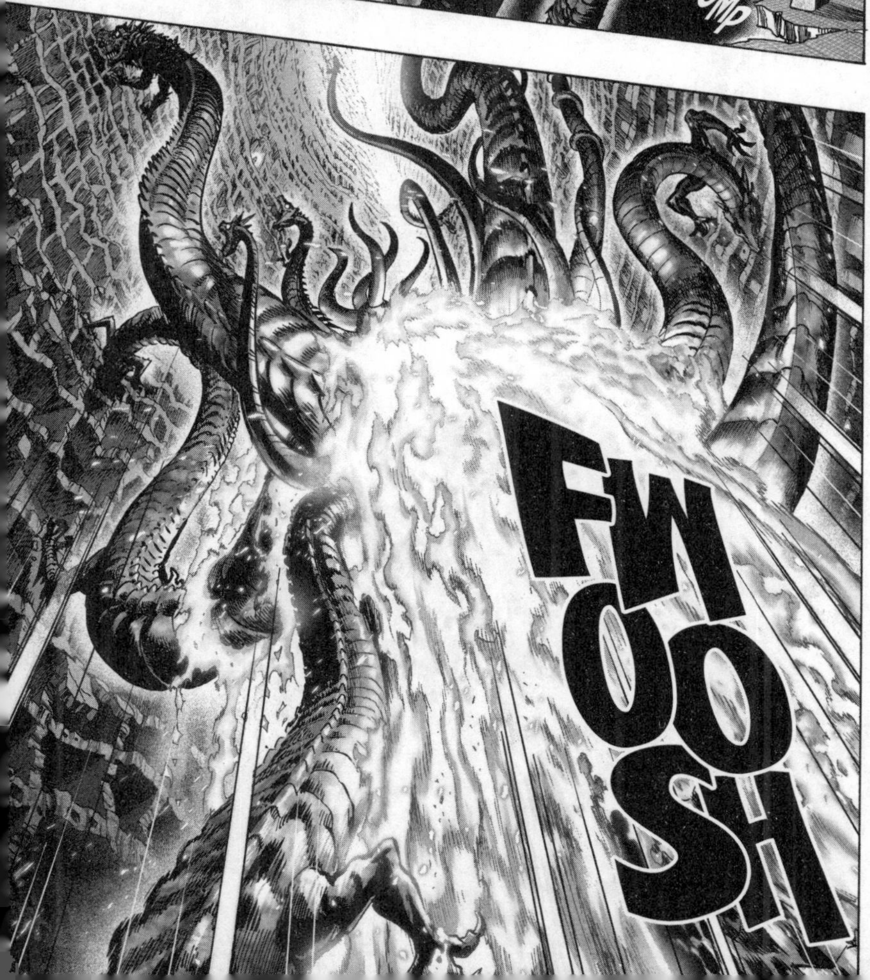
FWOOSH

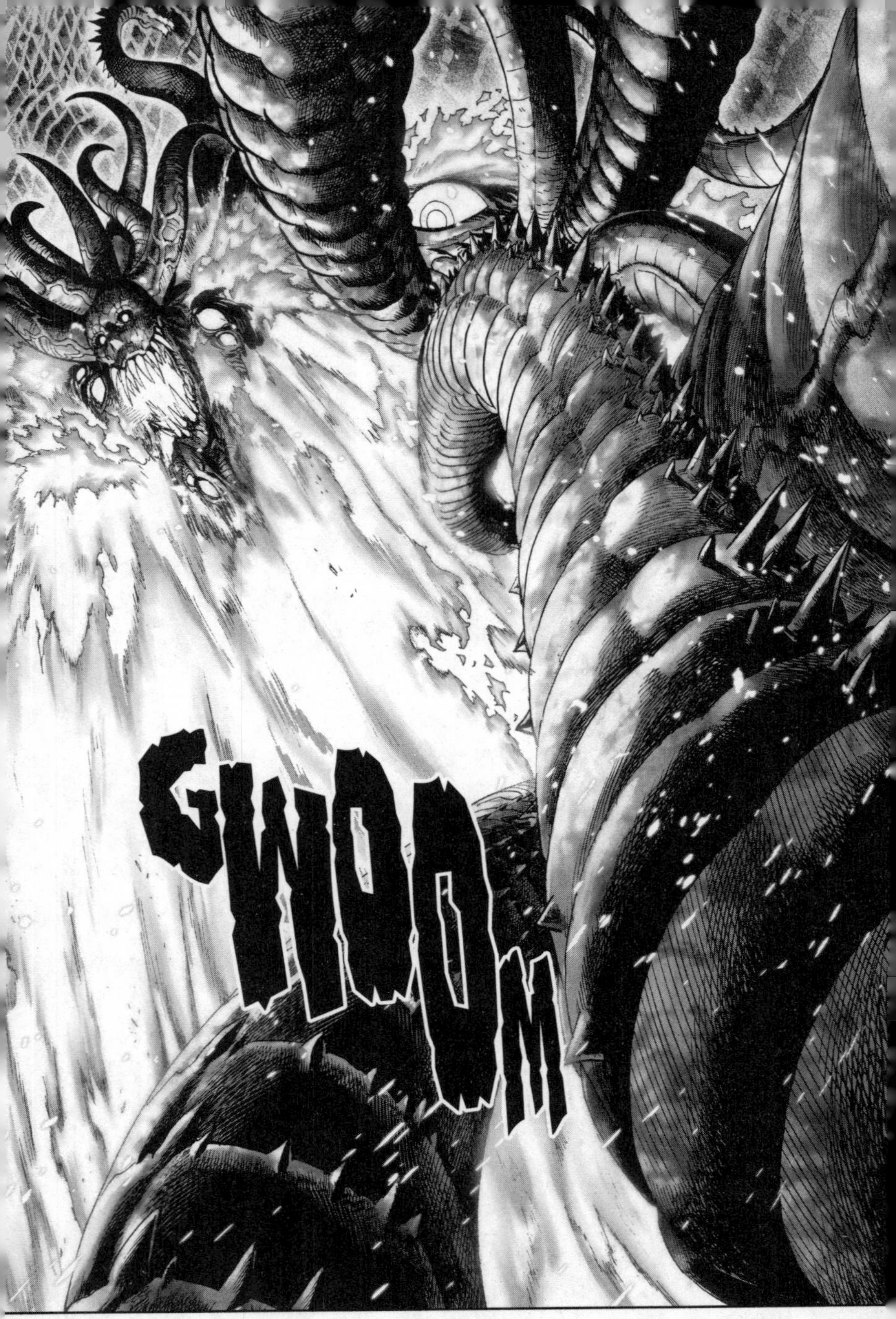
GWOOM

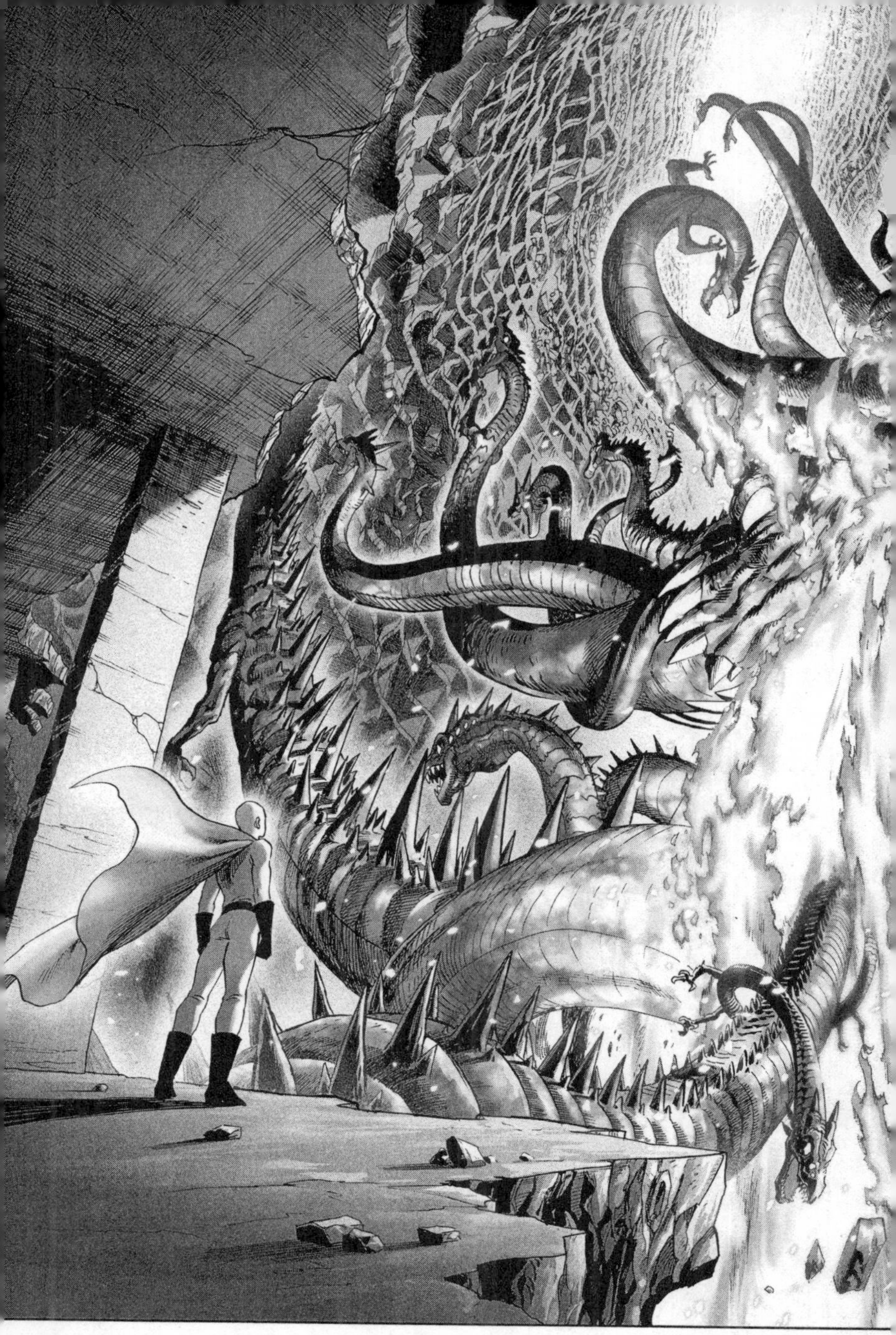

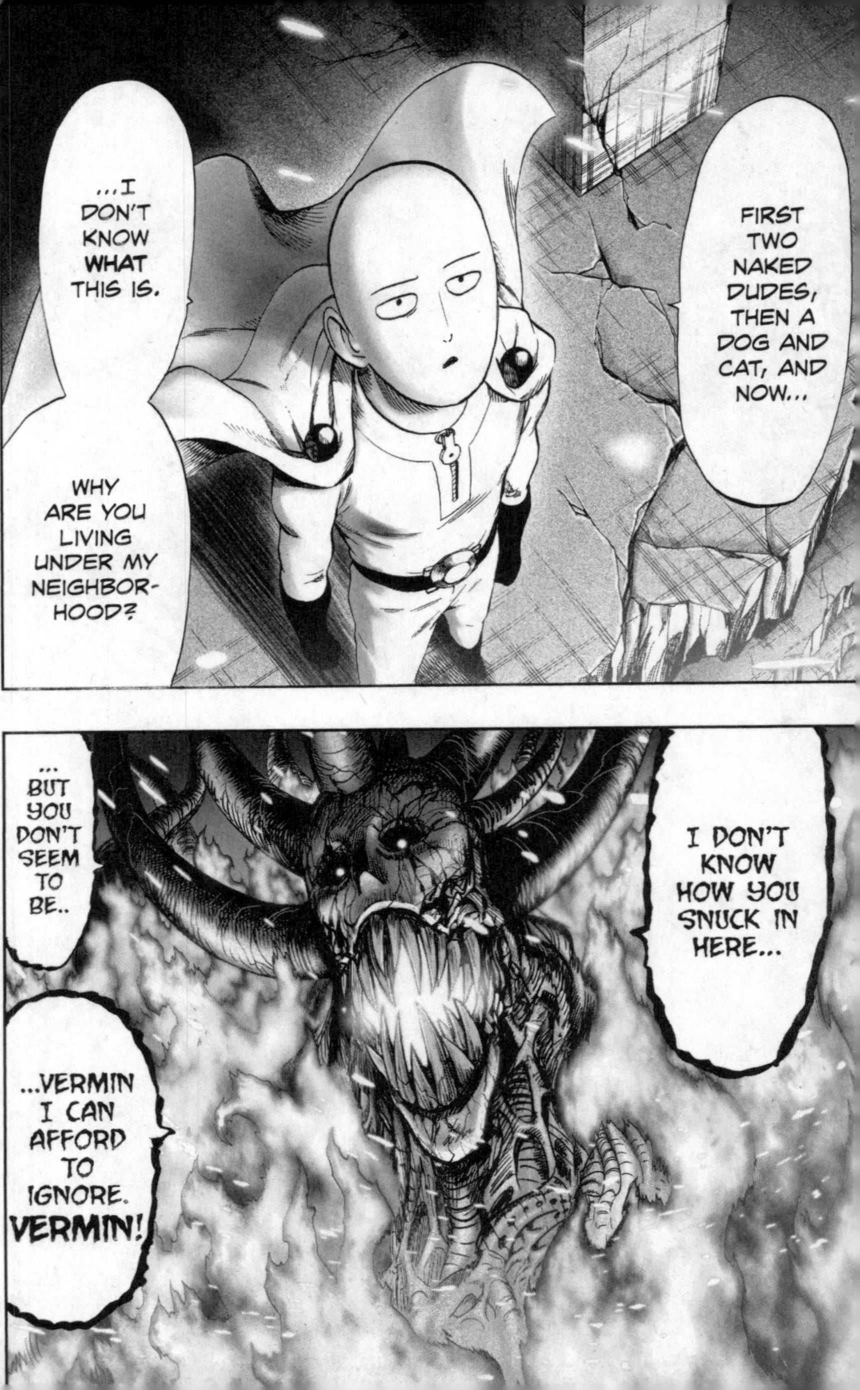
FIRST TWO NAKED DUDES, THEN A DOG AND CAT, AND NOW...
...I DON'T KNOW WHAT THIS IS.
WHY ARE YOU LIVING UNDER MY NEIGHBOR-HOOD?
I DON'T KNOW HOW YOU SNUCK IN HERE...
...BUT YOU DON'T SEEM TO BE..
...VERMIN I CAN AFFORD TO IGNORE. VERMIN!

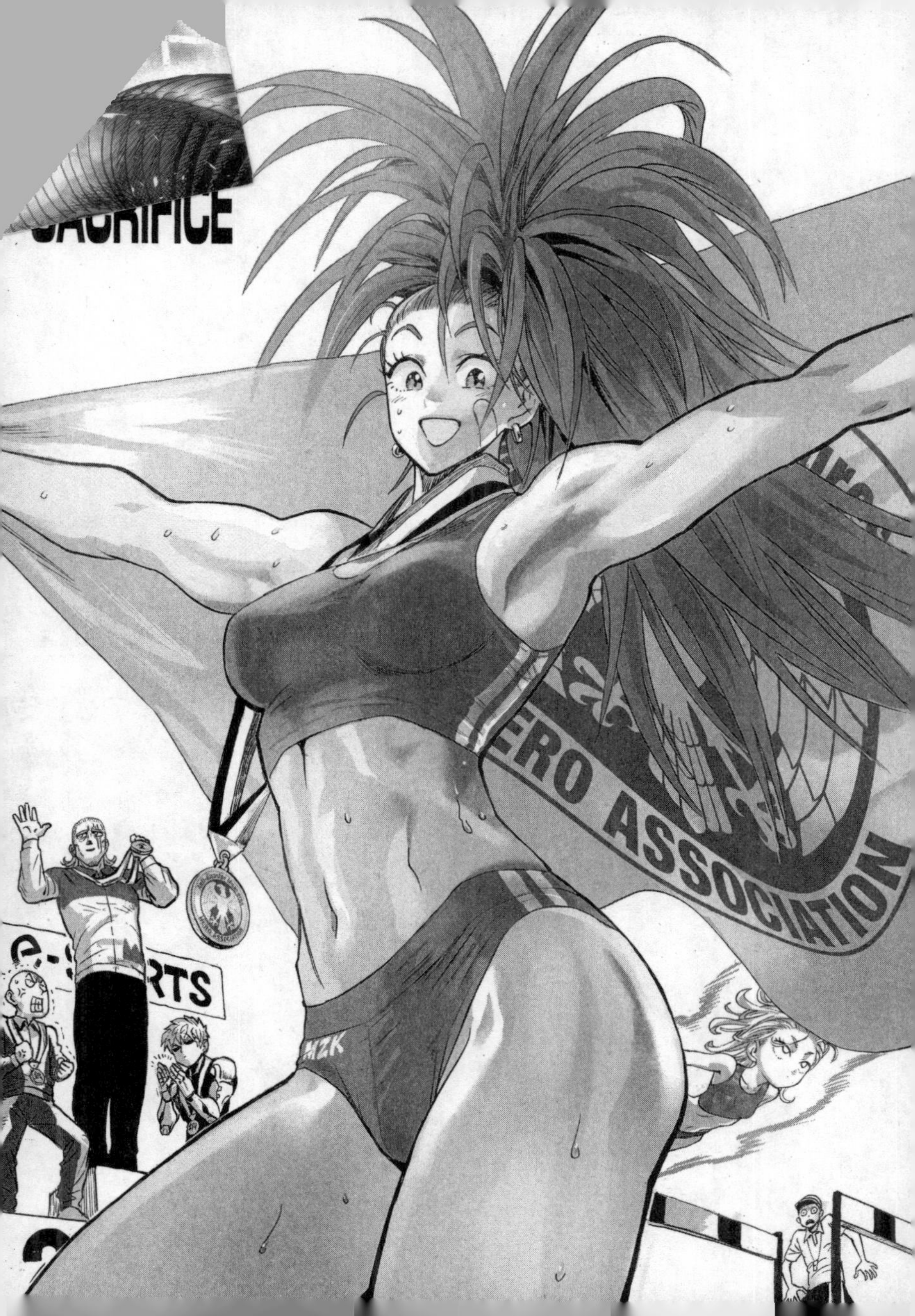
SACRIFICE
ERO ASSOCIATION
MZK

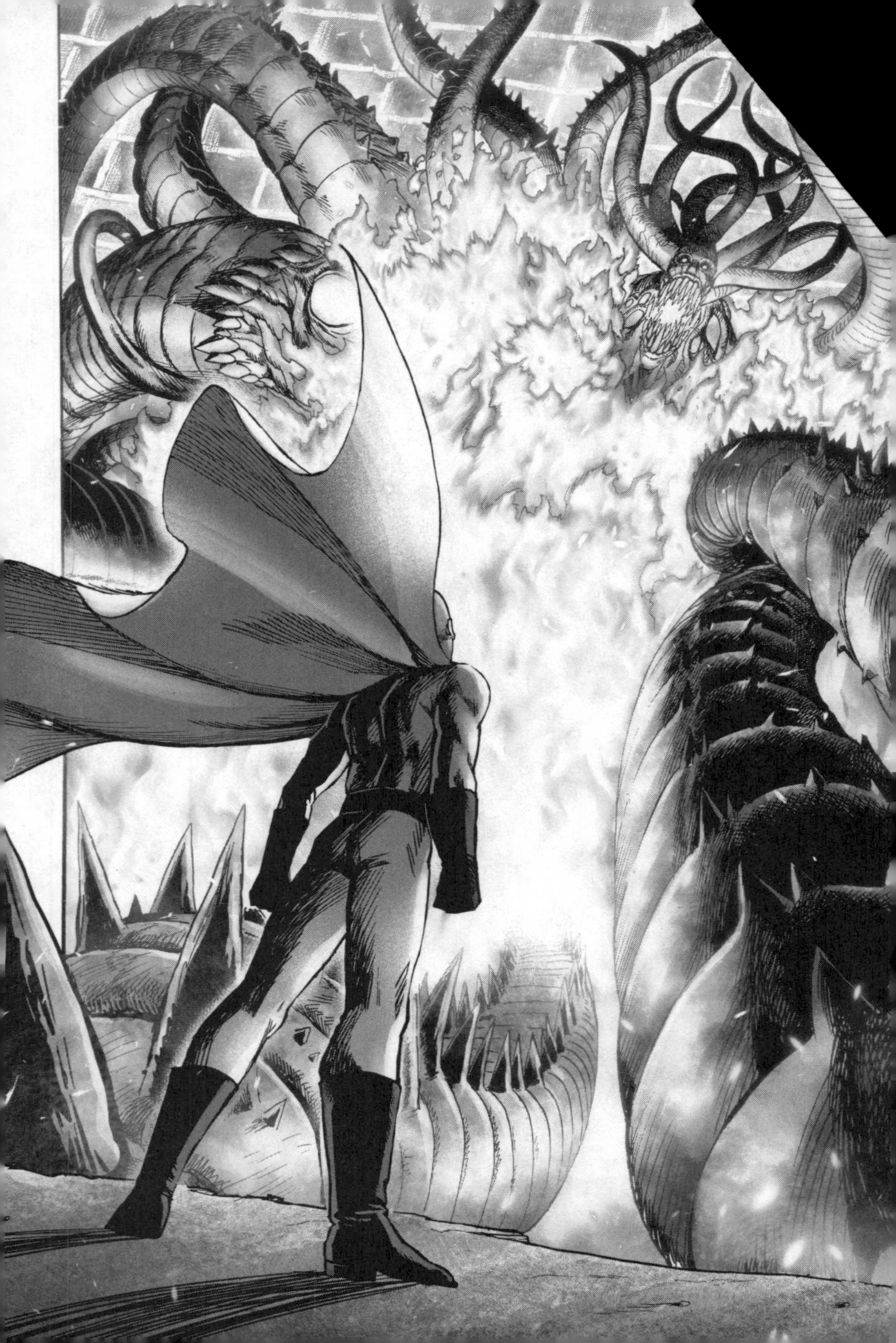

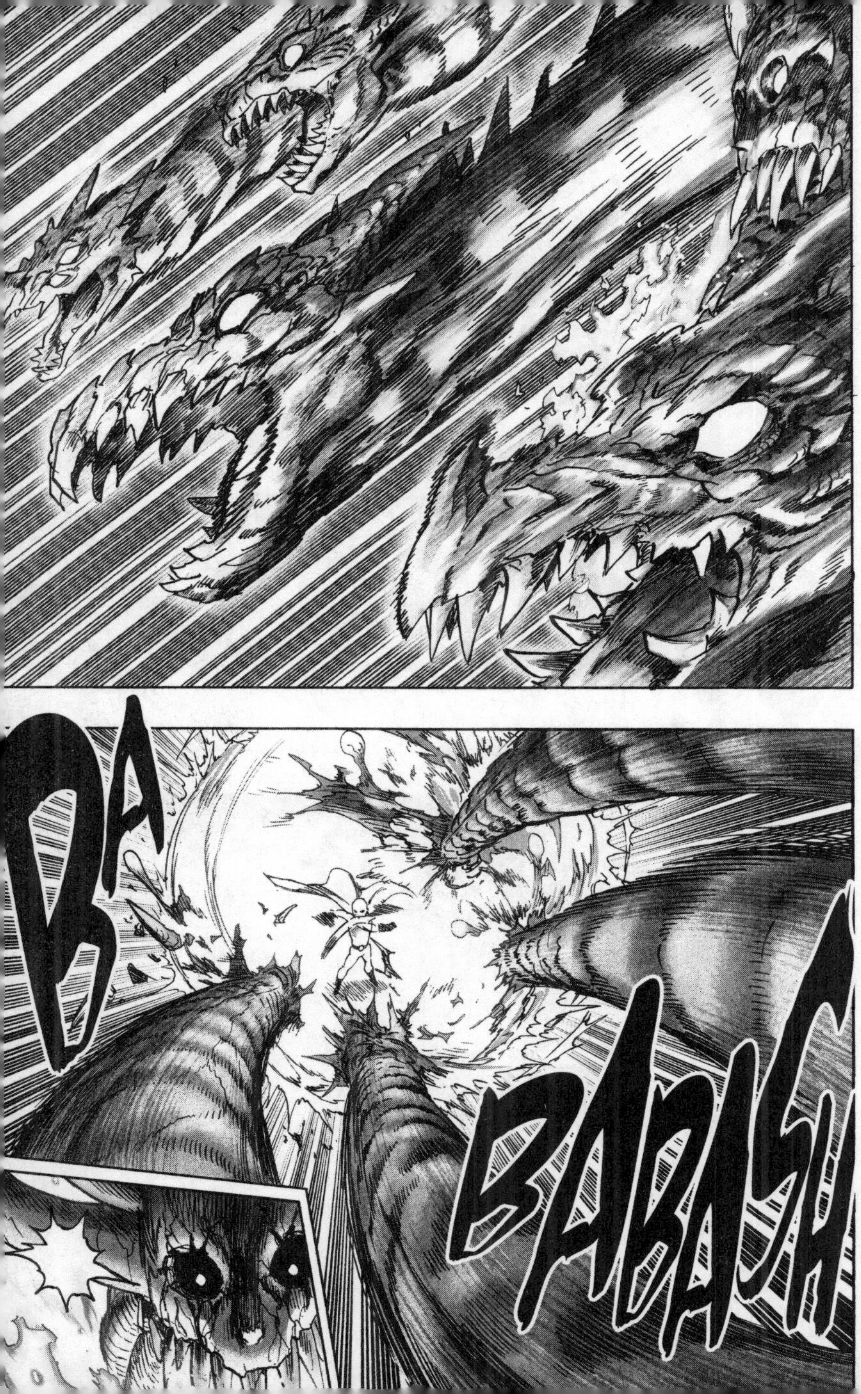
BA
BABASH

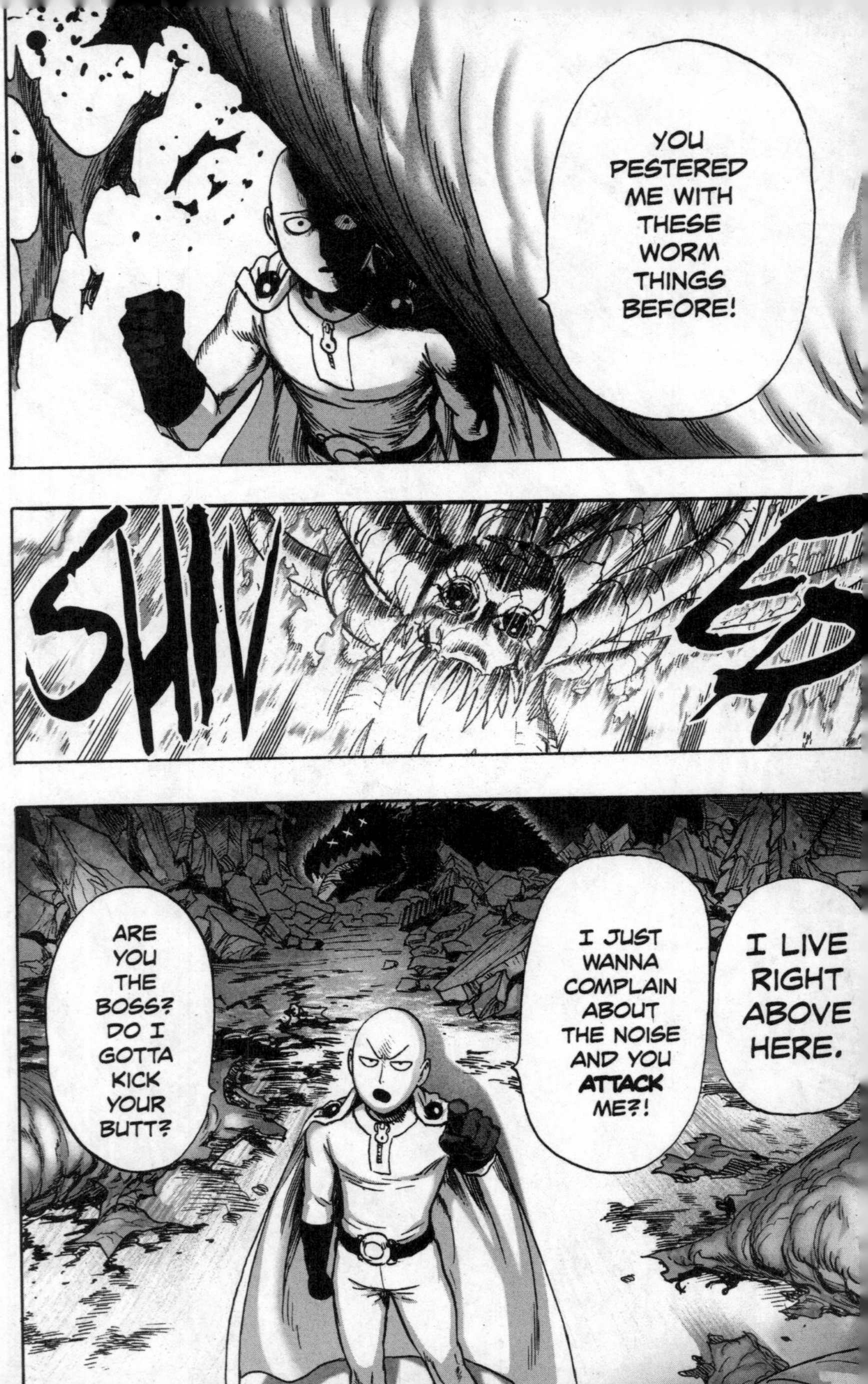
YOU PESTERED ME WITH THESE WORM THINGS BEFORE!
SHIV
I LIVE RIGHT ABOVE HERE.
I JUST WANNA COMPLAIN ABOUT THE NOISE AND YOU **ATTACK** ME?!
ARE YOU THE BOSS? DO I GOTTA KICK YOUR BUTT?

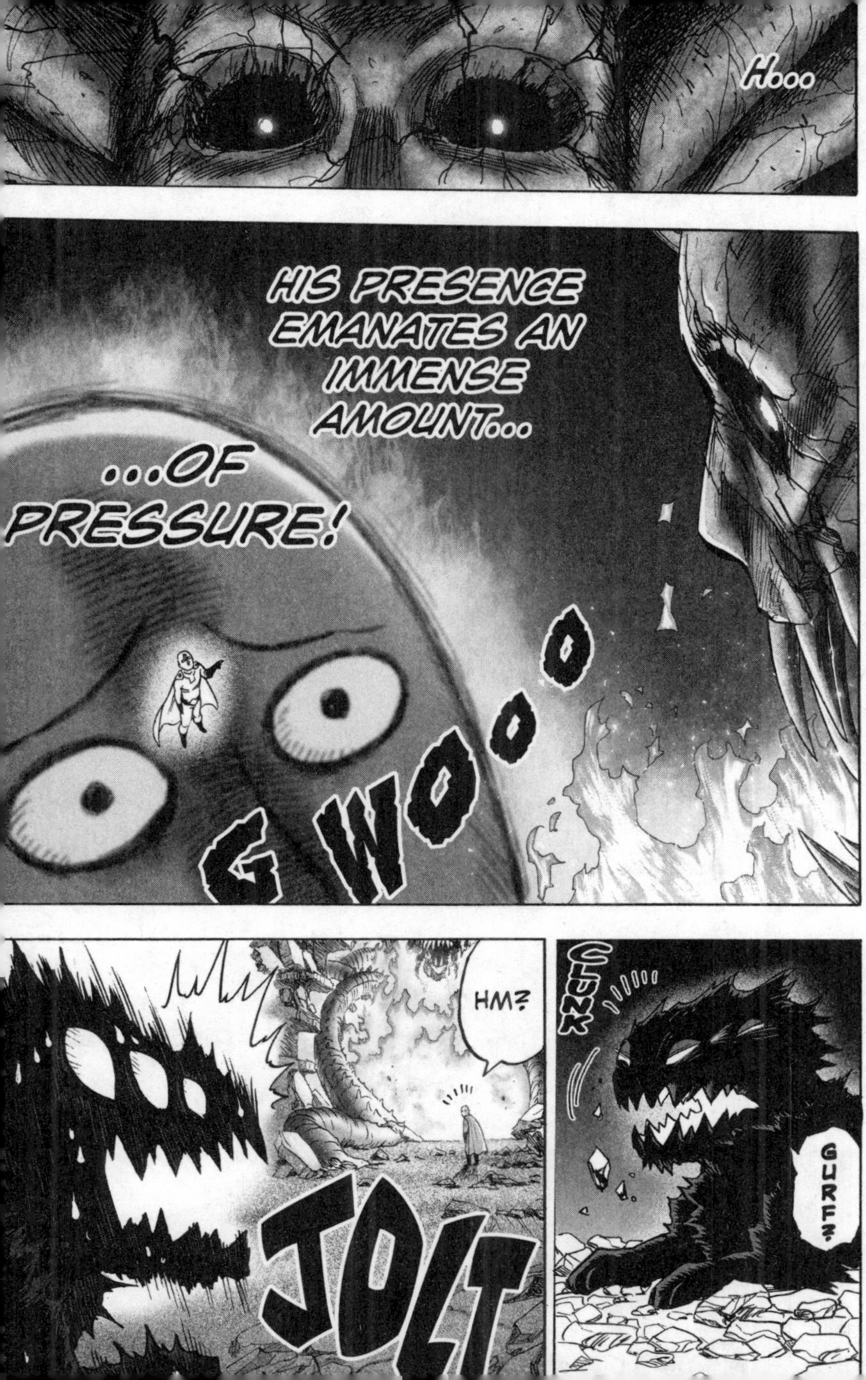
H...
HIS PRESENCE EMANATES AN IMMENSE AMOUNT...
...OF PRESSURE!
GWOOOO
CLUNK
GURF?
HM?
JOLT

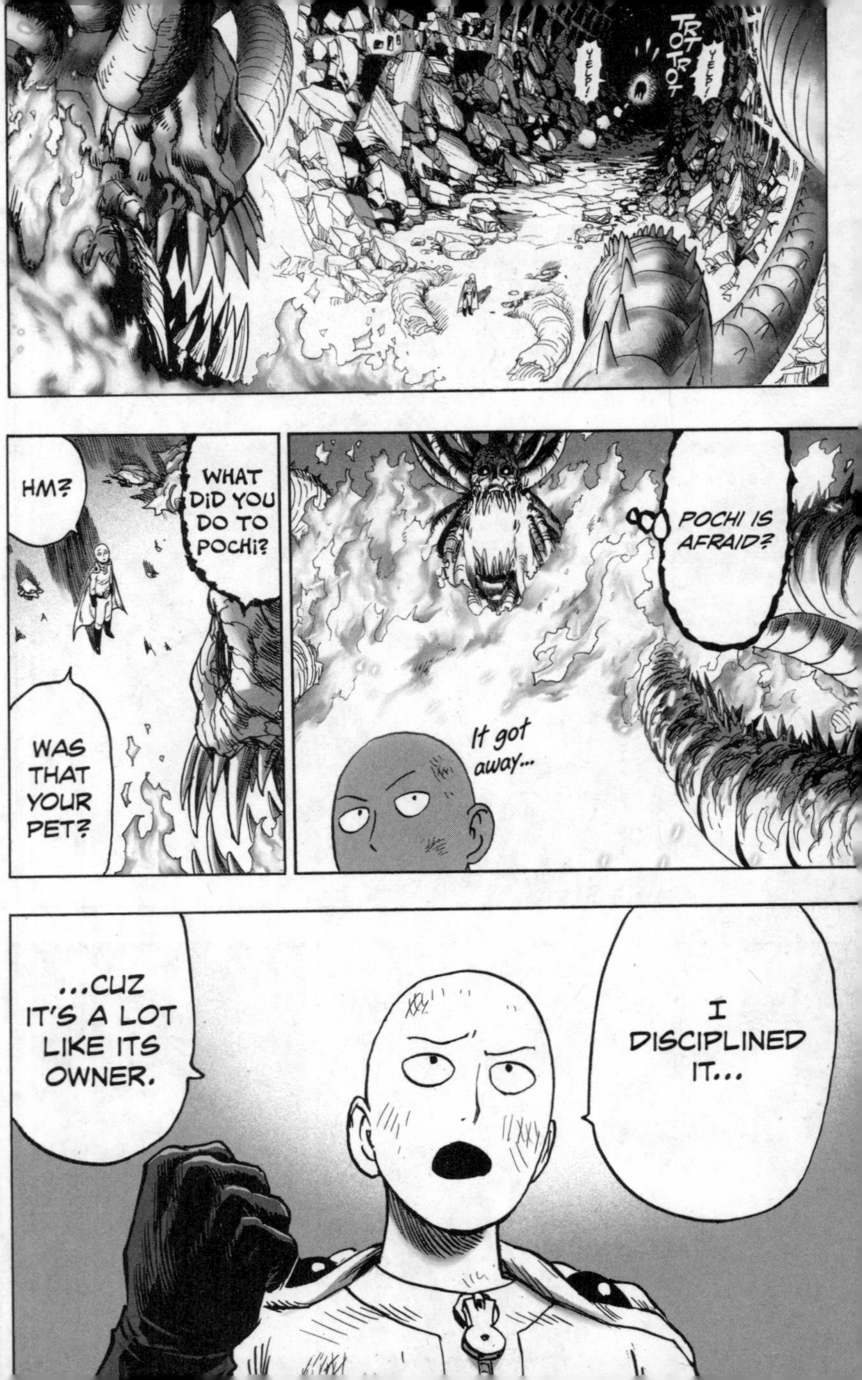
YELP!
TROT TROT
YELP!
POCHI IS AFRAID?
It got away...
WHAT DID YOU DO TO POCHI?
HM?
WAS THAT YOUR PET?
I DISCIPLINED IT...
...CUZ IT'S A LOT LIKE ITS OWNER.

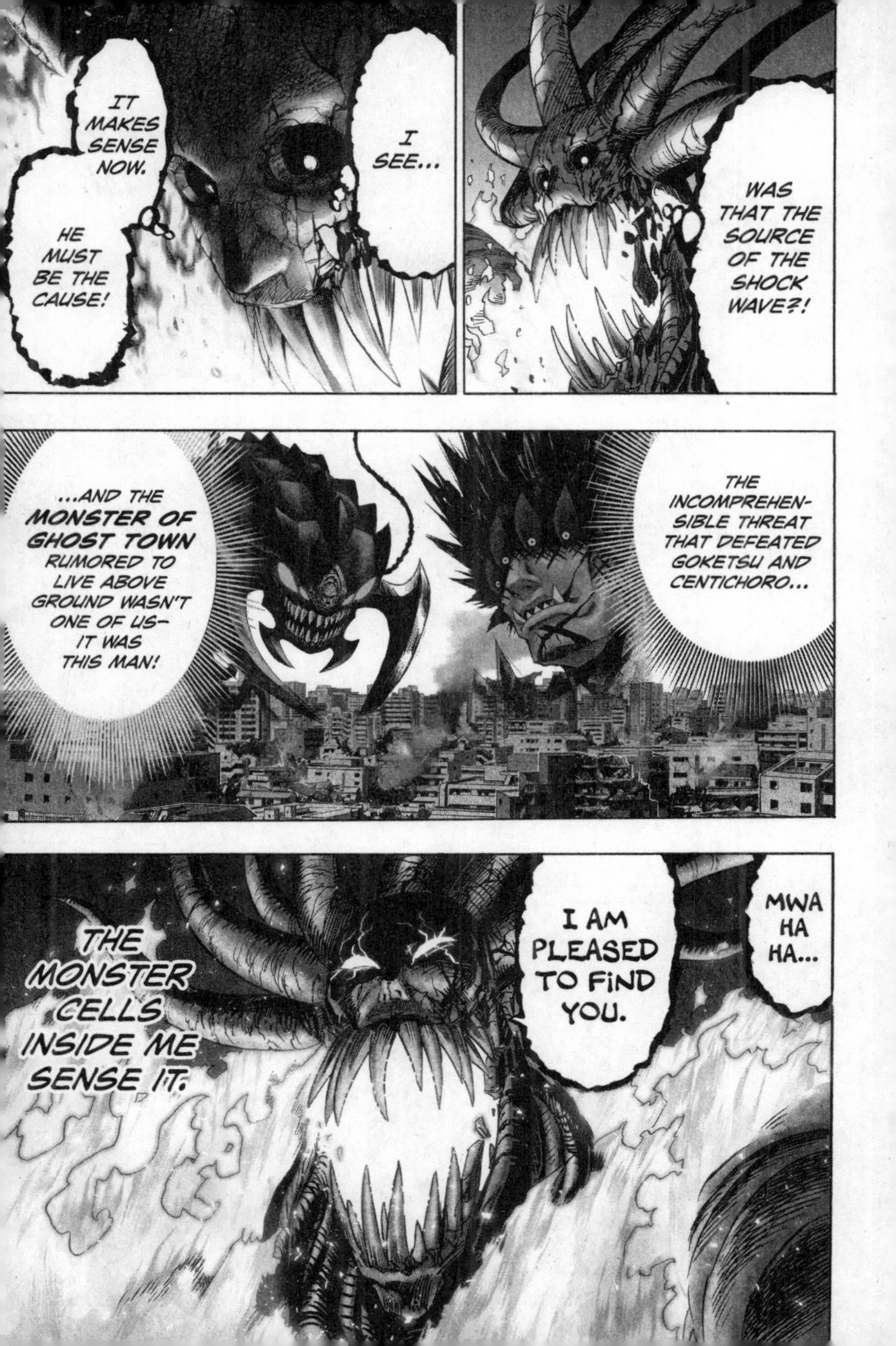
WAS THAT THE SOURCE OF THE SHOCK WAVE?!
I SEE...
IT MAKES SENSE NOW.
HE MUST BE THE CAUSE!
THE INCOMPREHENSIBLE THREAT THAT DEFEATED GOKETSU AND CENTICHORO...
...AND THE MONSTER OF GHOST TOWN RUMORED TO LIVE ABOVE GROUND WASN'T ONE OF US- IT WAS THIS MAN!
MWA HA HA...
I AM PLEASED TO FIND YOU.
THE MONSTER CELLS INSIDE ME SENSE IT.

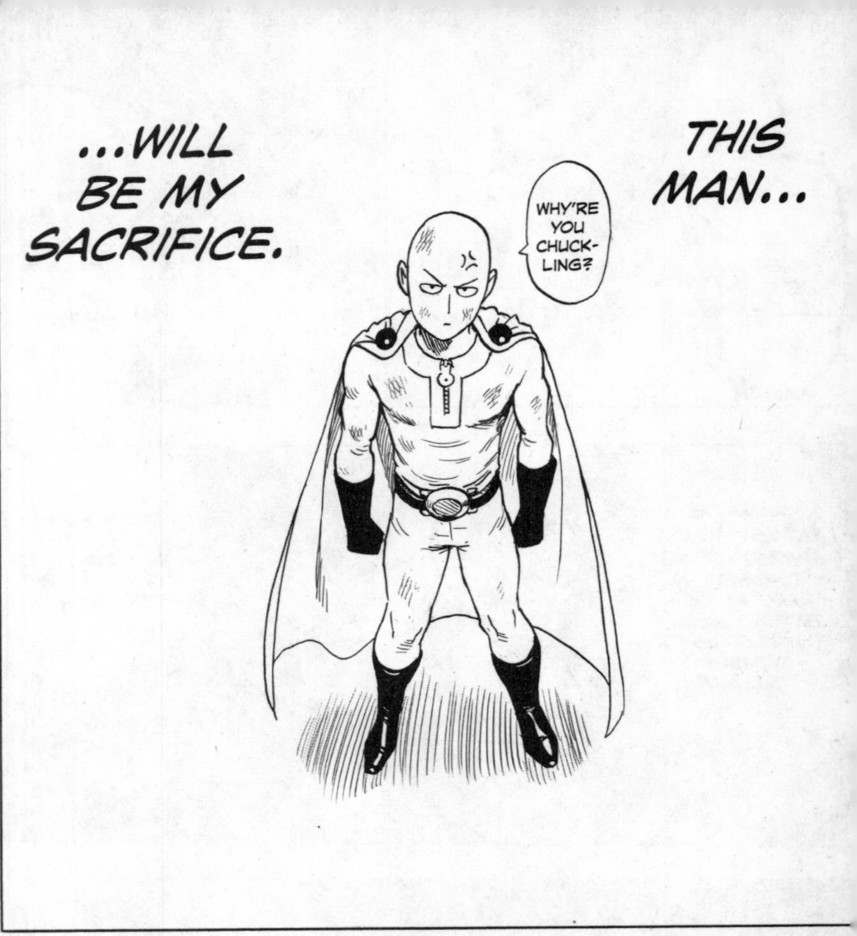
THIS MAN...
WHY'RE YOU CHUCK-LING?
...WILL BE MY SACRIFICE.
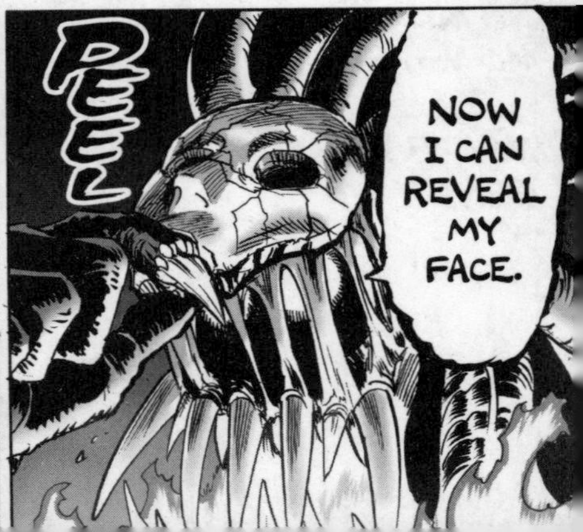
NOW I CAN REVEAL MY FACE.
PEEL
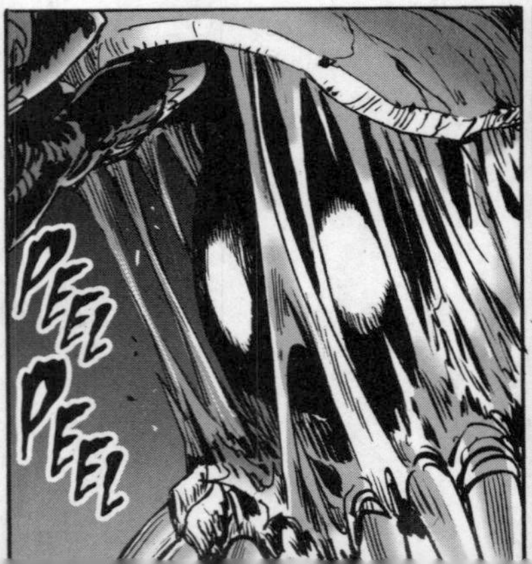
PEEL PEEL

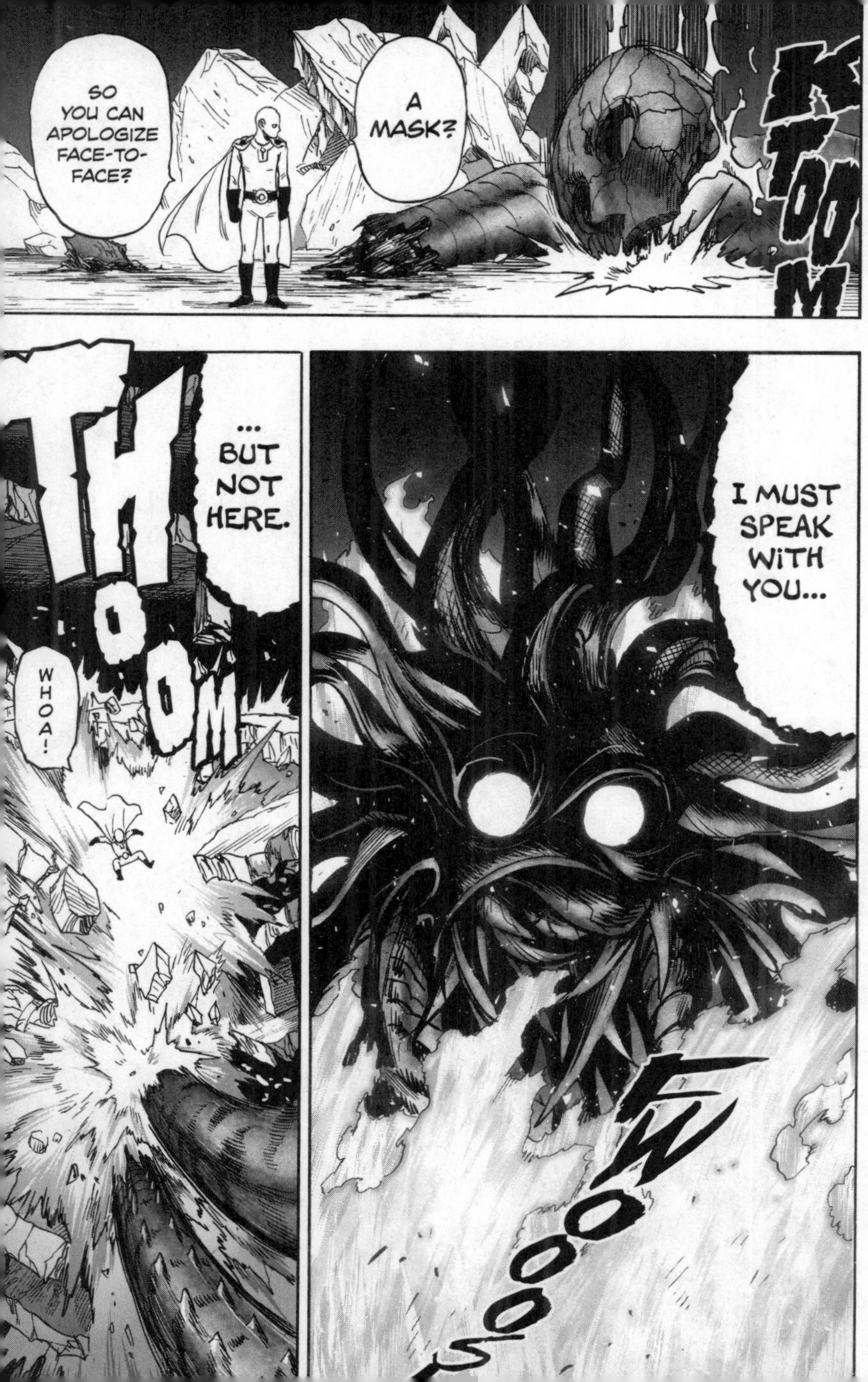
KTOOM
A MASK?
SO YOU CAN APOLOGIZE FACE-TO-FACE?
I MUST SPEAK WITH YOU...
FWOOOOS
... BUT NOT HERE.
THOOM
WHOA!

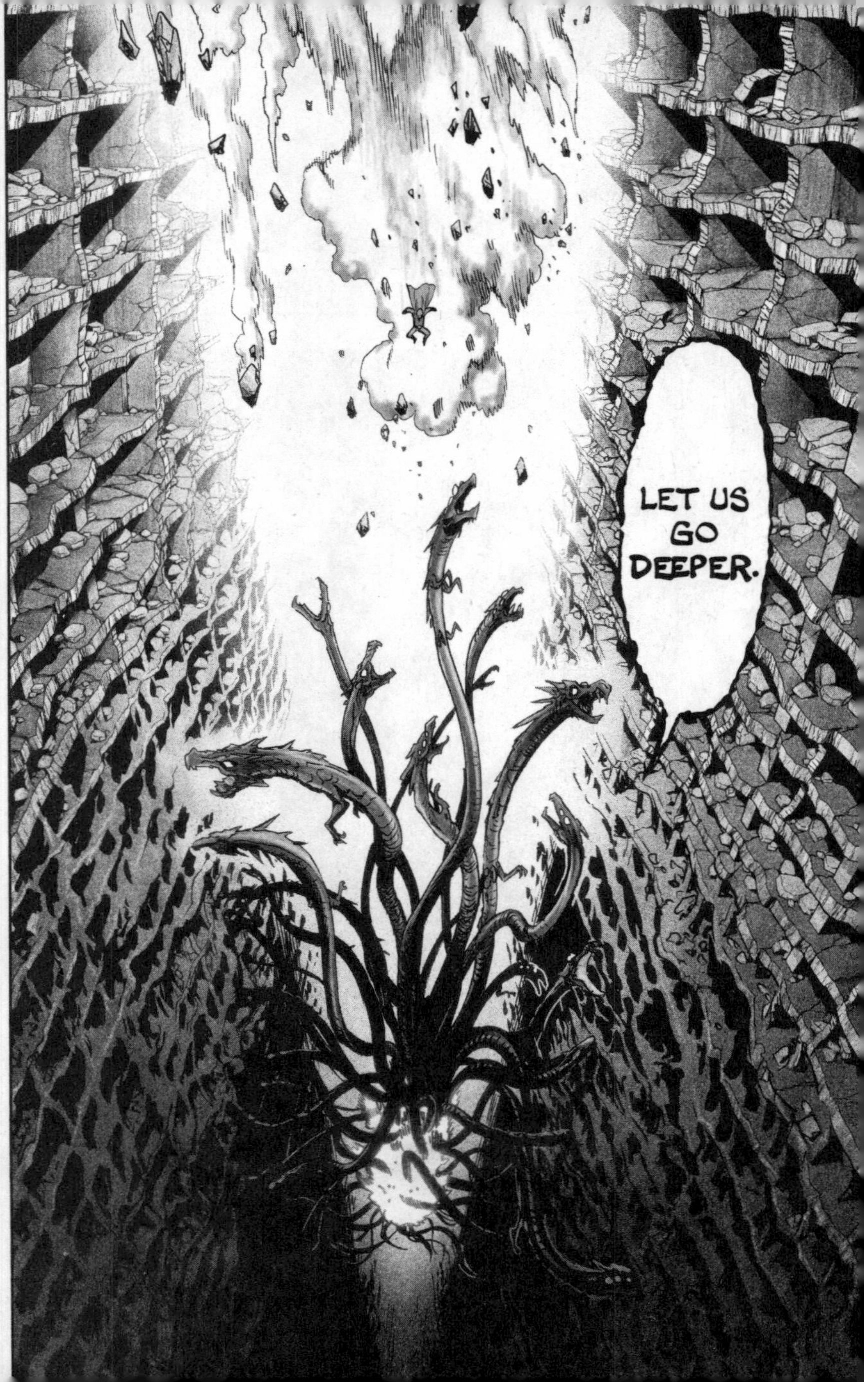
LET US GO DEEPER.

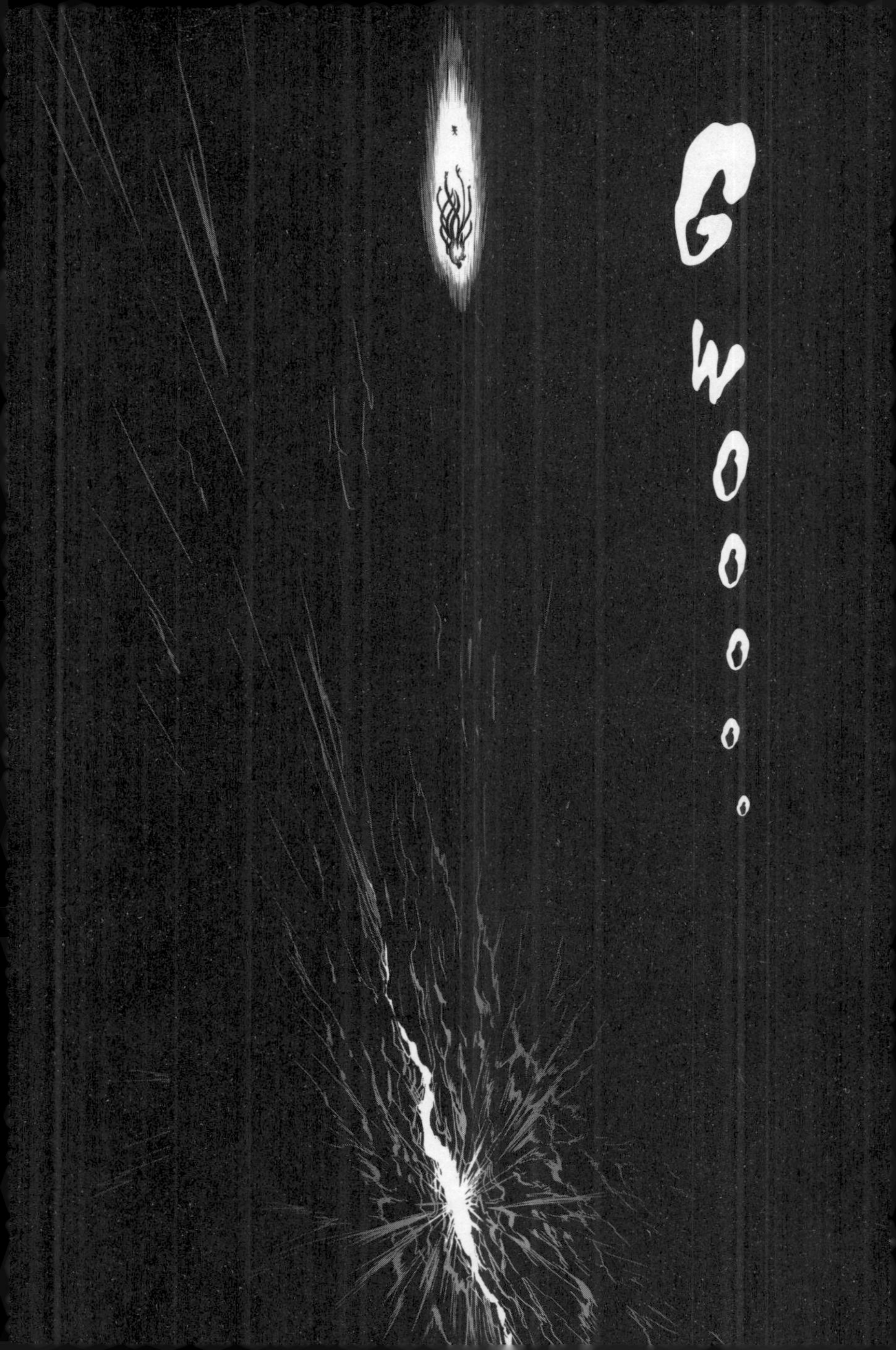
GWOOOOO

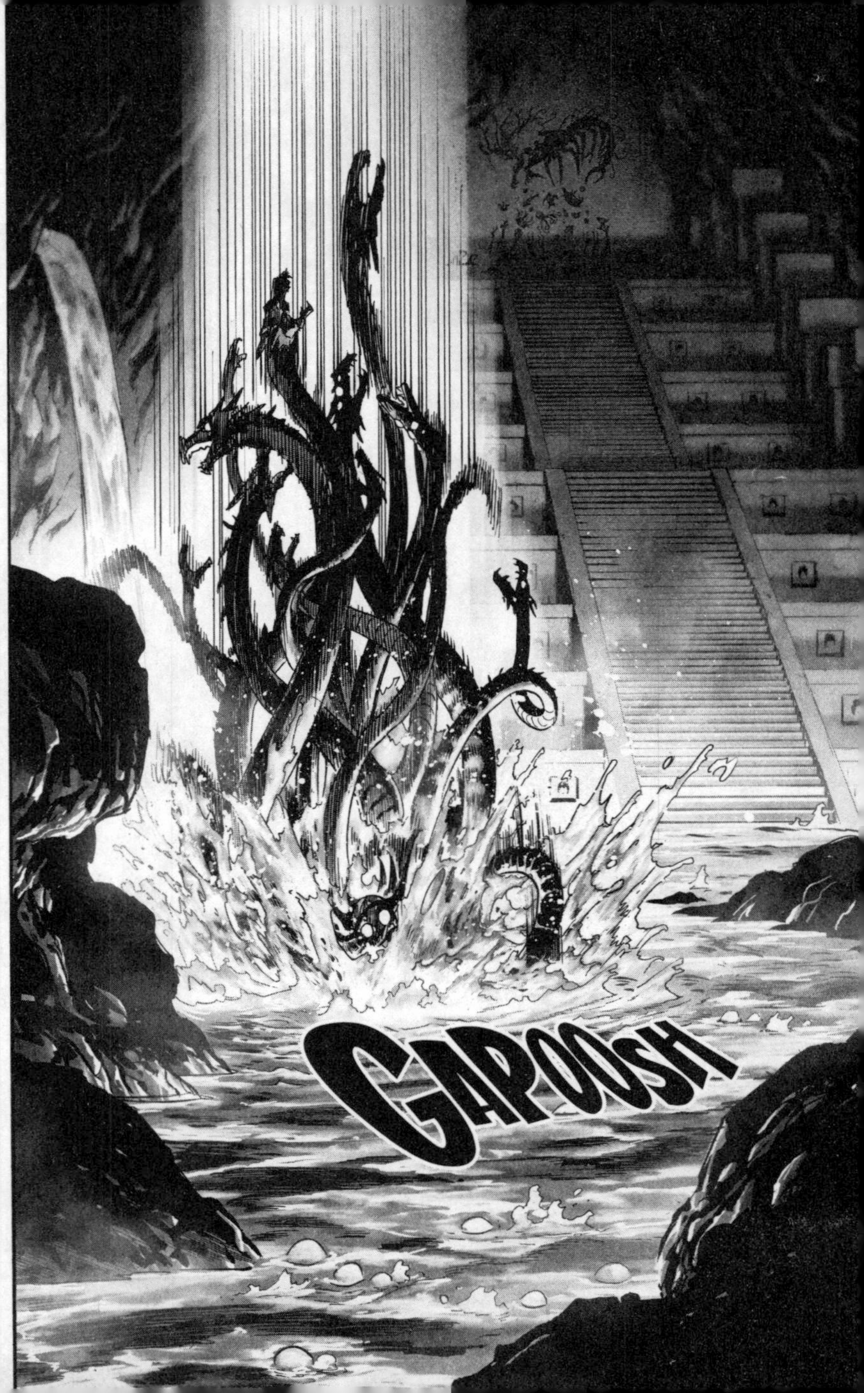
GAPOOSH

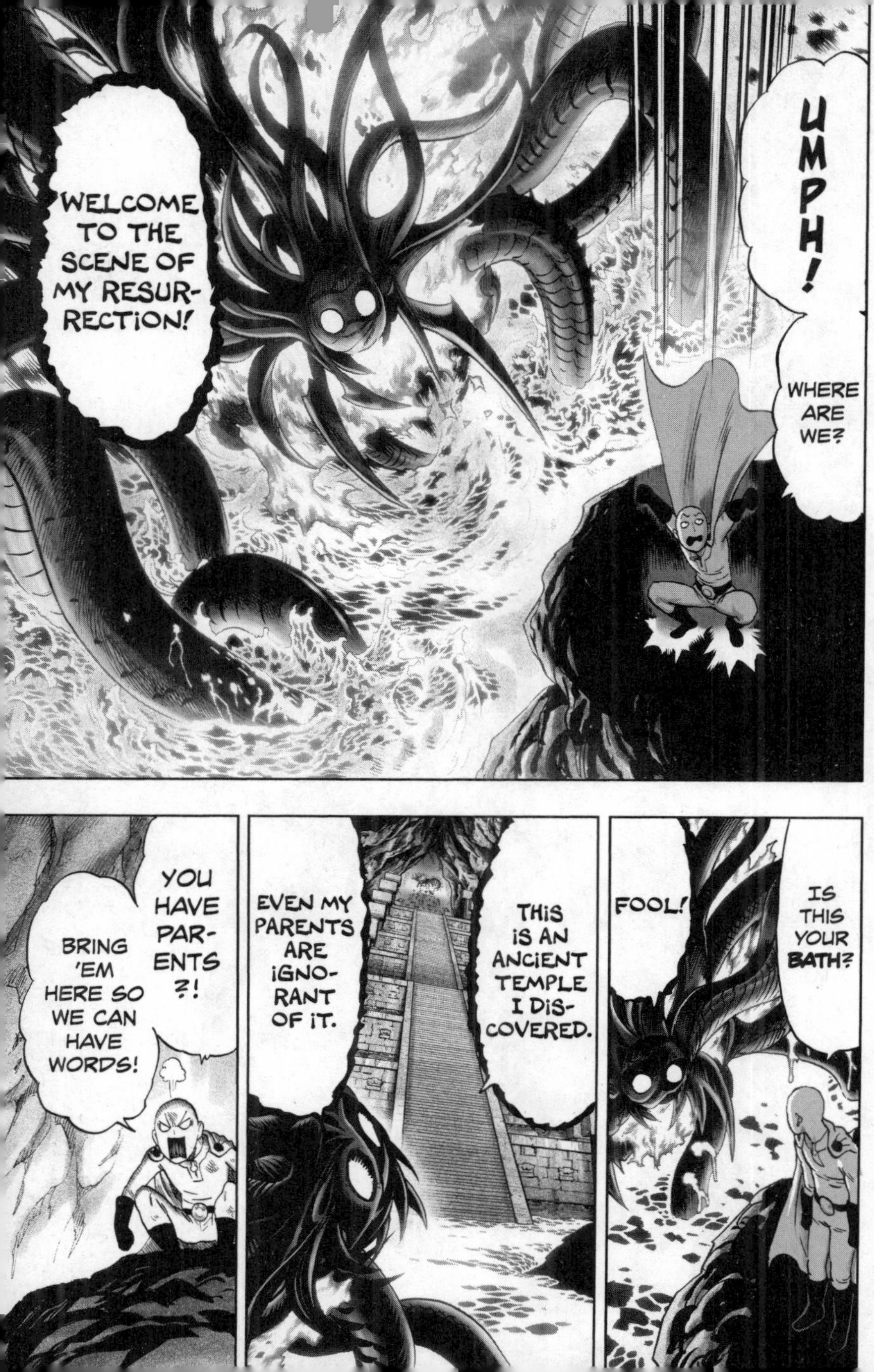
UMPH!
WHERE ARE WE?
WELCOME TO THE SCENE OF MY RESUR-RECTION!
IS THIS YOUR BATH?
FOOL!
THIS IS AN ANCIENT TEMPLE I DIS-COVERED.
EVEN MY PARENTS ARE IGNO-RANT OF IT.
YOU HAVE PAR-ENTS?!
BRING 'EM HERE SO WE CAN HAVE WORDS!

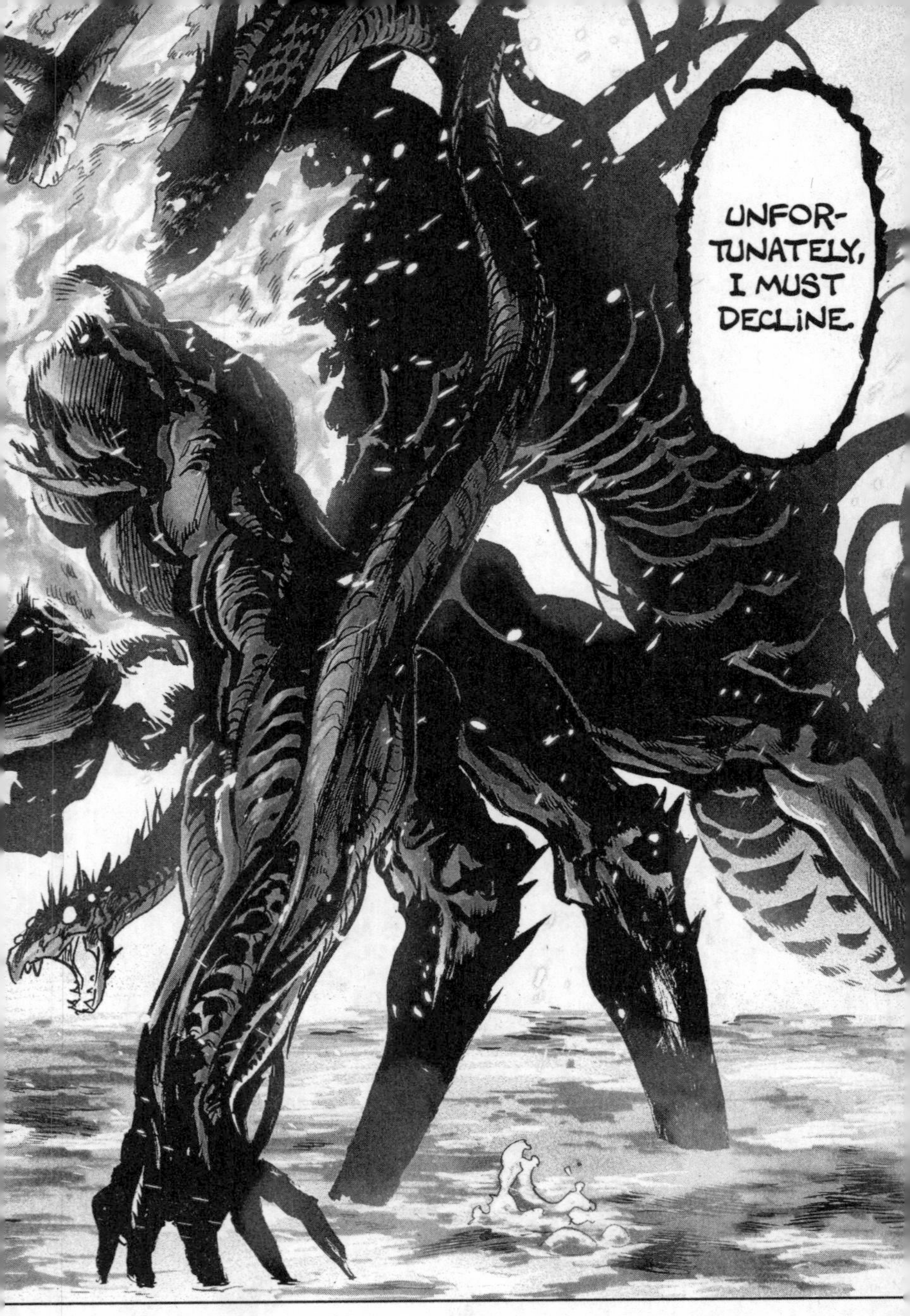
UNFOR-TUNATELY, I MUST DECLINE.

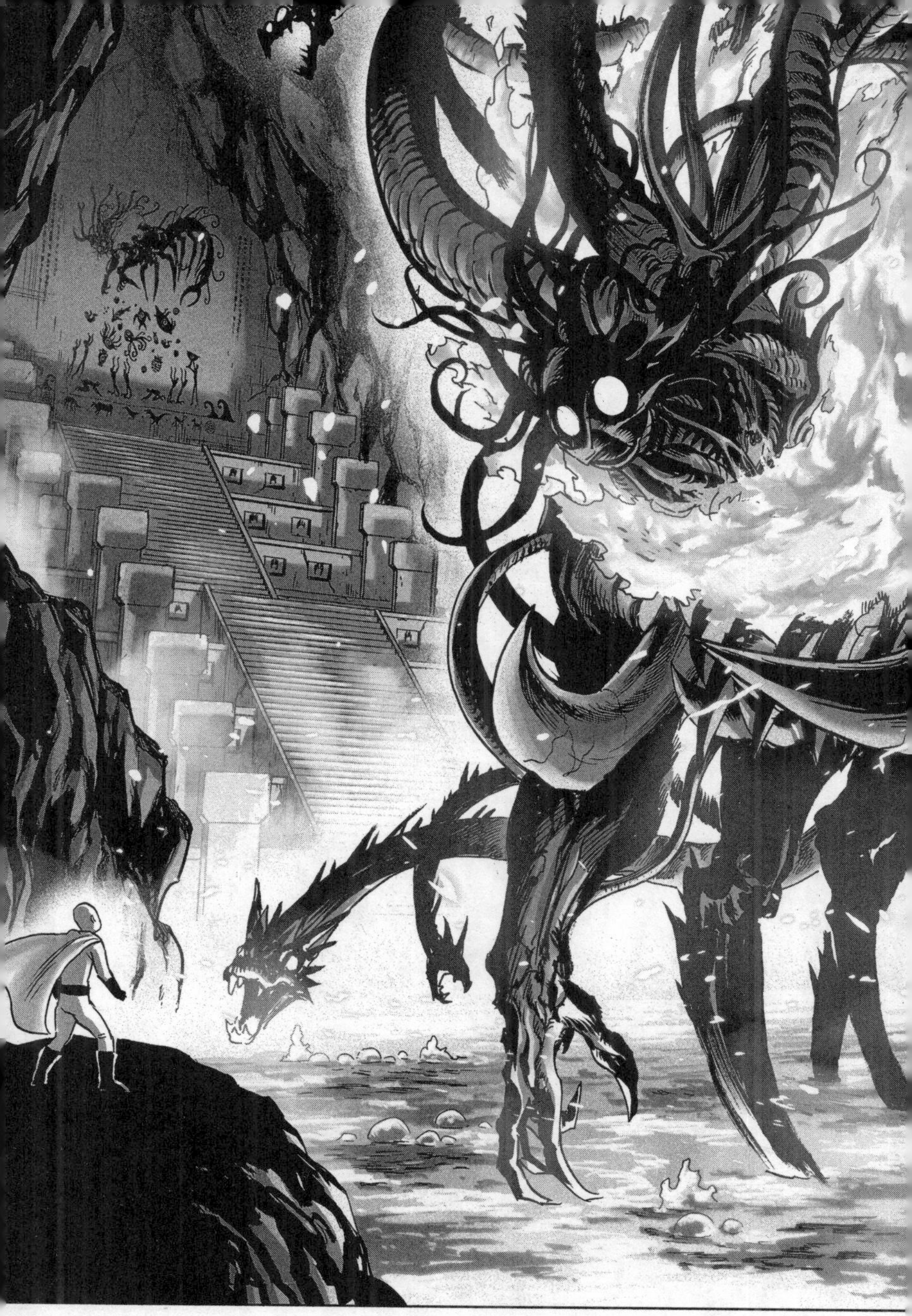

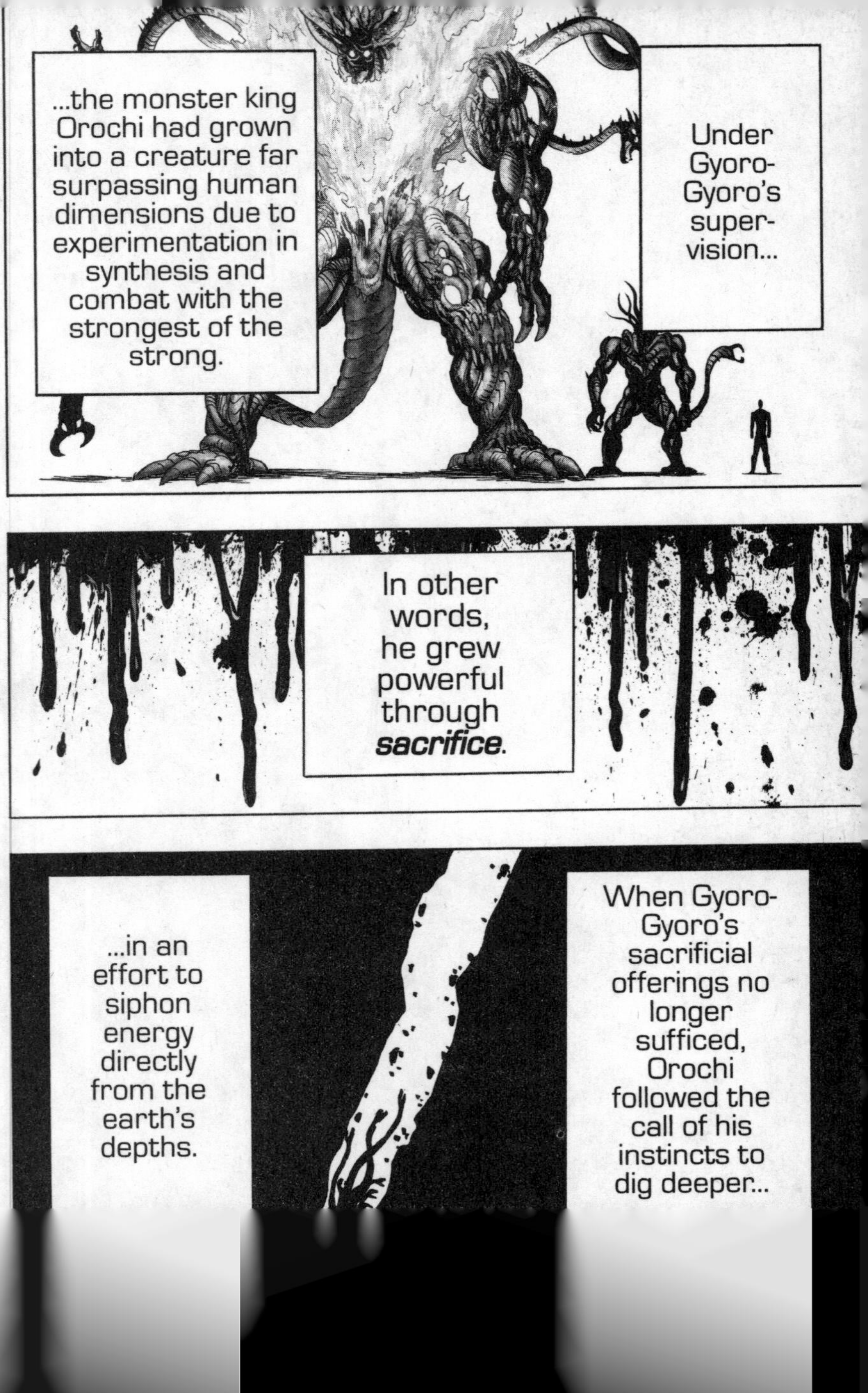
Under Gyoro-Gyoro's super-vision...
...the monster king Orochi had grown into a creature far surpassing human dimensions due to experimentation in synthesis and combat with the strongest of the strong.
In other words, he grew powerful through *sacrifice*.
When Gyoro-Gyoro's sacrificial offerings no longer sufficed, Orochi followed the call of his instincts to dig deeper...
...in an effort to siphon energy directly from the earth's depths.

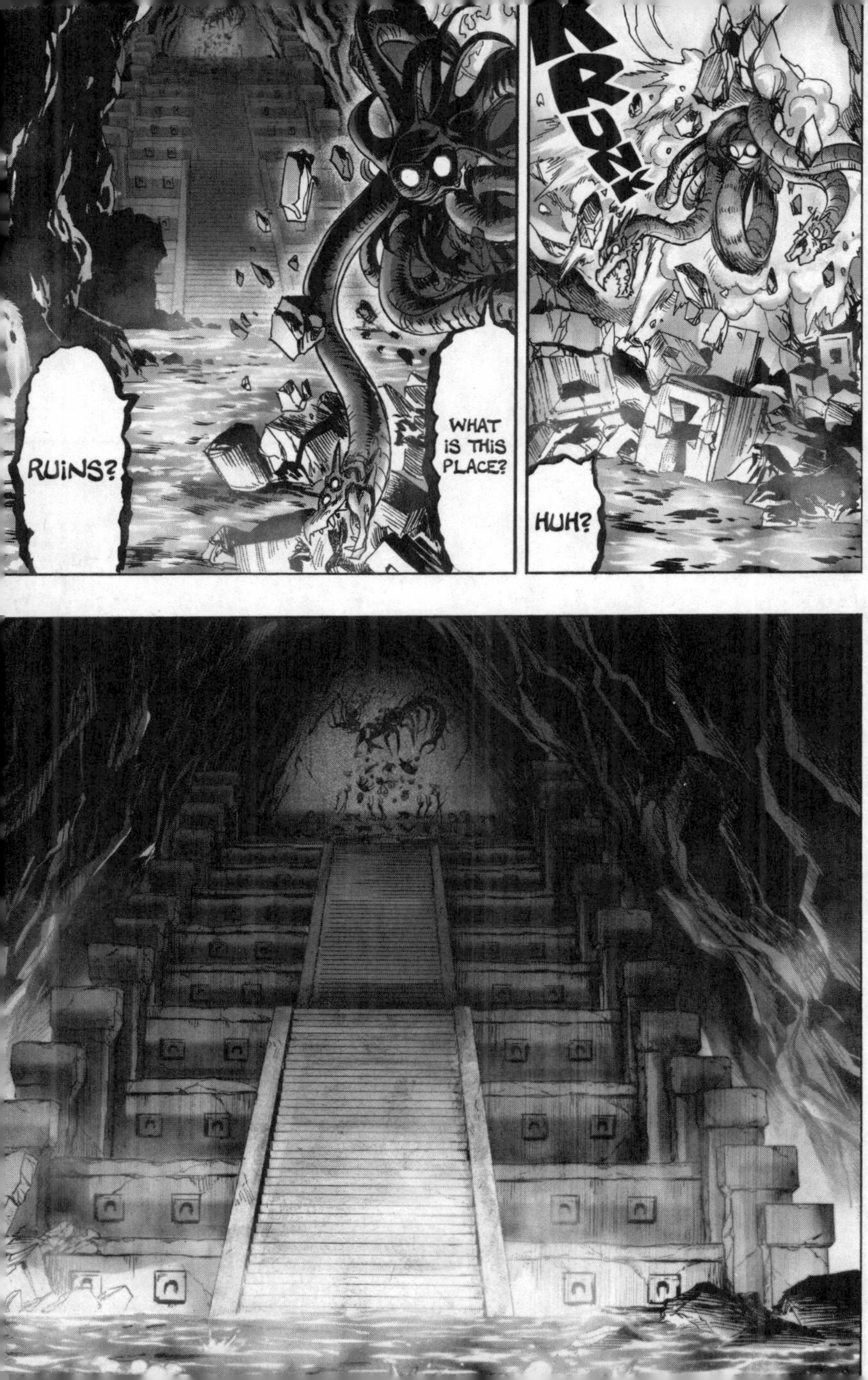
KRUNK
HUH?
WHAT IS THIS PLACE?
RUINS?

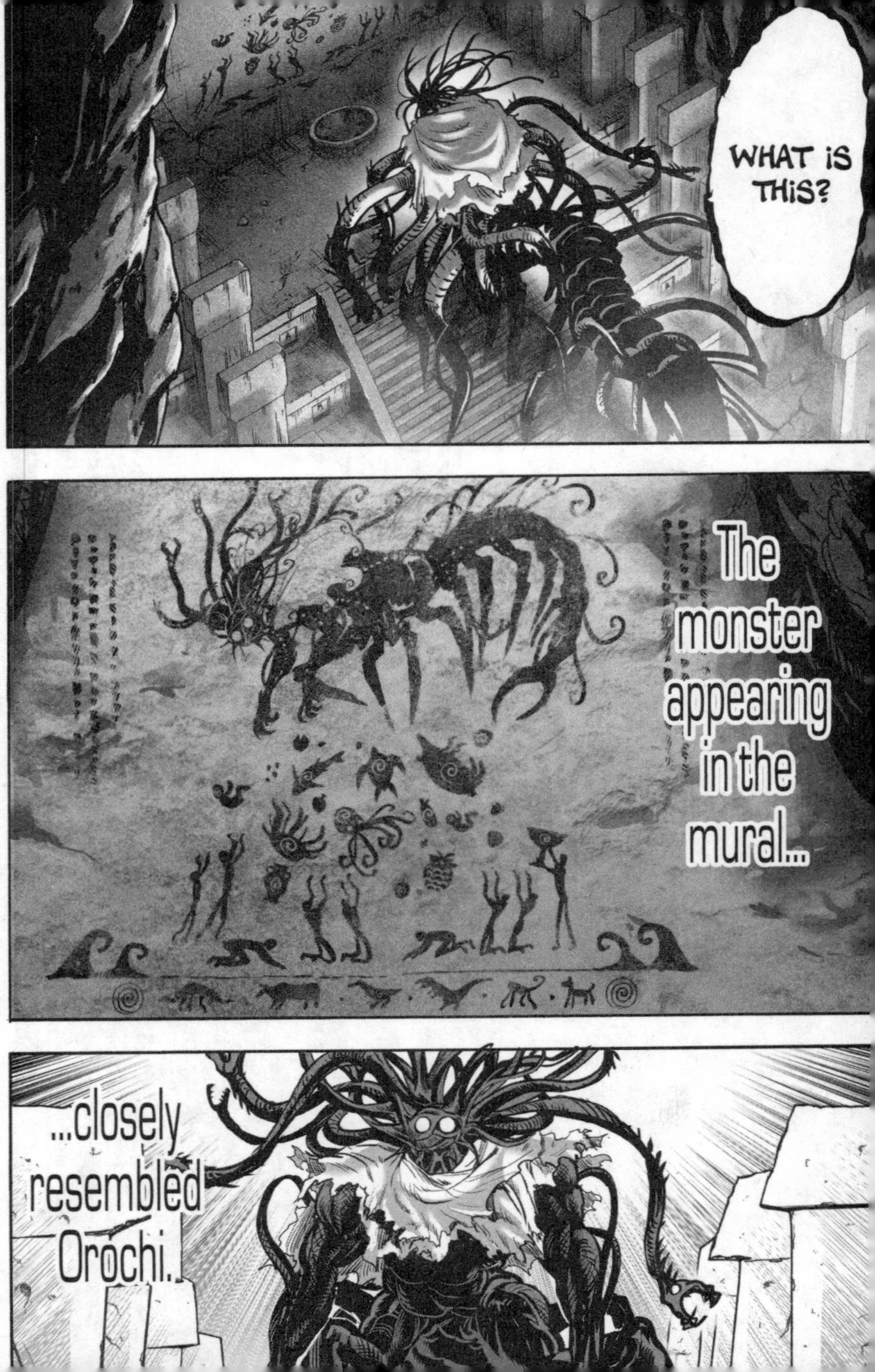
WHAT IS THIS?
The monster appearing in the mural...
...closely resembled Orochi.

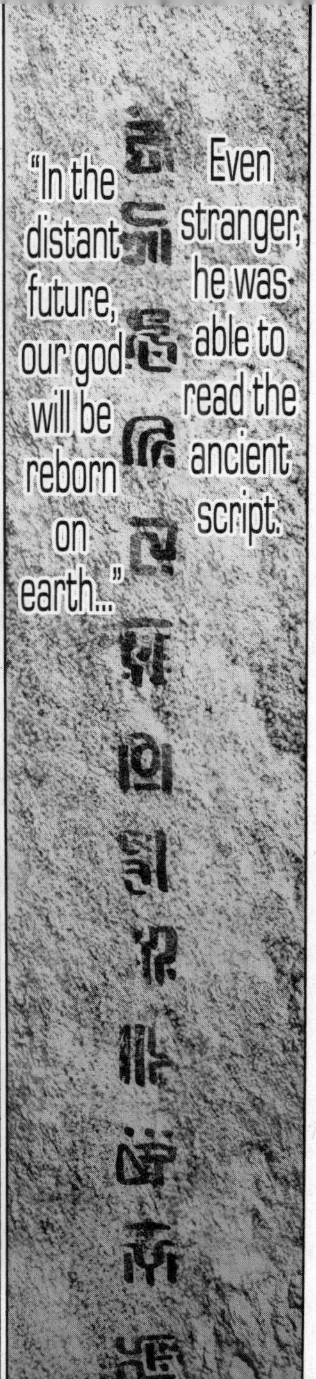
Even stranger, he was able to read the ancient script.
"In the distant future, our god will be reborn on earth..."
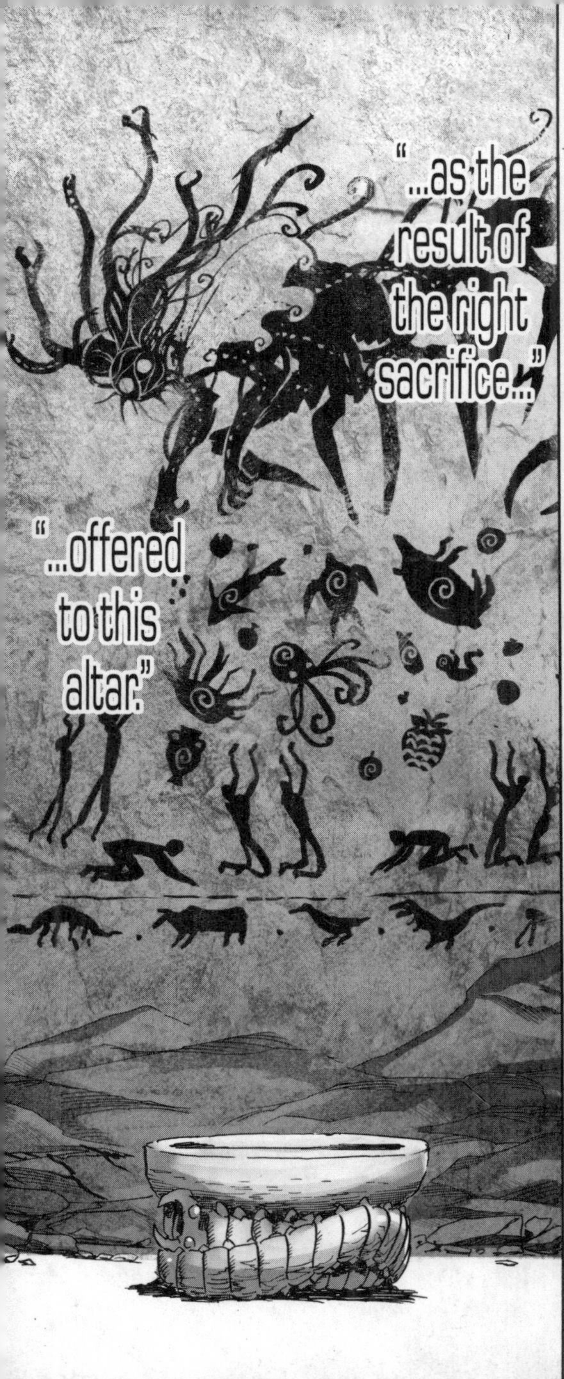
"...as the result of the right sacrifice..."
"...offered to this altar."

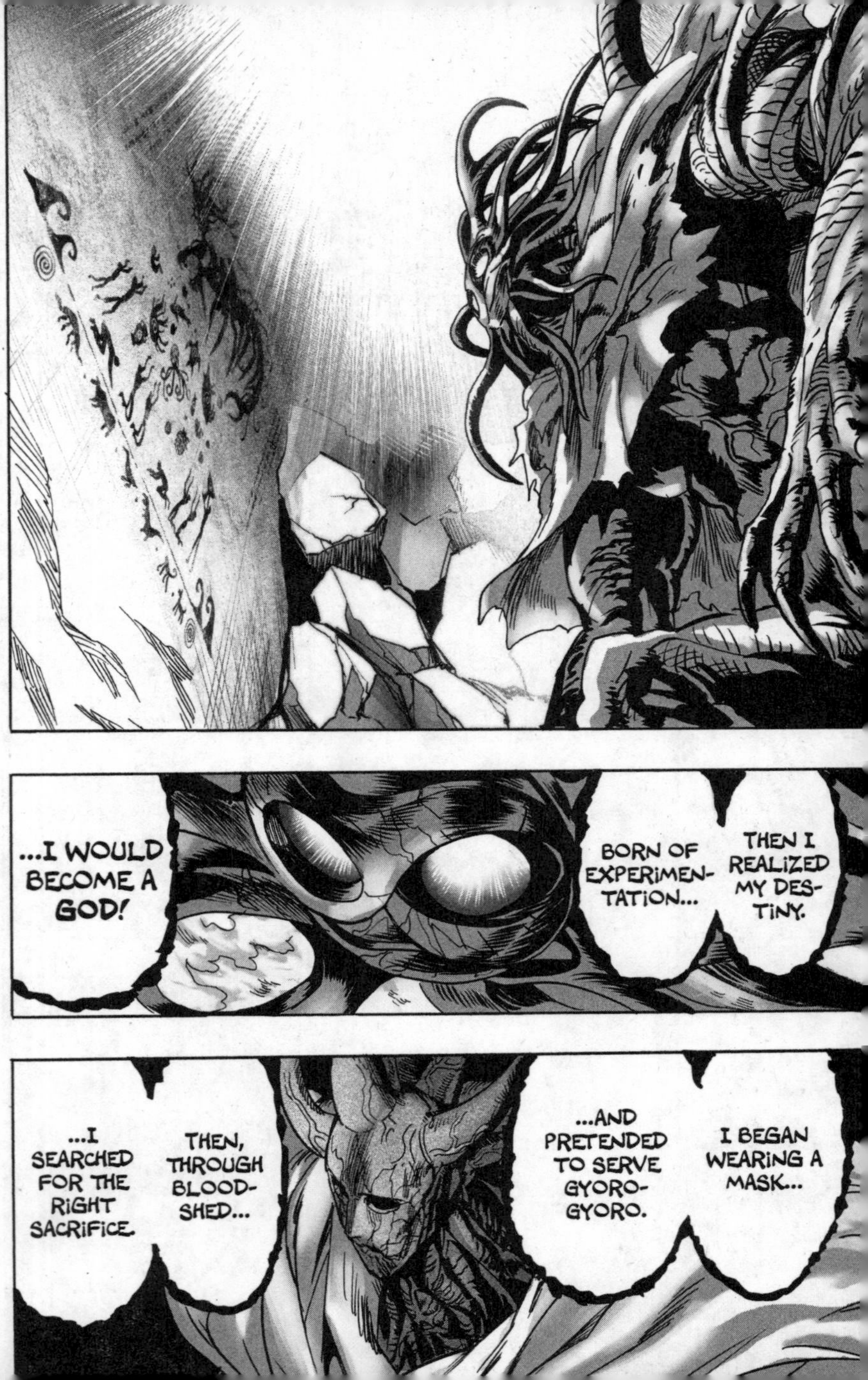
THEN I REALIZED MY DESTINY.
BORN OF EXPERIMENTATION...
...I WOULD BECOME A GOD!
I BEGAN WEARING A MASK...
...AND PRETENDED TO SERVE GYORO-GYORO.
THEN, THROUGH BLOODSHED...
...I SEARCHED FOR THE RIGHT SACRIFICE.

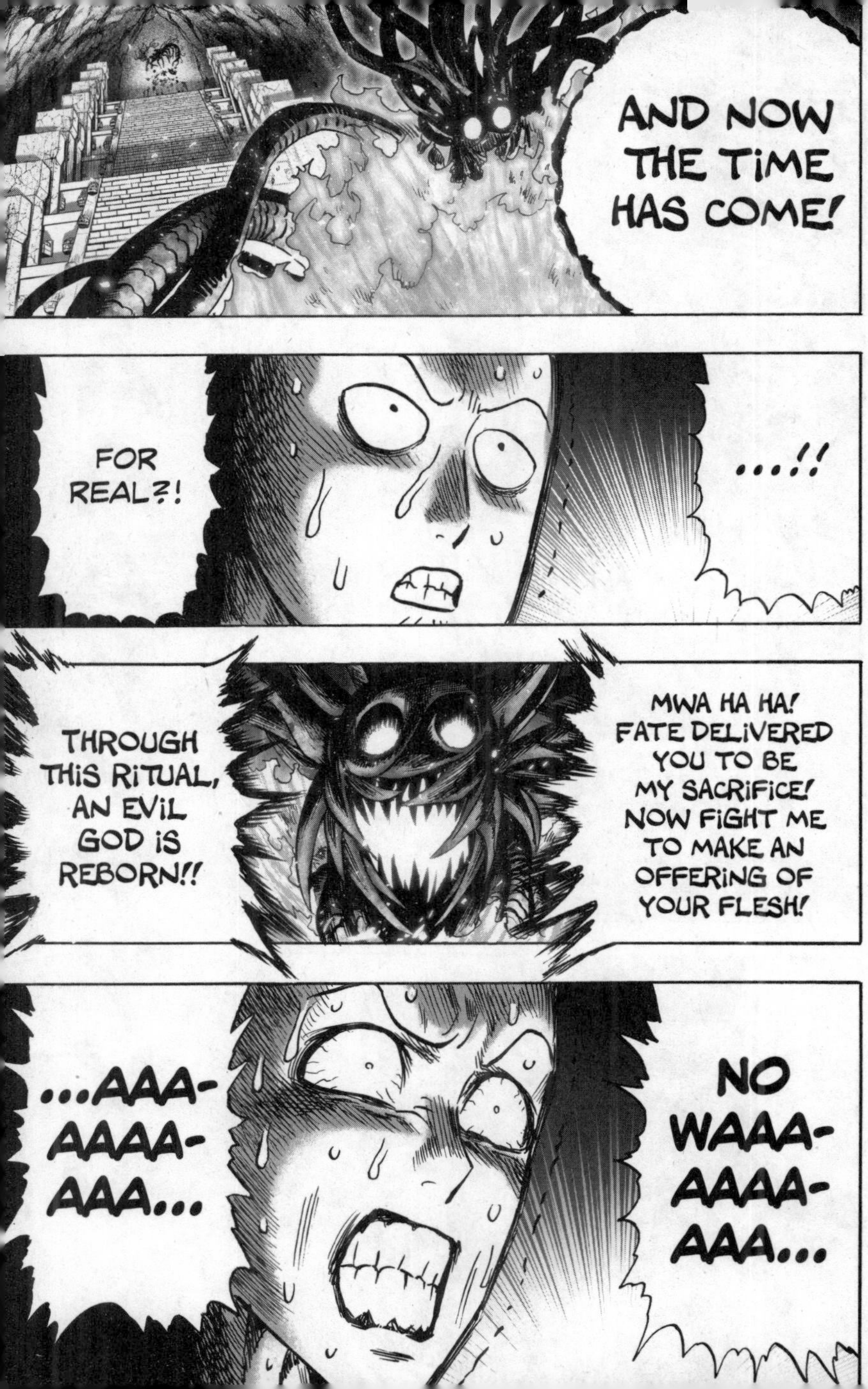
AND NOW THE TIME HAS COME!
...!!
FOR REAL?!
MWA HA HA! FATE DELIVERED YOU TO BE MY SACRIFICE! NOW FIGHT ME TO MAKE AN OFFERING OF YOUR FLESH!
THROUGH THIS RITUAL, AN EVIL GOD IS REBORN!!
NO WAAA-AAAA-AAA...
...AAA-AAAA-AAA...

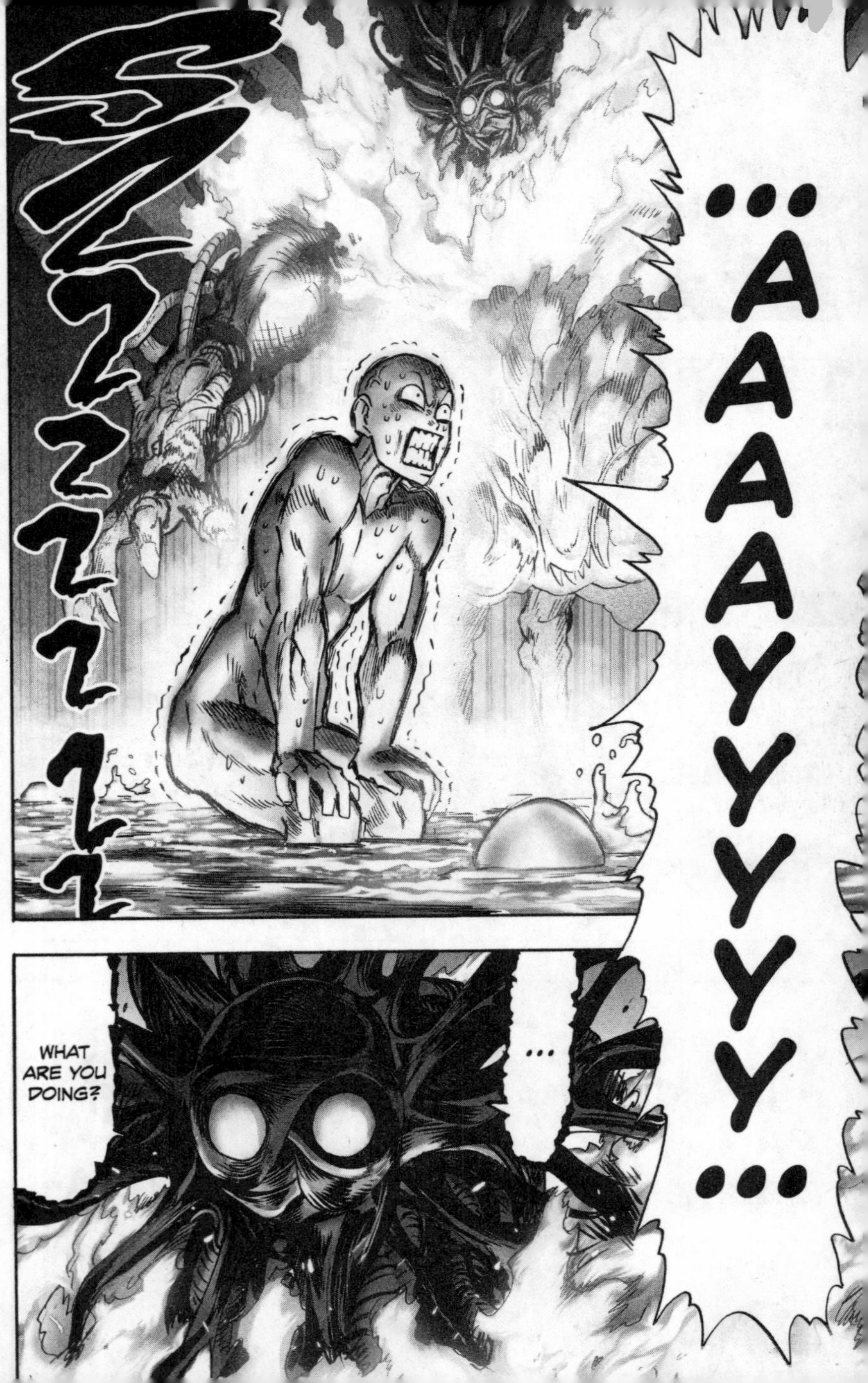
...AAAAYYYYY...
...
WHAT ARE YOU DOING?

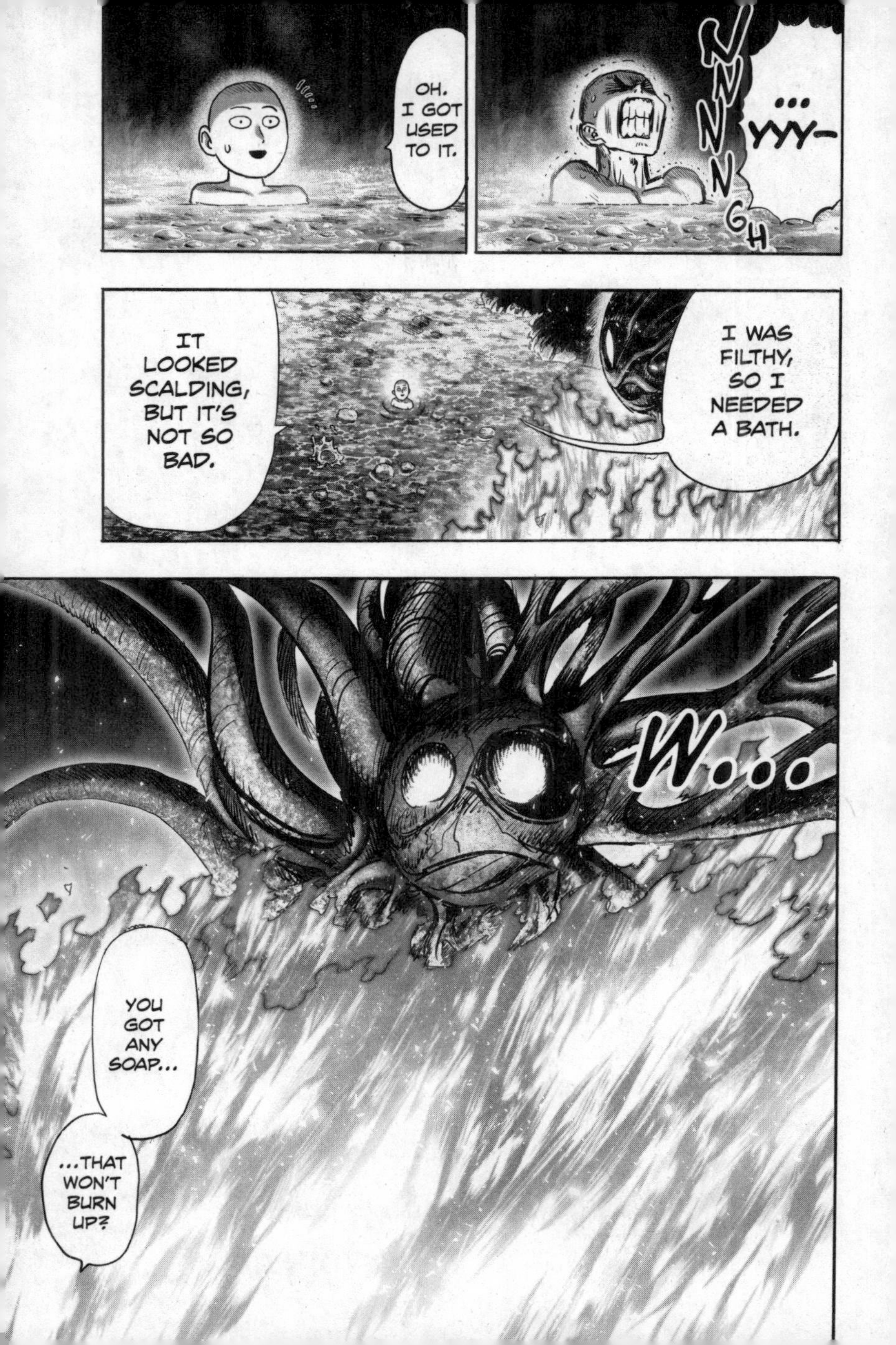
NNNNNGH
...YYY-
OH. I GOT USED TO IT.
I WAS FILTHY, SO I NEEDED A BATH.
IT LOOKED SCALDING, BUT IT'S NOT SO BAD.
W...
YOU GOT ANY SOAP...
...THAT WON'T BURN UP?

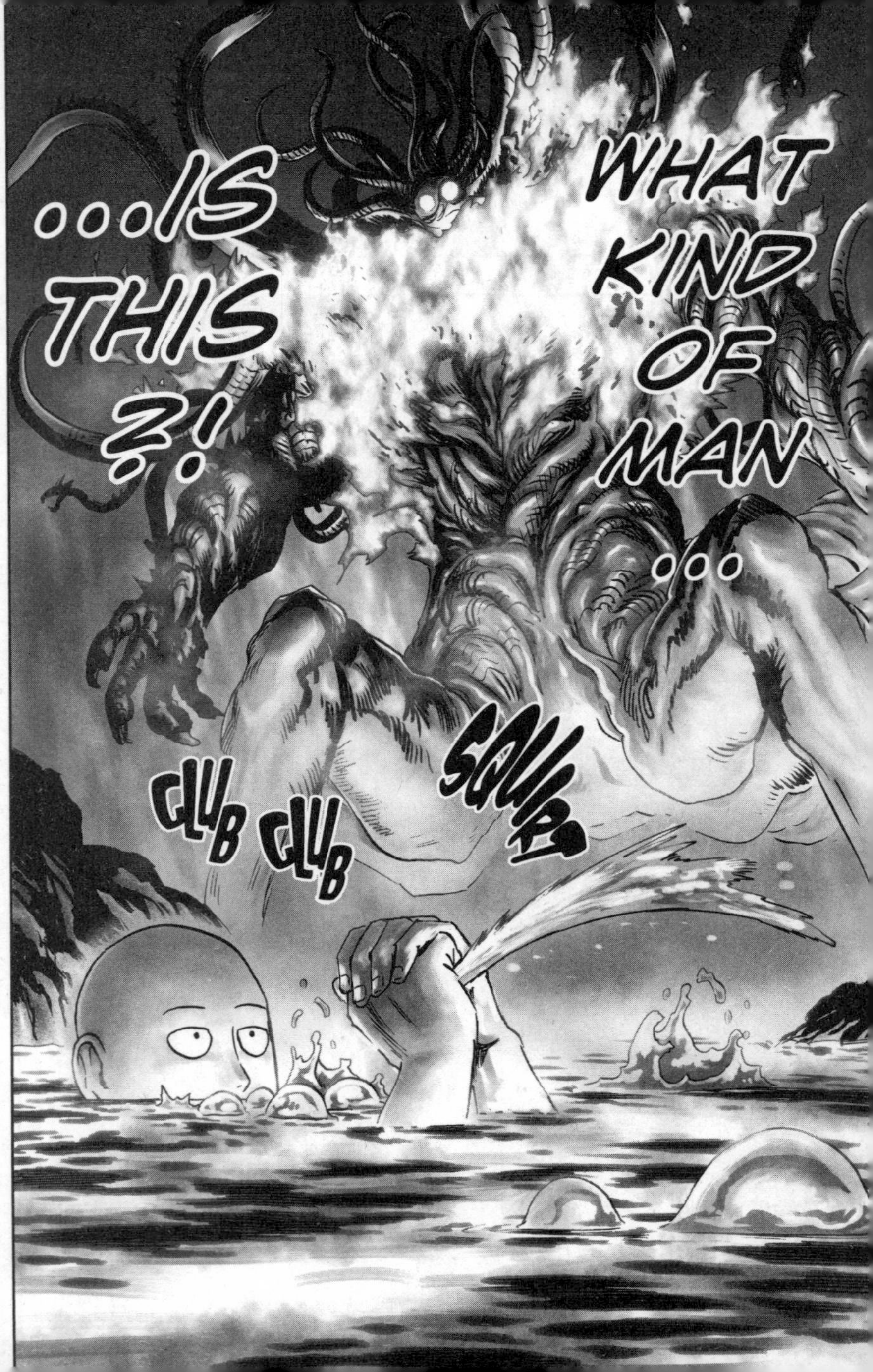
WHAT KIND OF MAN ...
...IS THIS?!
SQUIRT
GLUB GLUB

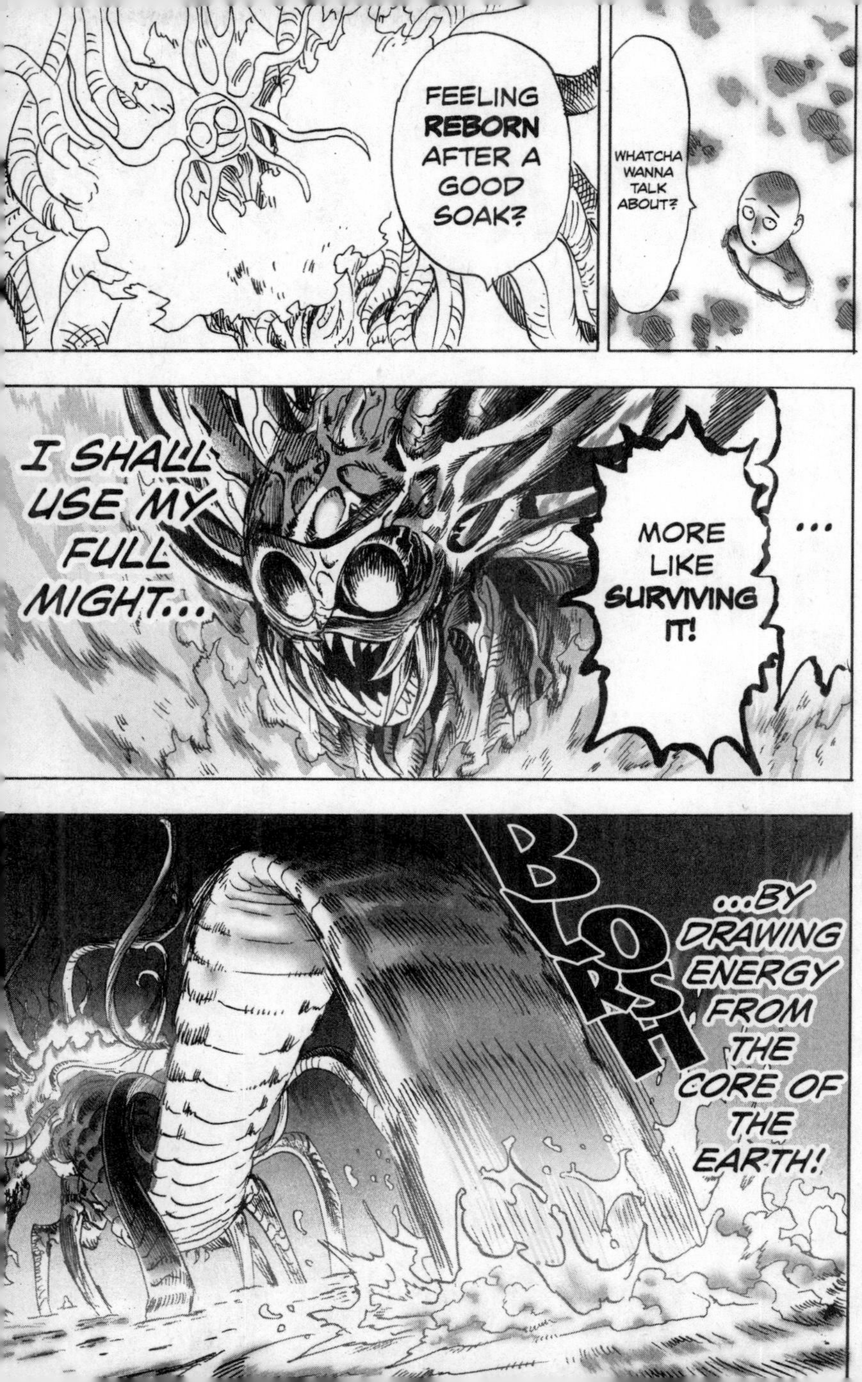
WHATCHA WANNA TALK ABOUT?
FEELING **REBORN** AFTER A GOOD SOAK?
...
MORE LIKE **SURVIVING** IT!
I SHALL USE MY FULL MIGHT...
BLORSH
...BY DRAWING ENERGY FROM THE CORE OF THE EARTH!

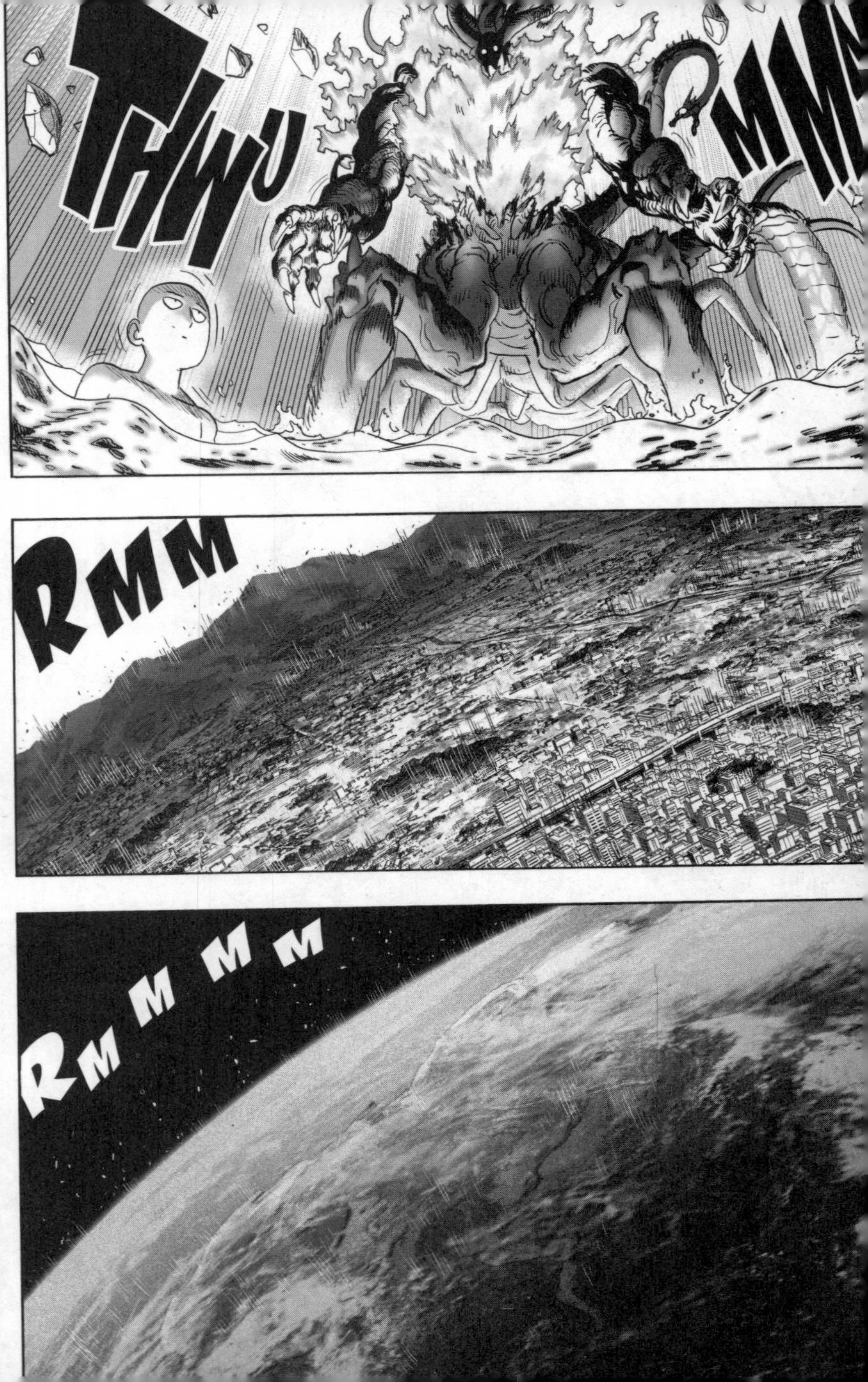
THWUMMM
RMM
RMMMM

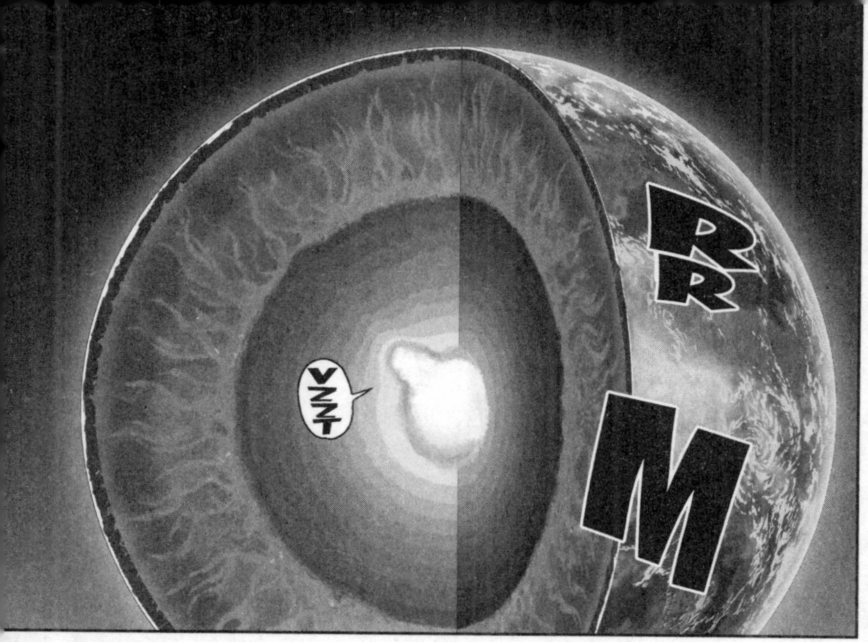
RRM
VZZT
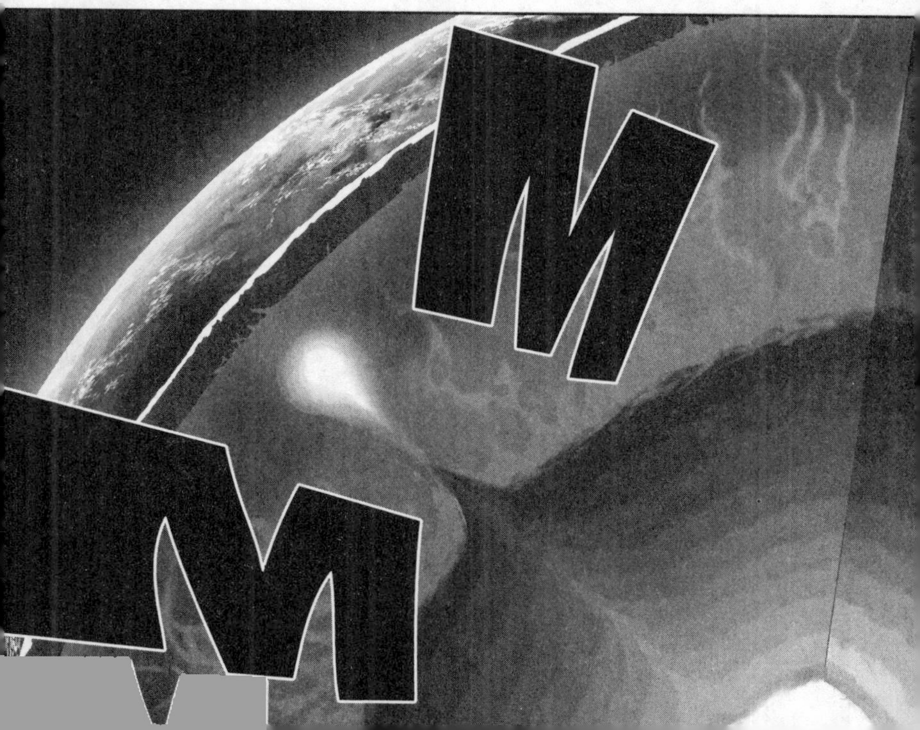
MMM

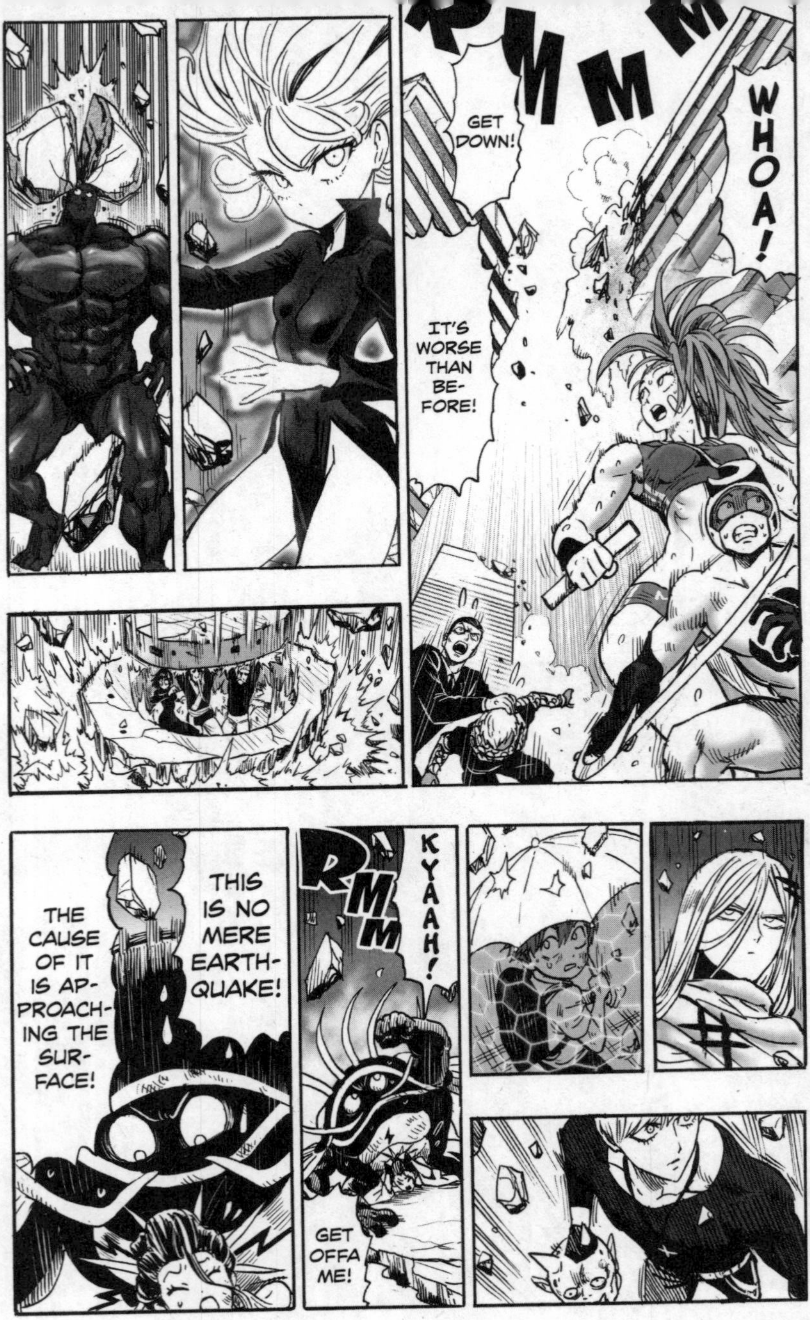
RMMMM
WHOA!
GET DOWN!
IT'S WORSE THAN BE-FORE!
KYAAH!
RMM
GET OFFA ME!
THIS IS NO MERE EARTH-QUAKE!
THE CAUSE OF IT IS AP-PROACH-ING THE SUR-FACE!

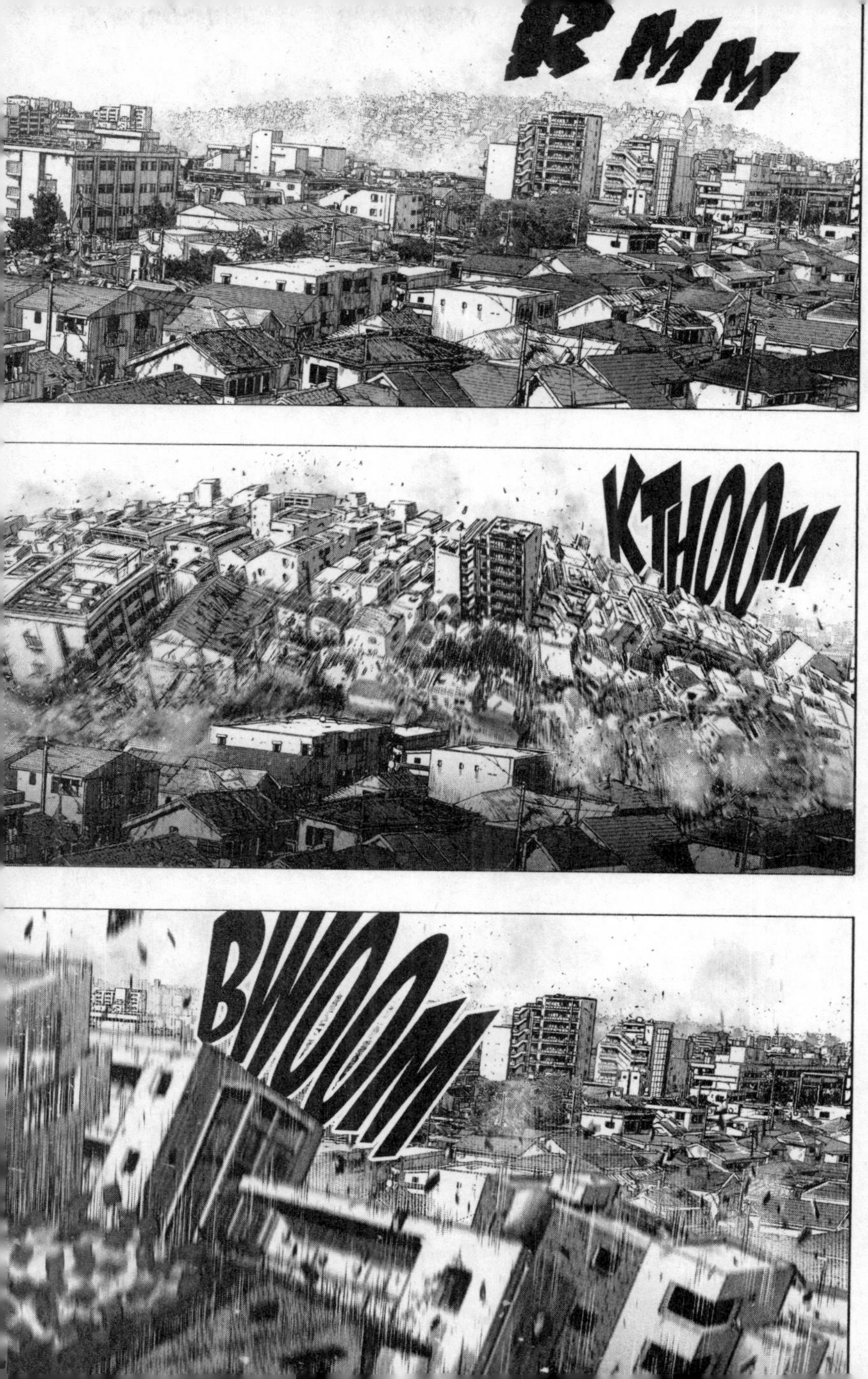
RMM
KTHOOM
BWOOM

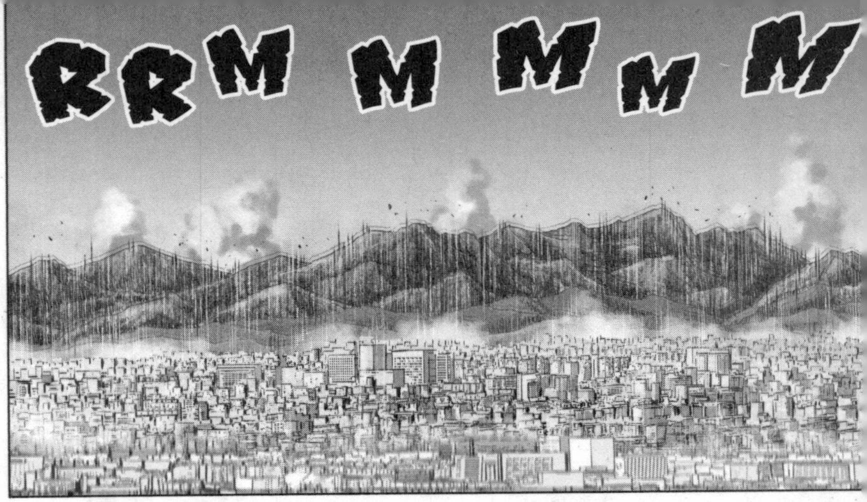
RRM M M M M
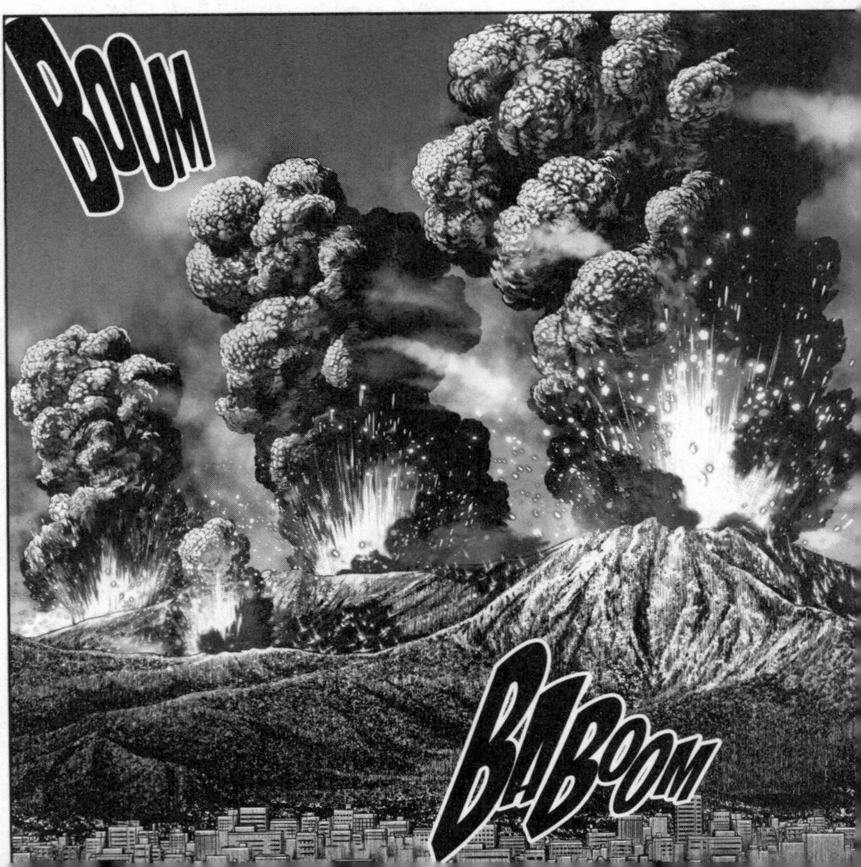
BOOM
BABOOM

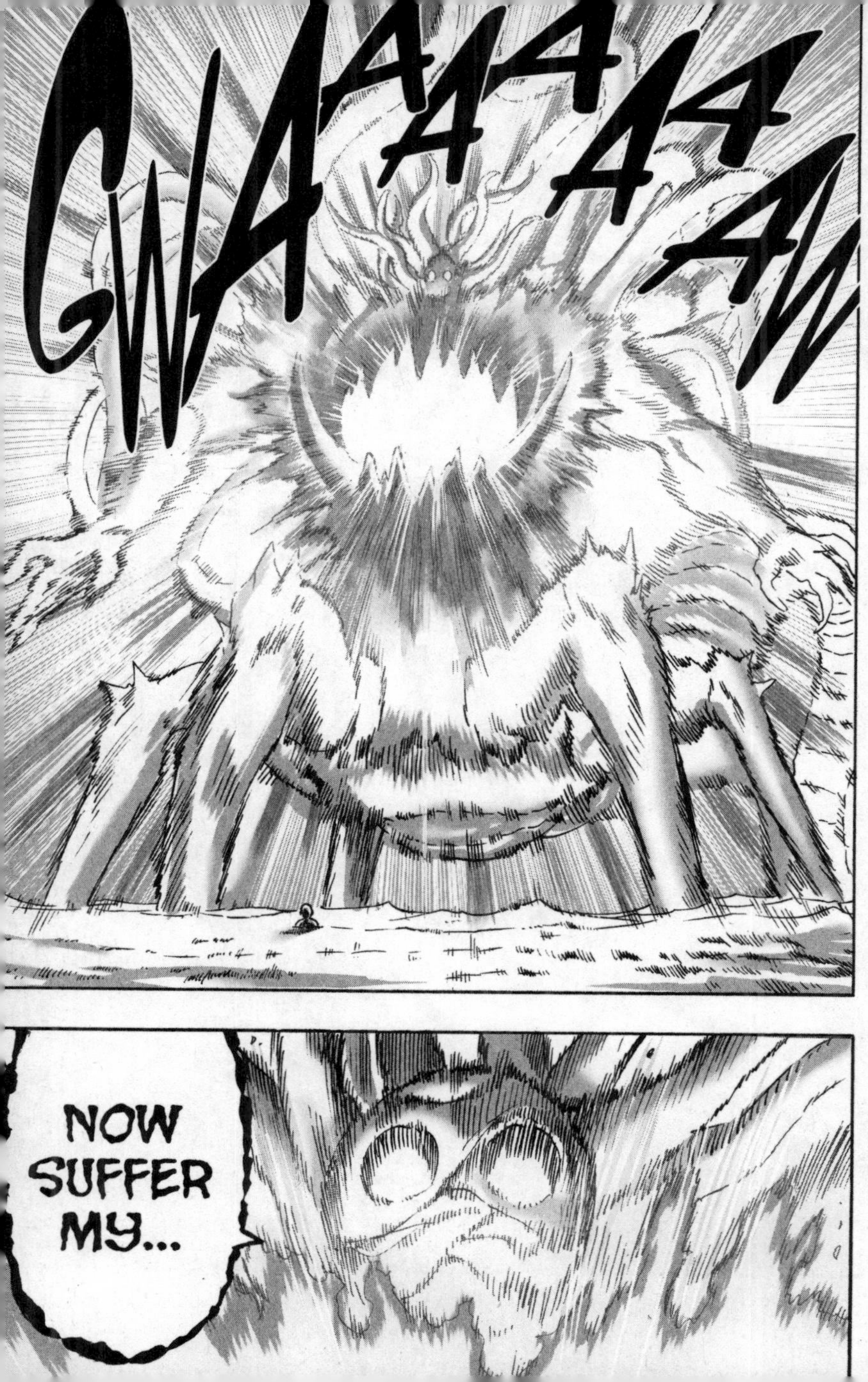
GWAAAAAAAN
NOW SUFFER MY...

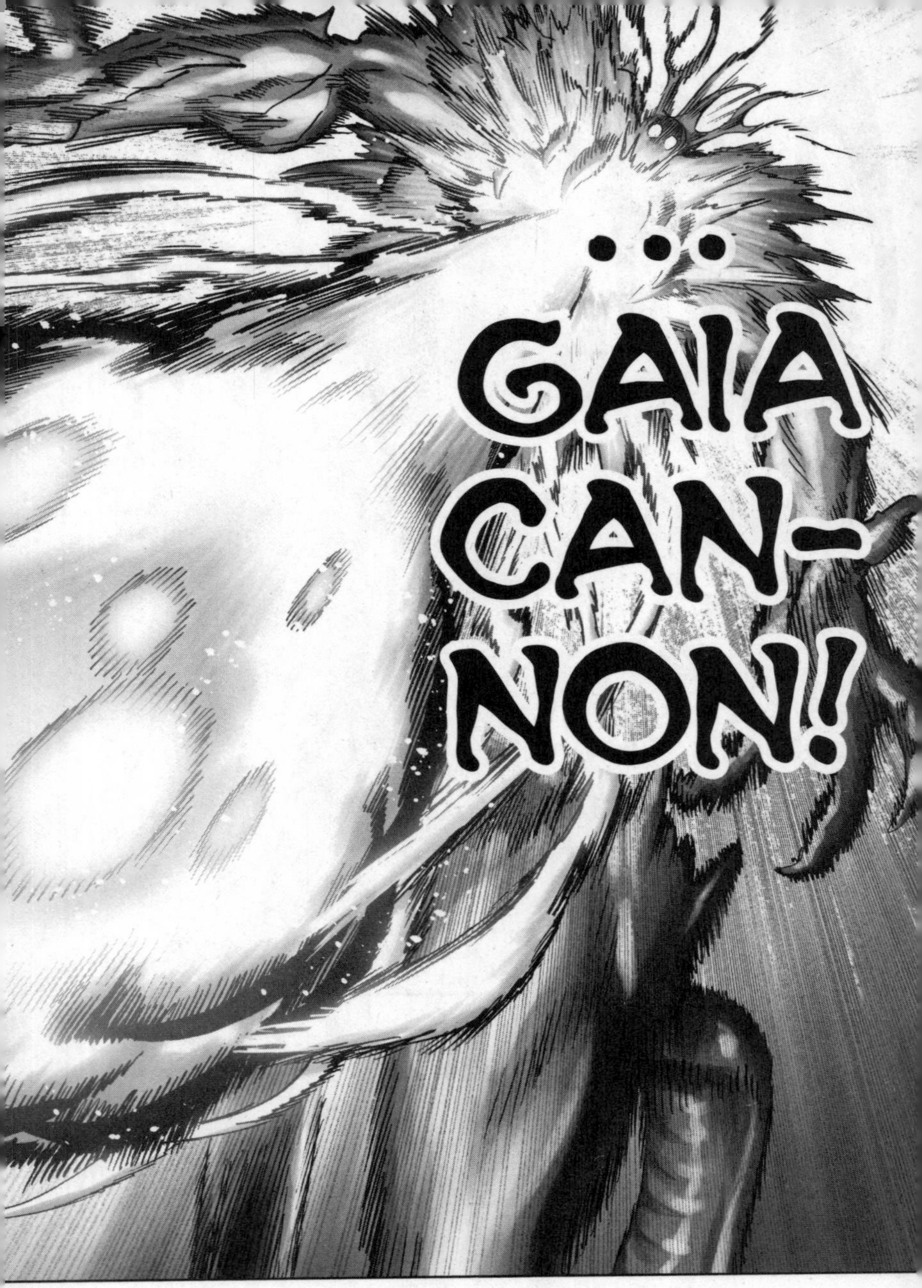
..GAIA CAN-NON!

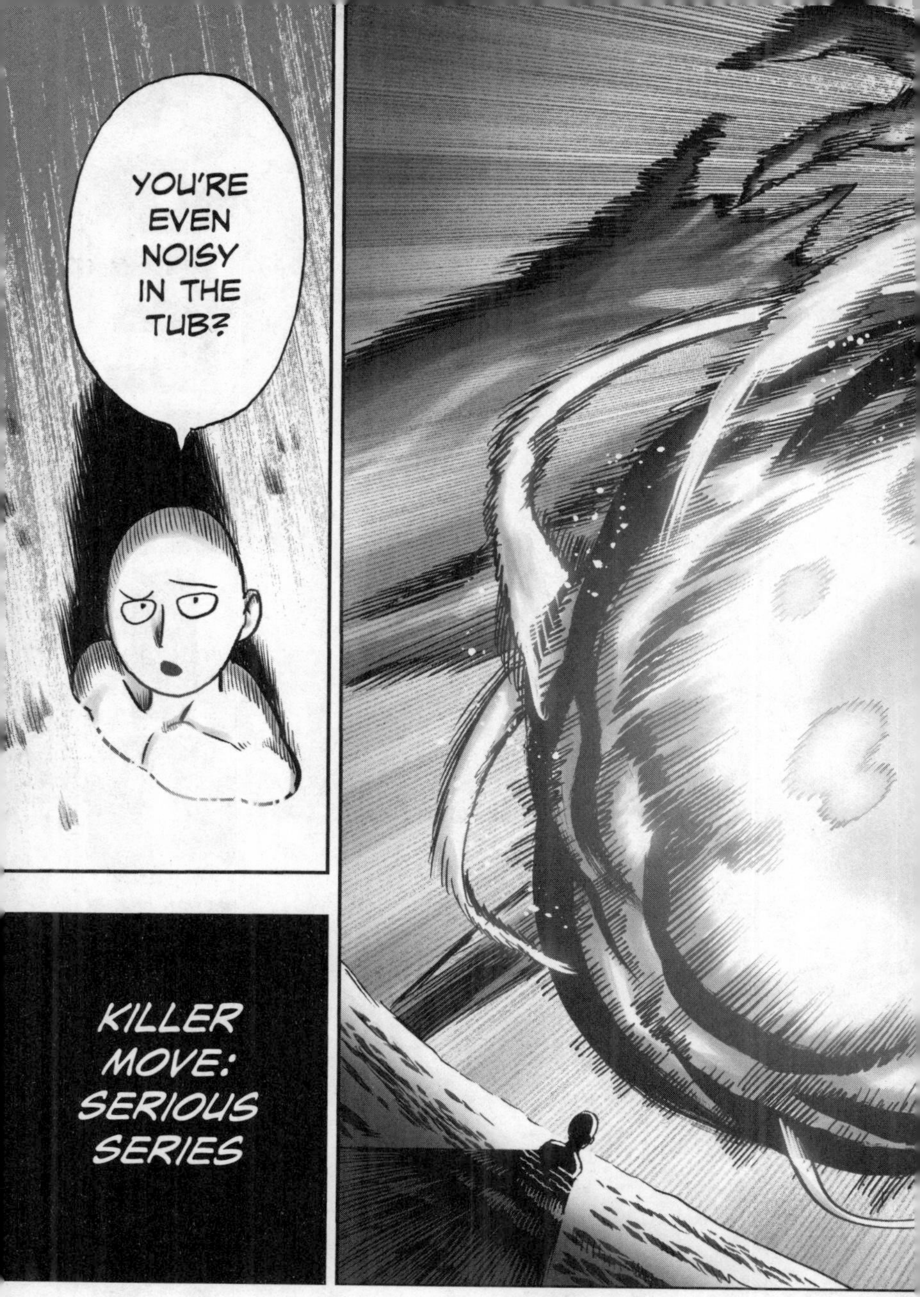
YOU'RE EVEN NOISY IN THE TUB?
KILLER MOVE: SERIOUS SERIES

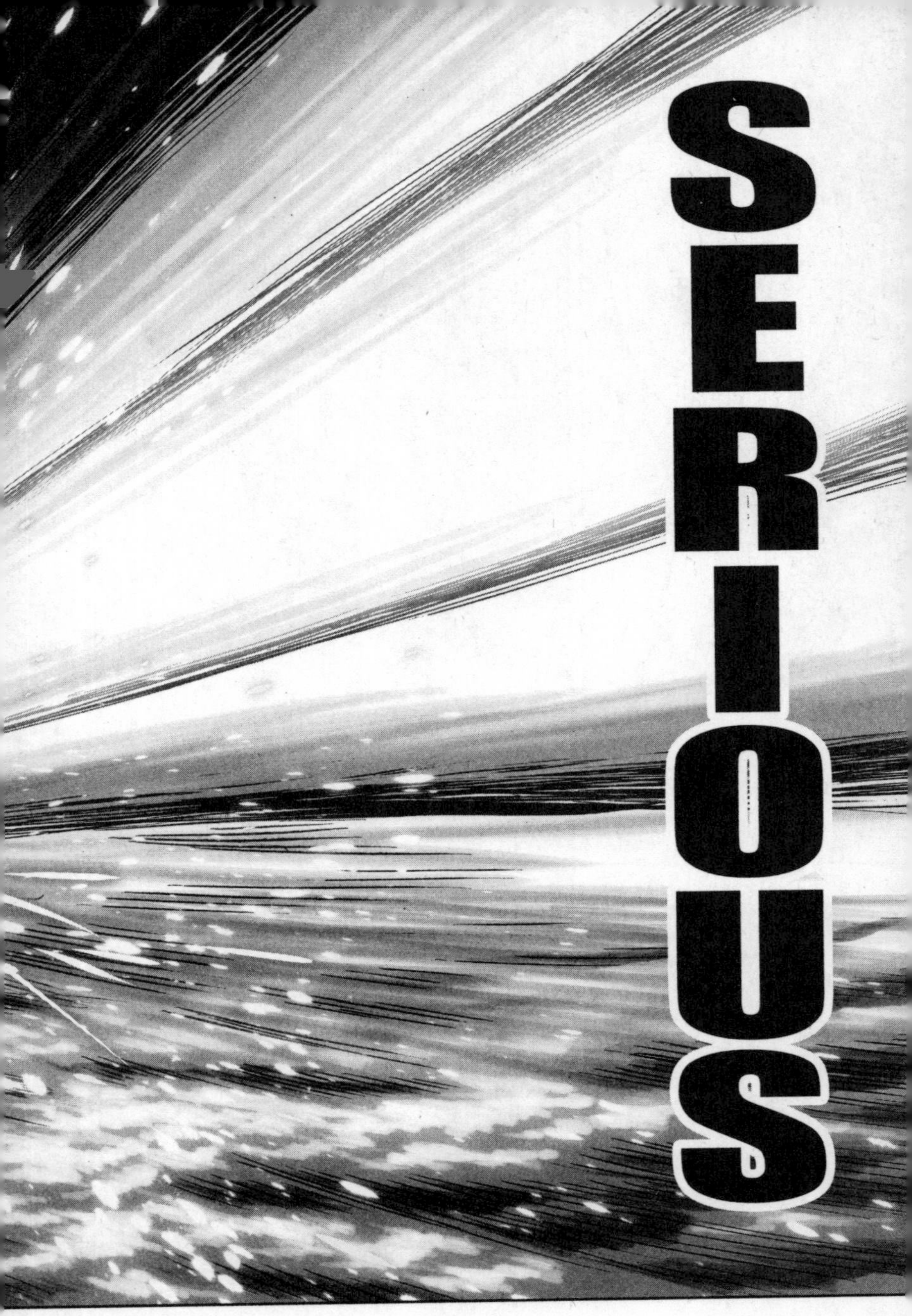
SERIOUS

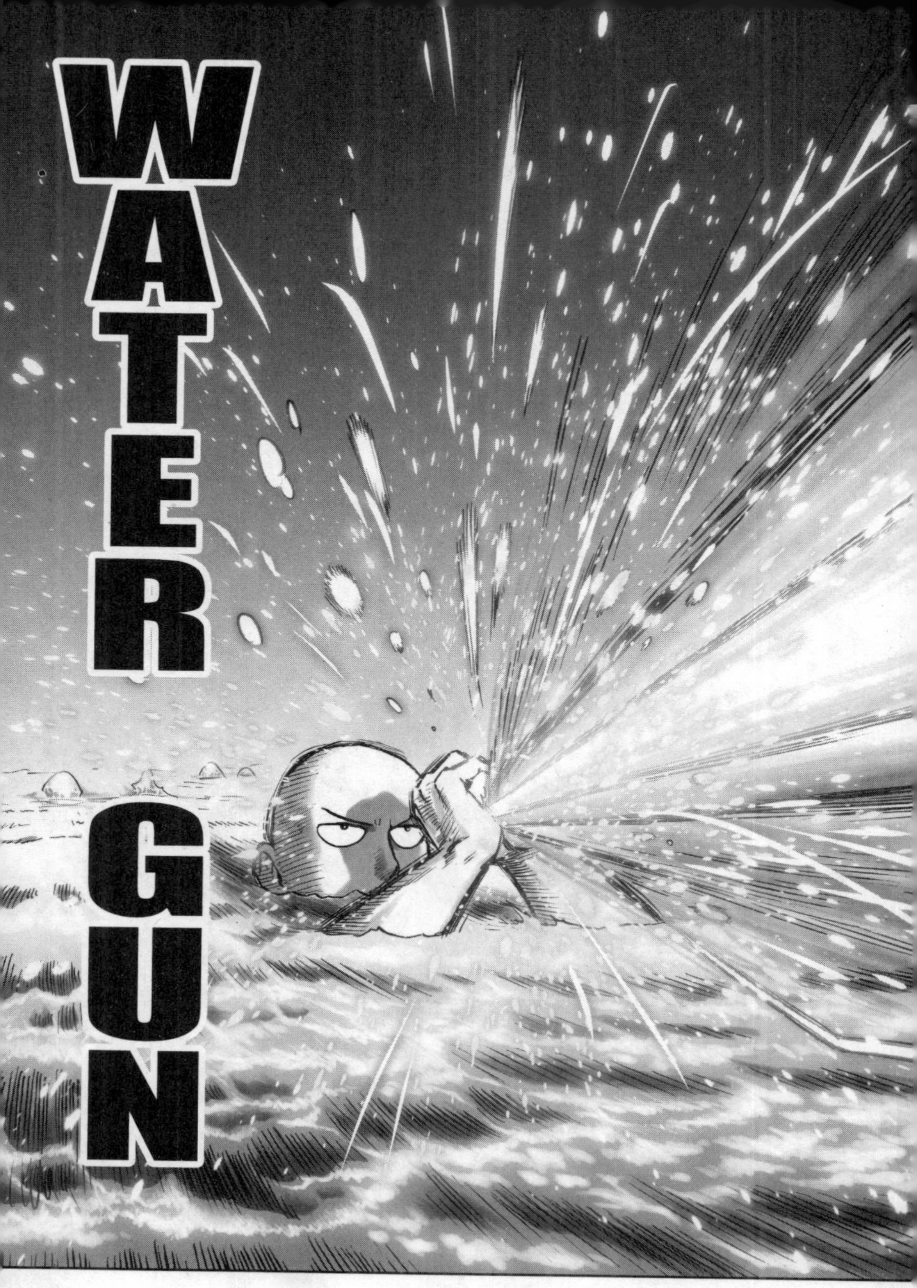
WATER
GUN

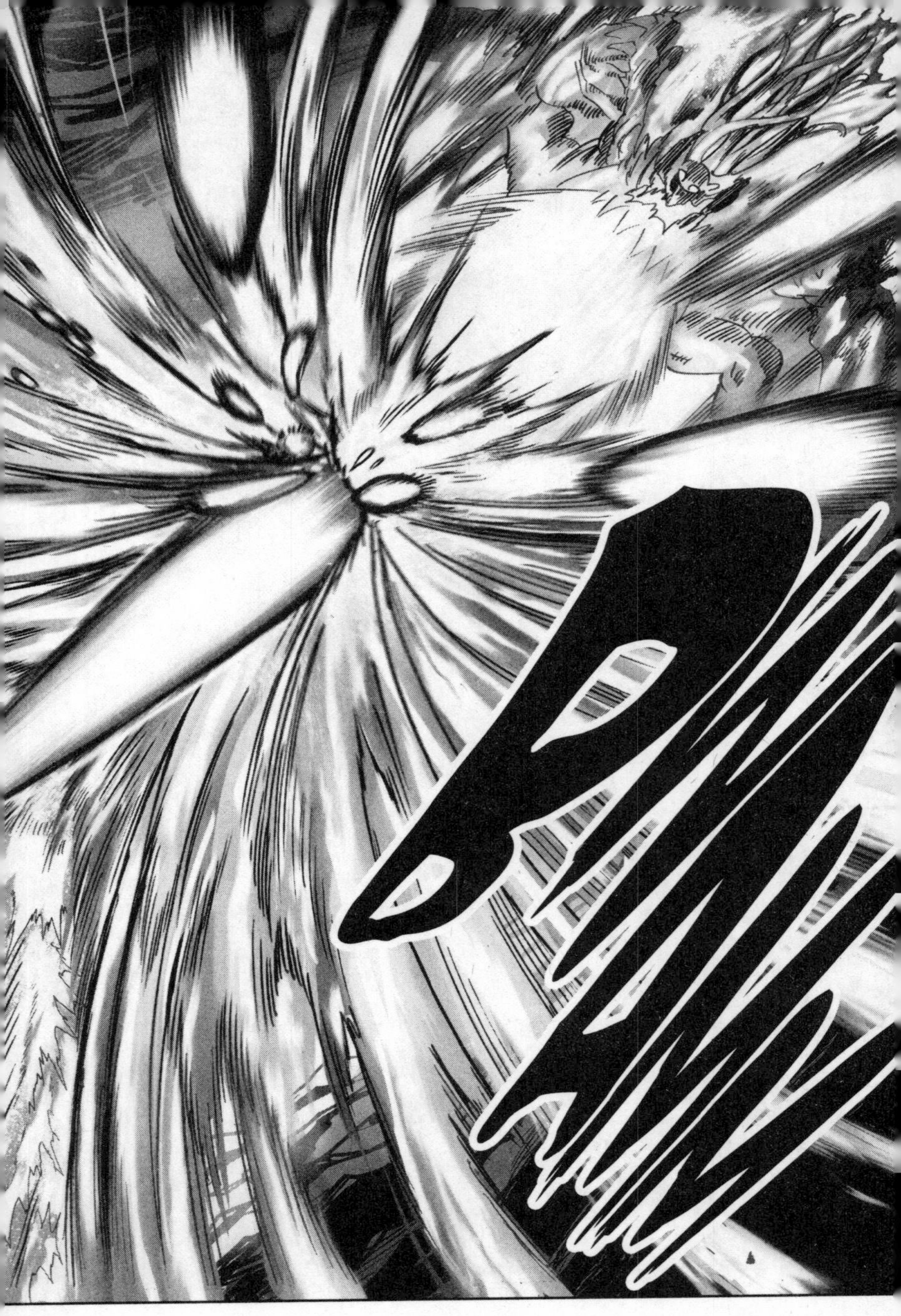

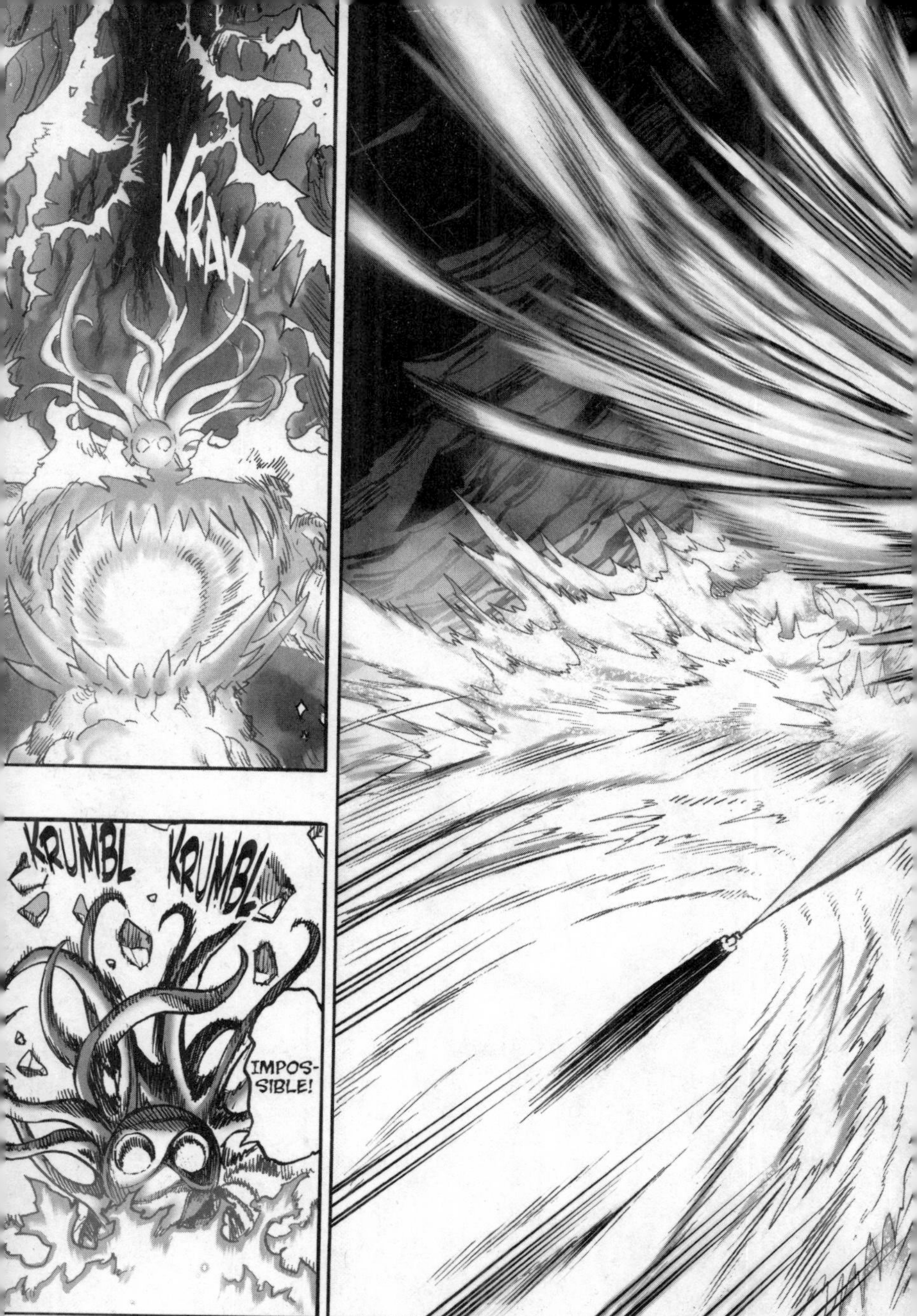
KRAK
KRUMBL KRUMBL
IMPOSSIBLE!

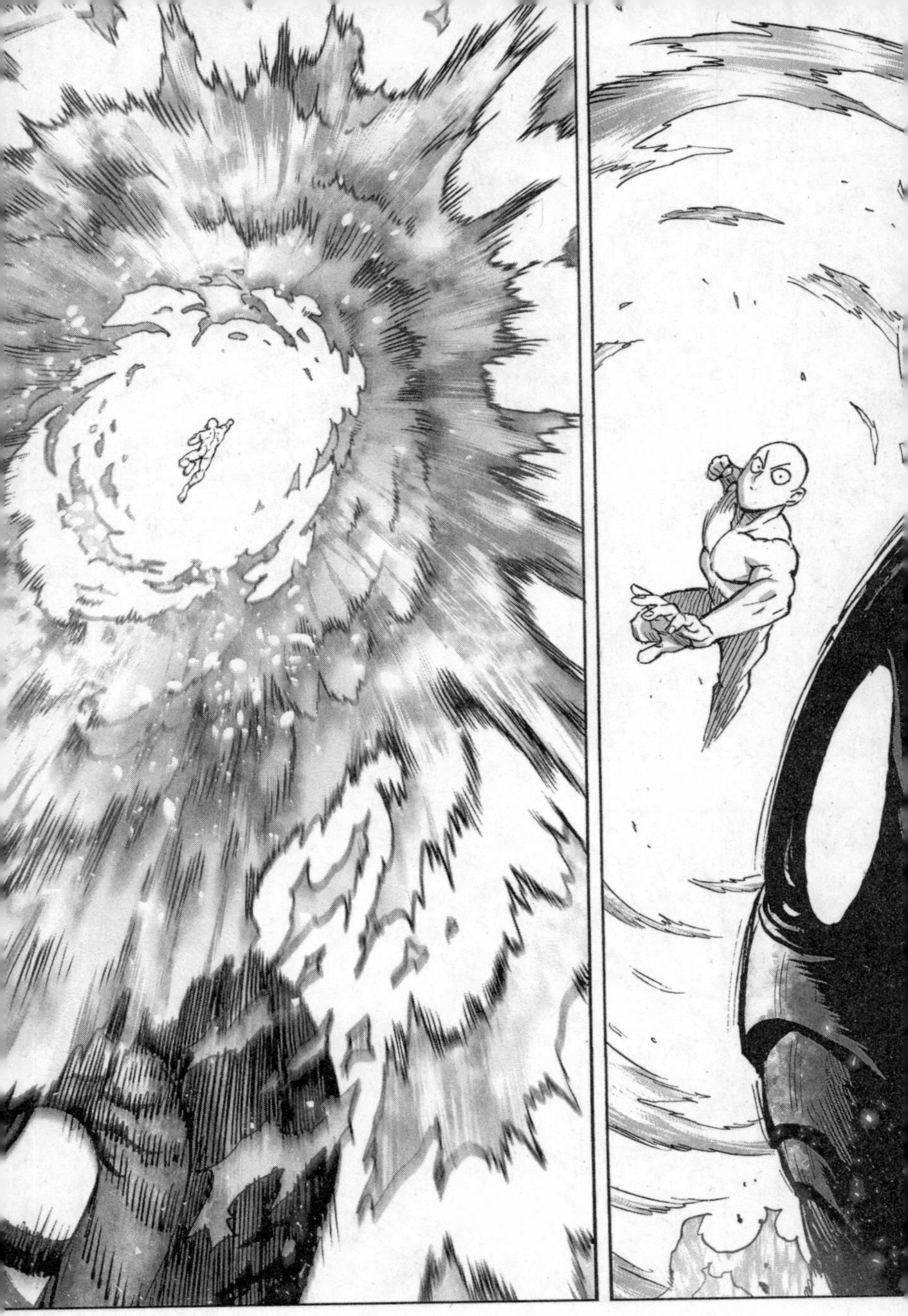

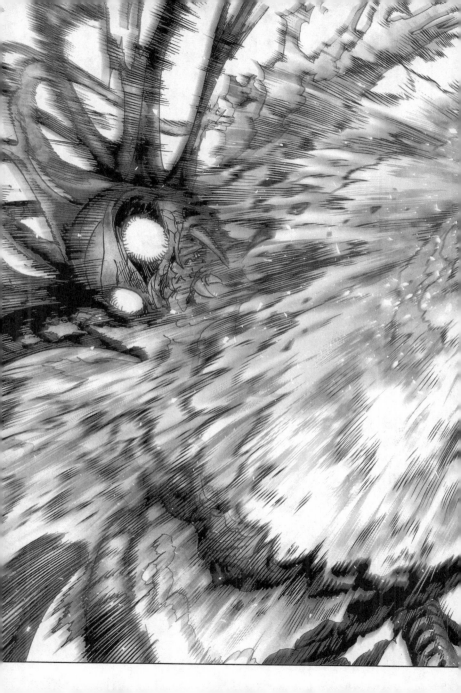

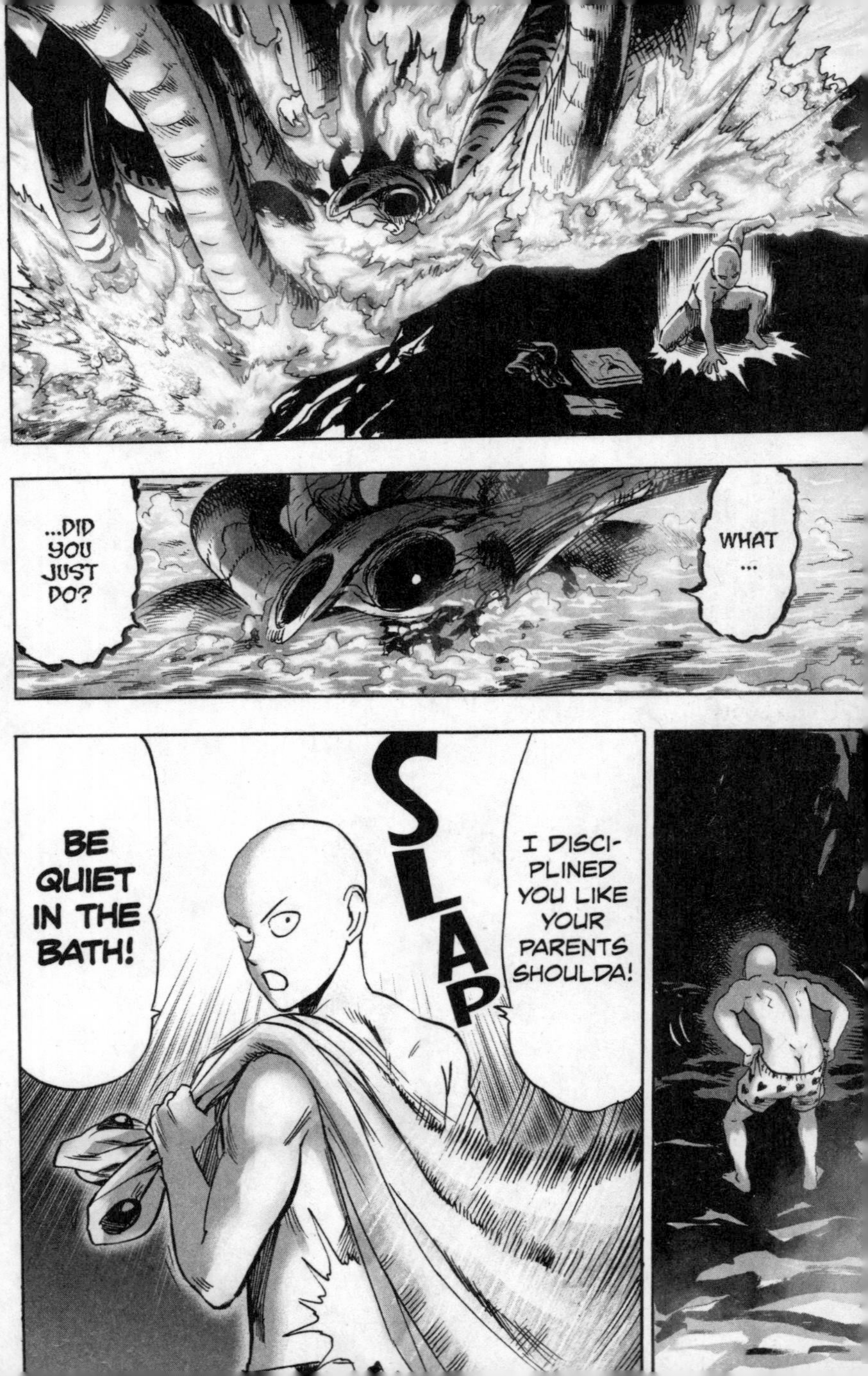
WHAT ...
...DID YOU JUST DO?
I DISCIPLINED YOU LIKE YOUR PARENTS SHOULDA!
SLAP
BE QUIET IN THE BATH!

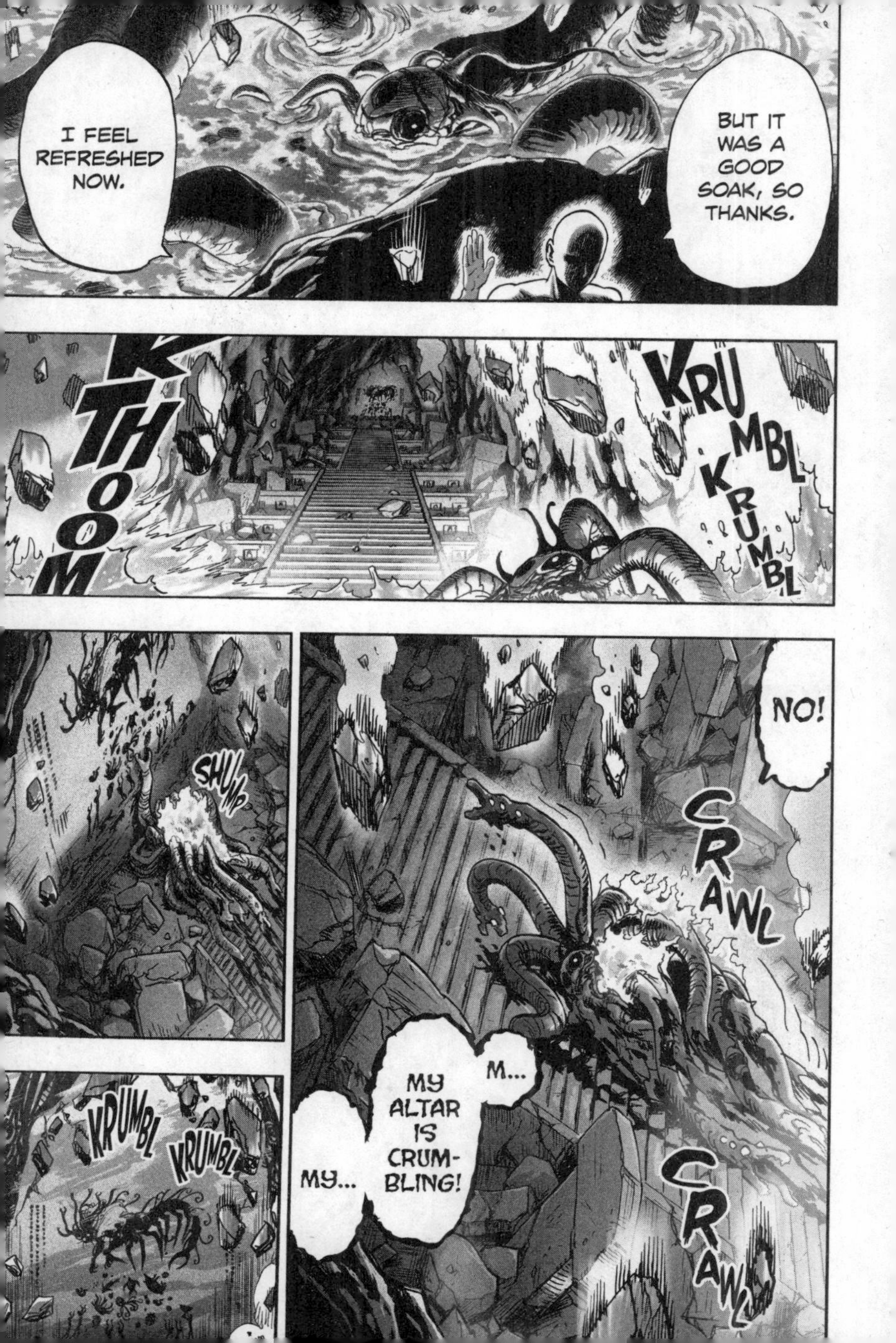
BUT IT WAS A GOOD SOAK, SO THANKS.
I FEEL REFRESHED NOW.
KRUMBL KRUMBL
KTHOOOM
NO!
CRAWL
M...
MY ALTAR IS CRUM-BLING!
MY...
CRAWL
SHUMP
KRUMBL
KRUMBL

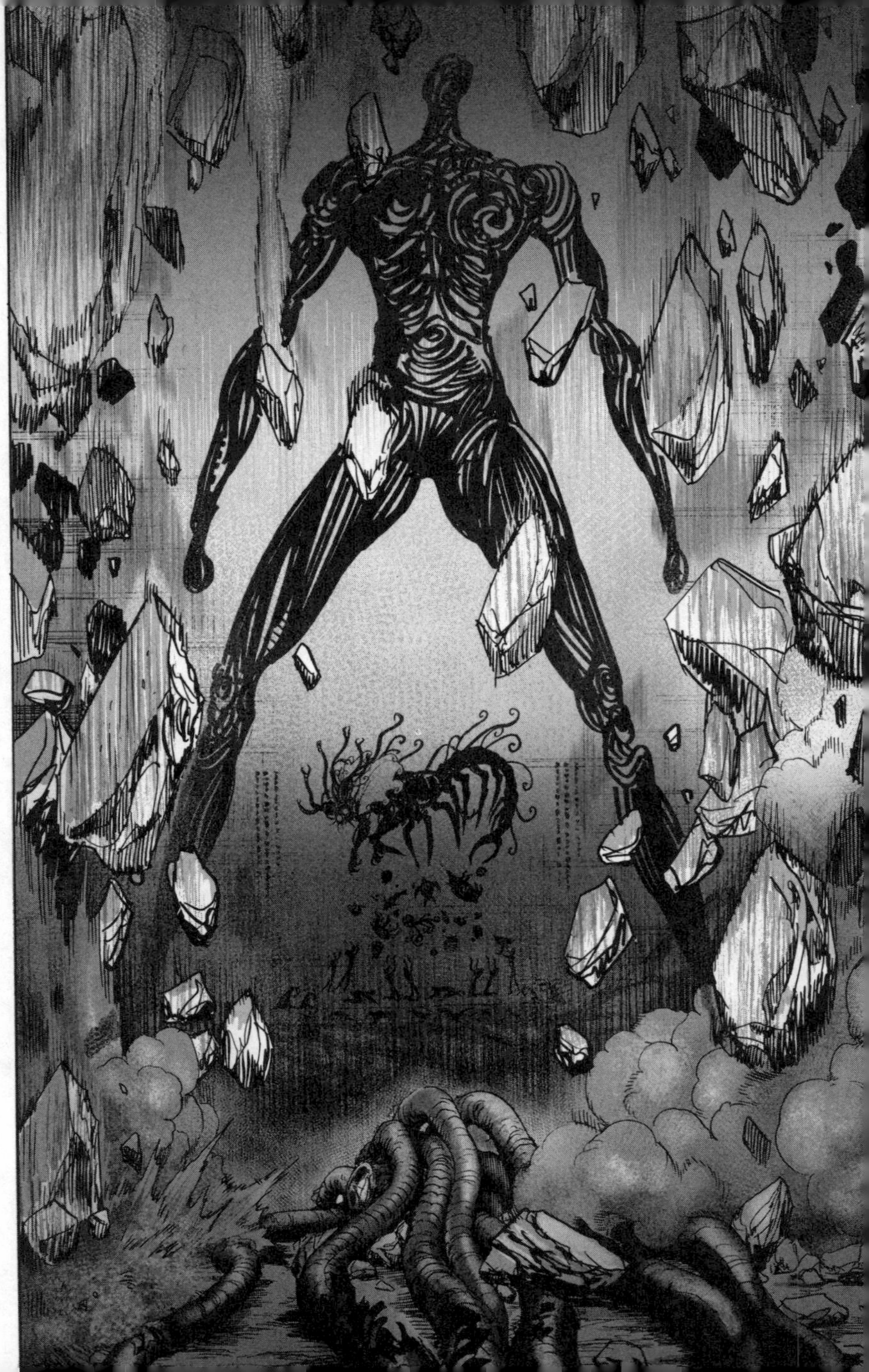

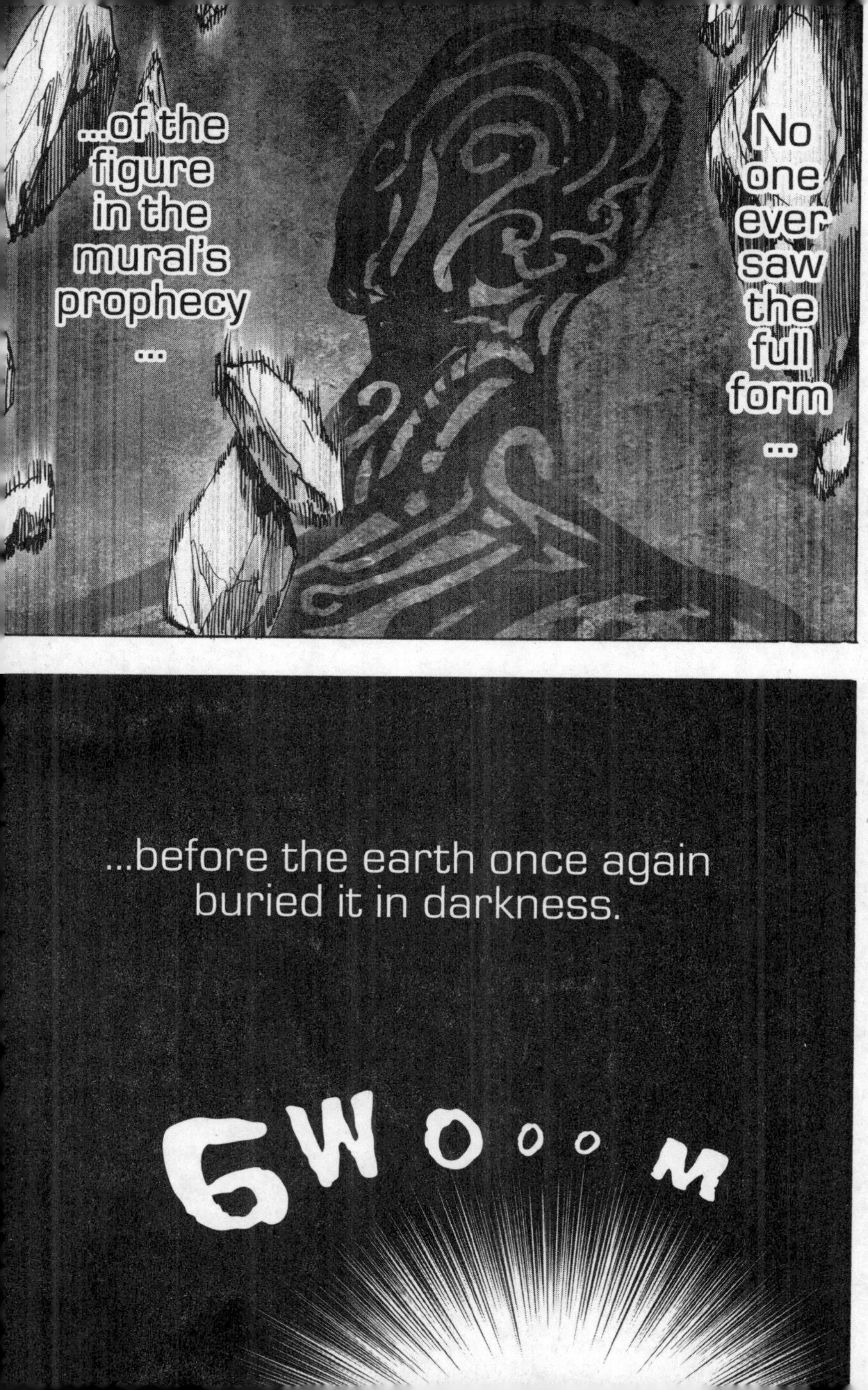
No one ever saw the full form...
...of the figure in the mural's prophecy...
...before the earth once again buried it in darkness.
GWOOOM

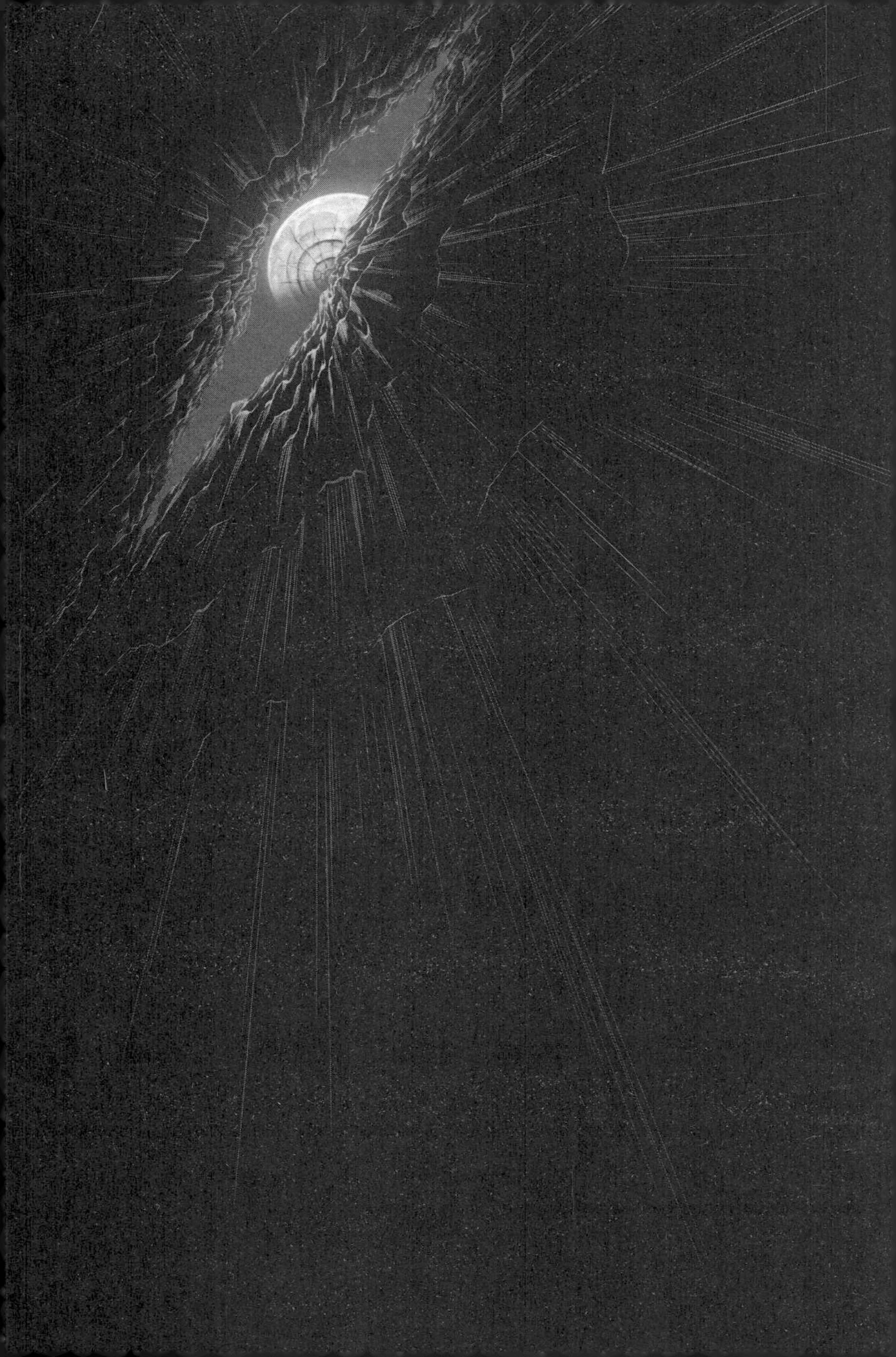

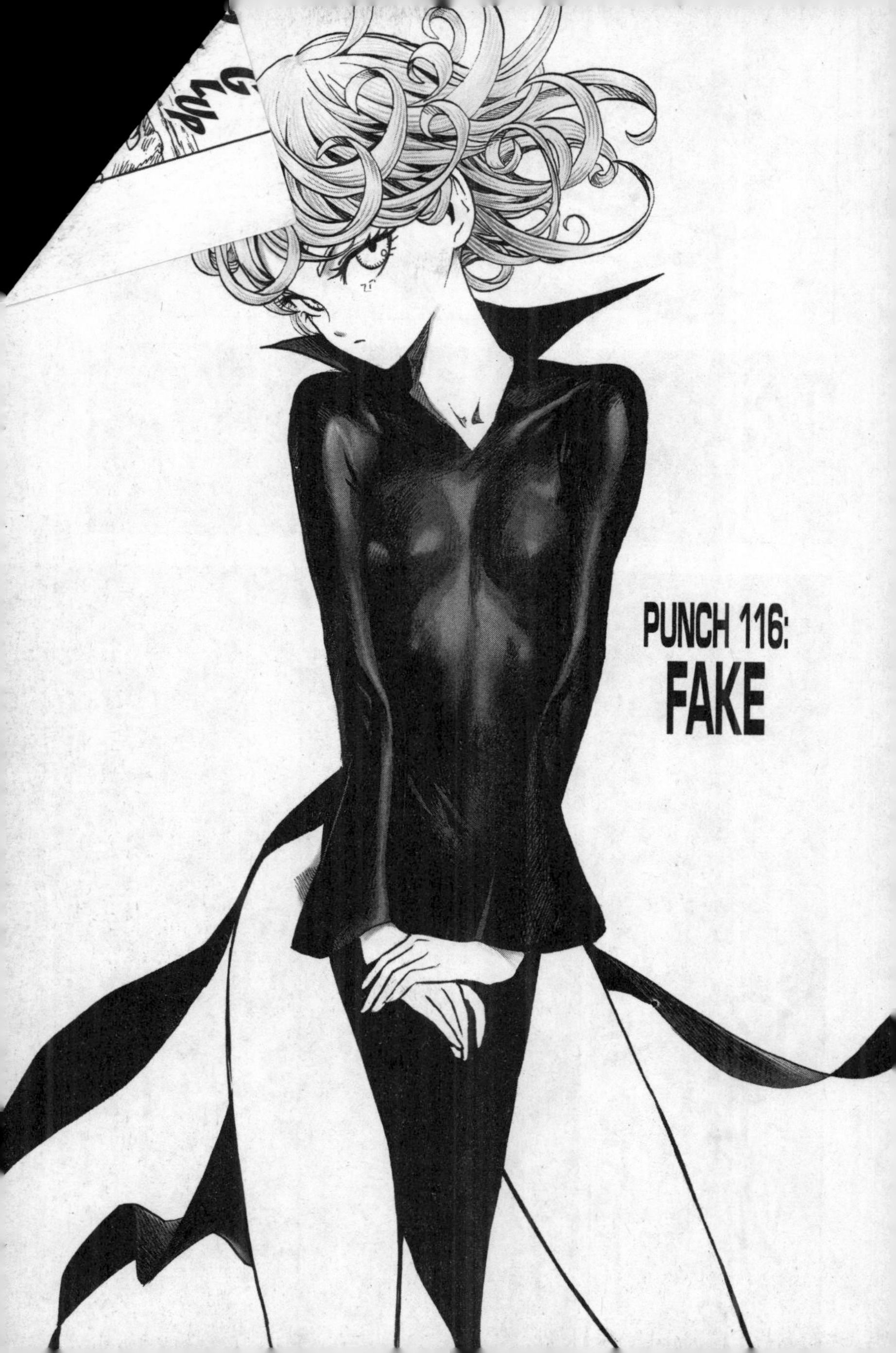

PUNCH 116: FAKE

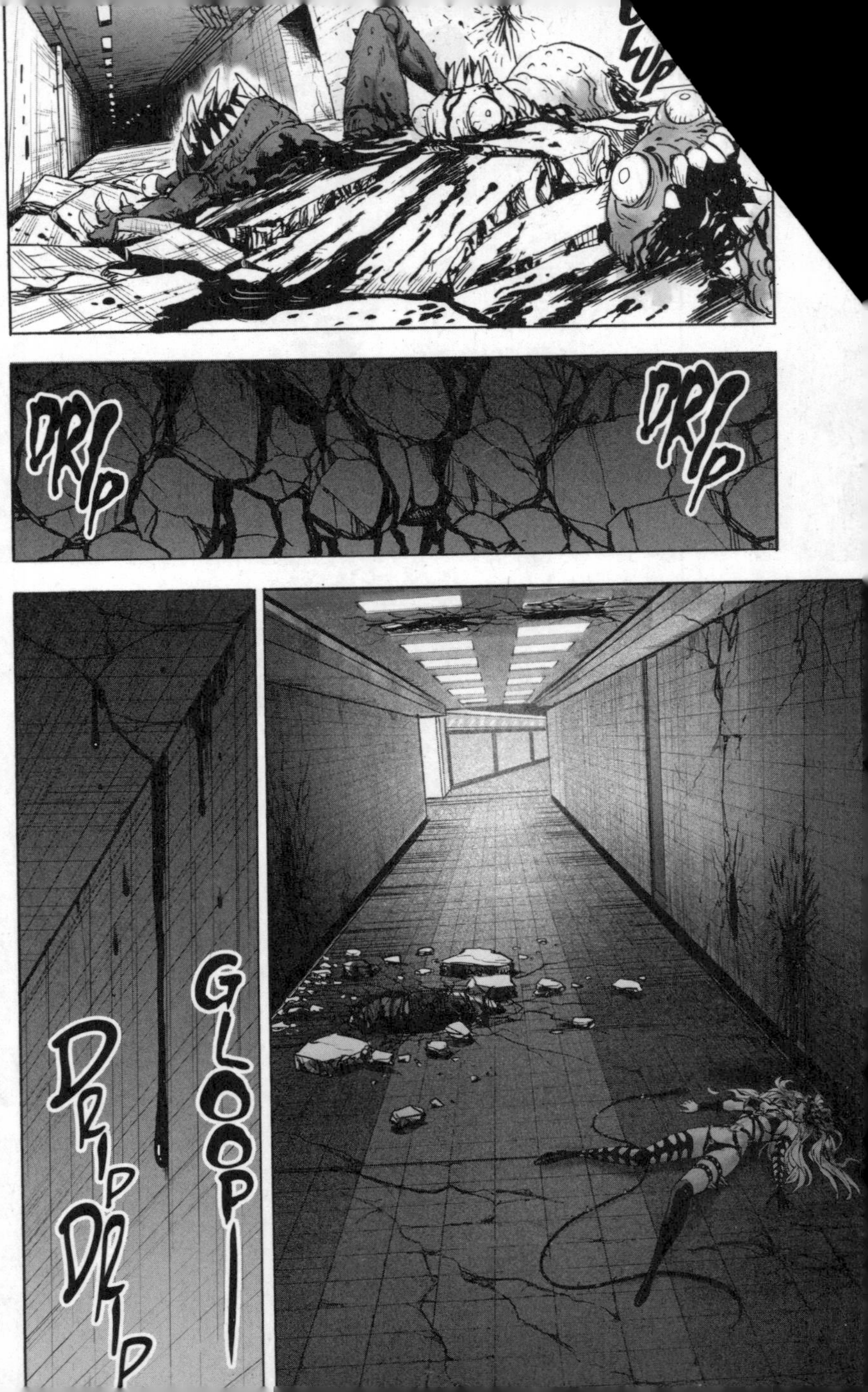
DRIP
DRIP
GLOOP!
DRIP DRIP

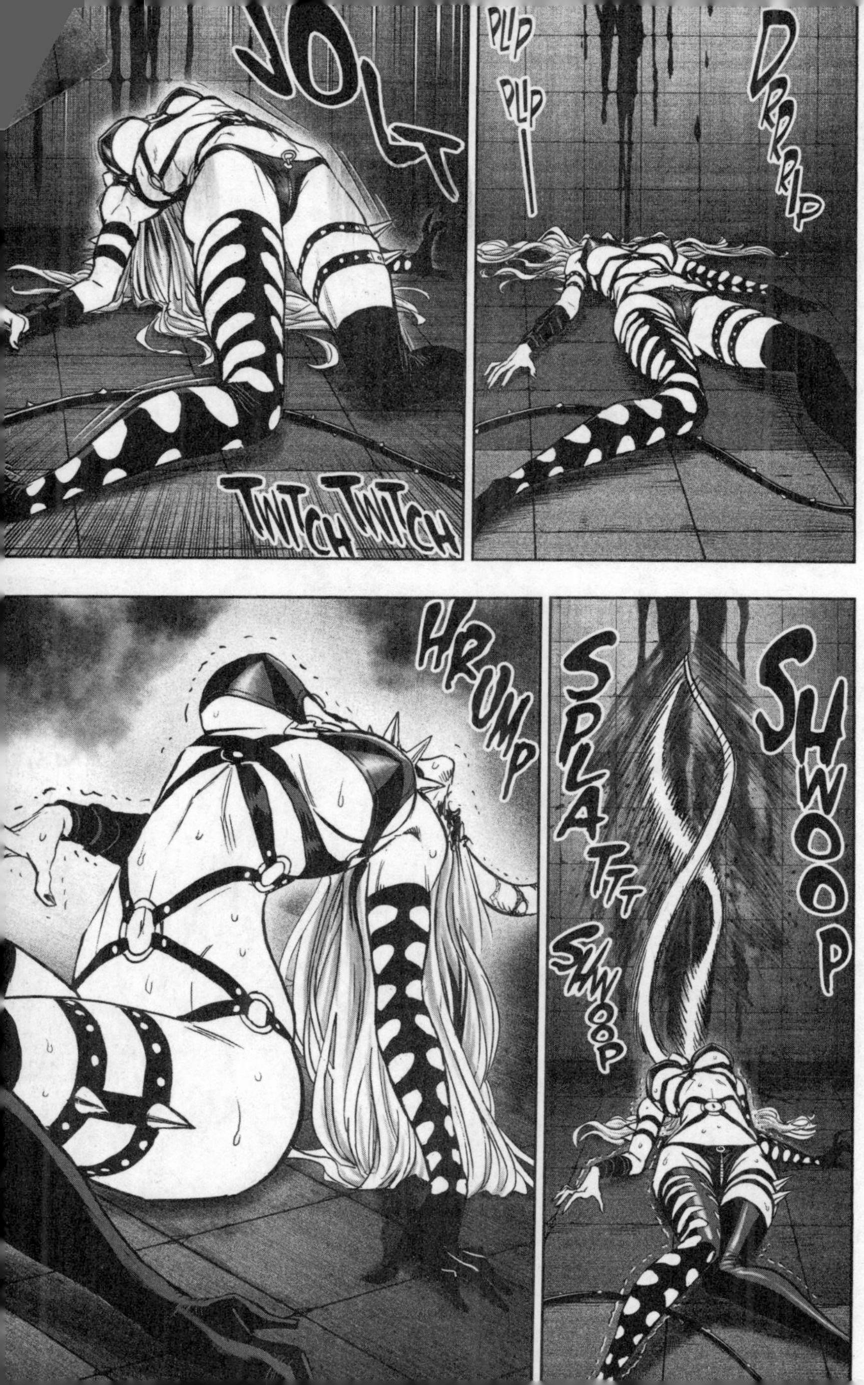
DRRRIP
PLIP PLIP
JOLT
TWITCH TWITCH
SHWOOP
SPLATTT
SHWOOP
HRUMP

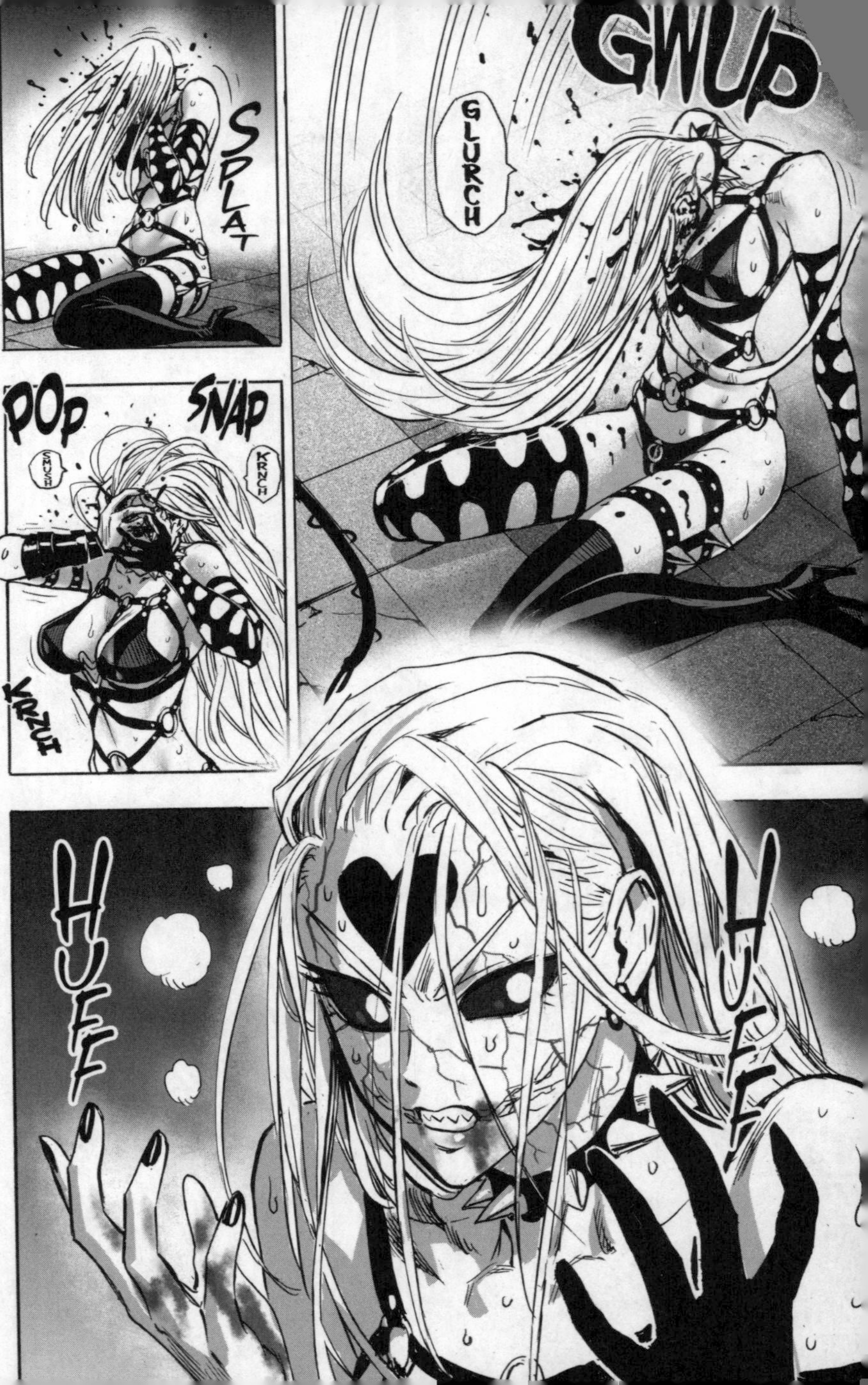
GWUP
GLURCH
SPLAT
SNAP
KRNCH
SMUSH
POP
KRNCH
HUFF
HUFF

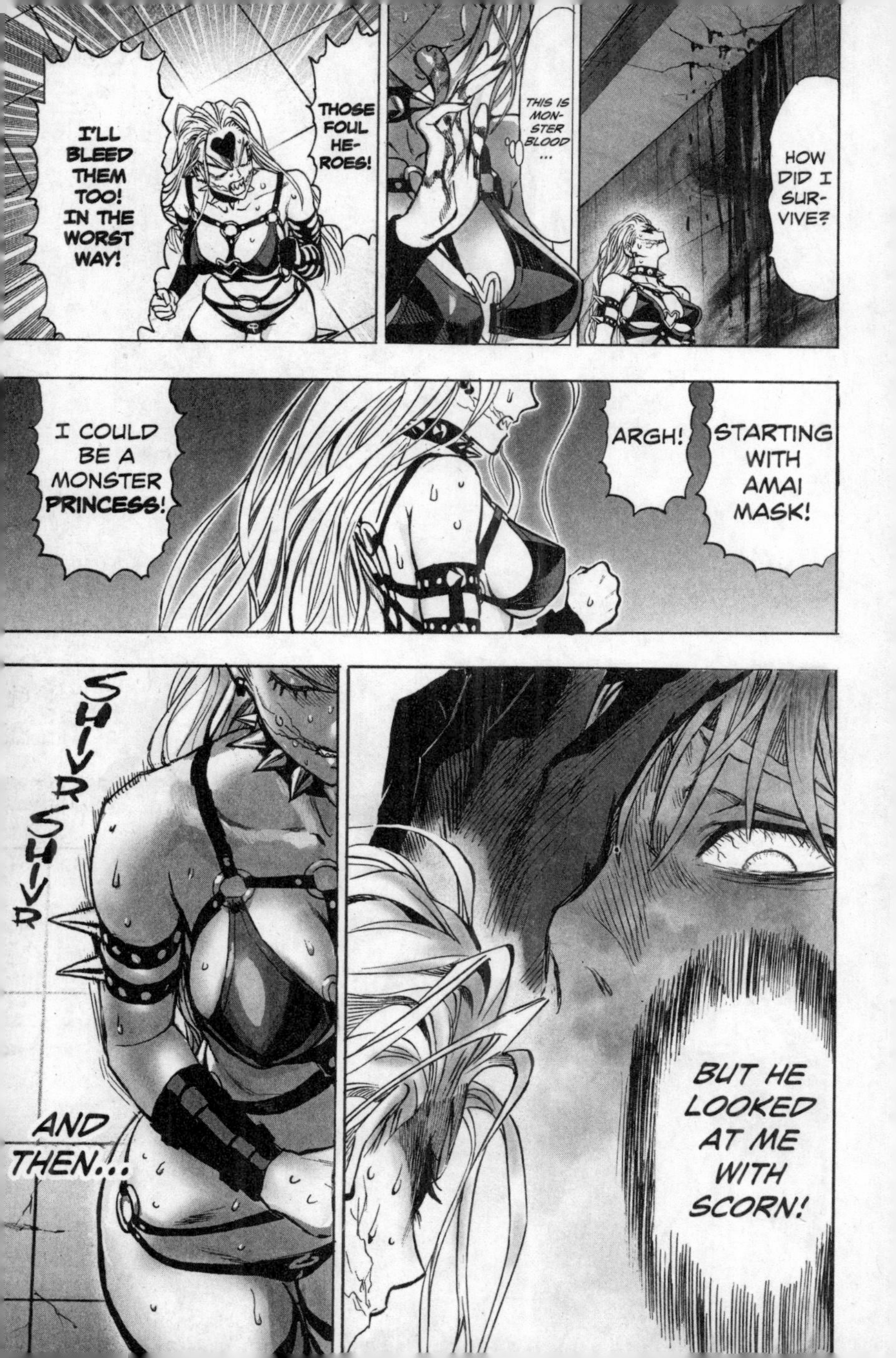
HOW DID I SURVIVE?
THIS IS MONSTER BLOOD...
THOSE FOUL HEROES!
I'LL BLEED THEM TOO! IN THE WORST WAY!
STARTING WITH AMAI MASK!
ARGH!
I COULD BE A MONSTER PRINCESS!
BUT HE LOOKED AT ME WITH SCORN!
SHIVR SHIVR
AND THEN...

...HE USED ALL HIS STRENGTH...

...TO CRUSH ME!

TREMBLE

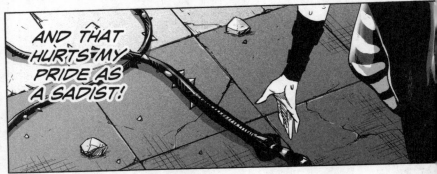

AND THAT HURTS MY PRIDE AS A SADIST!

...AMAI MASK.

SHWIP

JUST YOU WAIT...

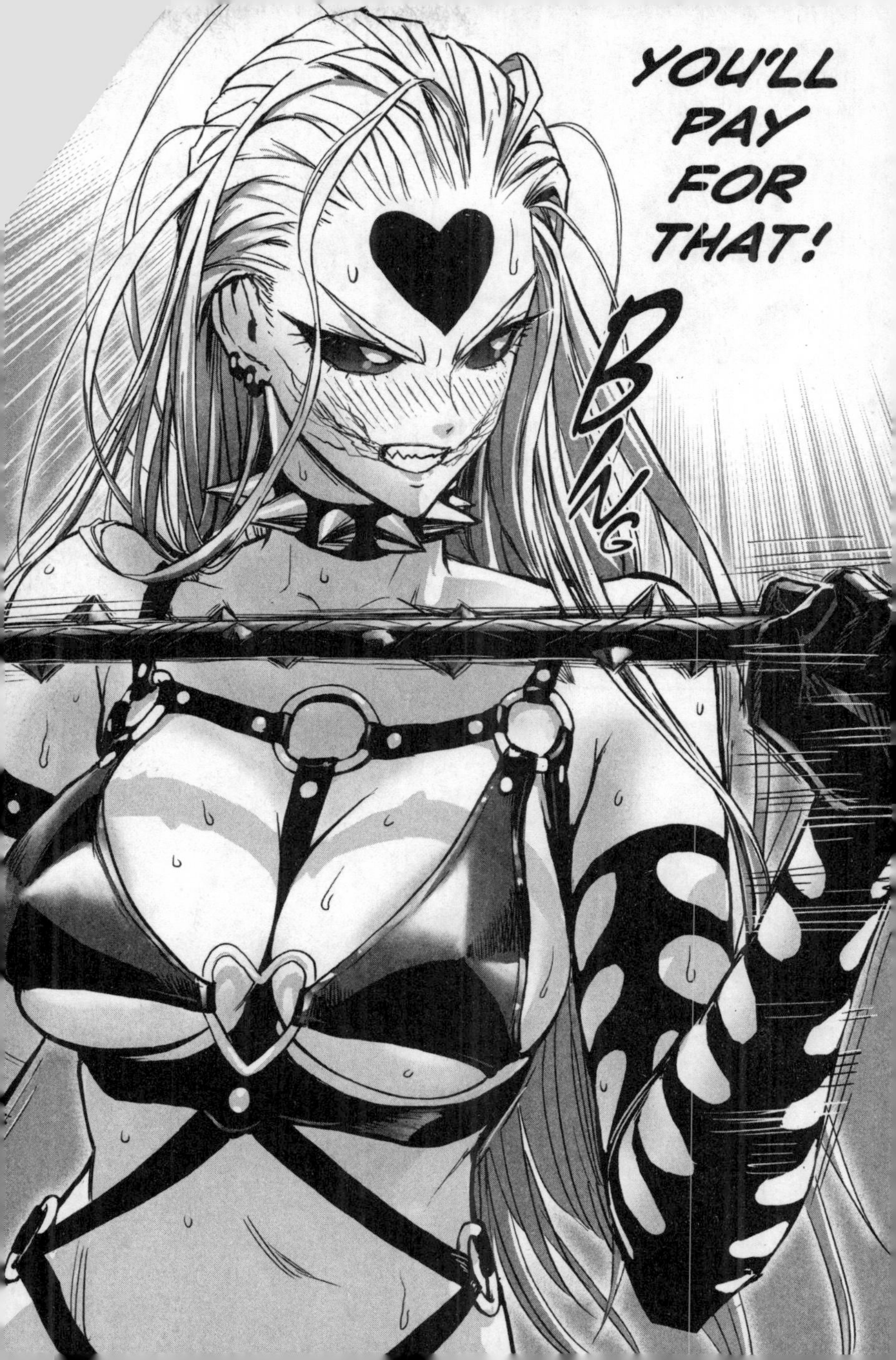
YOU'LL PAY FOR THAT!
BOING

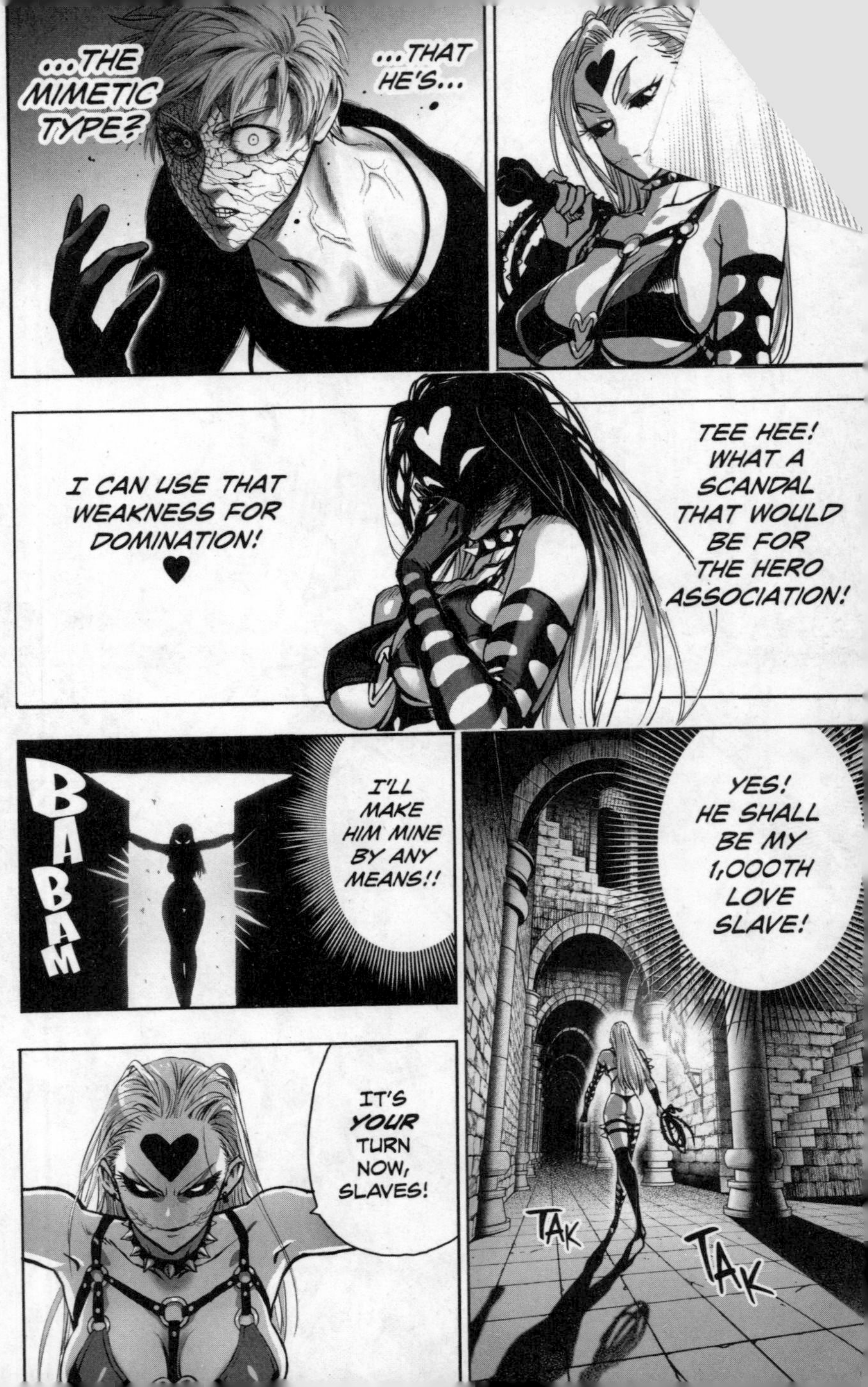
...THAT HE'S...
...THE MIMETIC TYPE?
TEE HEE! WHAT A SCANDAL THAT WOULD BE FOR THE HERO ASSOCIATION!
I CAN USE THAT WEAKNESS FOR DOMINATION! ♥
YES! HE SHALL BE MY 1,000TH LOVE SLAVE!
TAK
TAK
BABAM
I'LL MAKE HIM MINE BY ANY MEANS!!
IT'S YOUR TURN NOW, SLAVES!

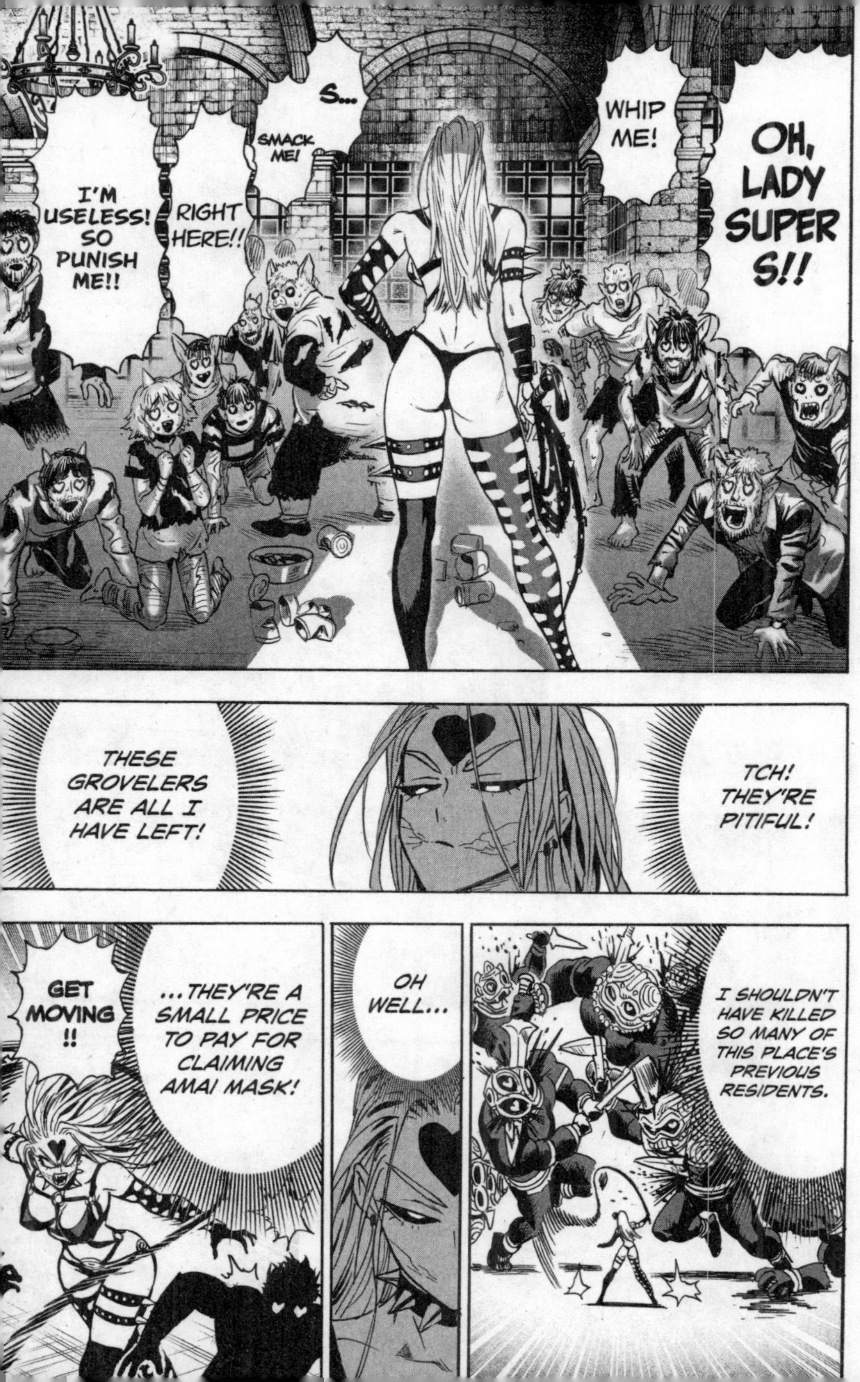

OH, LADY SUPER S!!
WHIP ME!
S...
SMACK ME!
RIGHT HERE!!
I'M USELESS! SO PUNISH ME!!
TCH! THEY'RE PITIFUL!
THESE GROVELERS ARE ALL I HAVE LEFT!
I SHOULDN'T HAVE KILLED SO MANY OF THIS PLACE'S PREVIOUS RESIDENTS.
OH WELL...
...THEY'RE A SMALL PRICE TO PAY FOR CLAIMING AMAI MASK!
GET MOVING !!

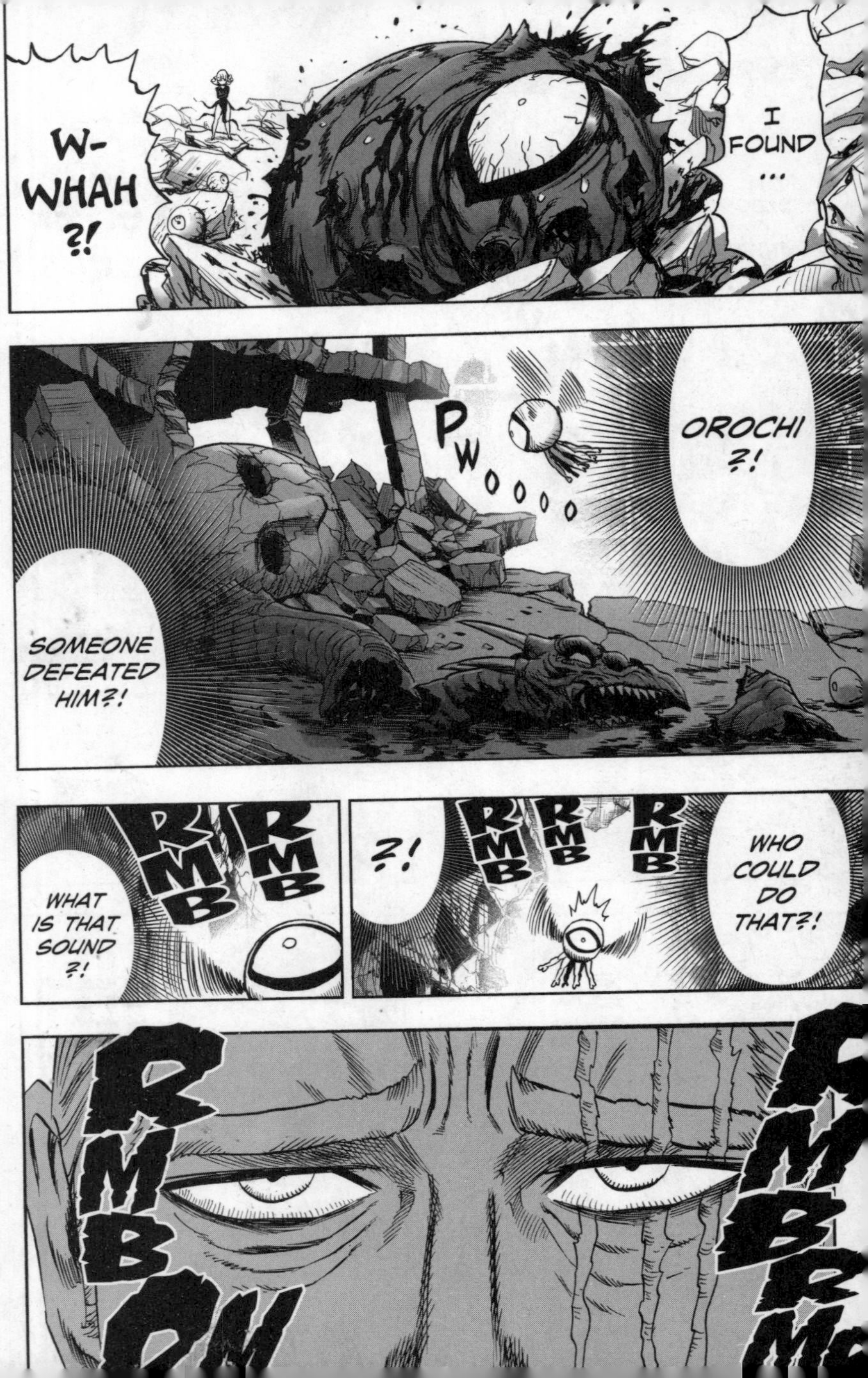

I FOUND ...
W- WHAH ?!
OROCHI ?!
PWOOOO
SOMEONE DEFEATED HIM?!
WHO COULD DO THAT?!
RMB RMB RMB
?!
RMB RMB
WHAT IS THAT SOUND ?!
RMB

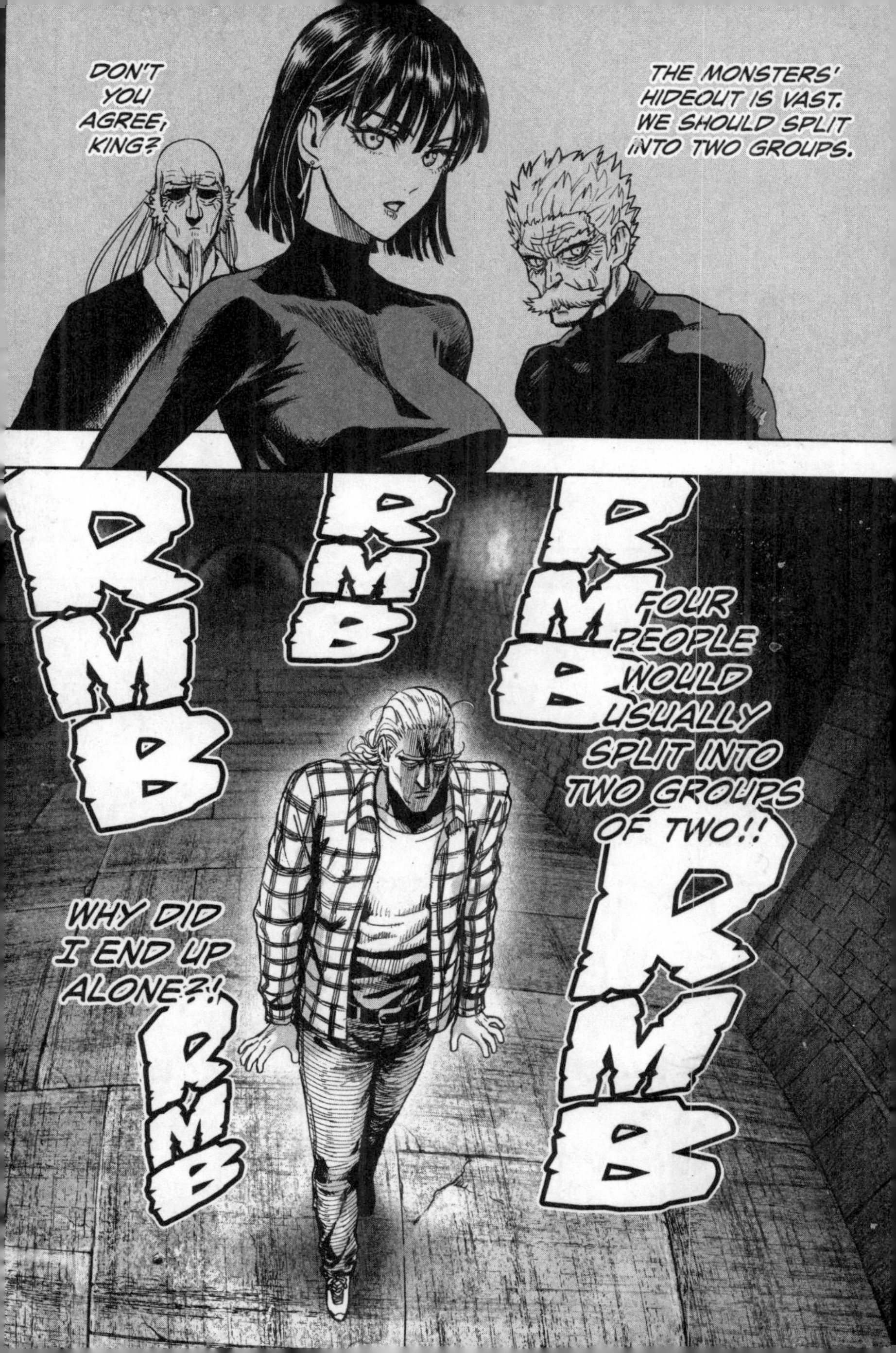
THE MONSTERS' HIDEOUT IS VAST. WE SHOULD SPLIT INTO TWO GROUPS.
DON'T YOU AGREE, KING?
RMB
RMB
RMB
FOUR PEOPLE WOULD USUALLY SPLIT INTO TWO GROUPS OF TWO!!
RMB
WHY DID I END UP ALONE?!
RMB

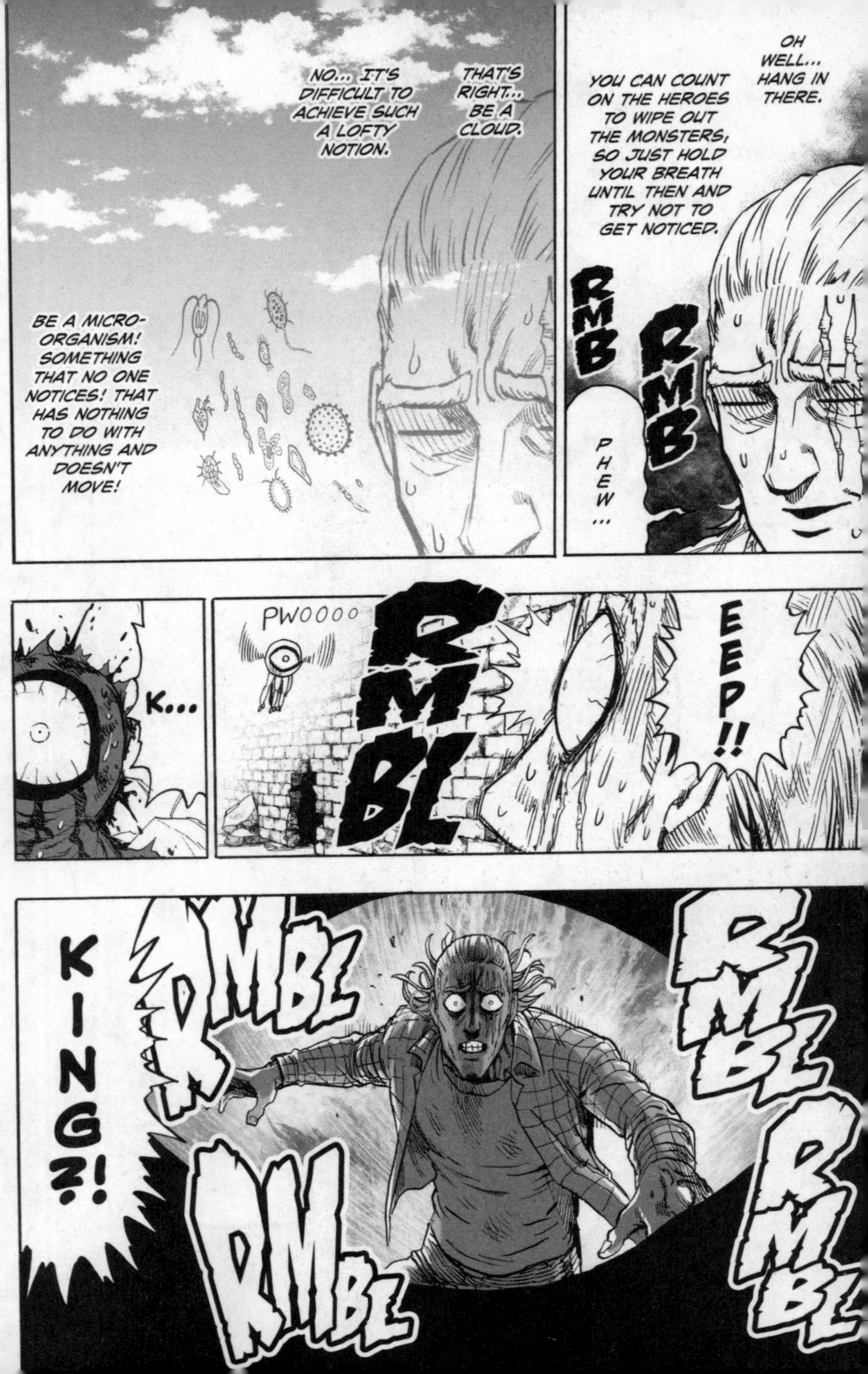

OH WELL... HANG IN THERE.
YOU CAN COUNT ON THE HEROES TO WIPE OUT THE MONSTERS, SO JUST HOLD YOUR BREATH UNTIL THEN AND TRY NOT TO GET NOTICED.
RMB
RMB
PHEW...
THAT'S RIGHT... BE A CLOUD.
NO... IT'S DIFFICULT TO ACHIEVE SUCH A LOFTY NOTION.
BE A MICRO-ORGANISM! SOMETHING THAT NO ONE NOTICES! THAT HAS NOTHING TO DO WITH ANYTHING AND DOESN'T MOVE!
EEP!!
RMBL
PWOOOO
K...
RMBLE
RMBLE
KING?!
RMBLE
RMBLE

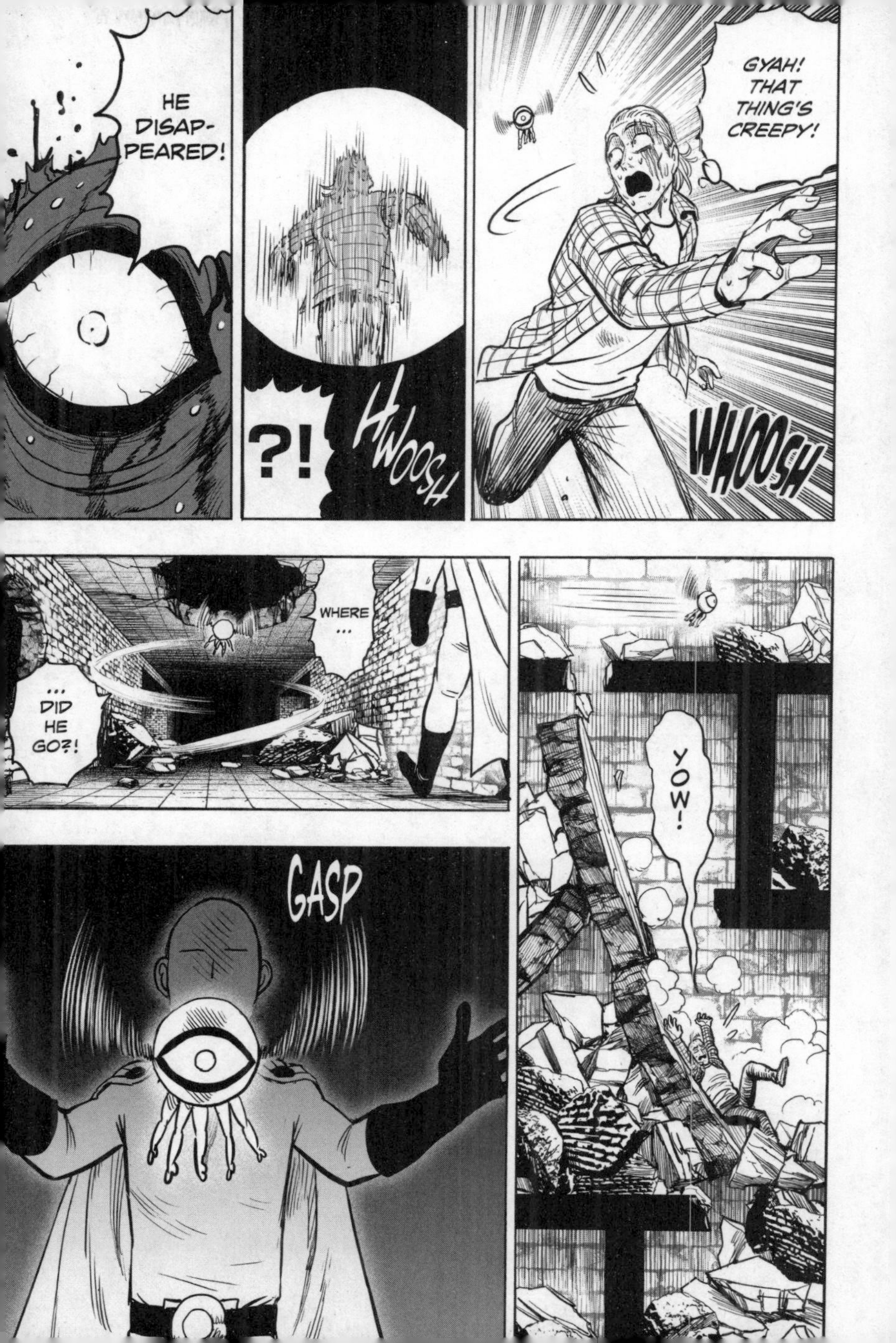
GYAH! THAT THING'S CREEPY!
WHOOSH
?!
HWOOSH
HE DISAP-PEARED!
YOW!
WHERE ...
... DID HE GO?!
GASP

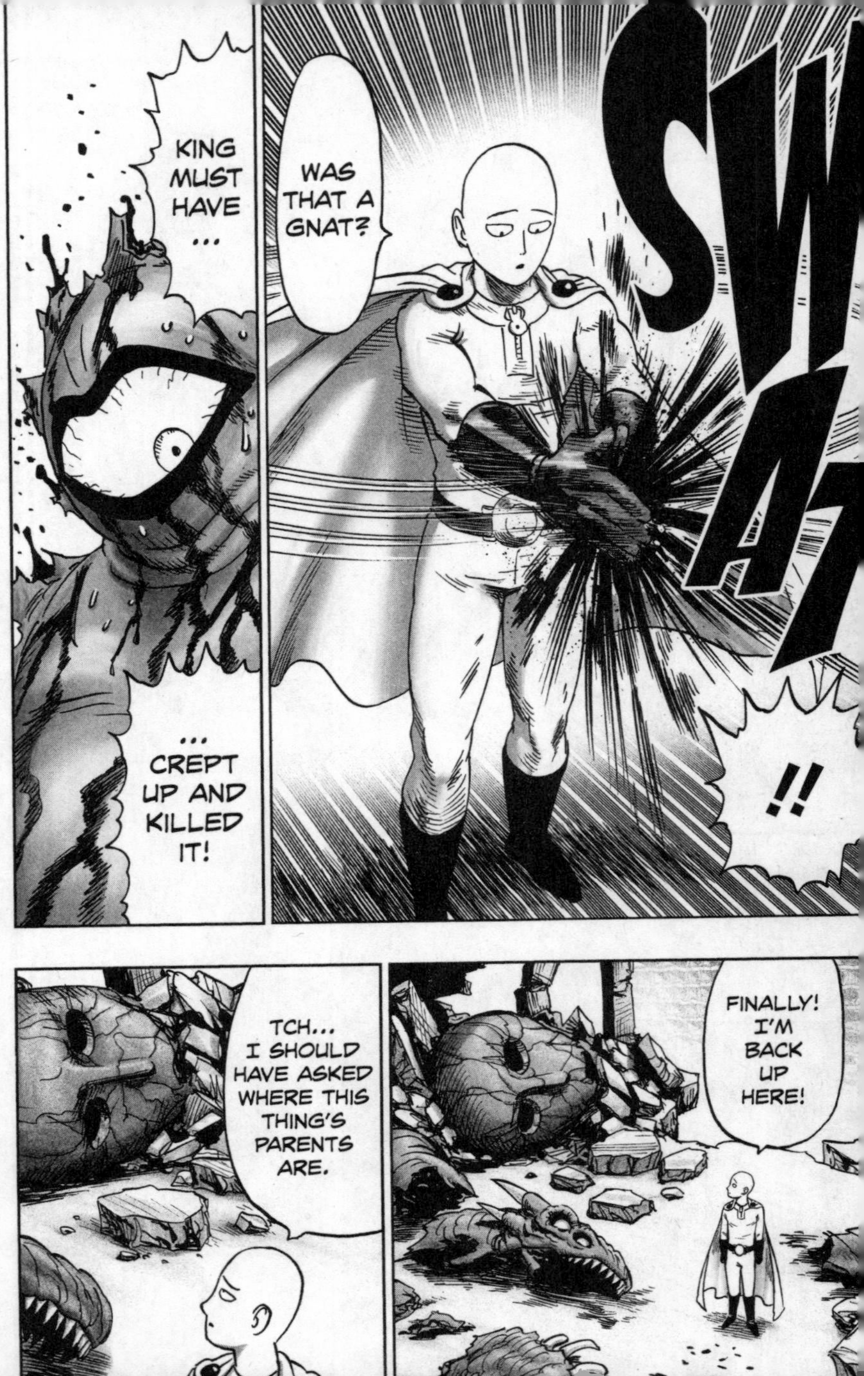
SWAT
WAS THAT A GNAT?
!!
KING MUST HAVE ...
... CREPT UP AND KILLED IT!
FINALLY! I'M BACK UP HERE!
TCH... I SHOULD HAVE ASKED WHERE THIS THING'S PARENTS ARE.

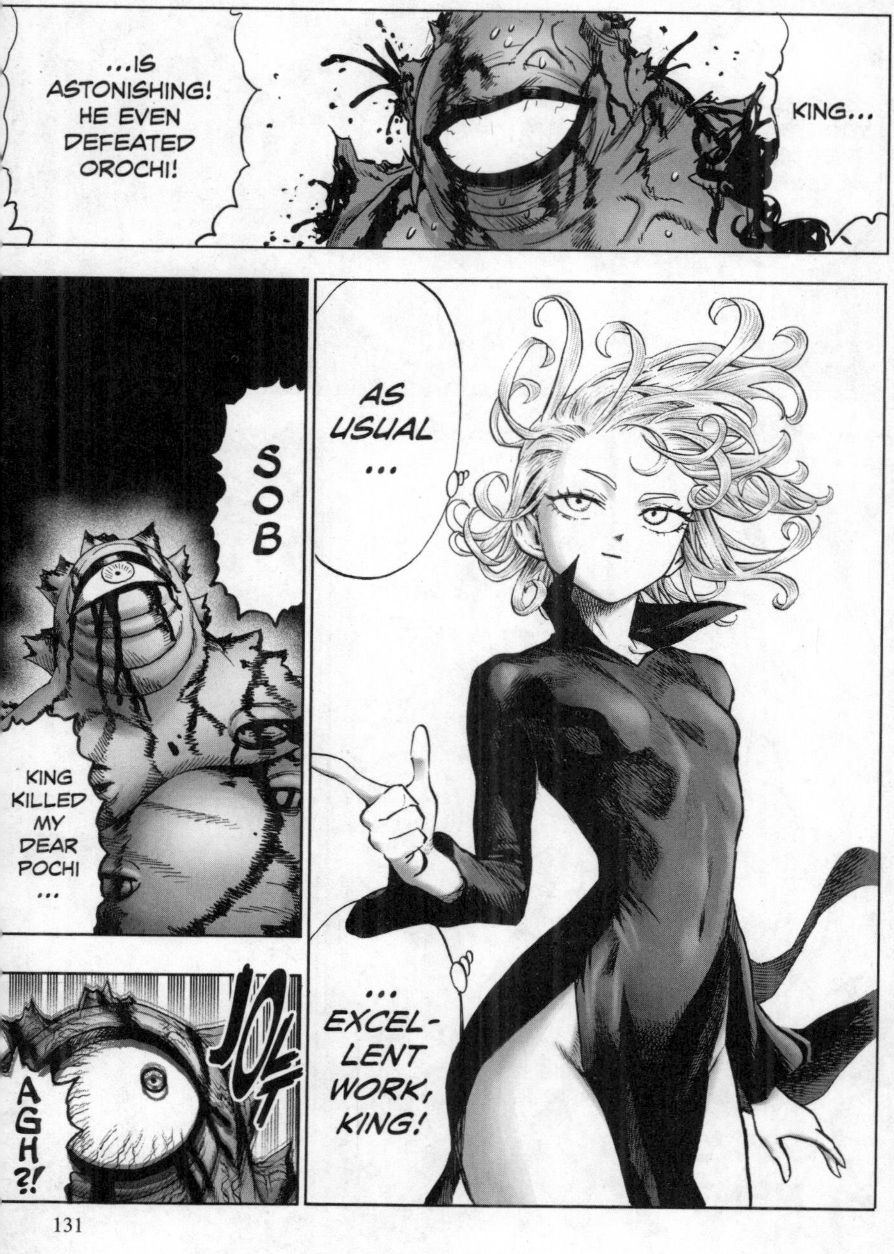
KING...
...IS ASTONISHING! HE EVEN DEFEATED OROCHI!
AS USUAL...
...EXCEL-LENT WORK, KING!
SOB
KING KILLED MY DEAR POCHI...
JOLT
AGH?!

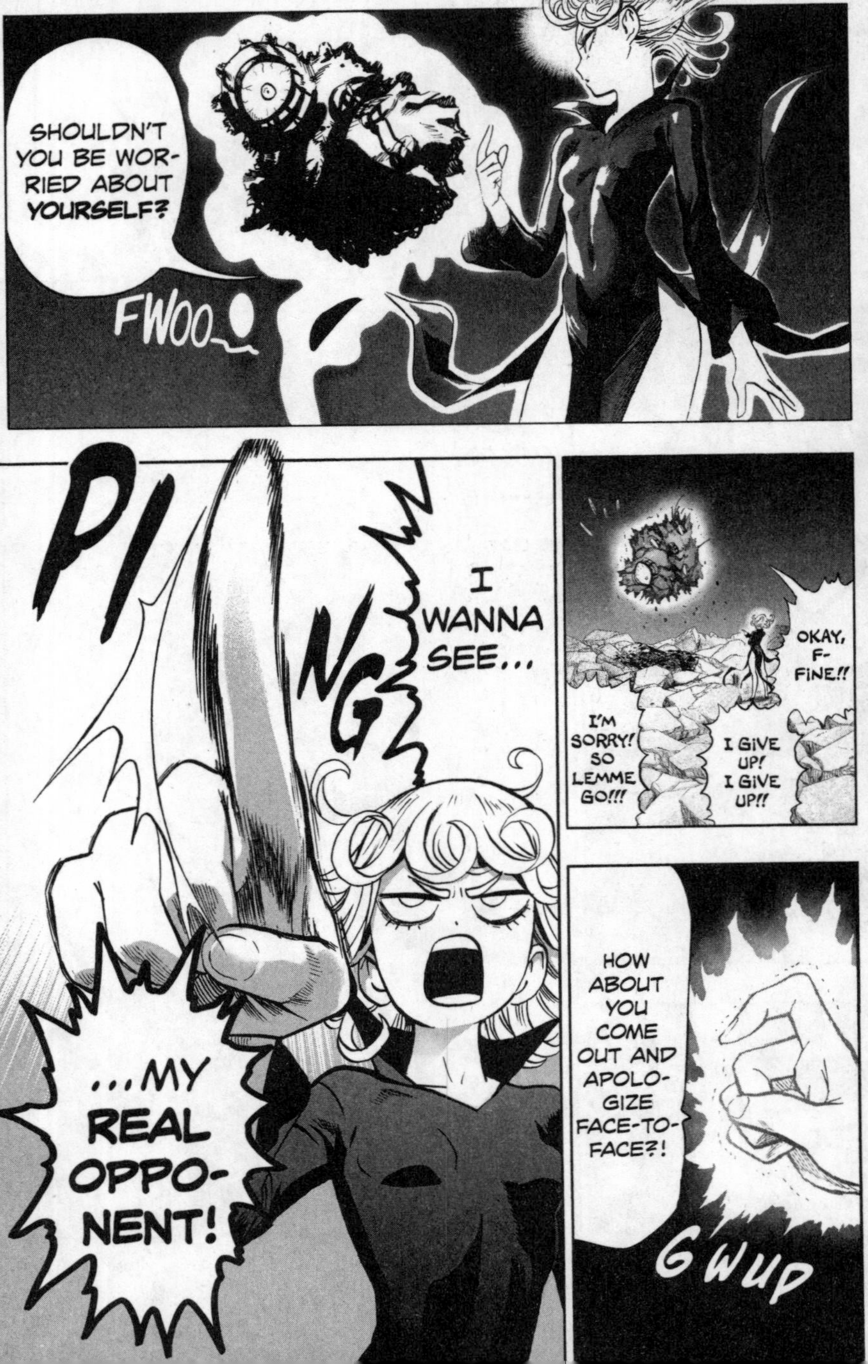
SHOULDN'T YOU BE WORRIED ABOUT YOURSELF?
FWOO
OKAY, F-FINE!!
I GIVE UP! I GIVE UP!!
I'M SORRY! SO LEMME GO!!!
HOW ABOUT YOU COME OUT AND APOLOGIZE FACE-TO-FACE?!
GWUP
PING
I WANNA SEE...
...MY REAL OPPONENT!

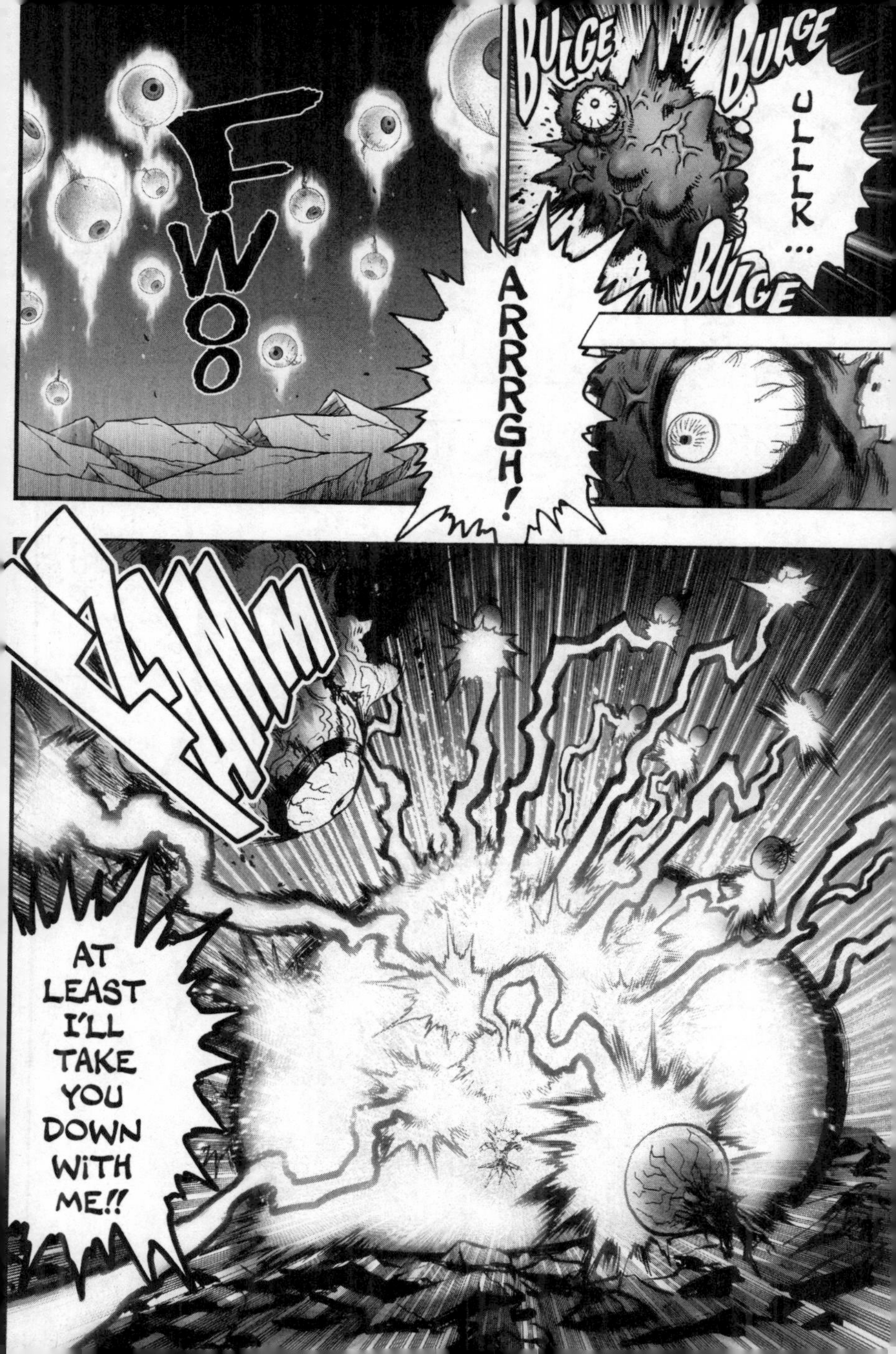
BULGE
BULGE
ULLLK...
BULGE
ARRRGH!
FWOO
AT LEAST I'LL TAKE YOU DOWN WITH ME!!

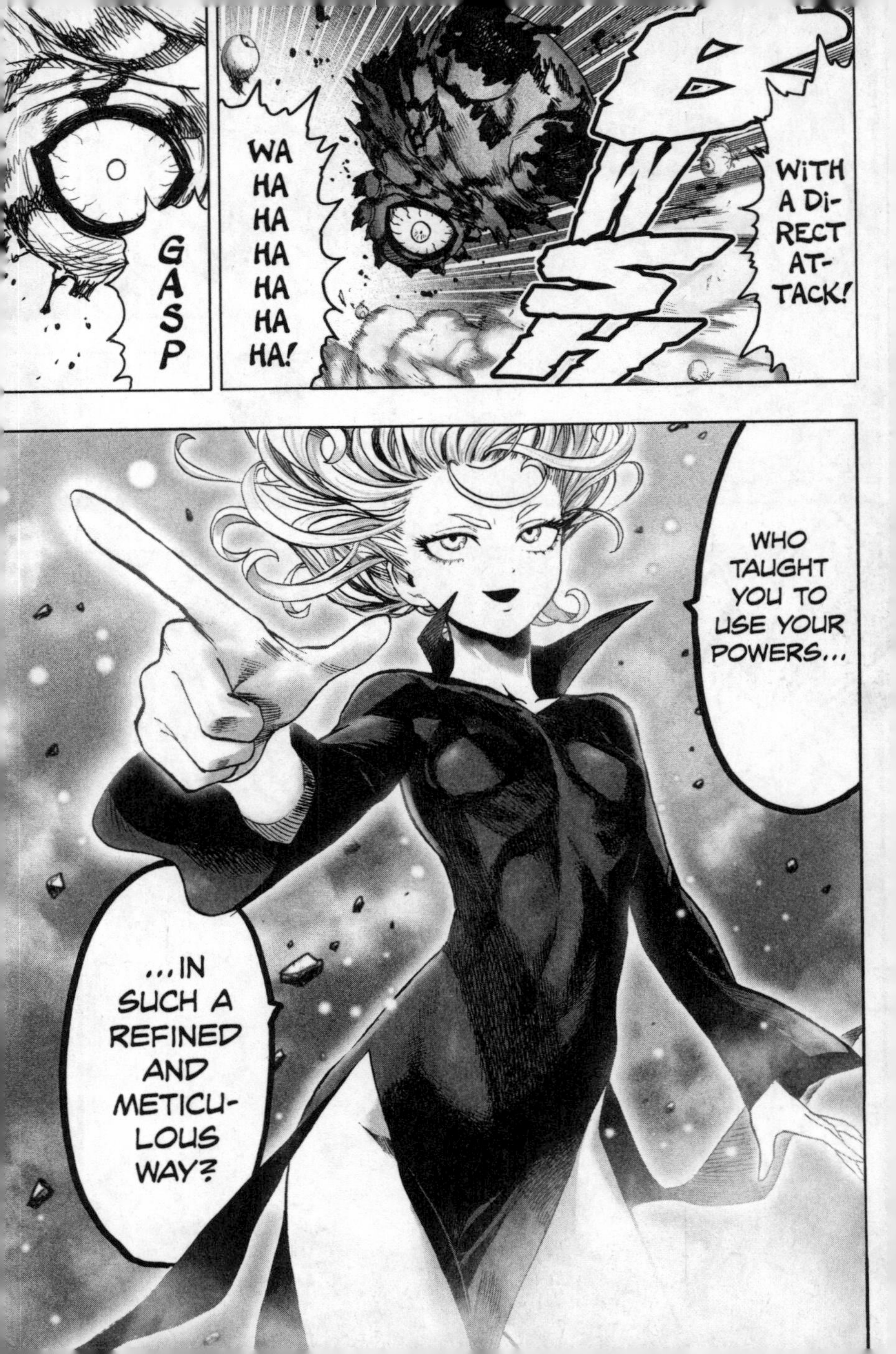
WITH A DIRECT ATTACK!
WA HA HA HA HA HA HA!
GASP
WHO TAUGHT YOU TO USE YOUR POWERS...
...IN SUCH A REFINED AND METICULOUS WAY?

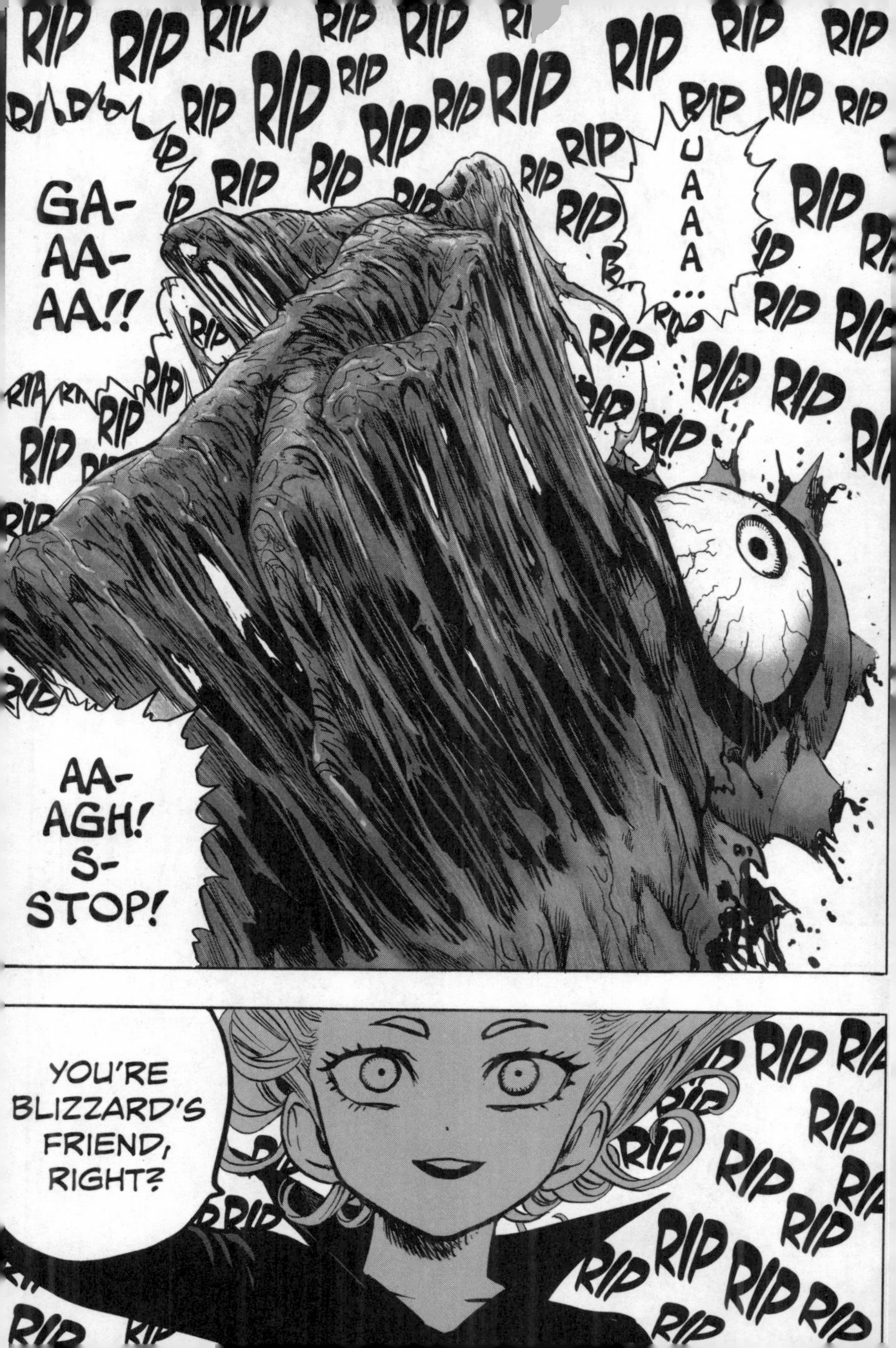
RIP RIP RIP RIP RIP RIP RIP RIP RIP RIP
UAAAA...
GA-AA-AA!!
AA-AGH! S-STOP!
RIP RIP RIP RIP RIP RIP RIP RIP
YOU'RE BLIZZARD'S FRIEND, RIGHT?

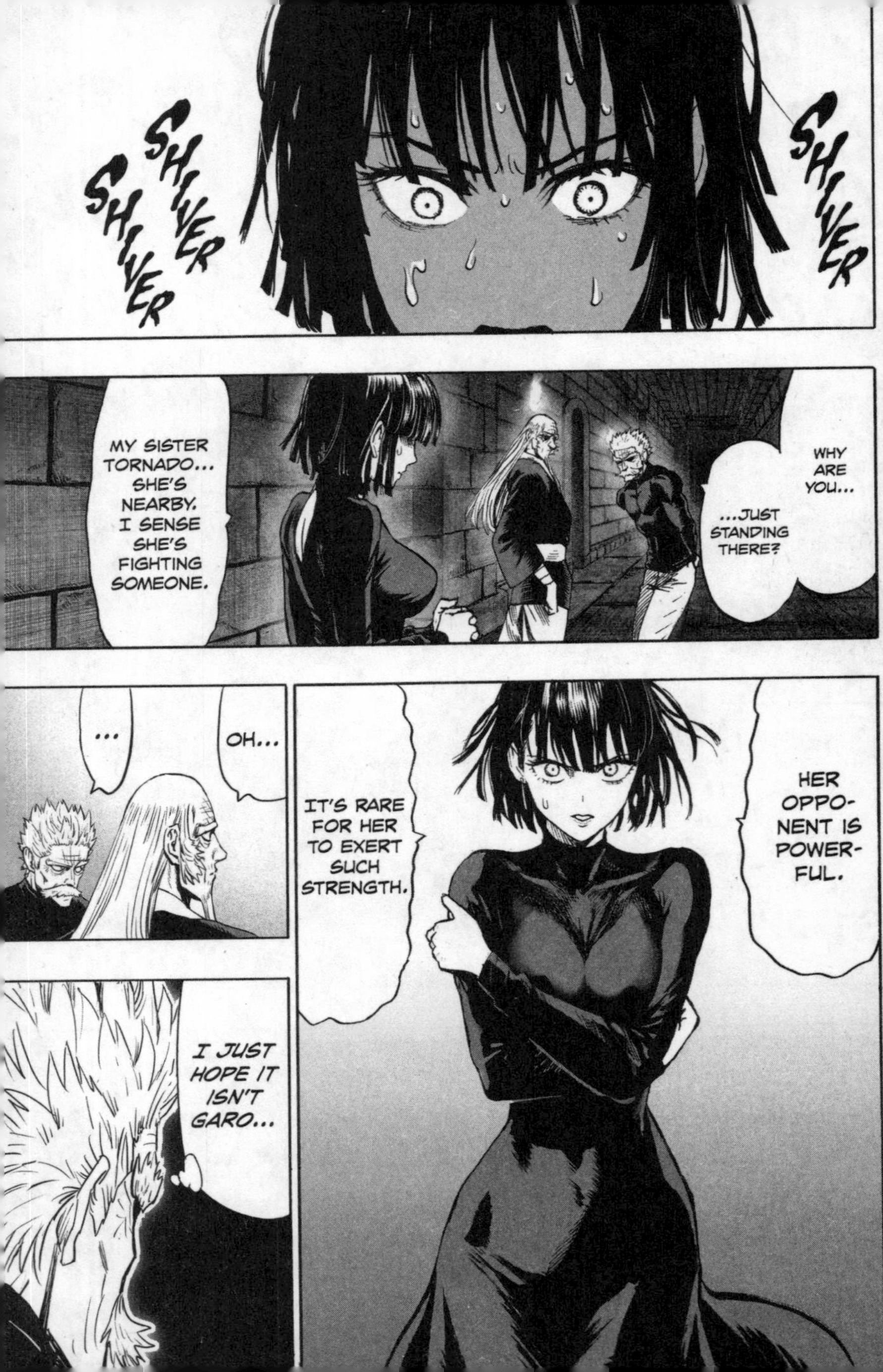
SHIVER SHIVER
SHIVER SHIVER
WHY ARE YOU...
...JUST STANDING THERE?
MY SISTER TORNADO... SHE'S NEARBY. I SENSE SHE'S FIGHTING SOMEONE.
HER OPPO-NENT IS POWER-FUL.
IT'S RARE FOR HER TO EXERT SUCH STRENGTH.
OH...
...
I JUST HOPE IT ISN'T GARO...

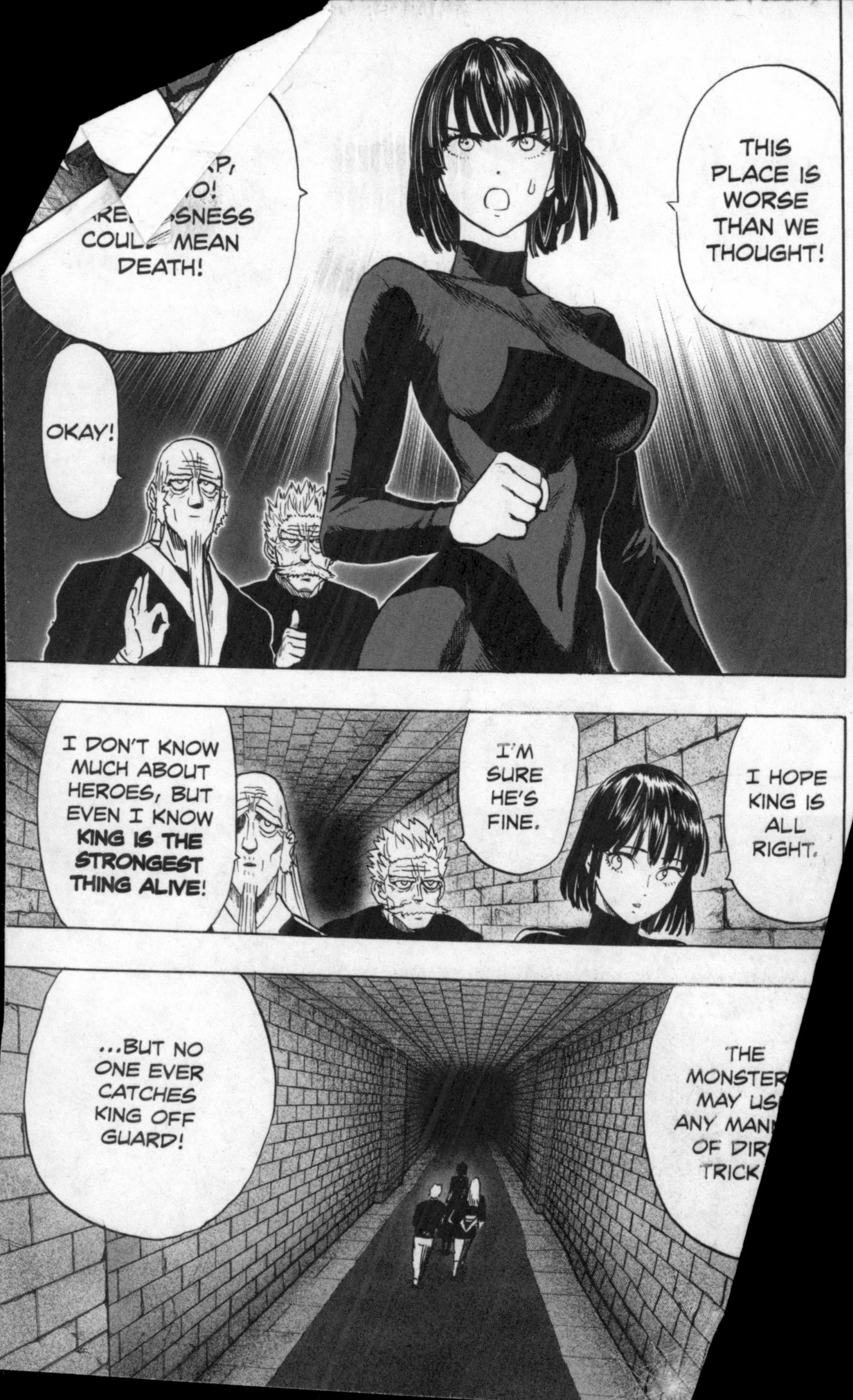
THIS PLACE IS WORSE THAN WE THOUGHT!
MEAN DEATH!
OKAY!
I HOPE KING IS ALL RIGHT.
I'M SURE HE'S FINE.
I DON'T KNOW MUCH ABOUT HEROES, BUT EVEN I KNOW **KING IS THE STRONGEST THING ALIVE!**
THE MONSTER MAY US ANY MANN OF DIRT TRICK
...BUT NO ONE EVER CATCHES KING OFF GUARD!

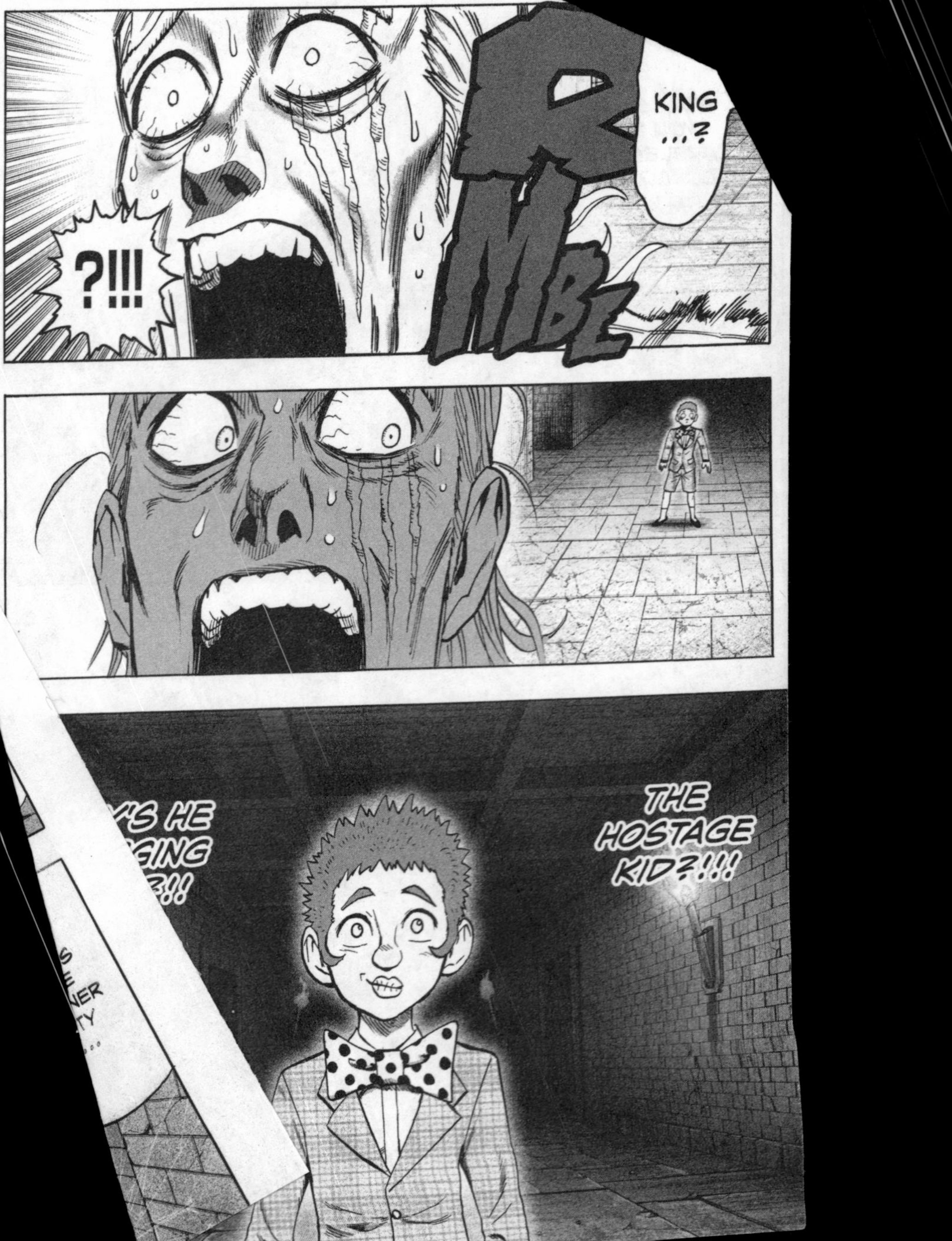
KING ...?
?!!!
THE HOSTAGE KID?!!!

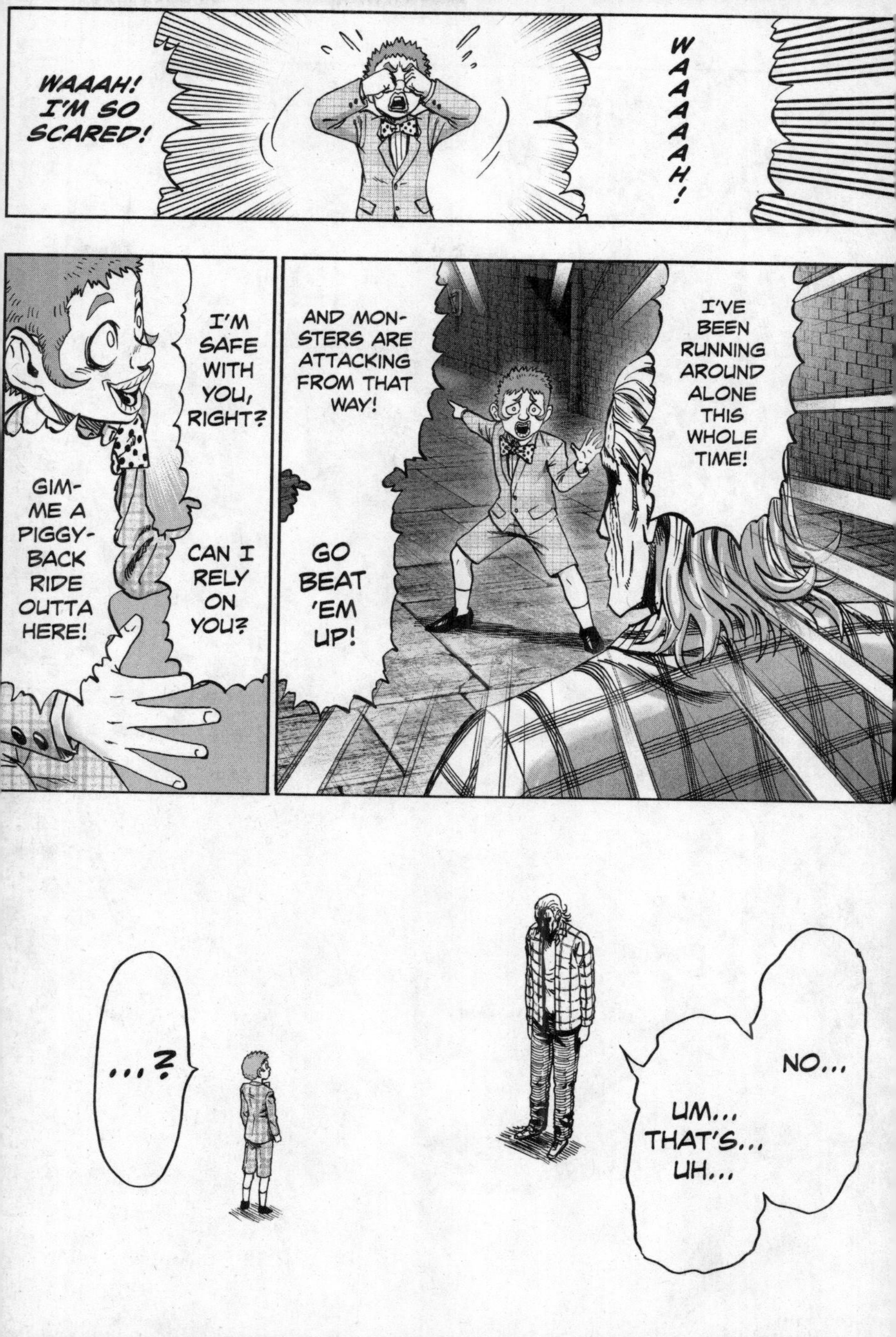
WAAAAAH!
WAAAH! I'M SO SCARED!
I'VE BEEN RUNNING AROUND ALONE THIS WHOLE TIME!
AND MONSTERS ARE ATTACKING FROM THAT WAY!
GO BEAT 'EM UP!
I'M SAFE WITH YOU, RIGHT?
CAN I RELY ON YOU?
GIMME A PIGGYBACK RIDE OUTTA HERE!
NO...
UM... THAT'S... UH...
...?

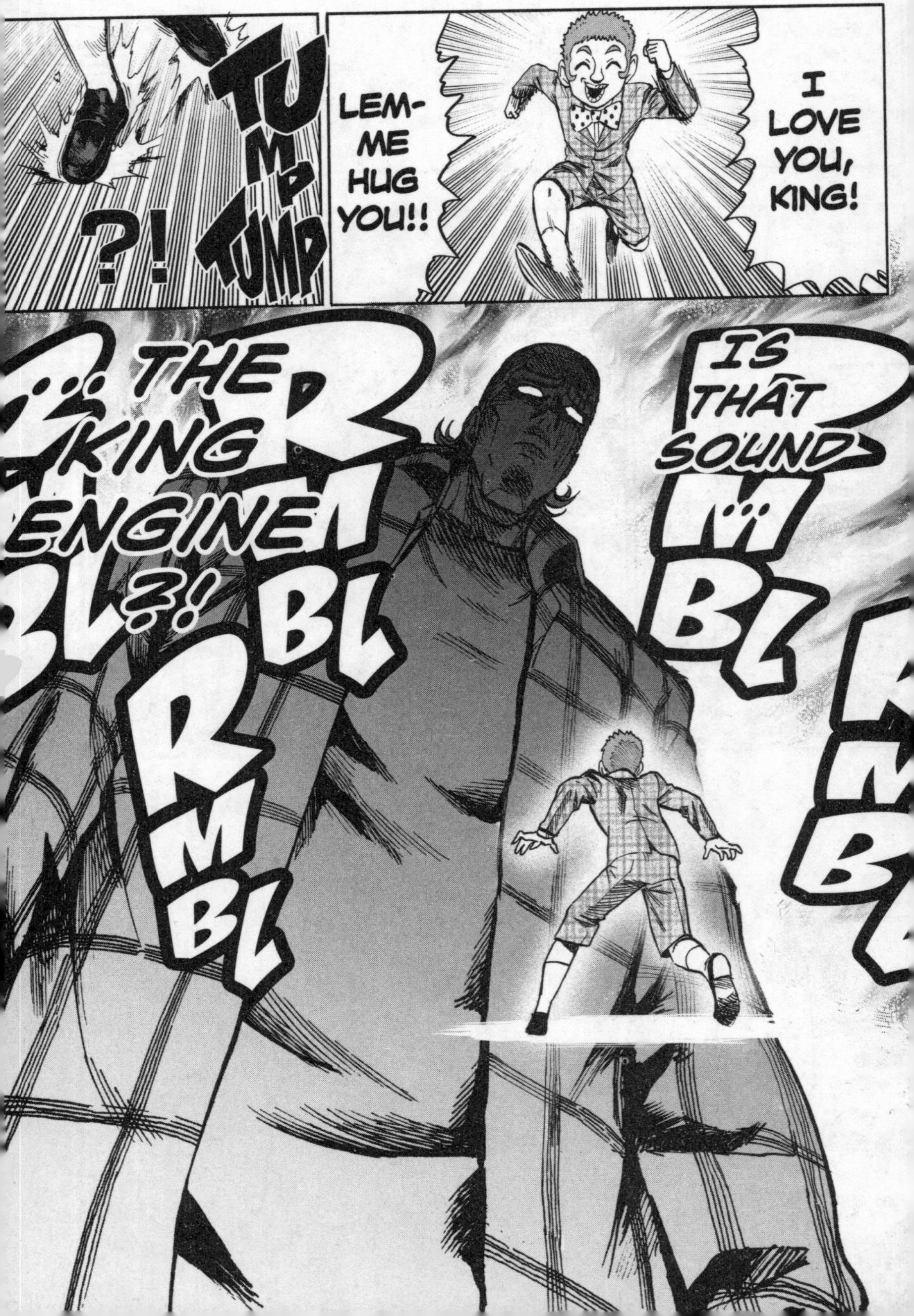

I LOVE YOU, KING!
LEM-ME HUG YOU!!
TUMP TUMP
?!
IS THAT SOUND...
...THE KING ENGINE?!
RMBL RMBL RMBL RMBL RMBL

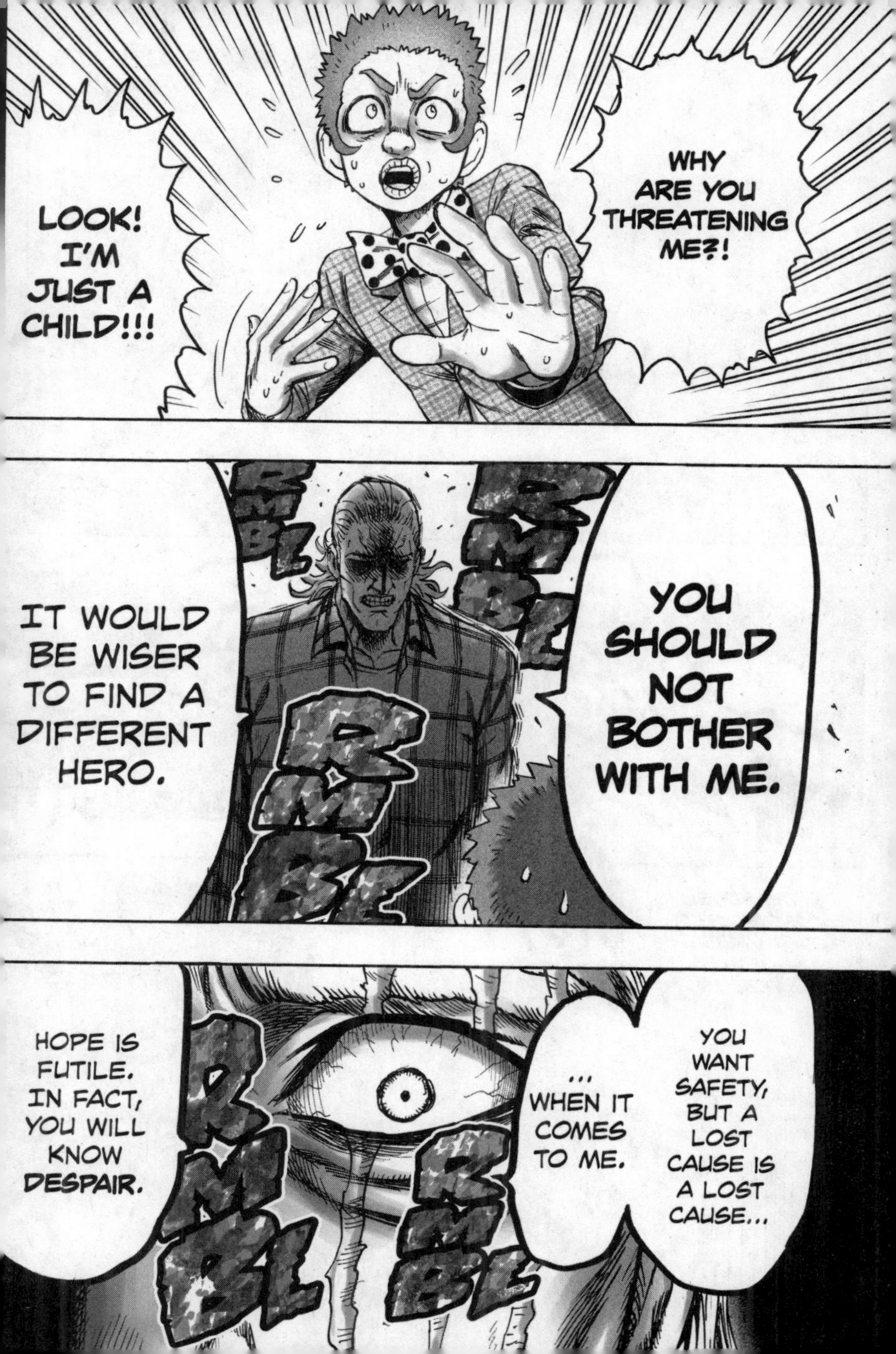
WHY ARE YOU THREATENING ME?!
LOOK! I'M JUST A CHILD!!!
YOU SHOULD NOT BOTHER WITH ME.
IT WOULD BE WISER TO FIND A DIFFERENT HERO.
YOU WANT SAFETY, BUT A LOST CAUSE IS A LOST CAUSE...
...WHEN IT COMES TO ME.
HOPE IS FUTILE. IN FACT, YOU WILL KNOW DESPAIR.

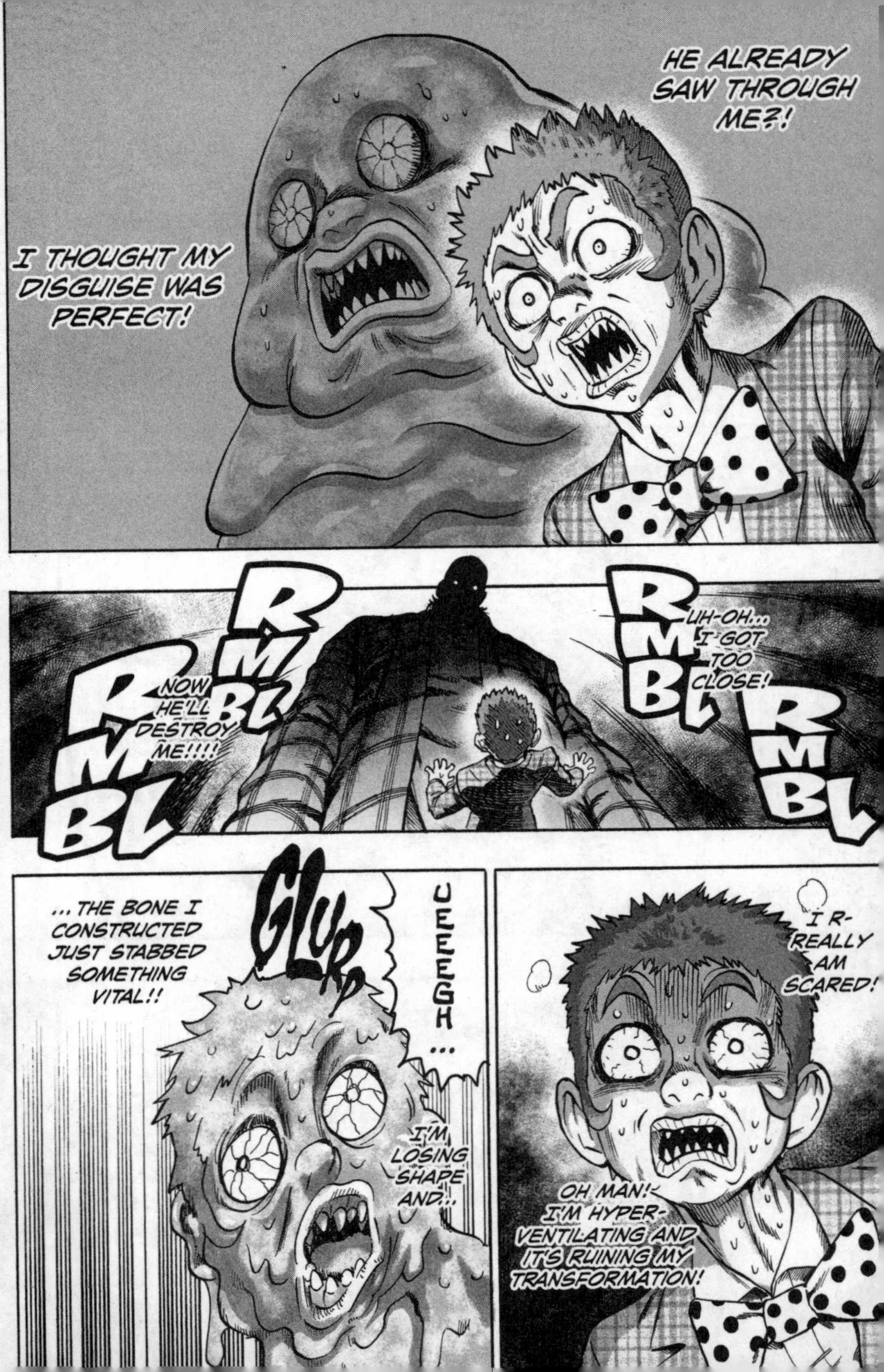
HE ALREADY SAW THROUGH ME?!
I THOUGHT MY DISGUISE WAS PERFECT!
RMBL
UH-OH... I GOT TOO CLOSE!
RMBL
RMBL
NOW HE'LL DESTROY ME!!!!
RMBL
I R-REALLY AM SCARED!
OH MAN! I'M HYPER-VENTILATING AND IT'S RUINING MY TRANSFORMATION!
UEEEGH...
GLURP
...THE BONE I CONSTRUCTED JUST STABBED SOMETHING VITAL!!
I'M LOSING SHAPE AND...

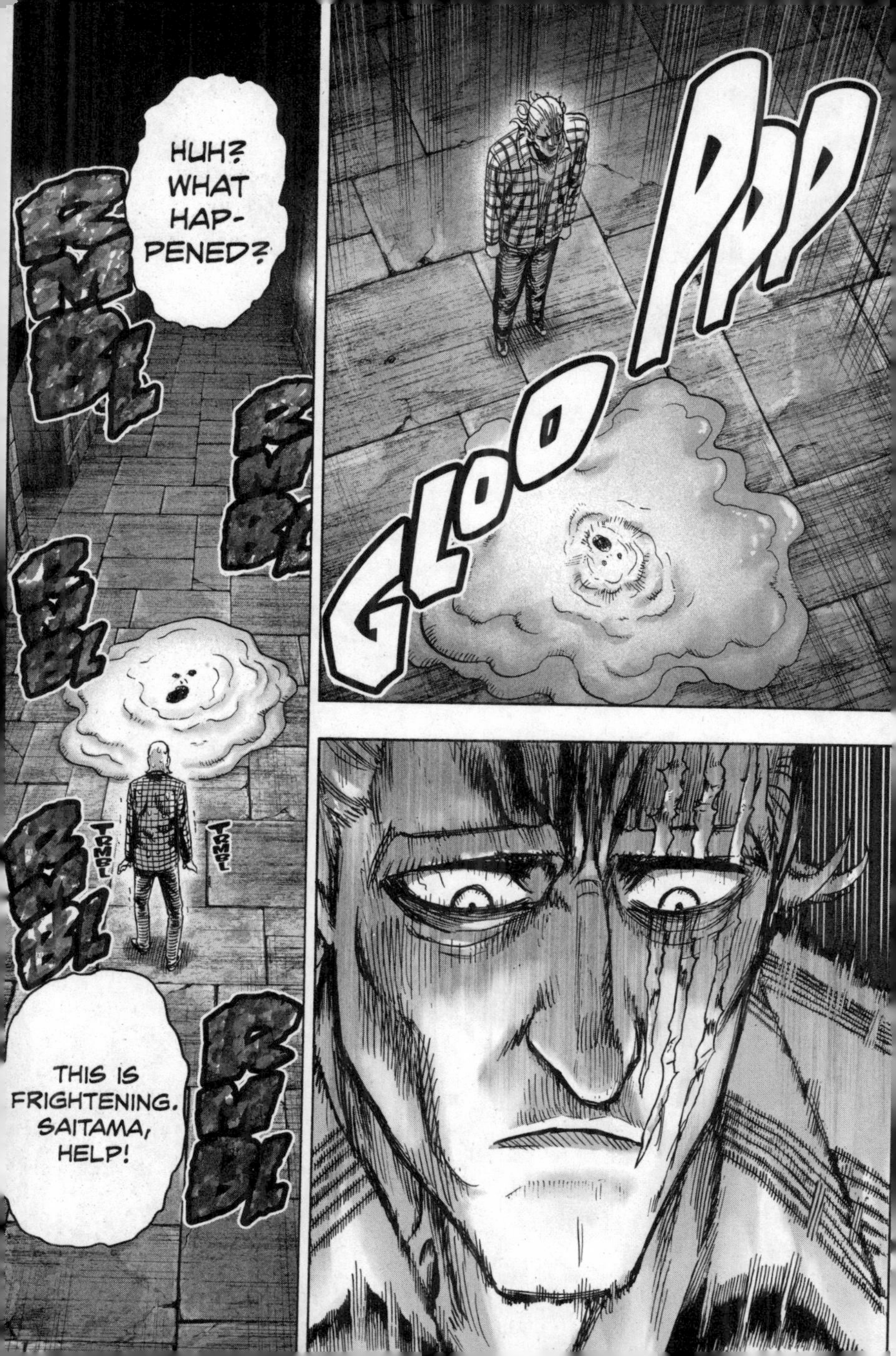
GLOOPPP
HUH? WHAT HAP-PENED?
TRMBL
TRMBL
THIS IS FRIGHTENING. SAITAMA, HELP!

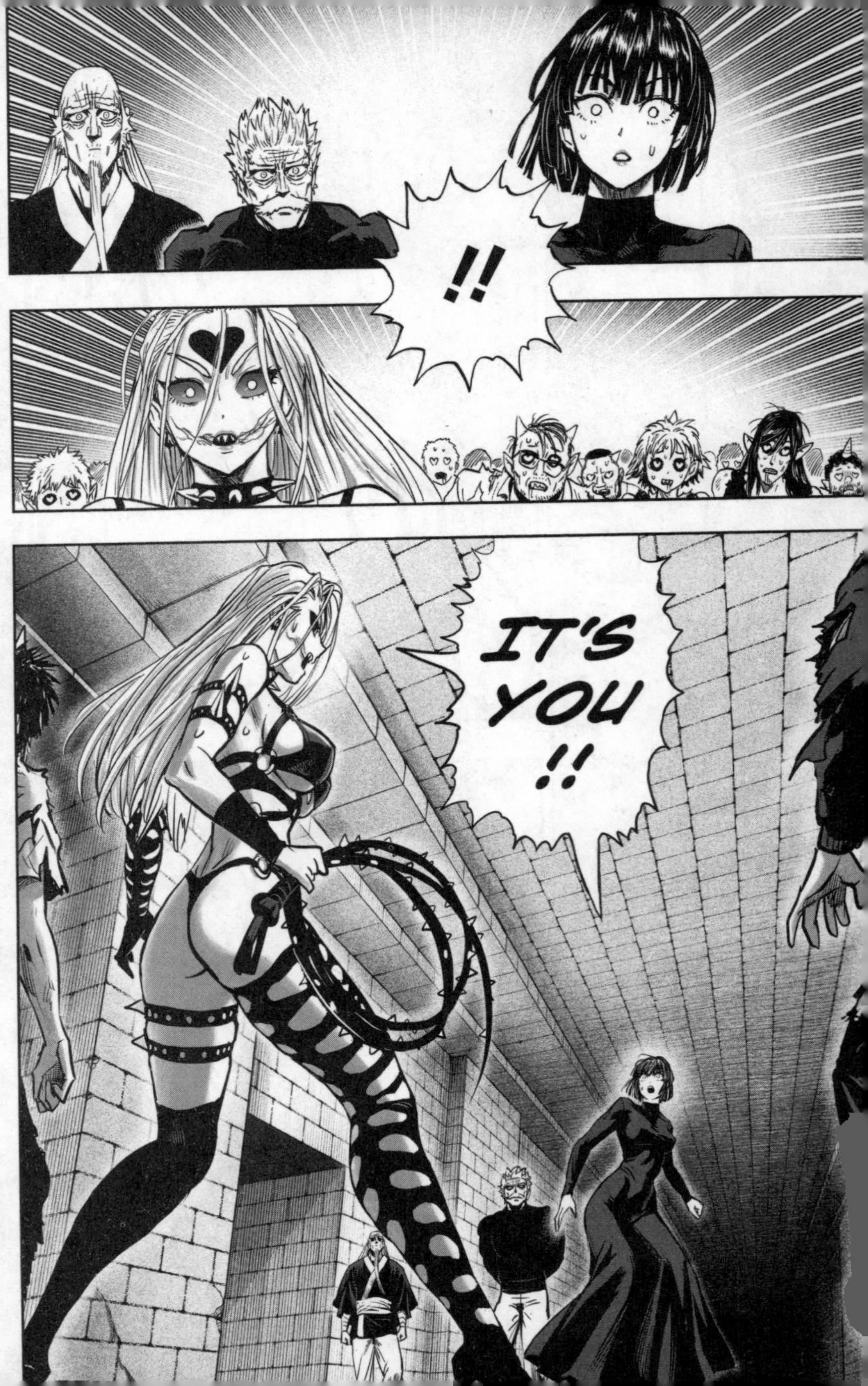
!!
IT'S YOU !!

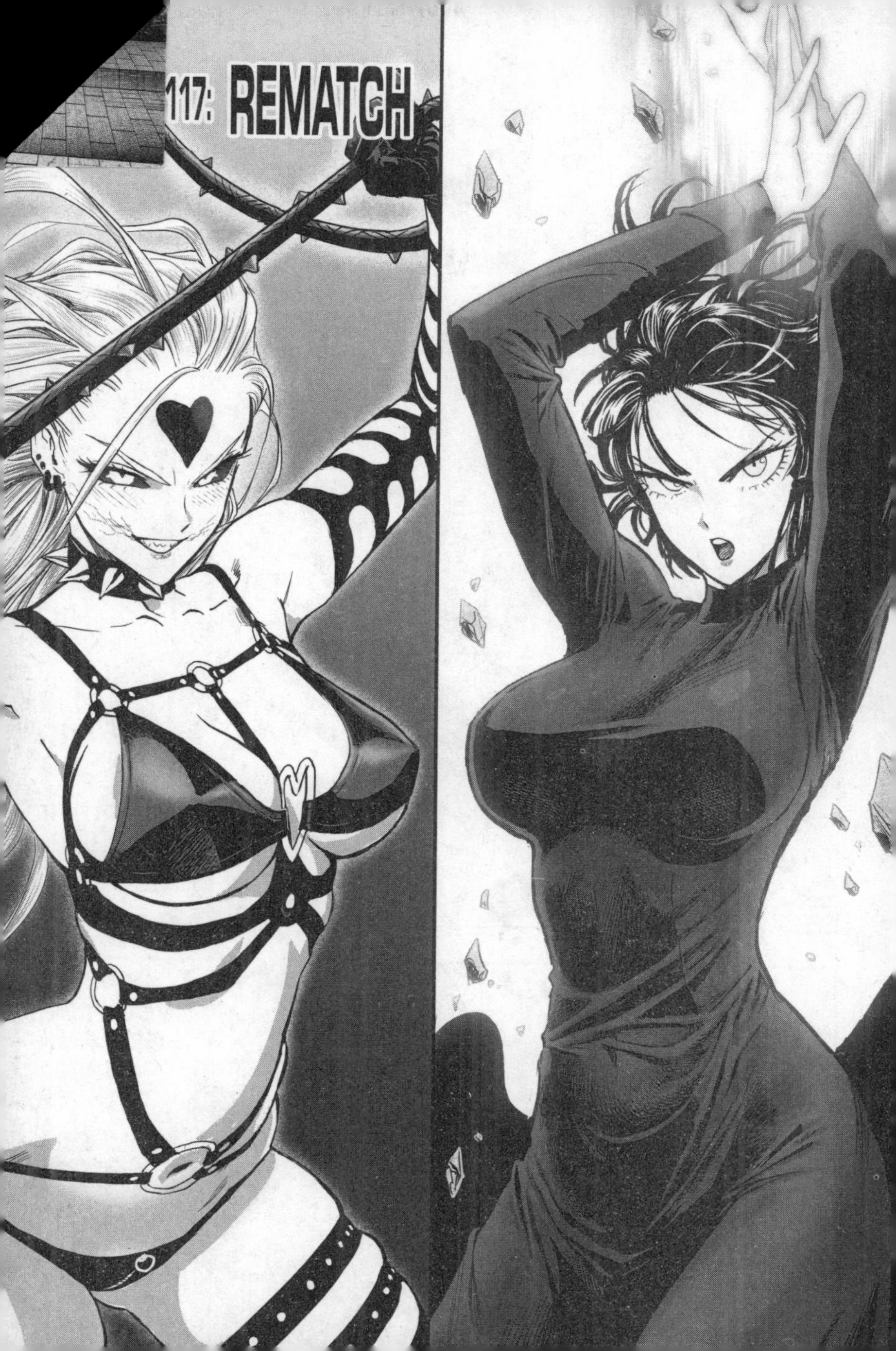
117: REMATCH

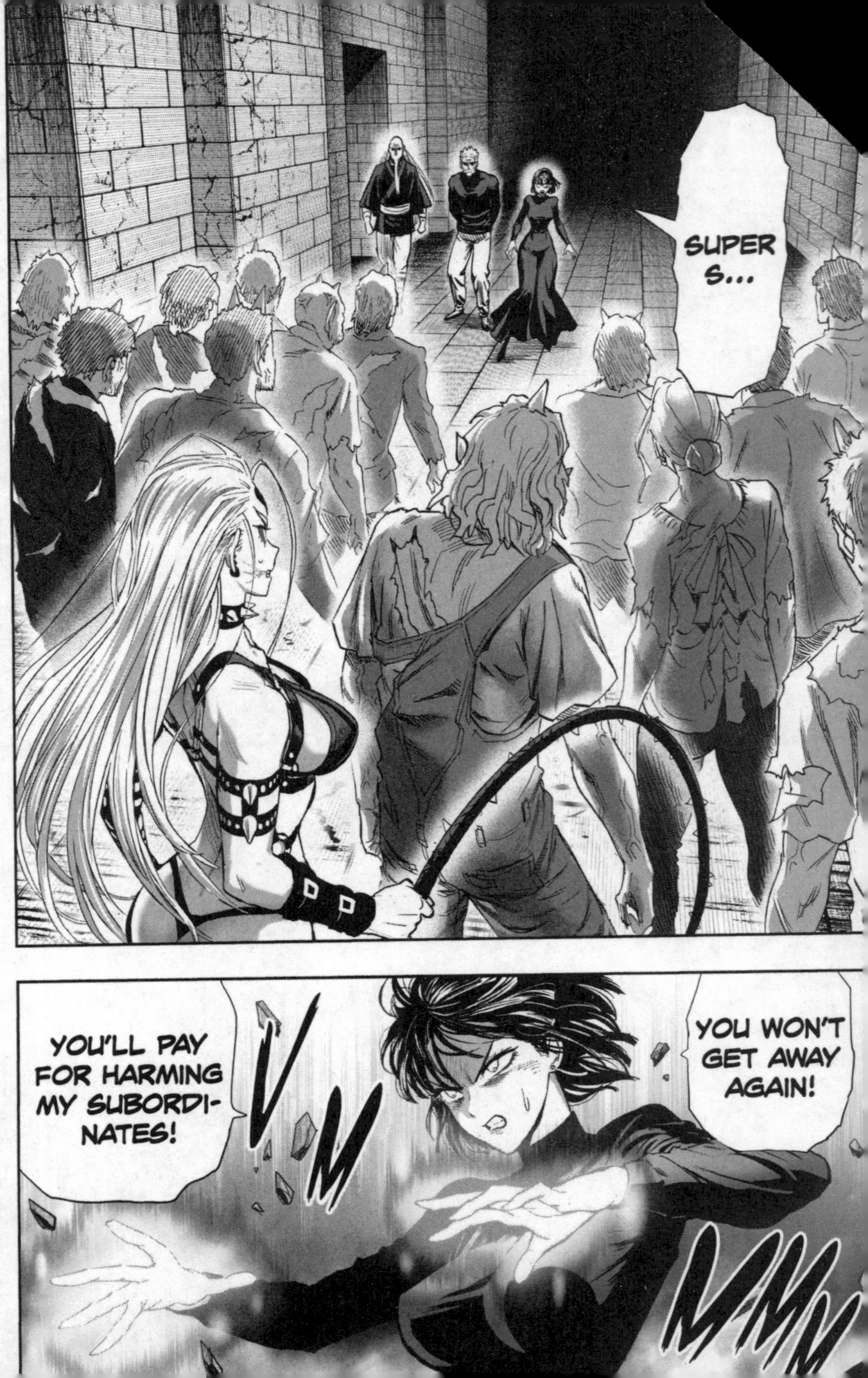
SUPER S...
YOU WON'T GET AWAY AGAIN!
YOU'LL PAY FOR HARMING MY SUBORDI- NATES!

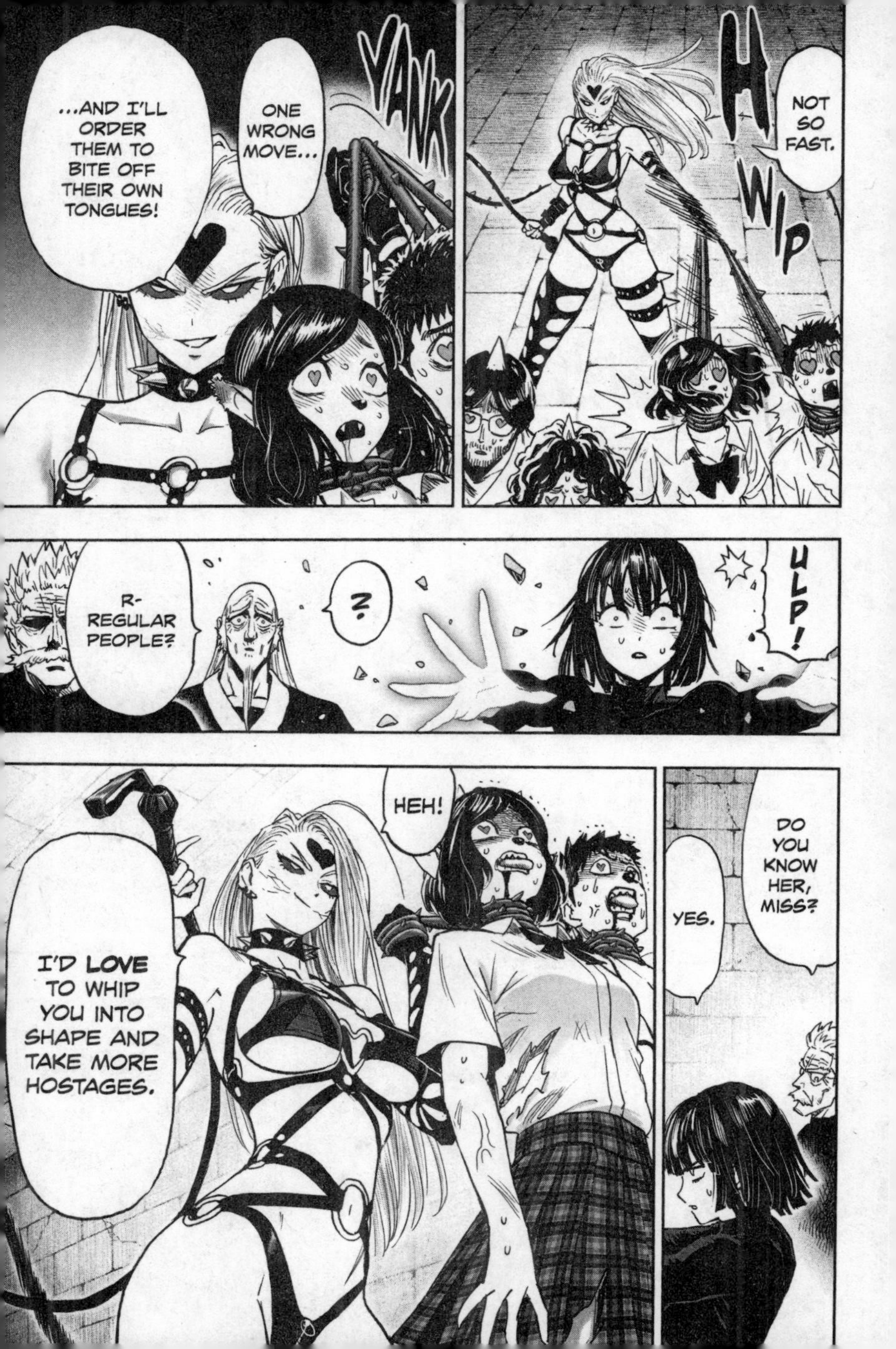
NOT SO FAST.
HWIP
YANK
ONE WRONG MOVE...
...AND I'LL ORDER THEM TO BITE OFF THEIR OWN TONGUES!
ULP!
?
R-REGULAR PEOPLE?
DO YOU KNOW HER, MISS?
YES.
HEH!
I'D **LOVE** TO WHIP YOU INTO SHAPE AND TAKE MORE HOSTAGES.

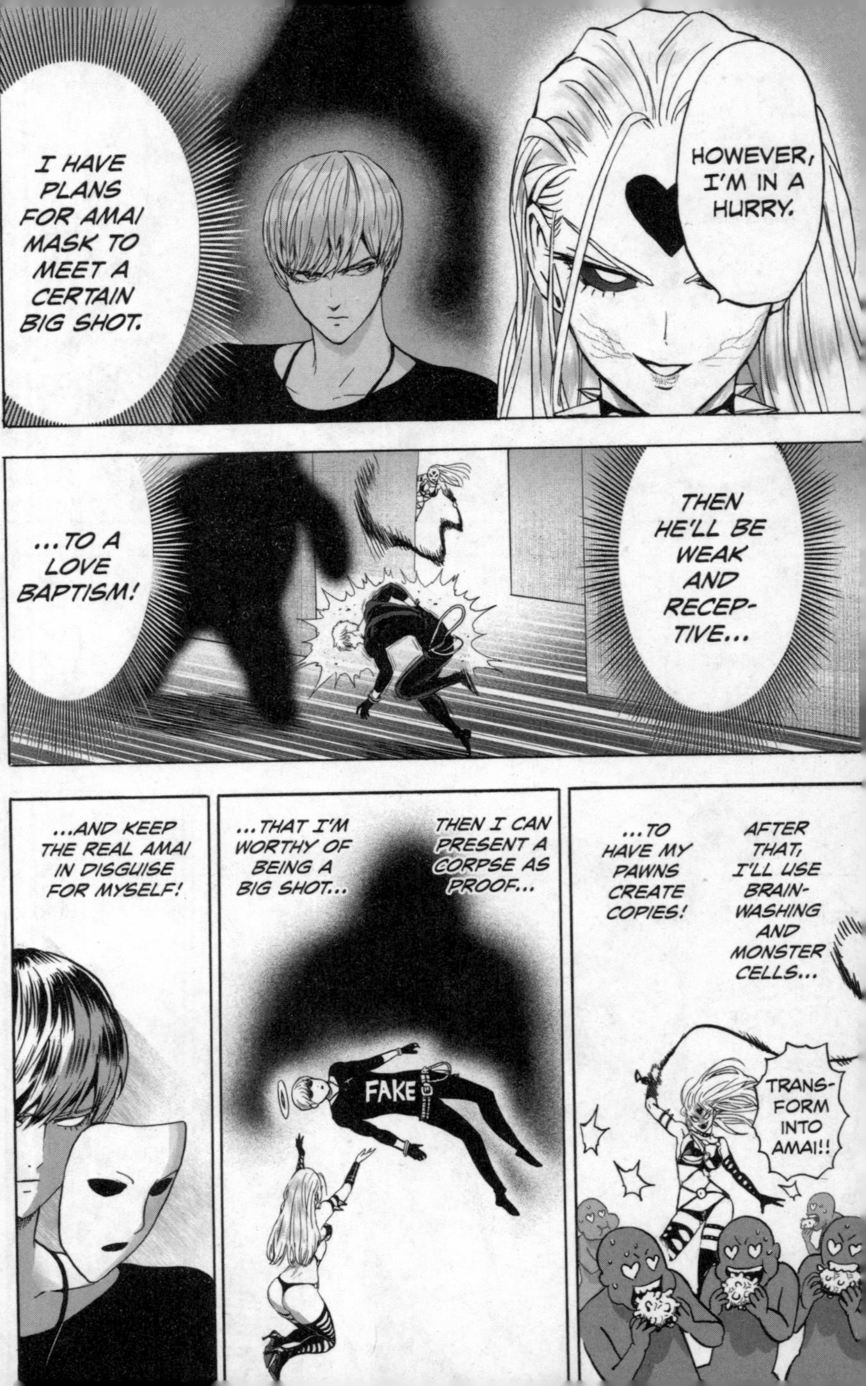
HOWEVER, I'M IN A HURRY.
I HAVE PLANS FOR AMAI MASK TO MEET A CERTAIN BIG SHOT.
THEN HE'LL BE WEAK AND RECEPTIVE...
...TO A LOVE BAPTISM!
AFTER THAT, I'LL USE BRAIN-WASHING AND MONSTER CELLS...
...TO HAVE MY PAWNS CREATE COPIES!
TRANS-FORM INTO AMAI!!
THEN I CAN PRESENT A CORPSE AS PROOF...
...THAT I'M WORTHY OF BEING A BIG SHOT...
FAKE
...AND KEEP THE REAL AMAI IN DISGUISE FOR MYSELF!

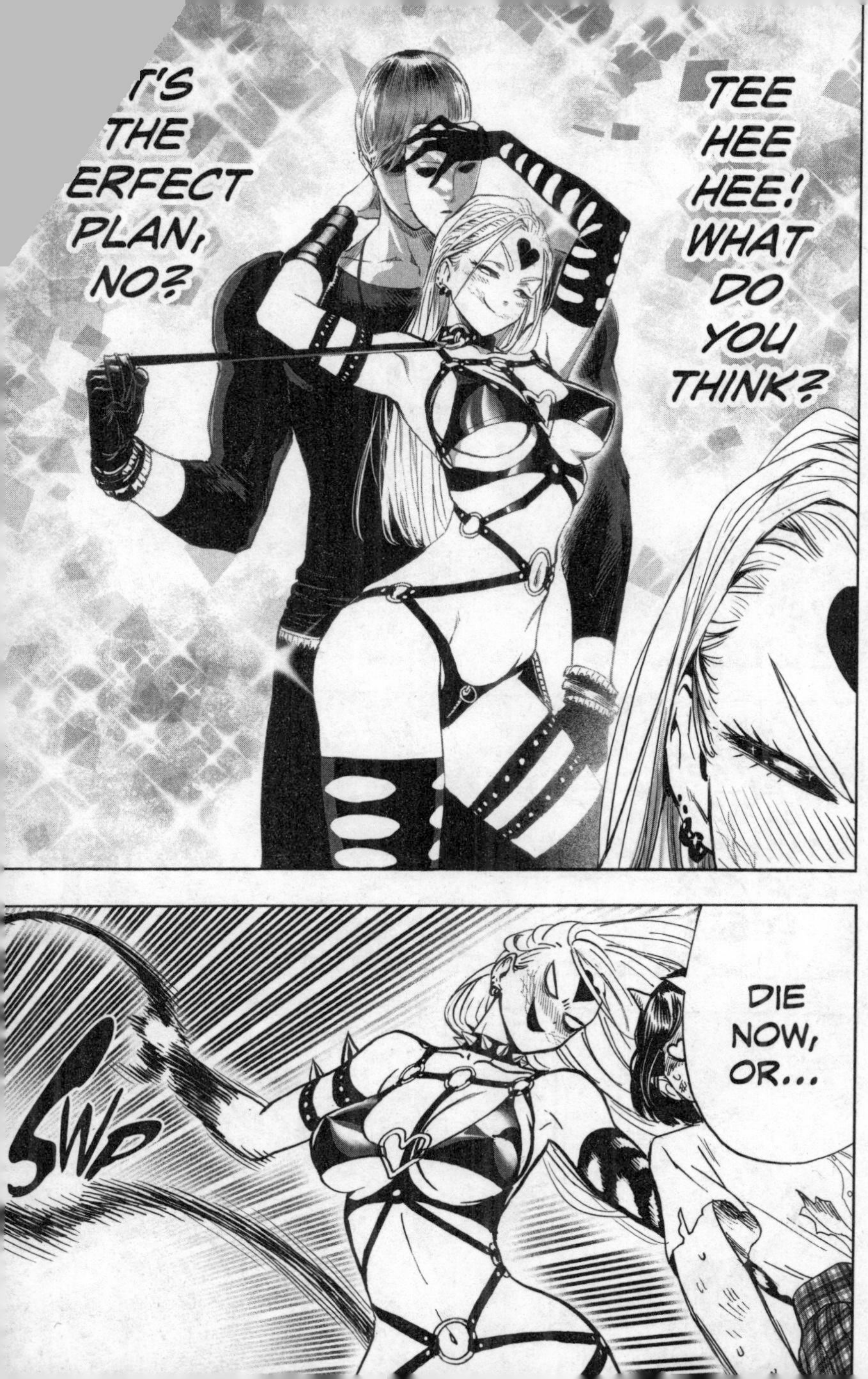
TEE HEE HEE! WHAT DO YOU THINK?
T'S THE ERFECT PLAN, NO?
DIE NOW, OR...
SWP

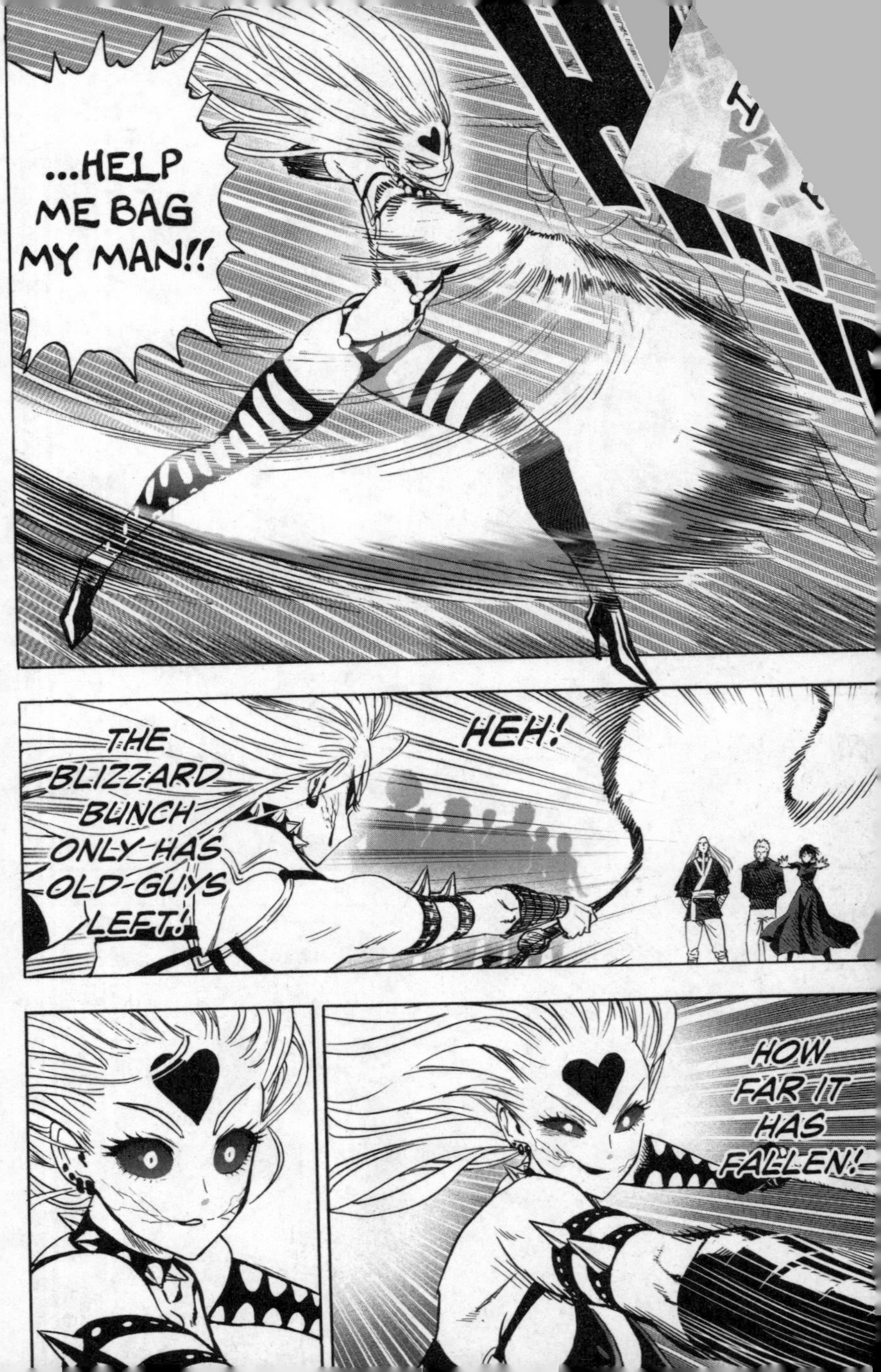
...HELP ME BAG MY MAN!!
HEH!
THE BLIZZARD BUNCH ONLY HAS OLD GUYS LEFT!
HOW FAR IT HAS FALLEN!

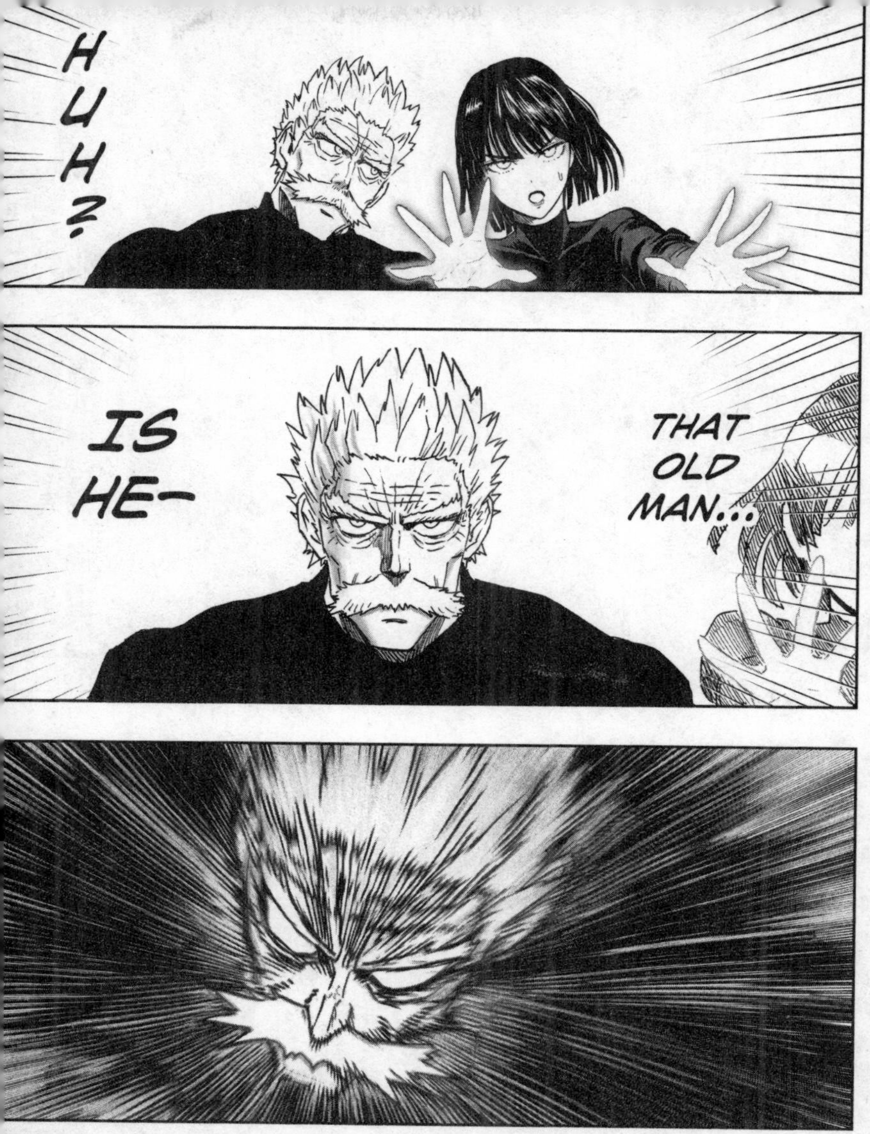
HUH?
THAT OLD MAN...
IS HE-

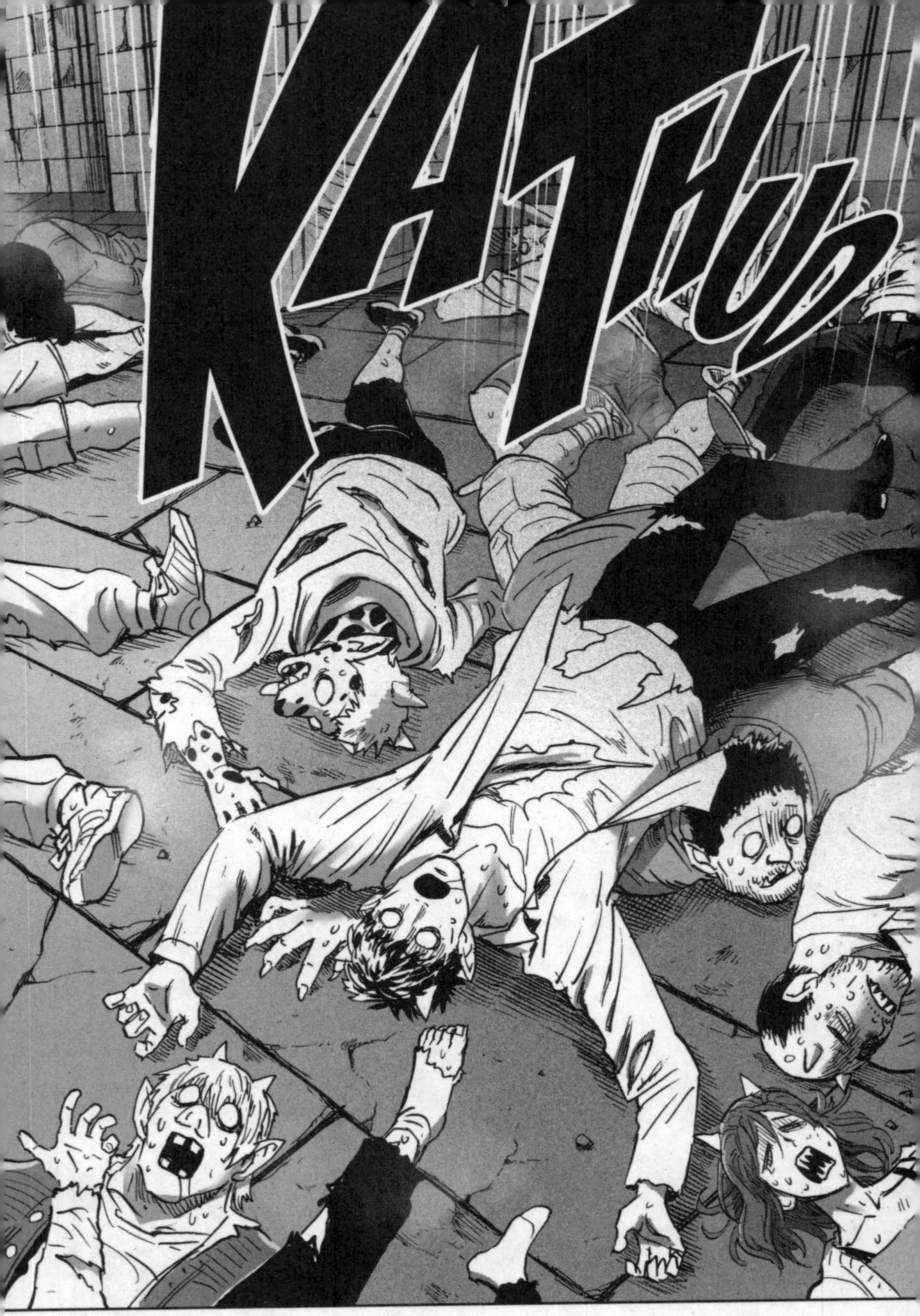
KATHUD

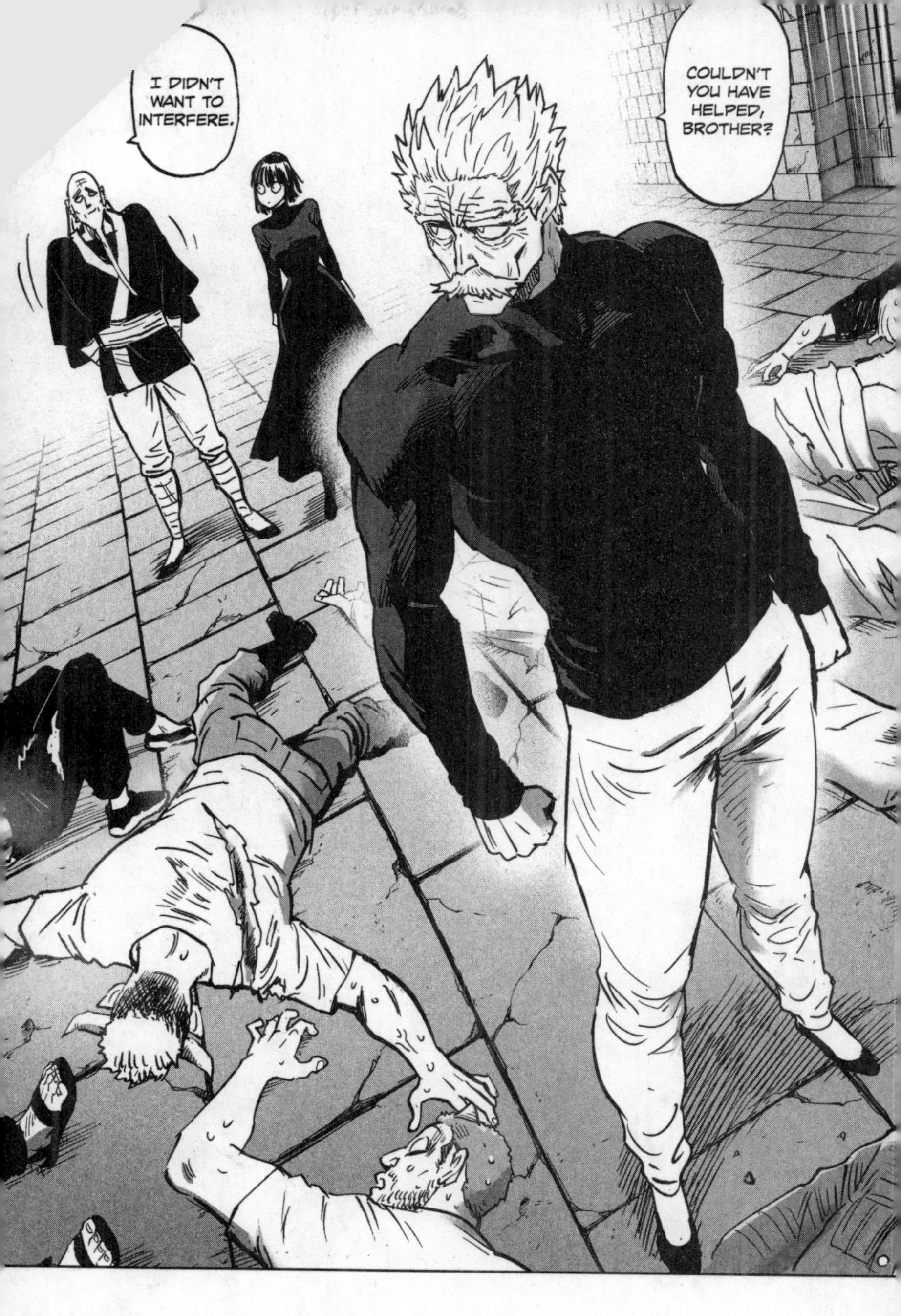
COULDN'T YOU HAVE HELPED, BROTHER?
I DIDN'T WANT TO INTERFERE.

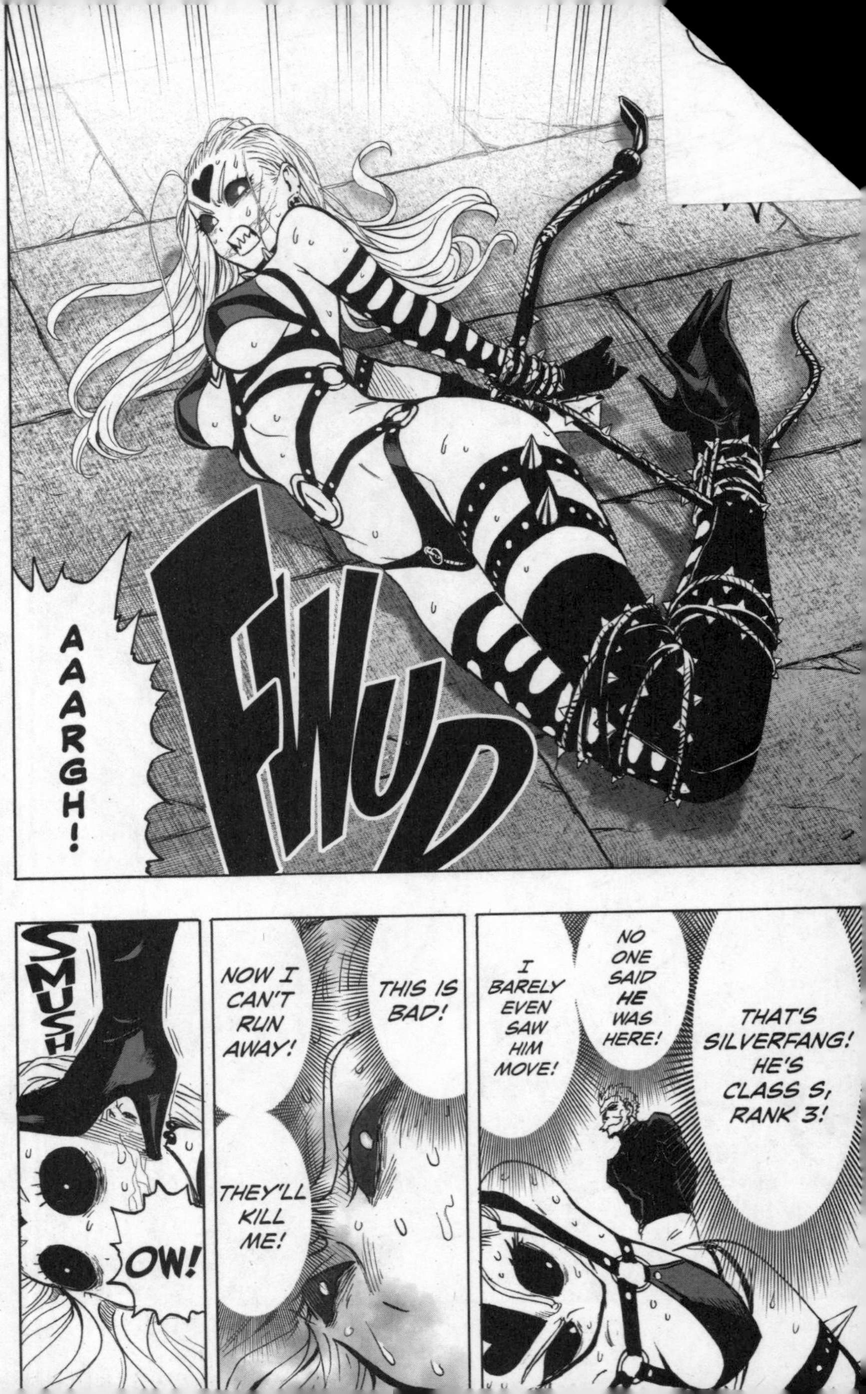
FWUD
AAARGH!
THAT'S SILVERFANG! HE'S CLASS S, RANK 3!
NO ONE SAID HE WAS HERE!
I BARELY EVEN SAW HIM MOVE!
THIS IS BAD!
NOW I CAN'T RUN AWAY!
THEY'LL KILL ME!
SMUSH
OW!

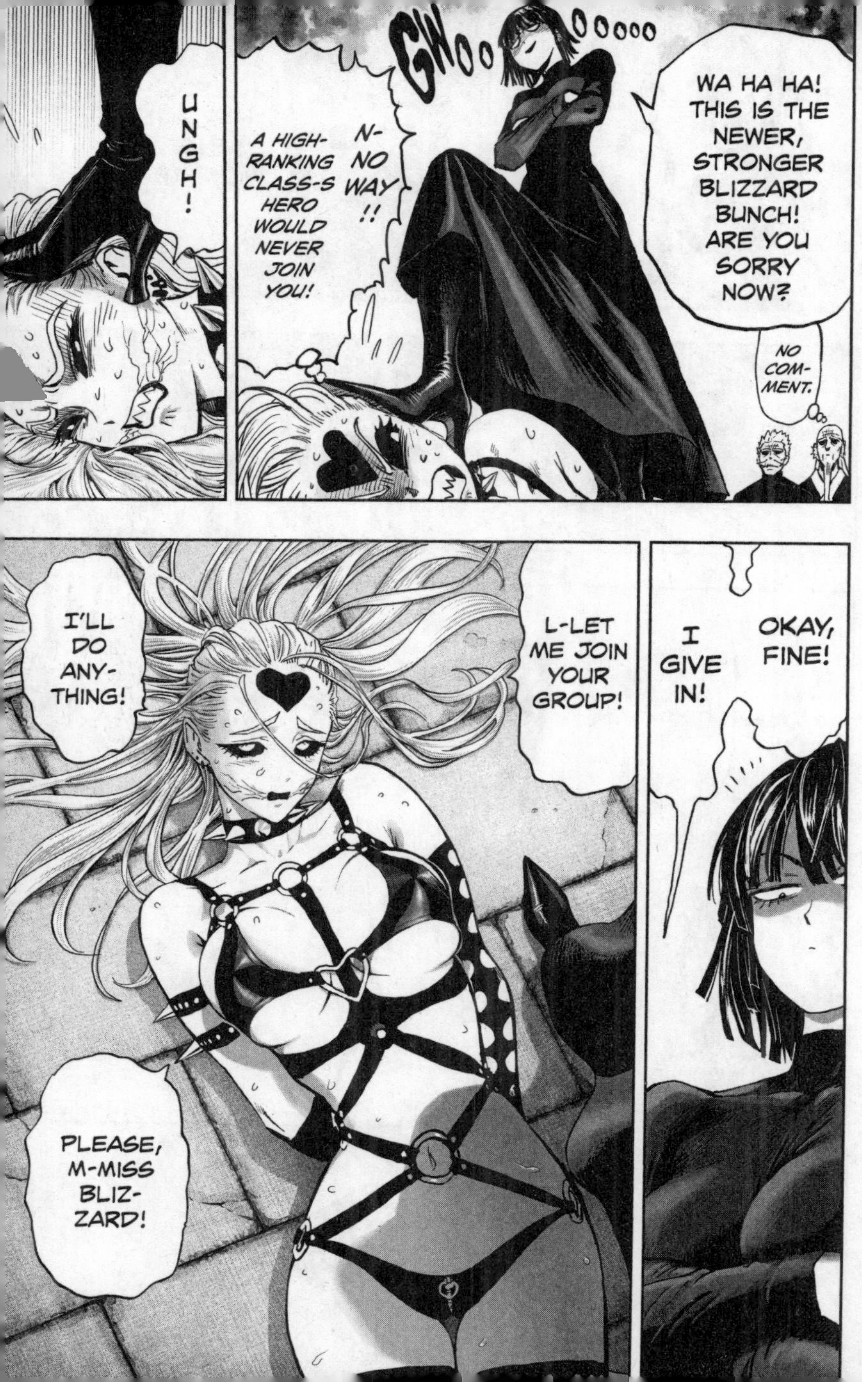
WA HA HA! THIS IS THE NEWER, STRONGER BLIZZARD BUNCH! ARE YOU SORRY NOW?
GWOOOOOOO
N-NO WAY!!
A HIGH-RANKING CLASS-S HERO WOULD NEVER JOIN YOU!
NO COMMENT.
UNGH!
OKAY, FINE!
I GIVE IN!
L-LET ME JOIN YOUR GROUP!
I'LL DO ANYTHING!
PLEASE, M-MISS BLIZZARD!

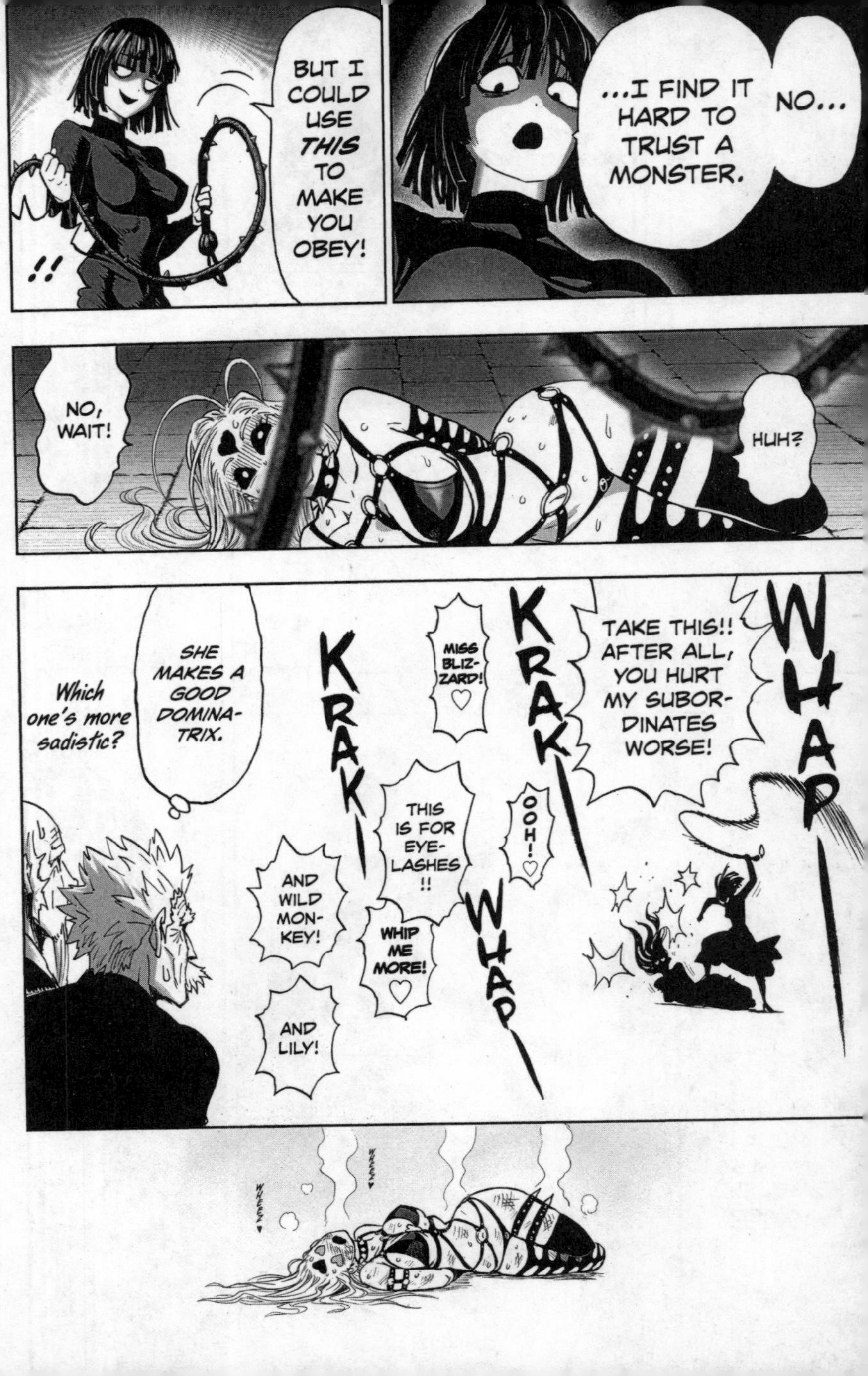
NO...
...I FIND IT HARD TO TRUST A MONSTER.
!!
BUT I COULD USE *THIS* TO MAKE YOU OBEY!
HUH?
NO, WAIT!
WHAP
TAKE THIS!! AFTER ALL, YOU HURT MY SUBOR-DINATES WORSE!
KRAK
MISS BLIZ-ZARD! ♡
OOH! ♡
WHAP
THIS IS FOR EYE-LASHES !!
KRAK
AND WILD MON-KEY!
WHIP ME MORE! ♡
AND LILY!
SHE MAKES A GOOD DOMINA-TRIX.
Which one's more sadistic?

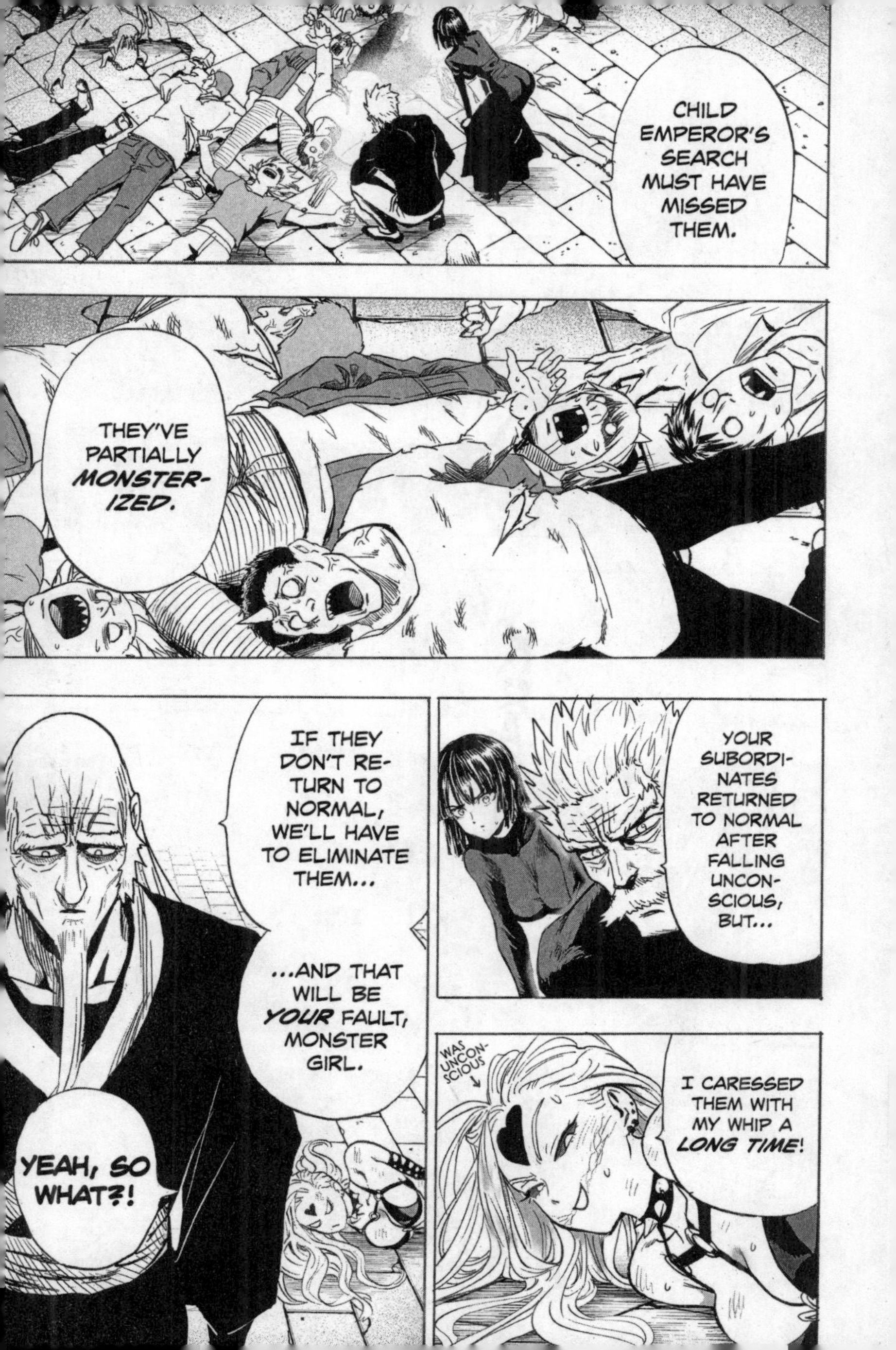
CHILD EMPEROR'S SEARCH MUST HAVE MISSED THEM.
THEY'VE PARTIALLY *MONSTER-IZED*.
YOUR SUBORDI-NATES RETURNED TO NORMAL AFTER FALLING UNCON-SCIOUS, BUT...
I CARESSED THEM WITH MY WHIP A *LONG TIME*!
WAS UNCON-SCIOUS
IF THEY DON'T RE-TURN TO NORMAL, WE'LL HAVE TO ELIMINATE THEM...
...AND THAT WILL BE *YOUR* FAULT, MONSTER GIRL.
YEAH, SO WHAT?!

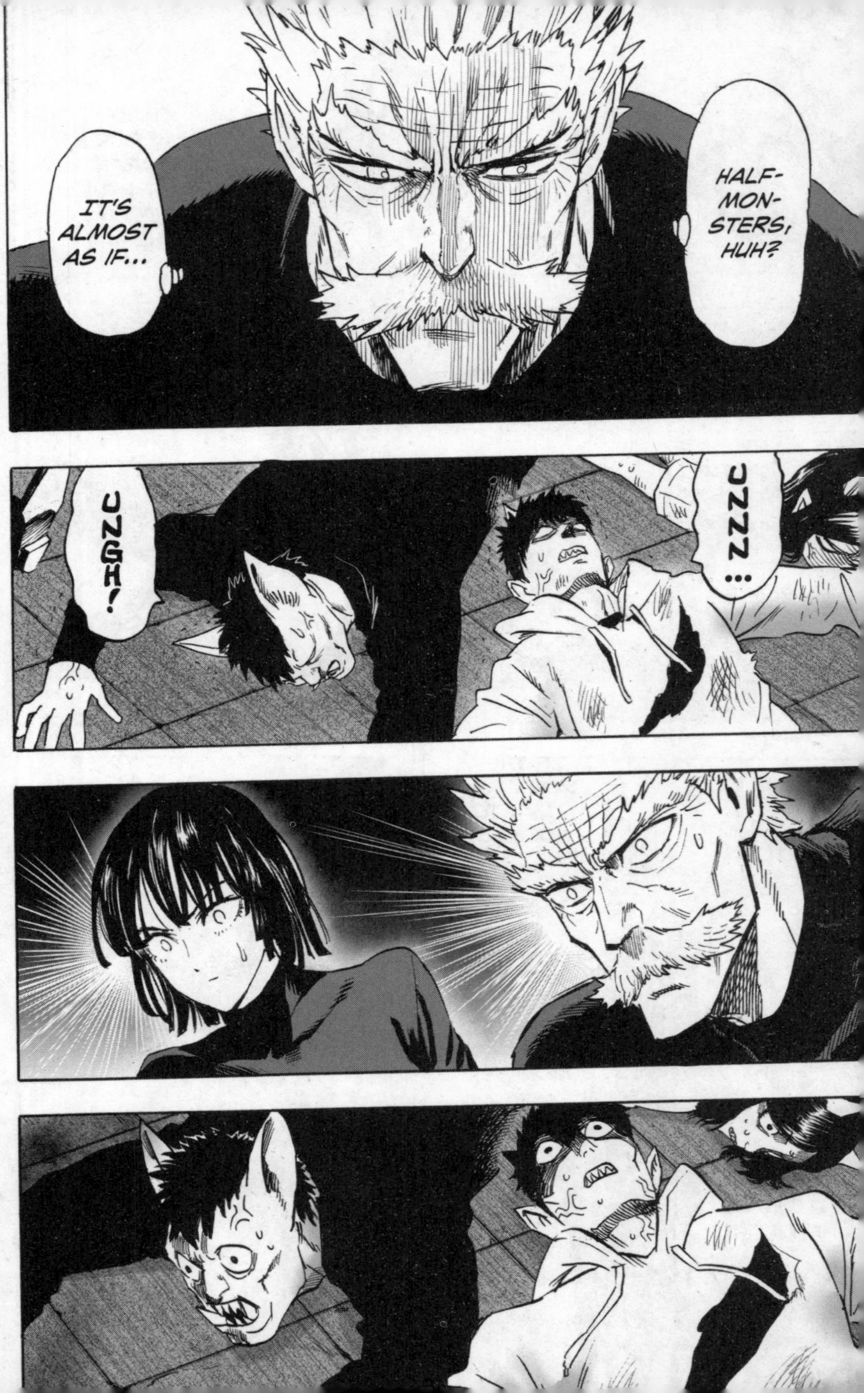
HALF-MONSTERS, HUH?
IT'S ALMOST AS IF...
UNNN...
UNGH!

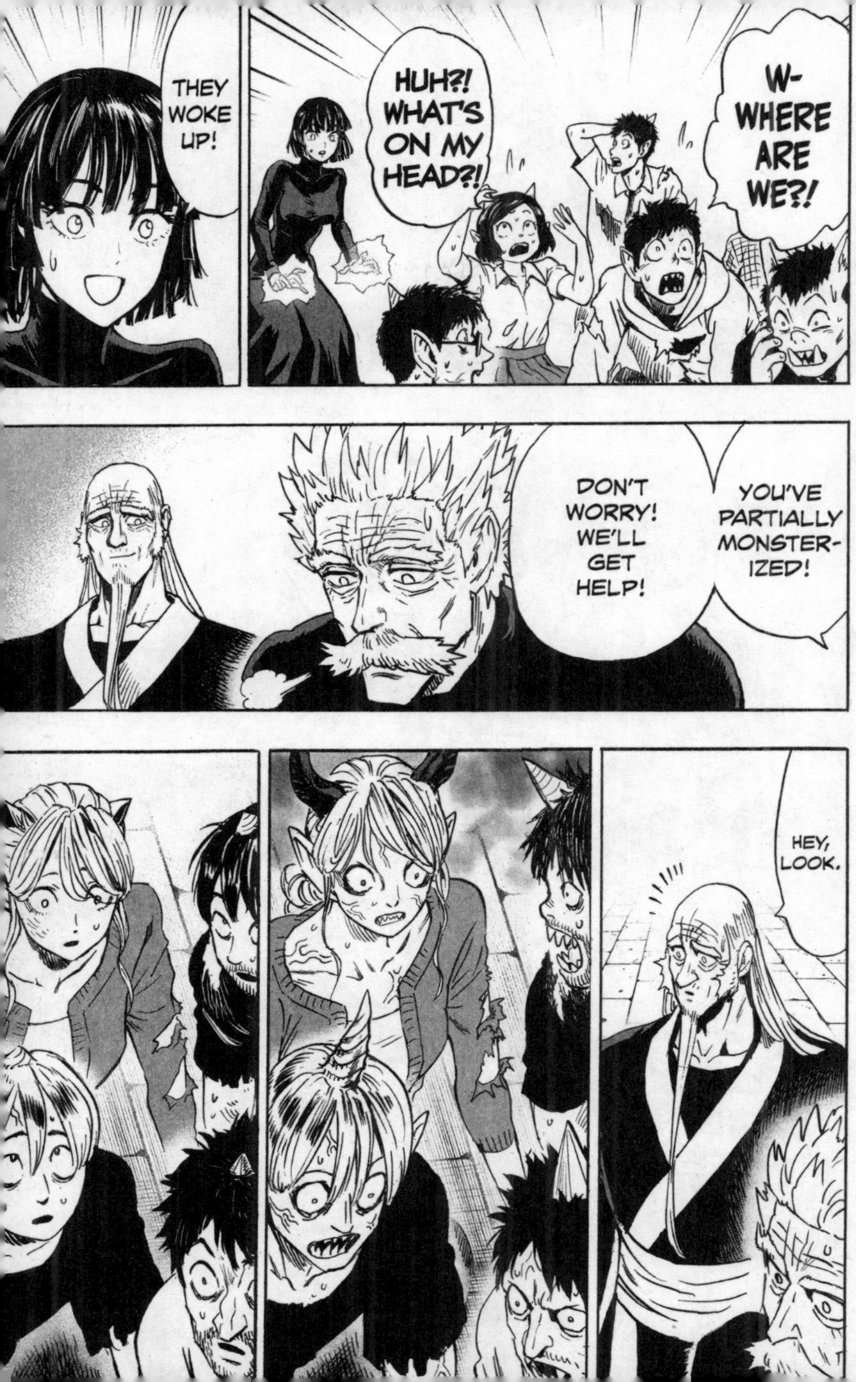
W- WHERE ARE WE?!
HUH?! WHAT'S ON MY HEAD?!
THEY WOKE UP!
YOU'VE PARTIALLY MONSTER-IZED!
DON'T WORRY! WE'LL GET HELP!
HEY, LOOK.

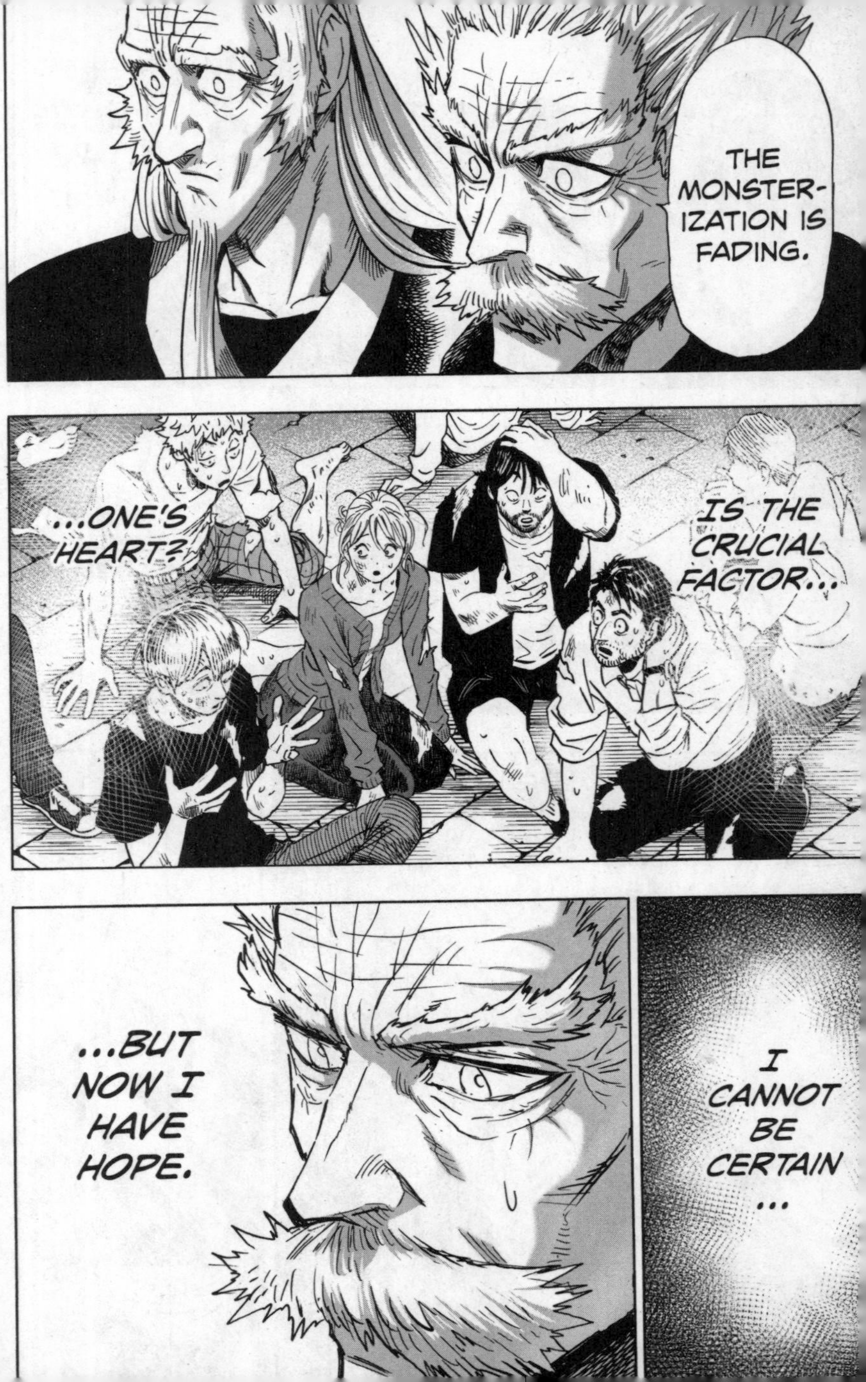
THE MONSTER-IZATION IS FADING.
IS THE CRUCIAL FACTOR...
...ONE'S HEART?
I CANNOT BE CERTAIN...
...BUT NOW I HAVE HOPE.

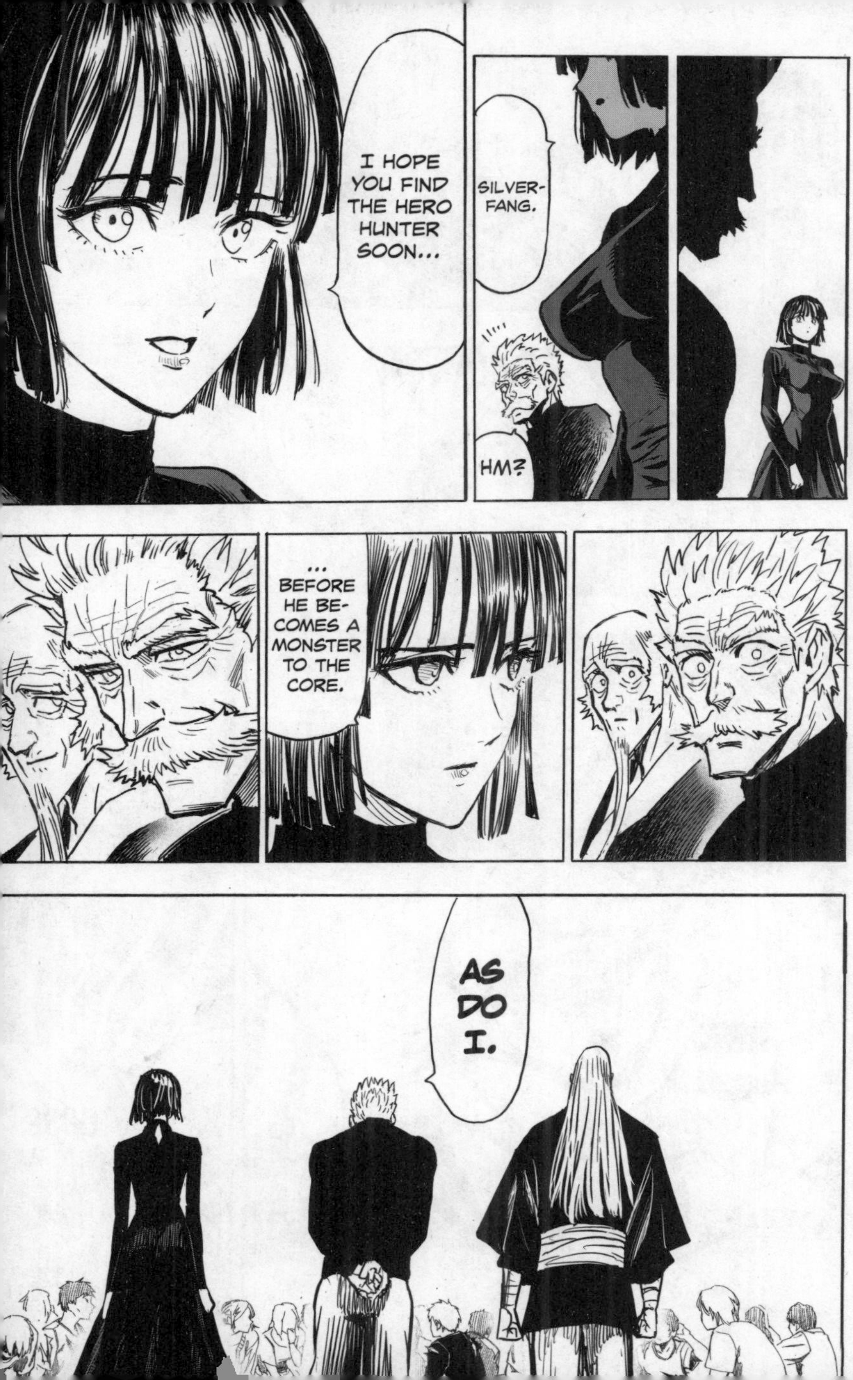
SILVER-FANG.
HM?
I HOPE YOU FIND THE HERO HUNTER SOON...
... BEFORE HE BE-COMES A MONSTER TO THE CORE.
AS DO I.

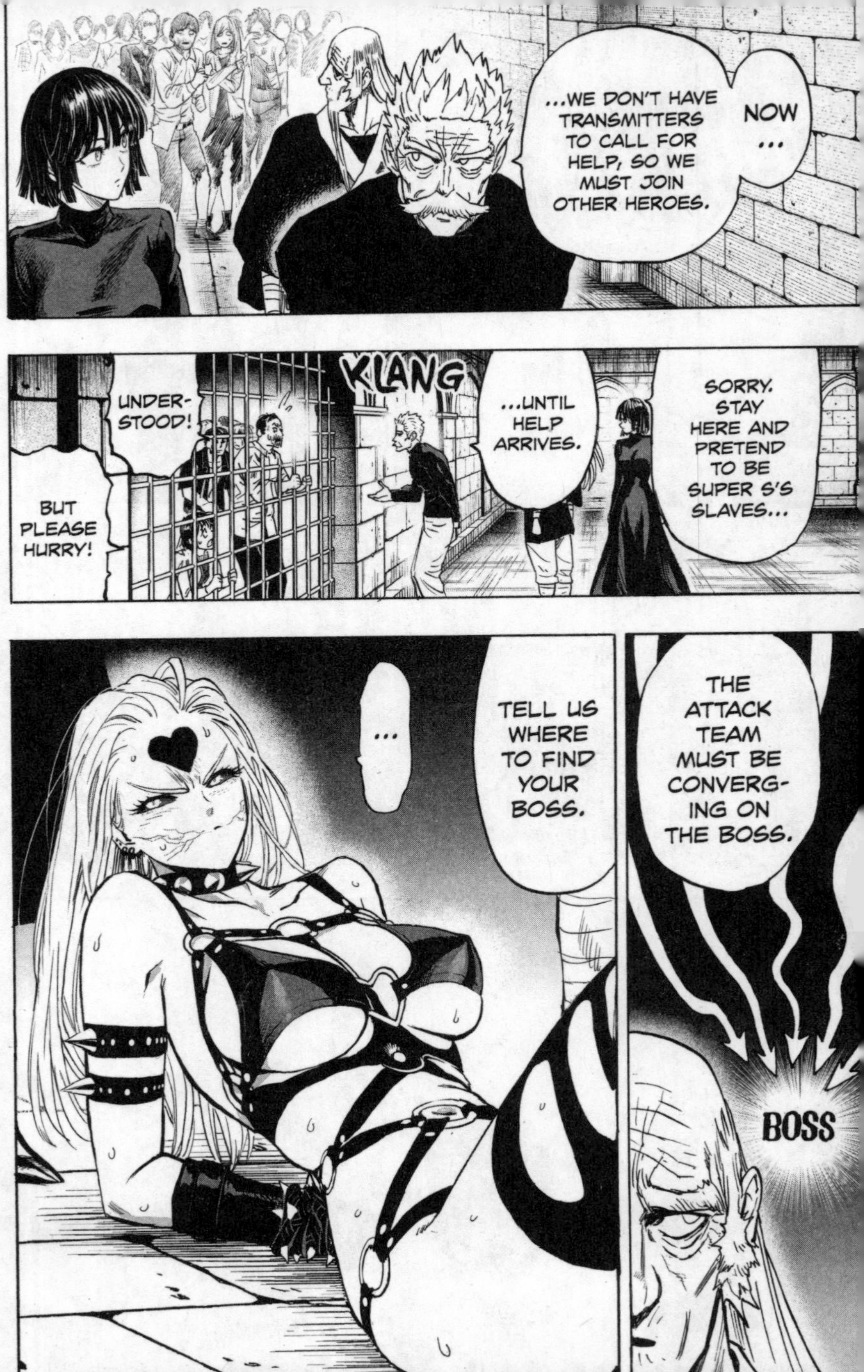
NOW ...
...WE DON'T HAVE TRANSMITTERS TO CALL FOR HELP, SO WE MUST JOIN OTHER HEROES.
SORRY. STAY HERE AND PRETEND TO BE SUPER S'S SLAVES...
...UNTIL HELP ARRIVES.
KLANG
UNDER-STOOD!
BUT PLEASE HURRY!
THE ATTACK TEAM MUST BE CONVERG-ING ON THE BOSS.
BOSS
TELL US WHERE TO FIND YOUR BOSS.
...

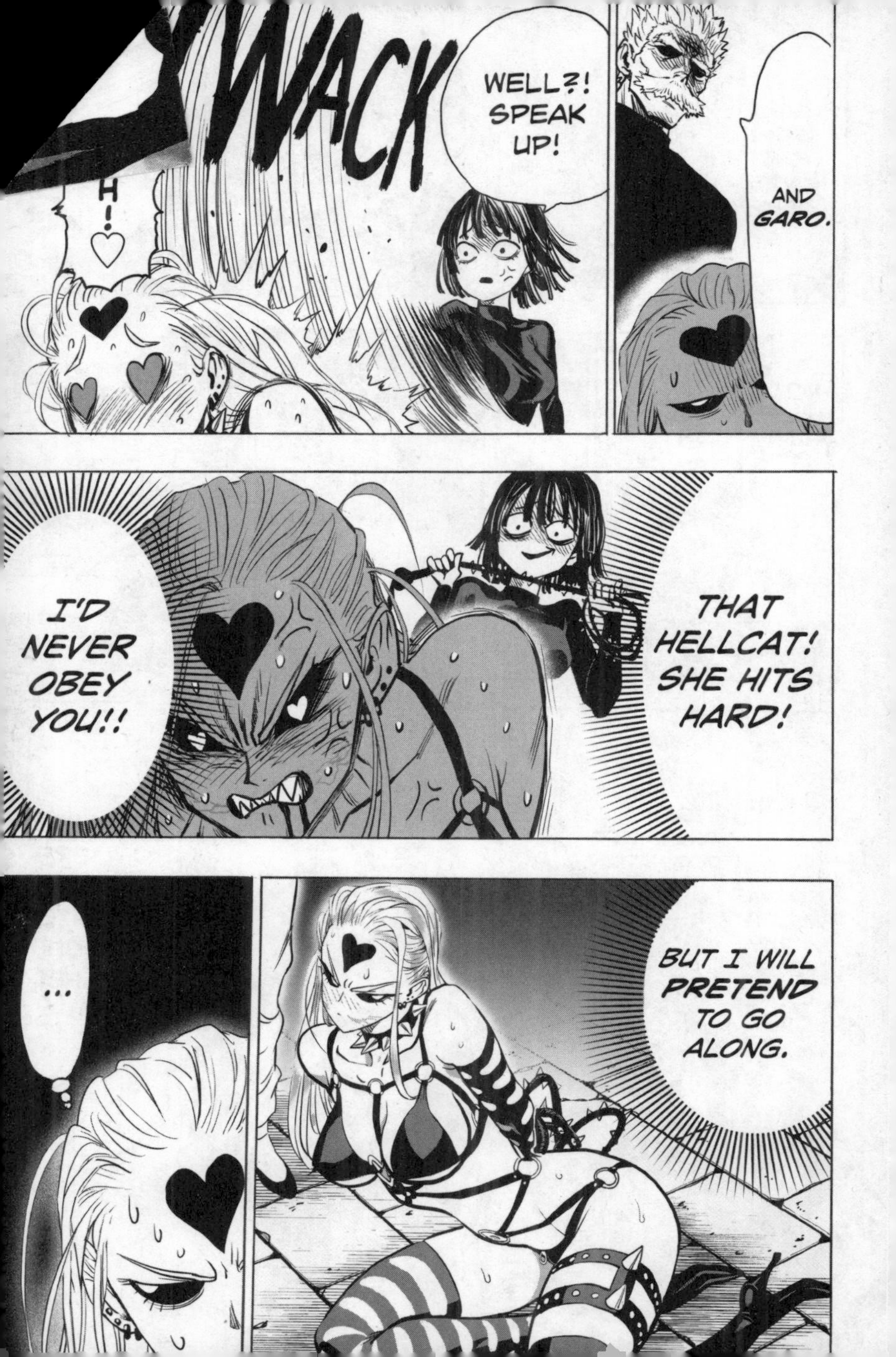

AND GARO.
WELL?! SPEAK UP!
WACK
H! ♡
THAT HELLCAT! SHE HITS HARD!
I'D NEVER OBEY YOU!!
BUT I WILL PRETEND TO GO ALONG.
...

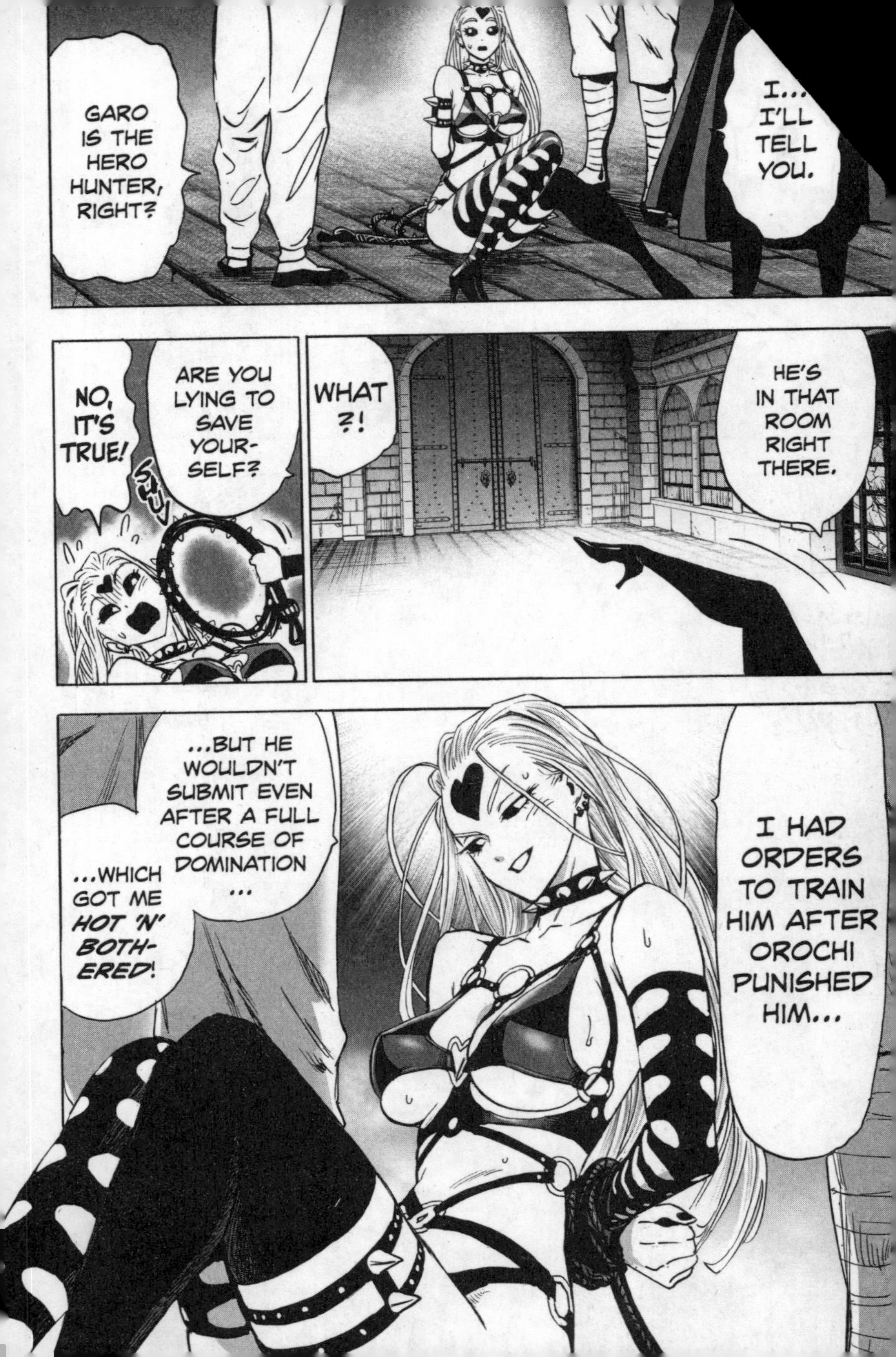
I... I'LL TELL YOU.
GARO IS THE HERO HUNTER, RIGHT?
HE'S IN THAT ROOM RIGHT THERE.
WHAT ?!
ARE YOU LYING TO SAVE YOUR-SELF?
NO, IT'S TRUE!
I HAD ORDERS TO TRAIN HIM AFTER OROCHI PUNISHED HIM...
...BUT HE WOULDN'T SUBMIT EVEN AFTER A FULL COURSE OF DOMINATION...
...WHICH GOT ME *HOT 'N' BOTHERED*!

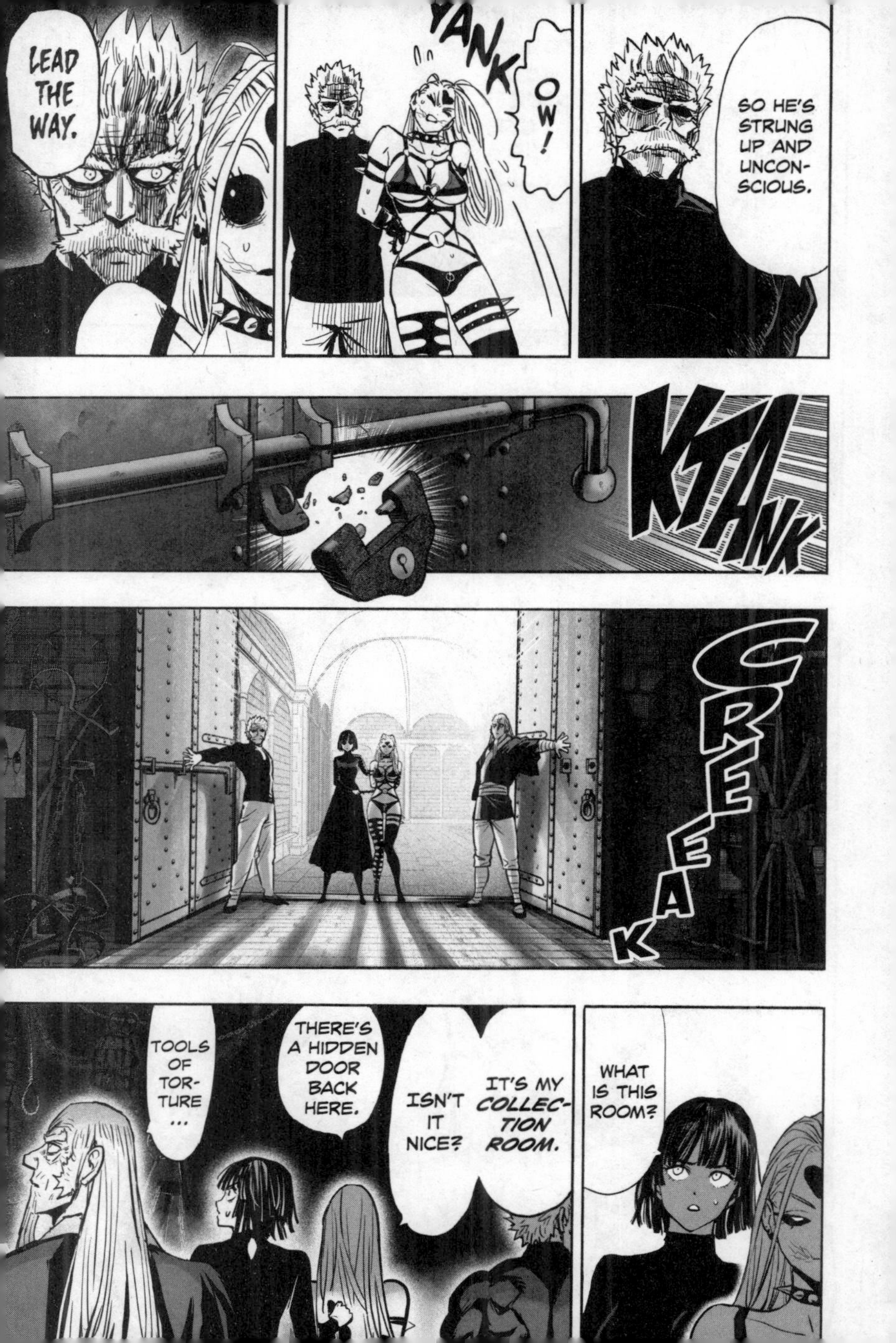
SO HE'S STRUNG UP AND UNCON-SCIOUS.
YANK
OW!
LEAD THE WAY.
KLANK
CREEAK
WHAT IS THIS ROOM?
IT'S MY COLLEC-TION ROOM.
ISN'T IT NICE?
THERE'S A HIDDEN DOOR BACK HERE.
TOOLS OF TOR-TURE ...

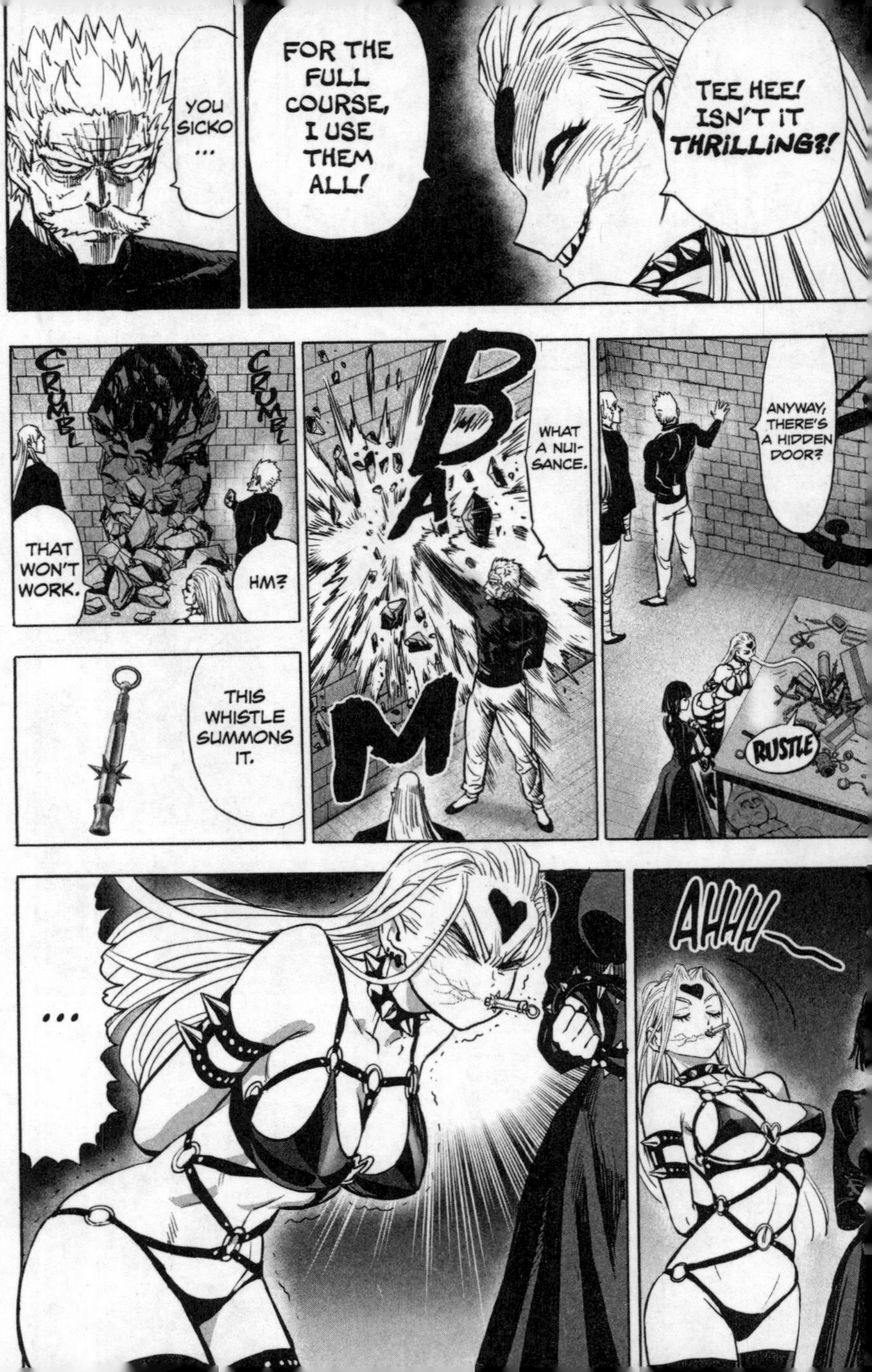
TEE HEE! ISN'T IT THRILLING?!
FOR THE FULL COURSE, I USE THEM ALL!
YOU SICKO ...
ANYWAY, THERE'S A HIDDEN DOOR?
RUSTLE
WHAT A NUI-SANCE.
BAM
CRUMBL
CRUMBL
HM?
THAT WON'T WORK.
THIS WHISTLE SUMMONS IT.
AHHH
...

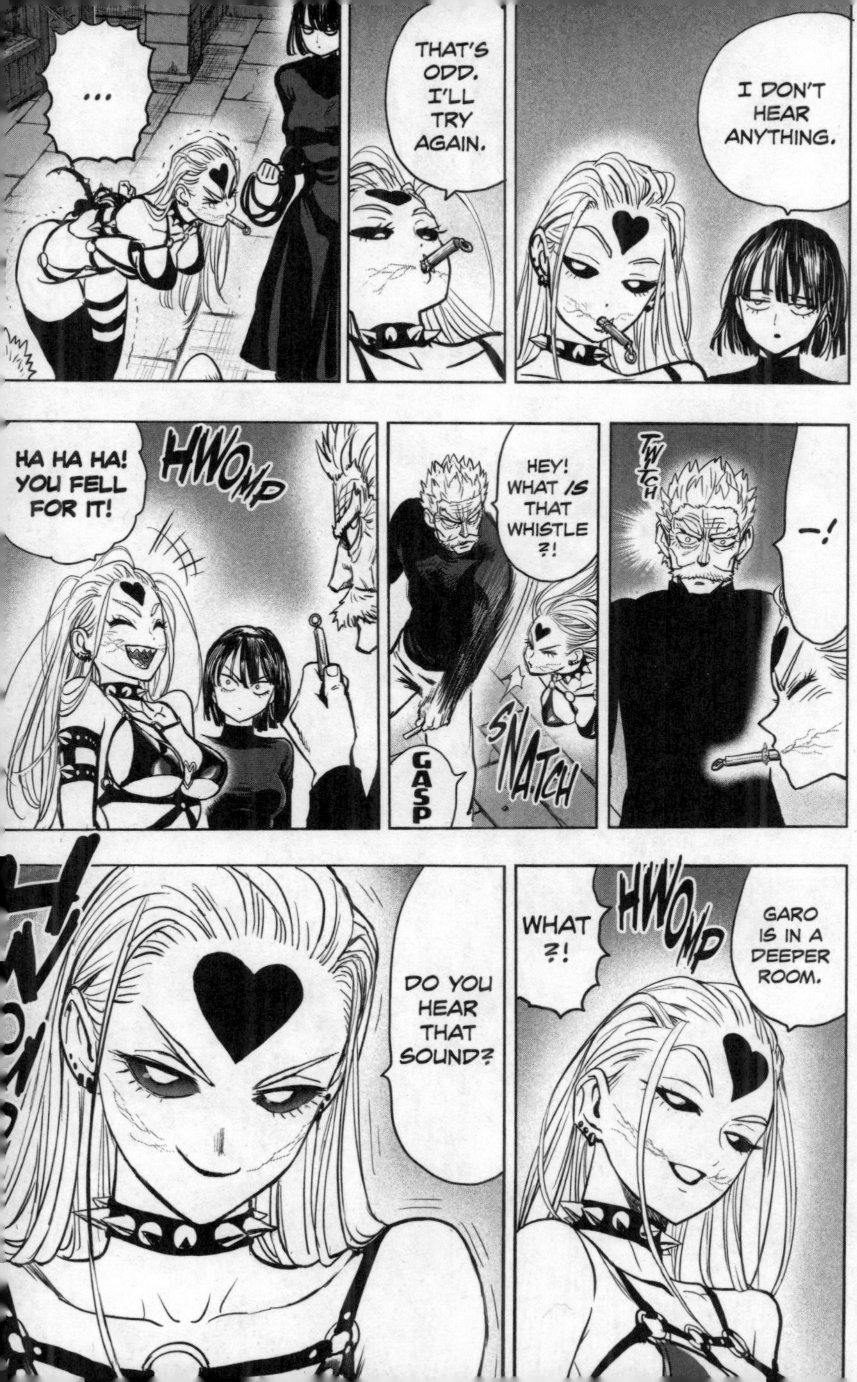
I DON'T HEAR ANYTHING.
THAT'S ODD. I'LL TRY AGAIN.
...
TWITCH
—!
HEY! WHAT IS THAT WHISTLE ?!
SNATCH
GASP
HWOMP
HA HA HA! YOU FELL FOR IT!
GARO IS IN A DEEPER ROOM.
HWOMP
WHAT ?!
DO YOU HEAR THAT SOUND?

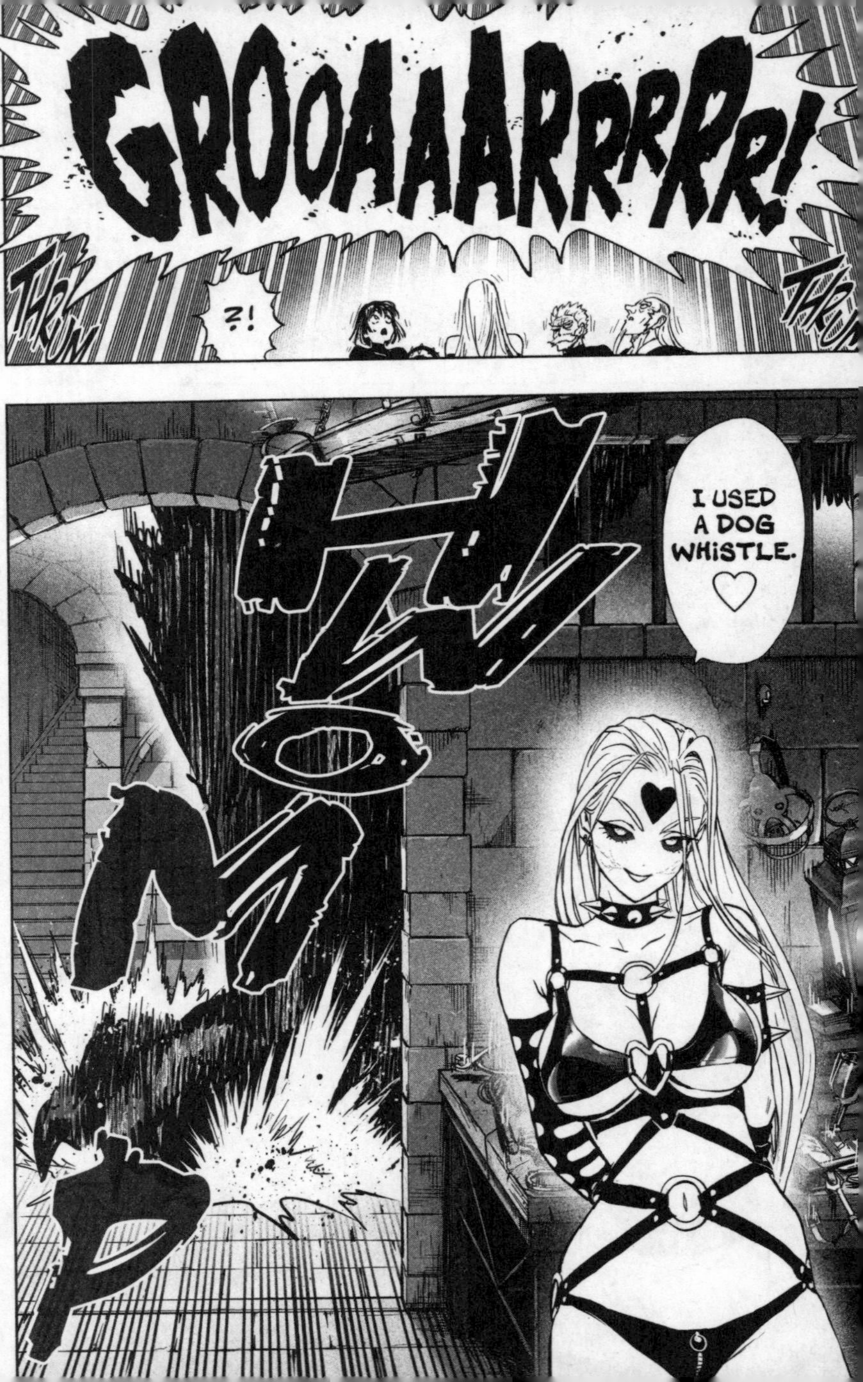
GROOAARRRR!
THRUM
THRUM
?!
I USED A DOG WHISTLE. ♡

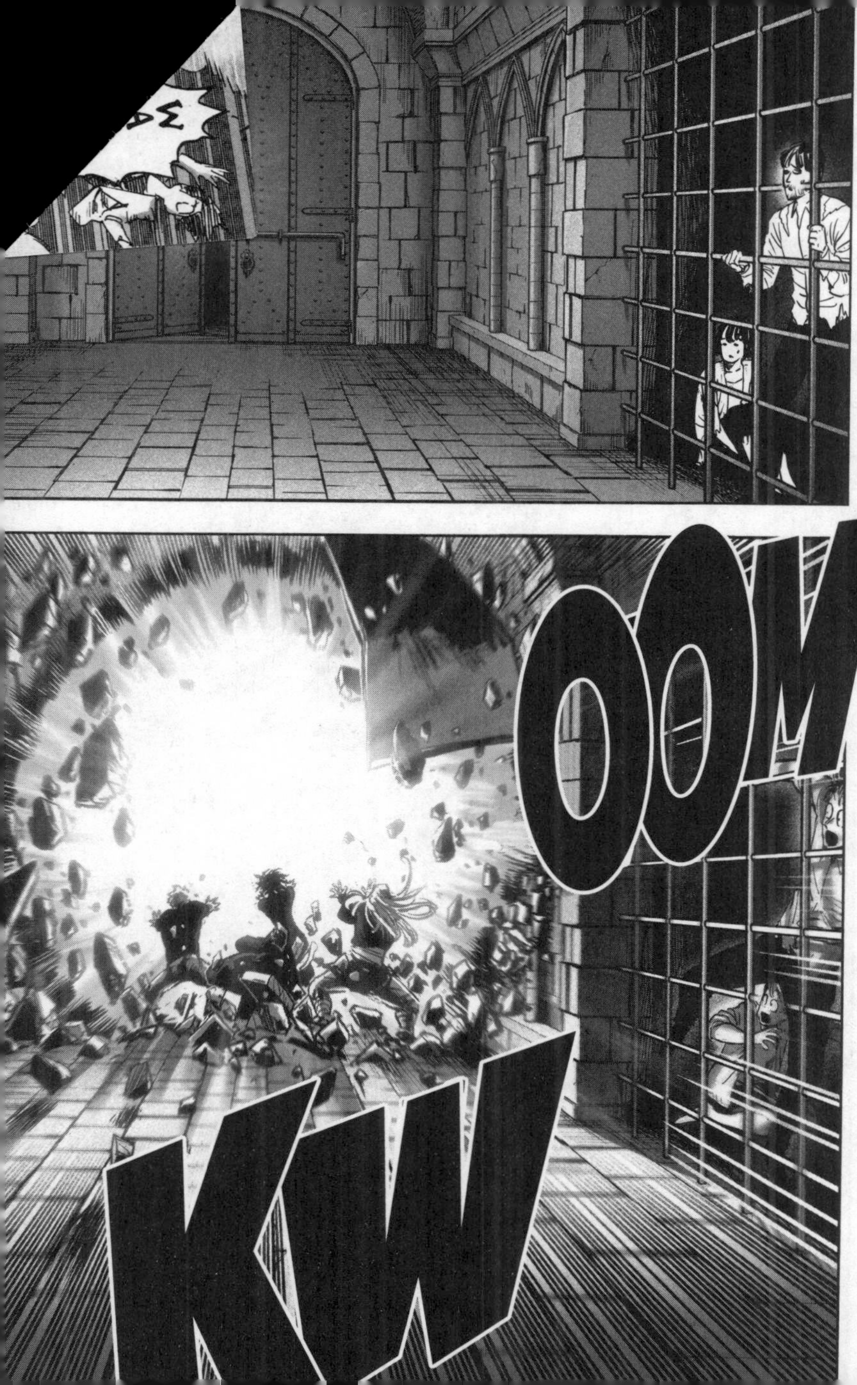
KWOOM

AAGH!

UH-OH!

SKRRR

UMF!

SWOOSH

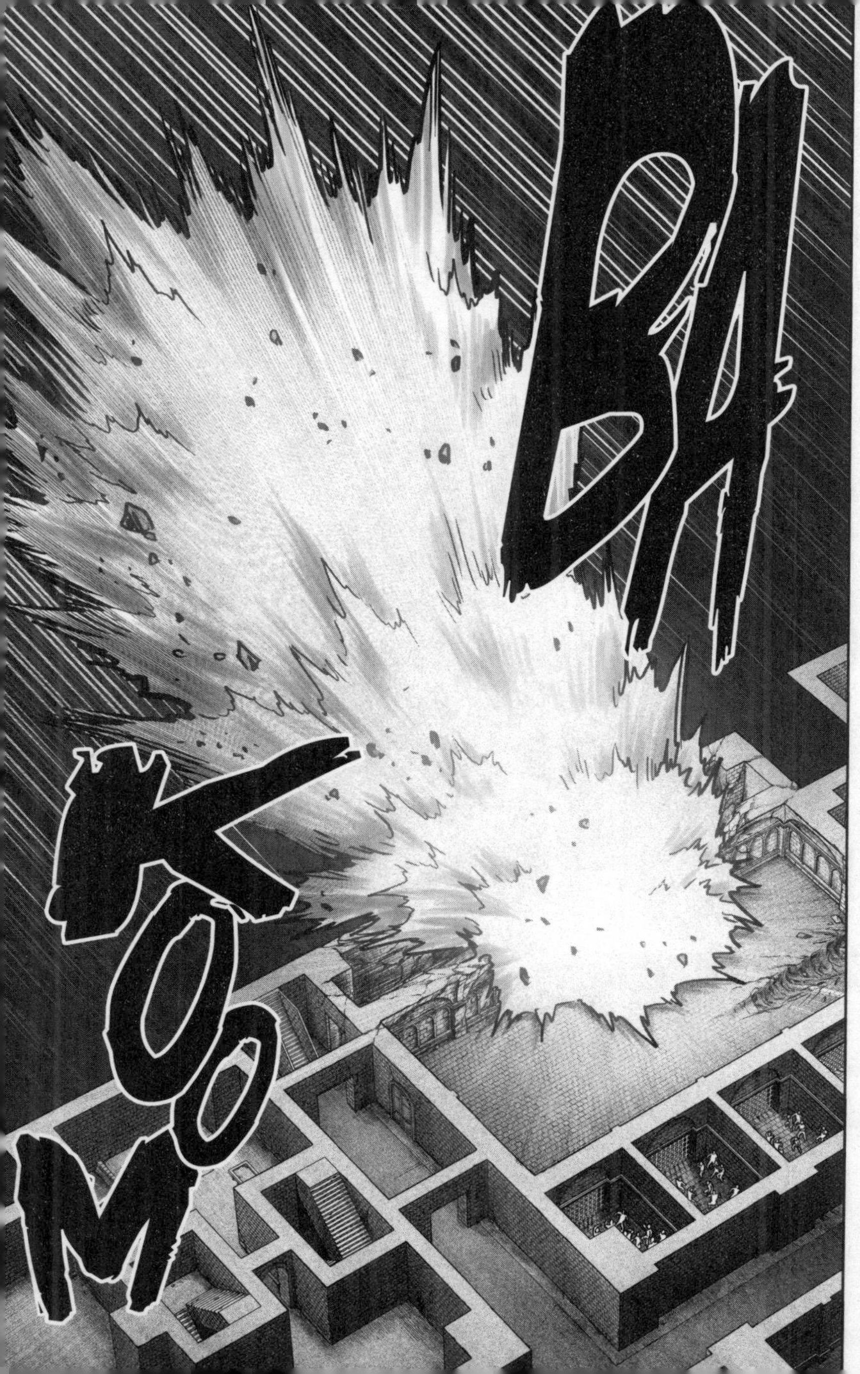
BA
KOOM

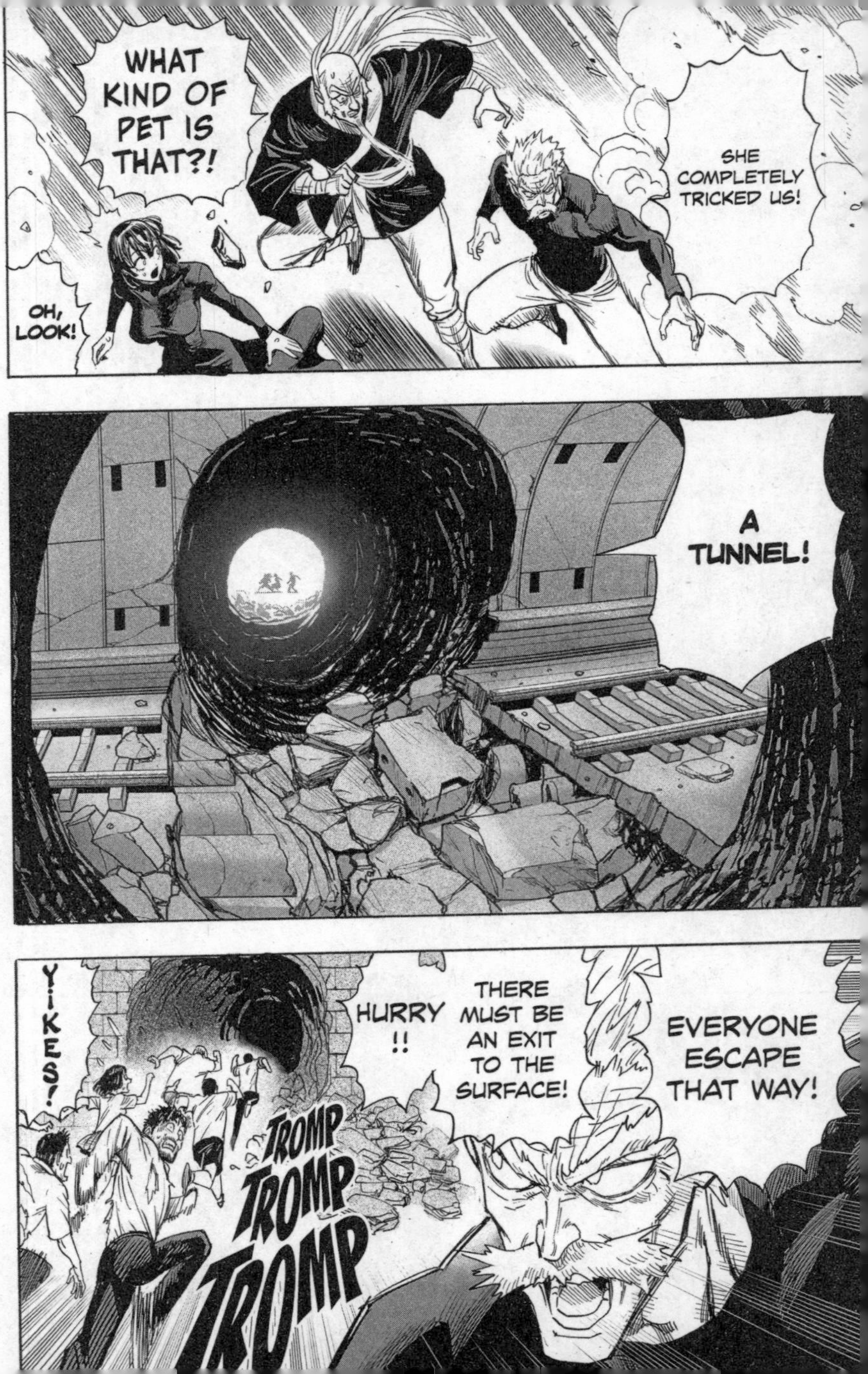
SHE COMPLETELY TRICKED US!
WHAT KIND OF PET IS THAT?!
OH, LOOK!
A TUNNEL!
EVERYONE ESCAPE THAT WAY!
THERE MUST BE AN EXIT TO THE SURFACE!
HURRY!!
YIKES!
TROMP
TROMP
TROMP
TROMP

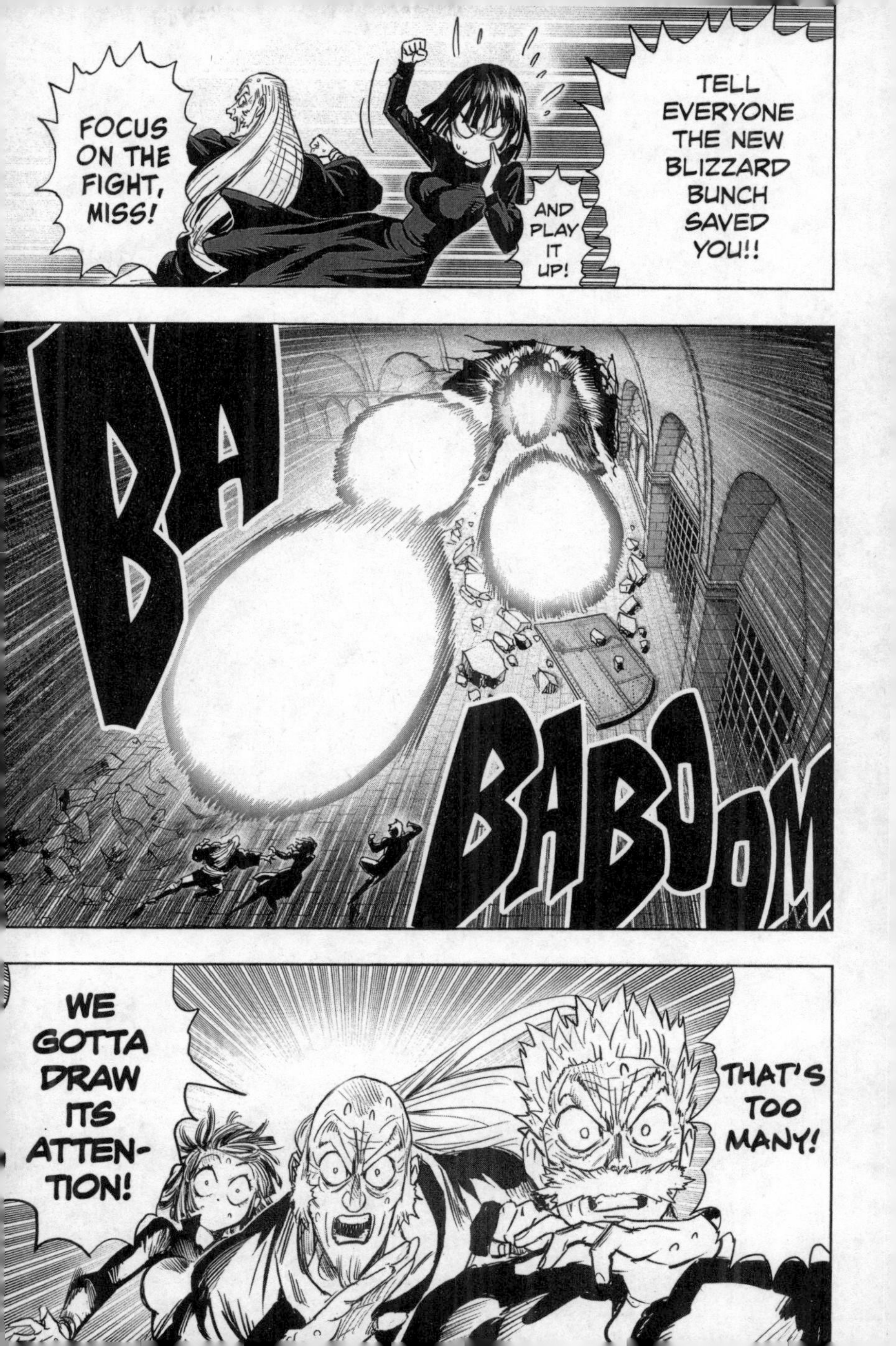
TELL EVERYONE THE NEW BLIZZARD BUNCH SAVED YOU!!
AND PLAY IT UP!
FOCUS ON THE FIGHT, MISS!
BA
BABOOM
THAT'S TOO MANY!
WE GOTTA DRAW ITS ATTENTION!

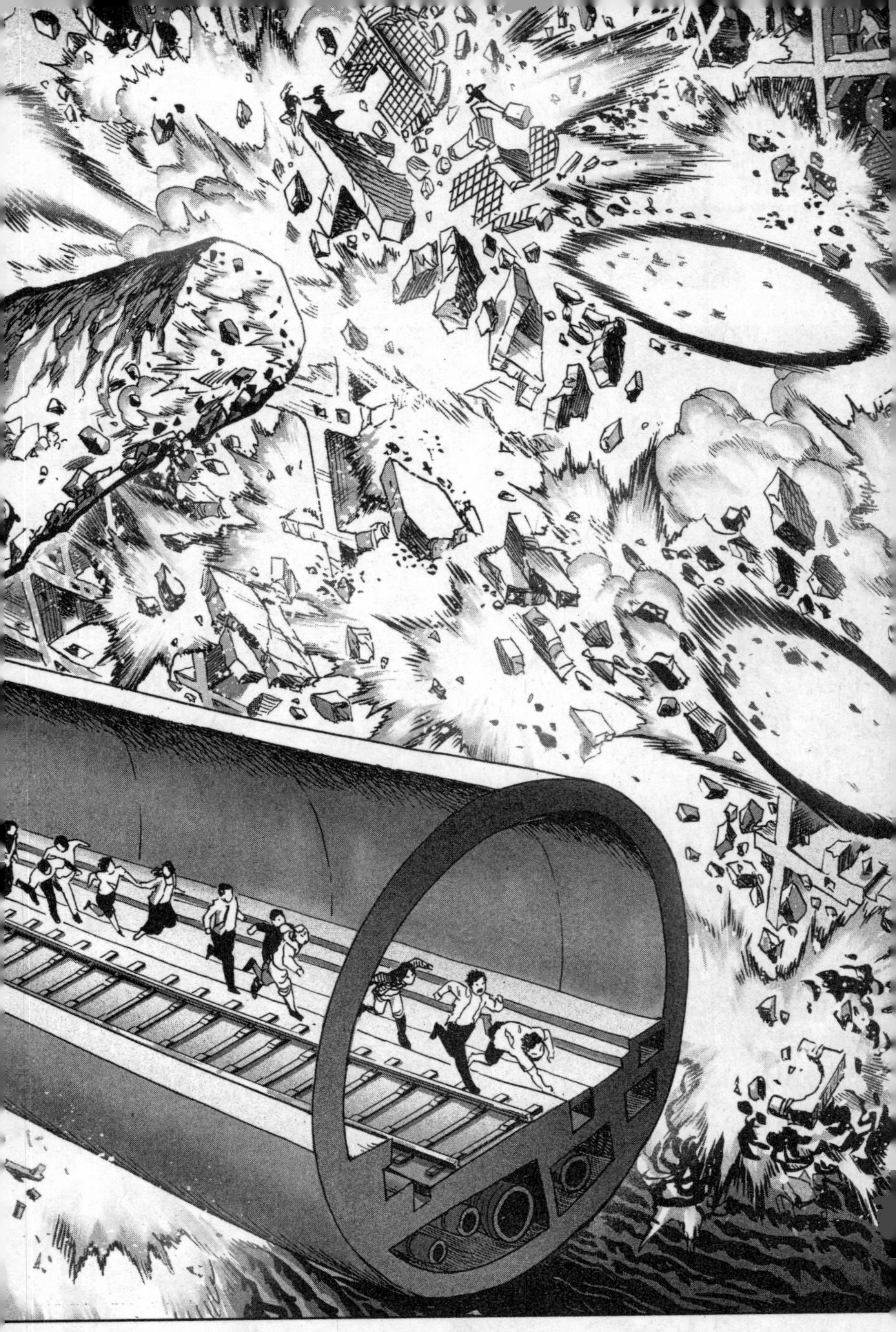

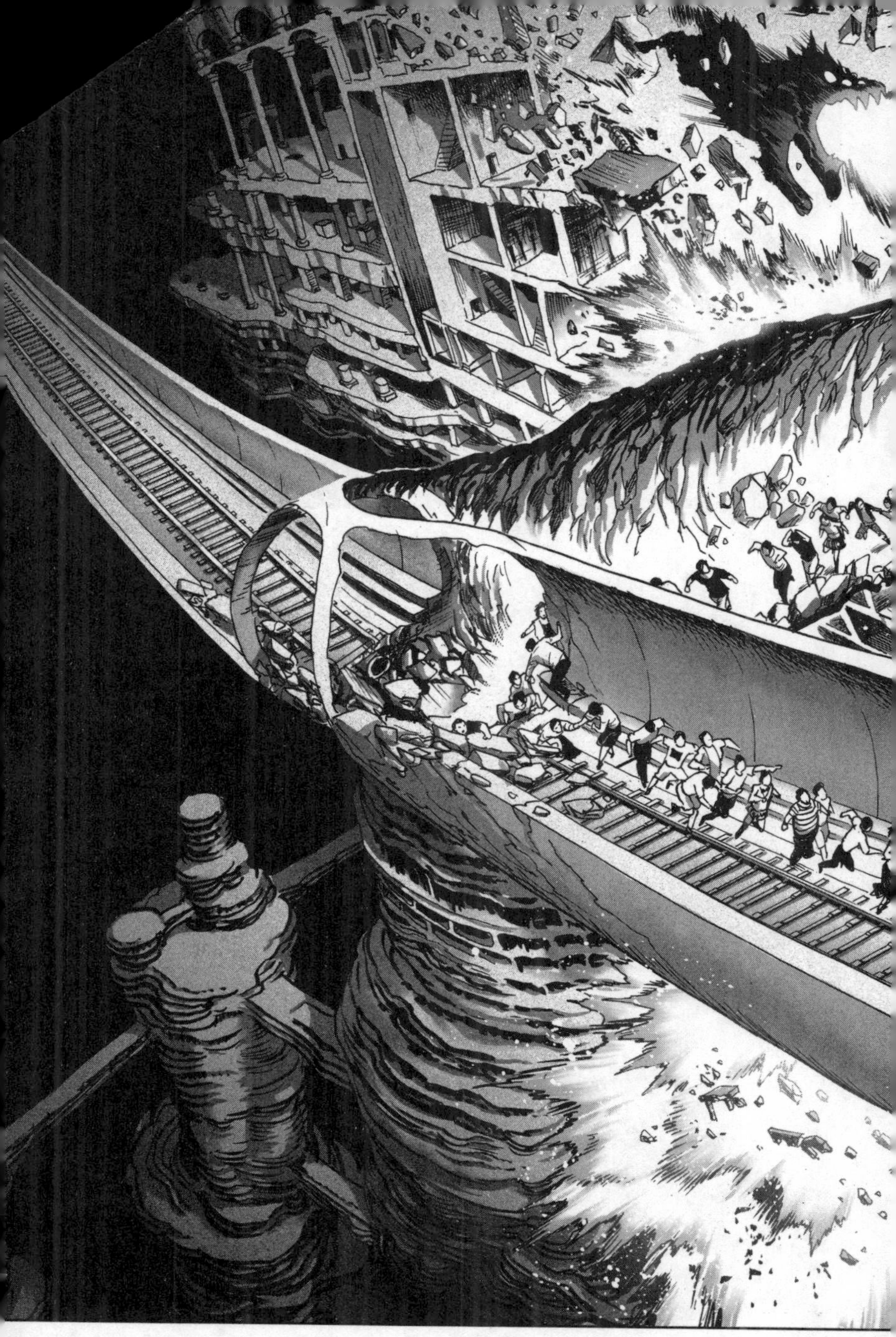

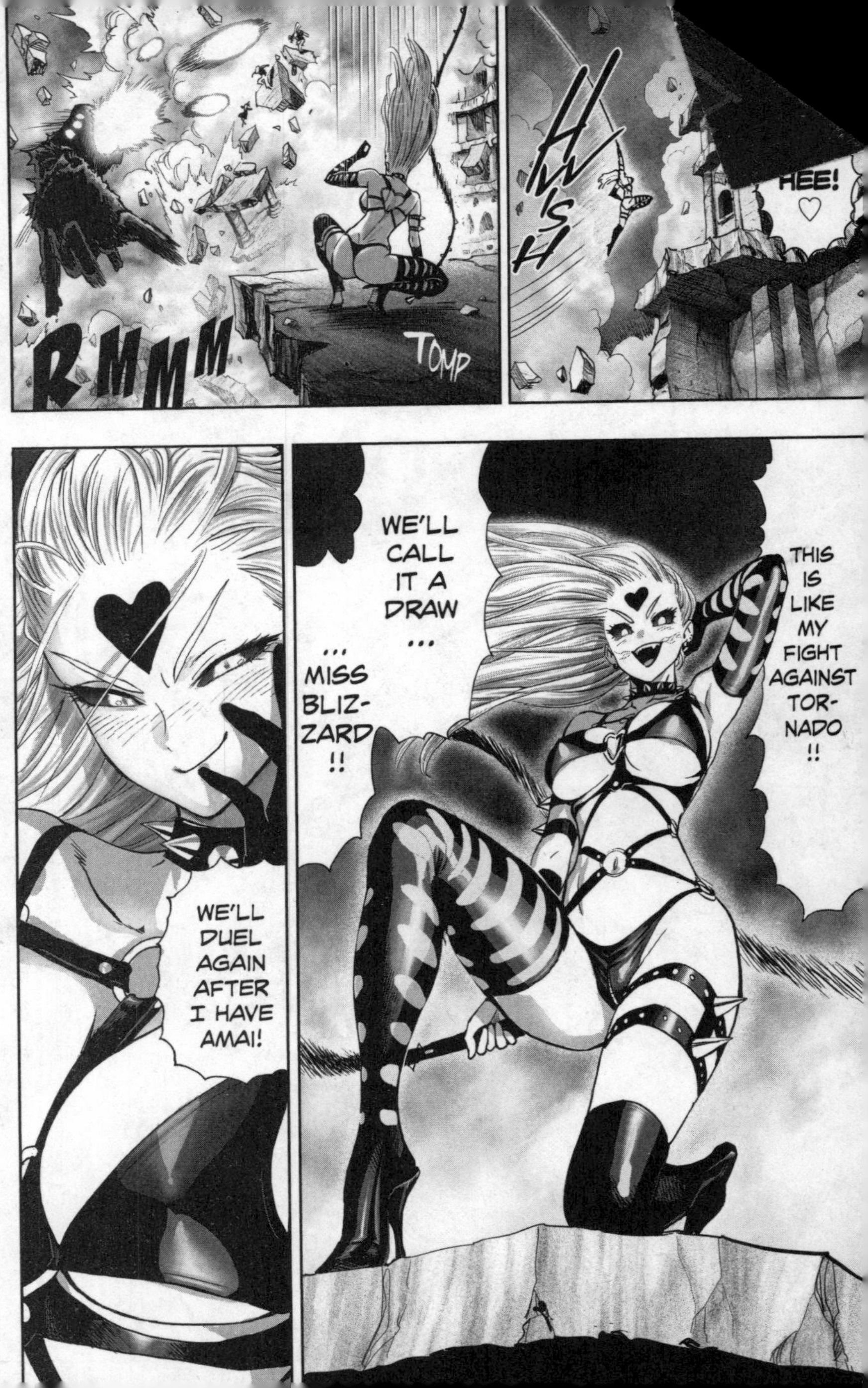
HEE! ♡
WHSH
RMMM
TOMP
THIS IS LIKE MY FIGHT AGAINST TORNADO!!
WE'LL CALL IT A DRAW...
... MISS BLIZZARD!!
WE'LL DUEL AGAIN AFTER I HAVE AMAI!

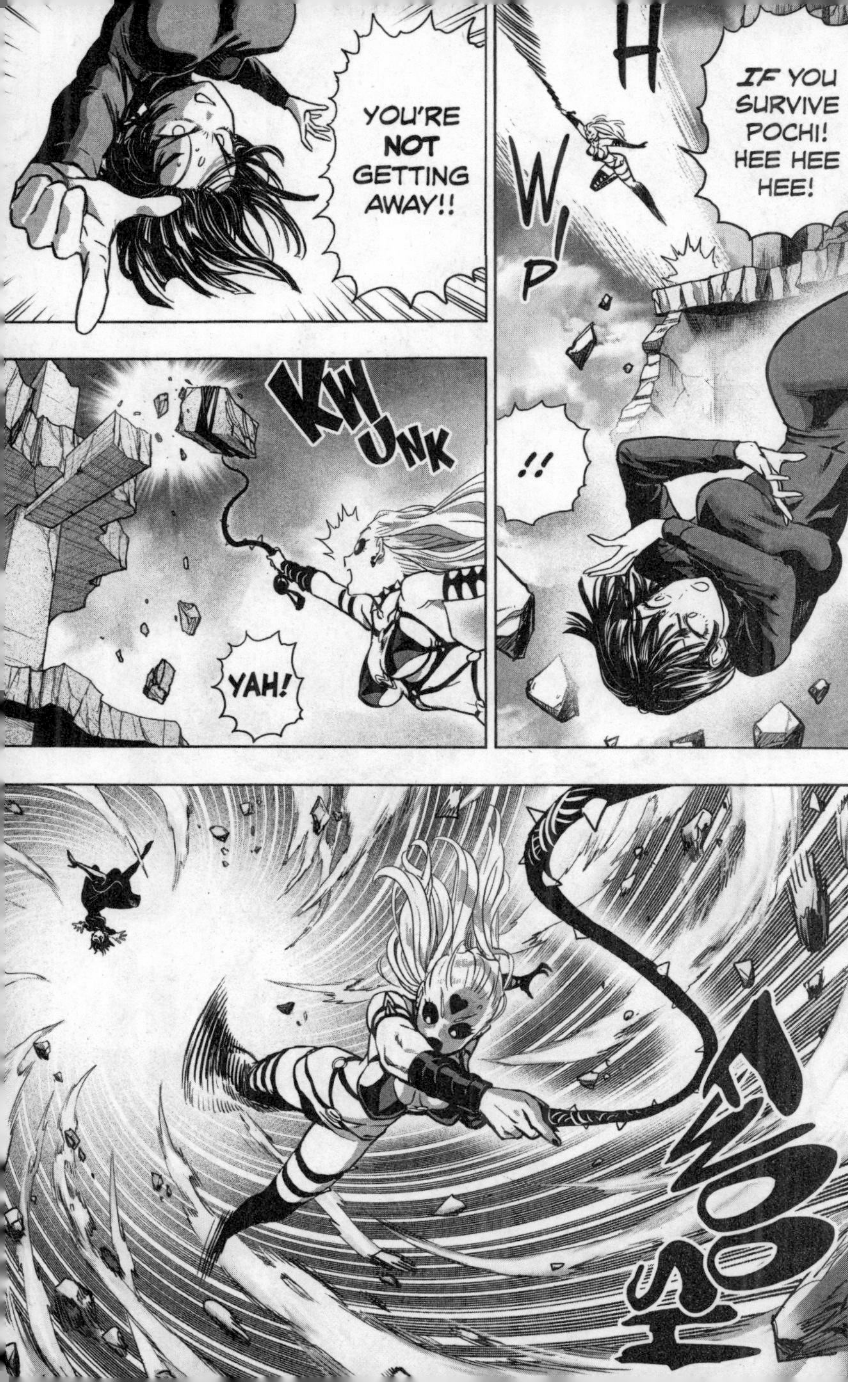
WHIP
IF YOU SURVIVE POCHI! HEE HEE HEE!
!!
YOU'RE NOT GETTING AWAY!!
KWUNK
YAH!
FWOOSH

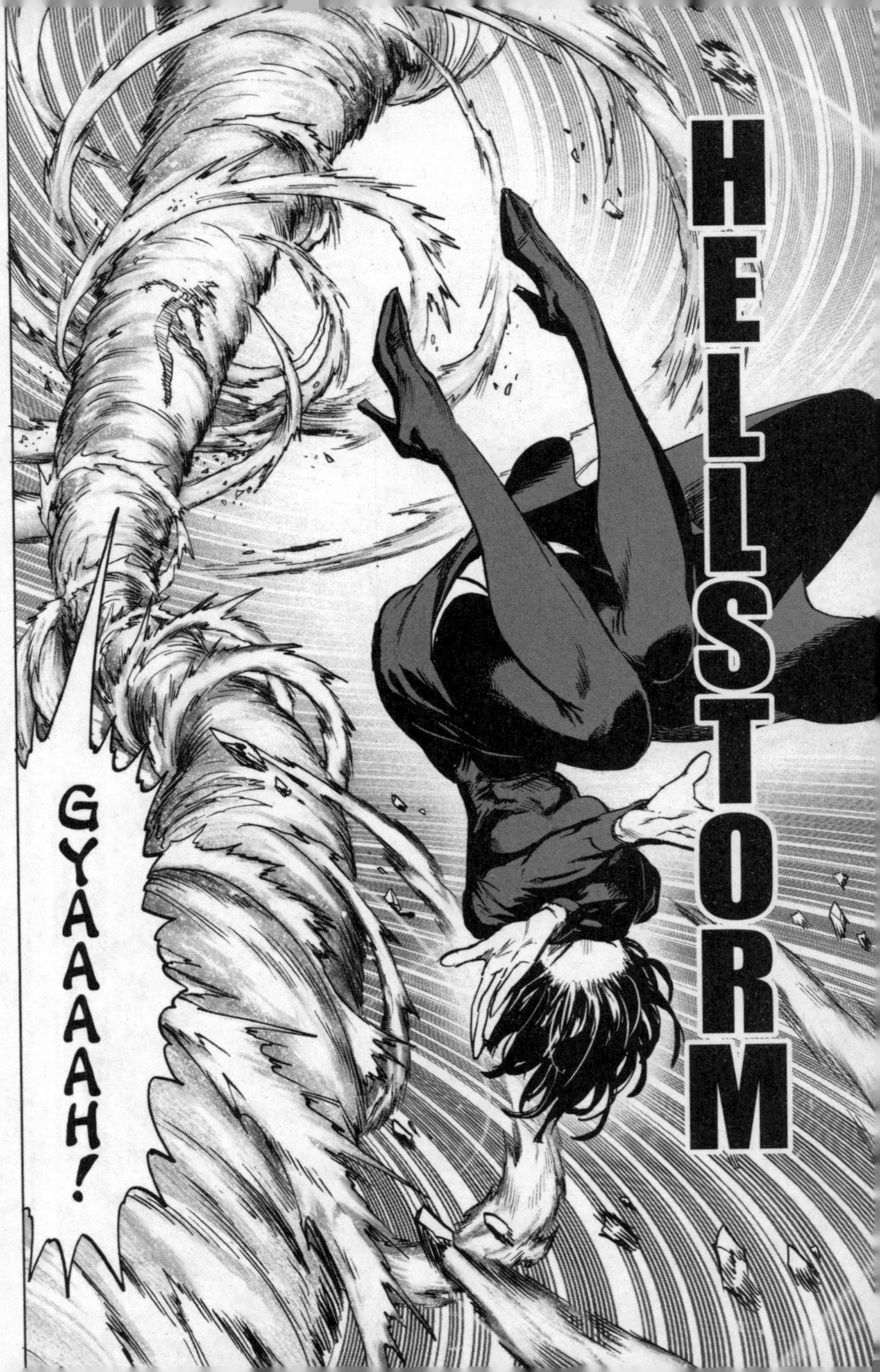
HELLSTORM
GYAAAAH!

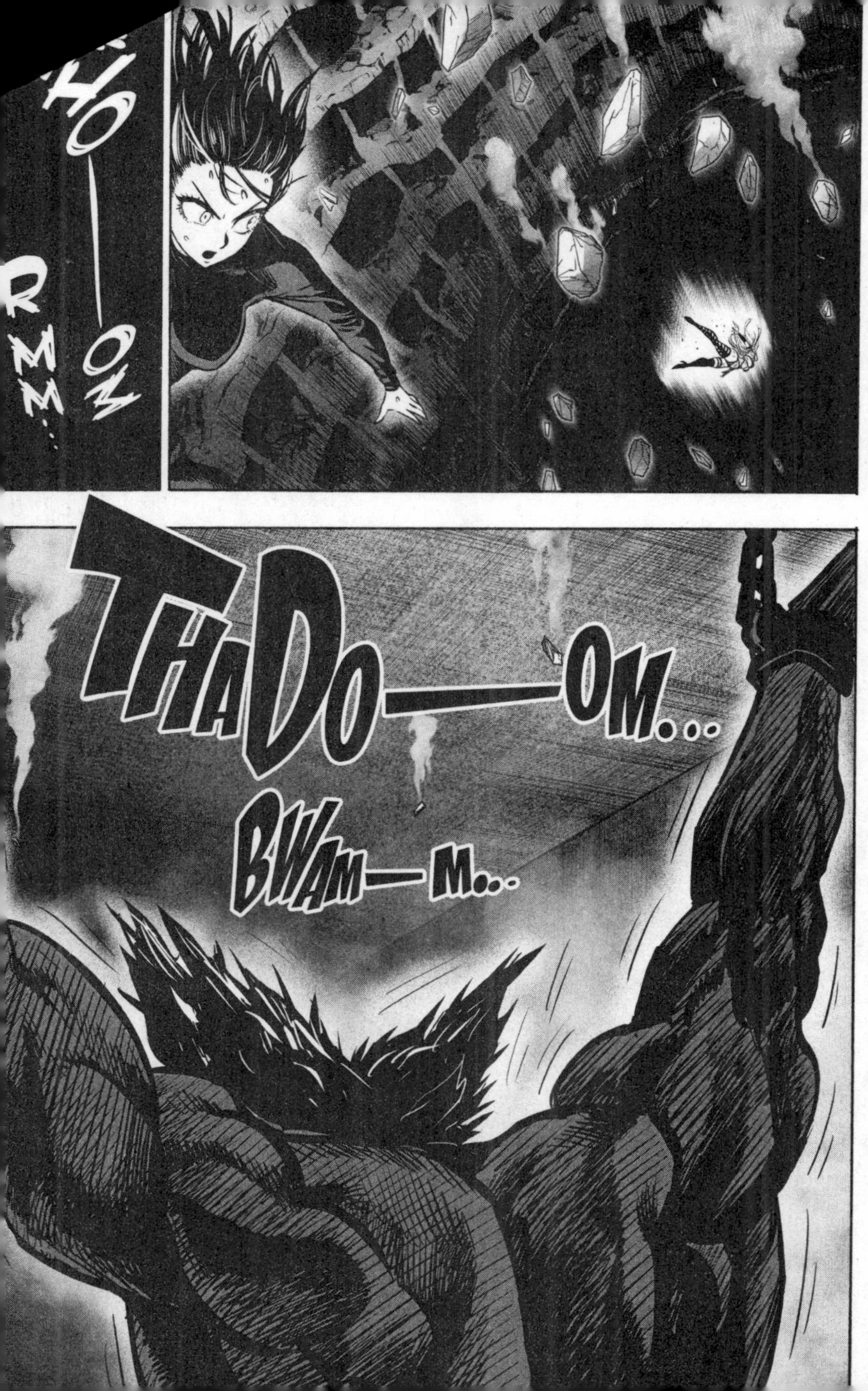
HO——OM
RMM..
THADO——OM...
BWAM—M..

SUPER S
DRESSED UP

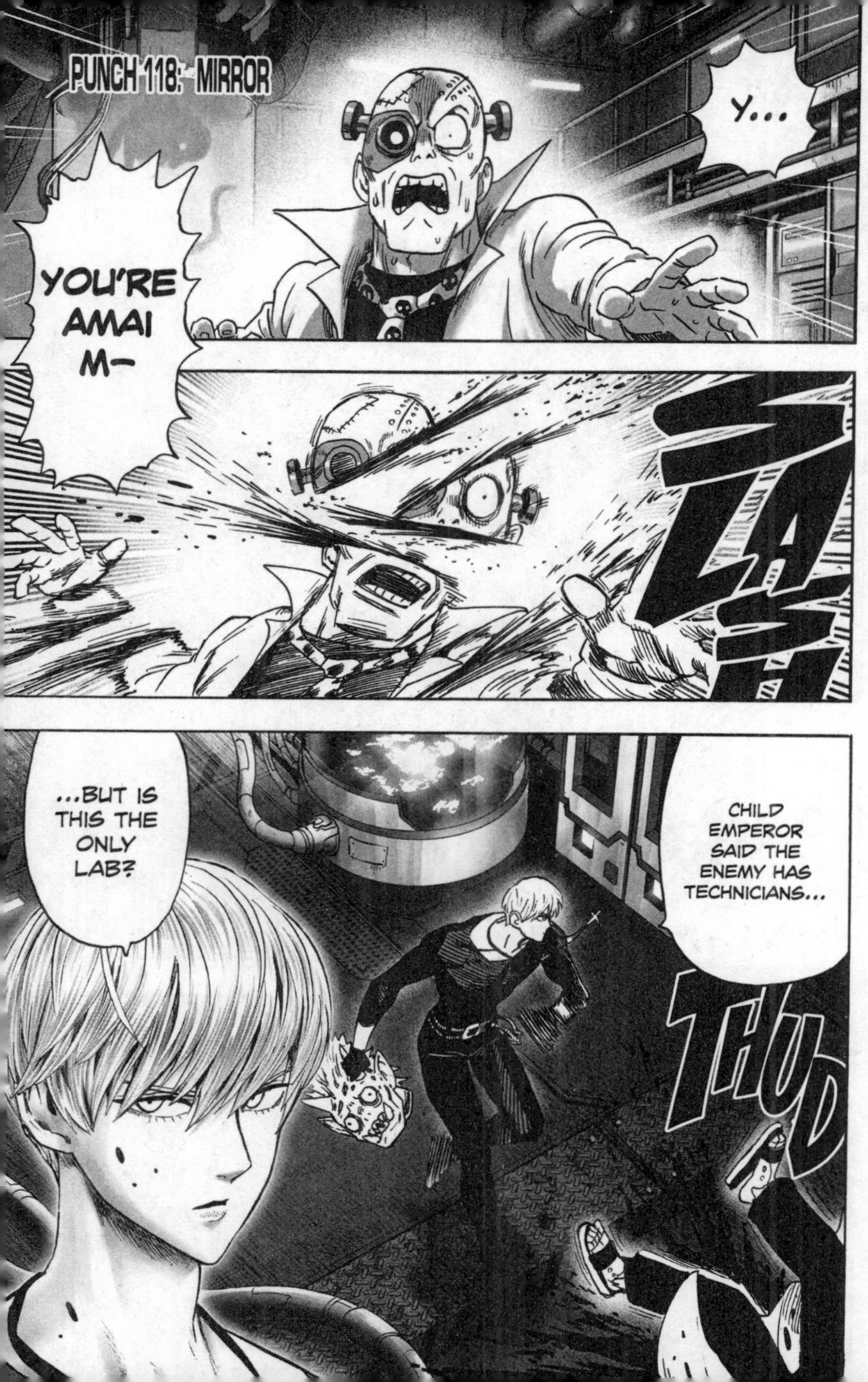
PUNCH 118: MIRROR
Y...
YOU'RE AMAI M-
ZASH
CHILD EMPEROR SAID THE ENEMY HAS TECHNICIANS...
THUD
...BUT IS THIS THE ONLY LAB?

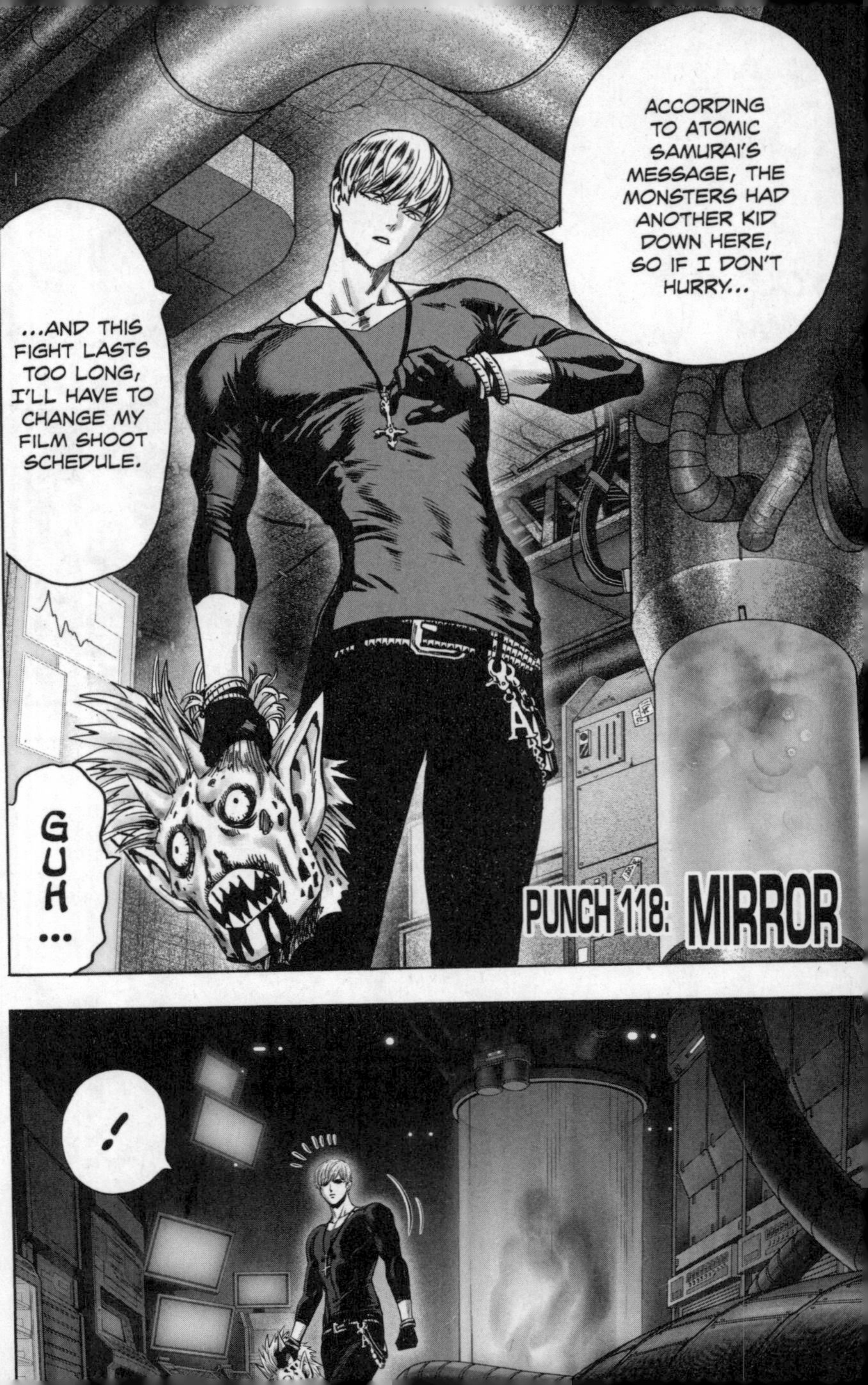
ACCORDING TO ATOMIC SAMURAI'S MESSAGE, THE MONSTERS HAD ANOTHER KID DOWN HERE, SO IF I DON'T HURRY...
...AND THIS FIGHT LASTS TOO LONG, I'LL HAVE TO CHANGE MY FILM SHOOT SCHEDULE.
GUH...
PUNCH 118: MIRROR
!

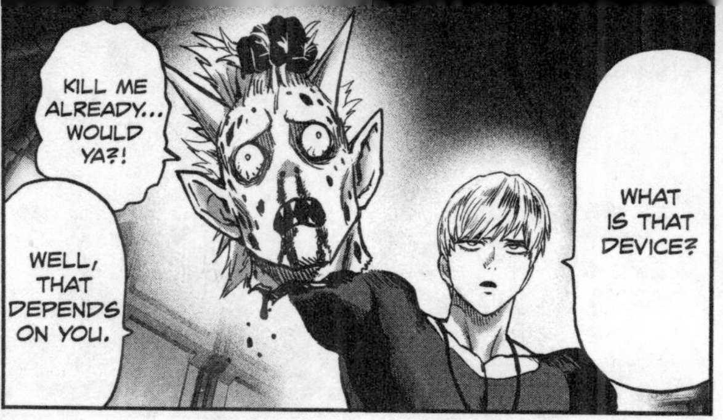
KILL ME ALREADY... WOULD YA?!
WELL, THAT DEPENDS ON YOU.
WHAT IS THAT DEVICE?
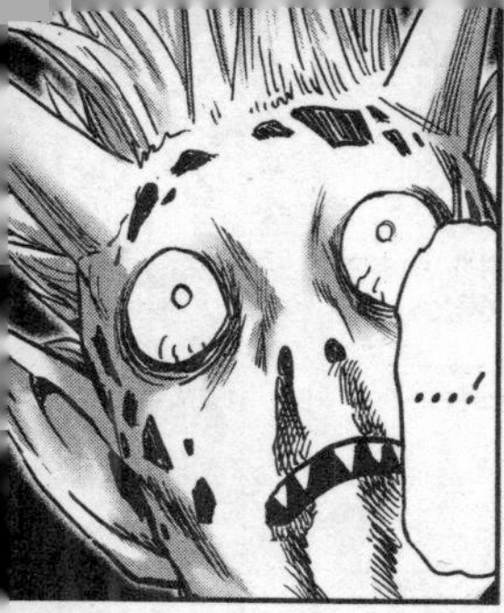
...!
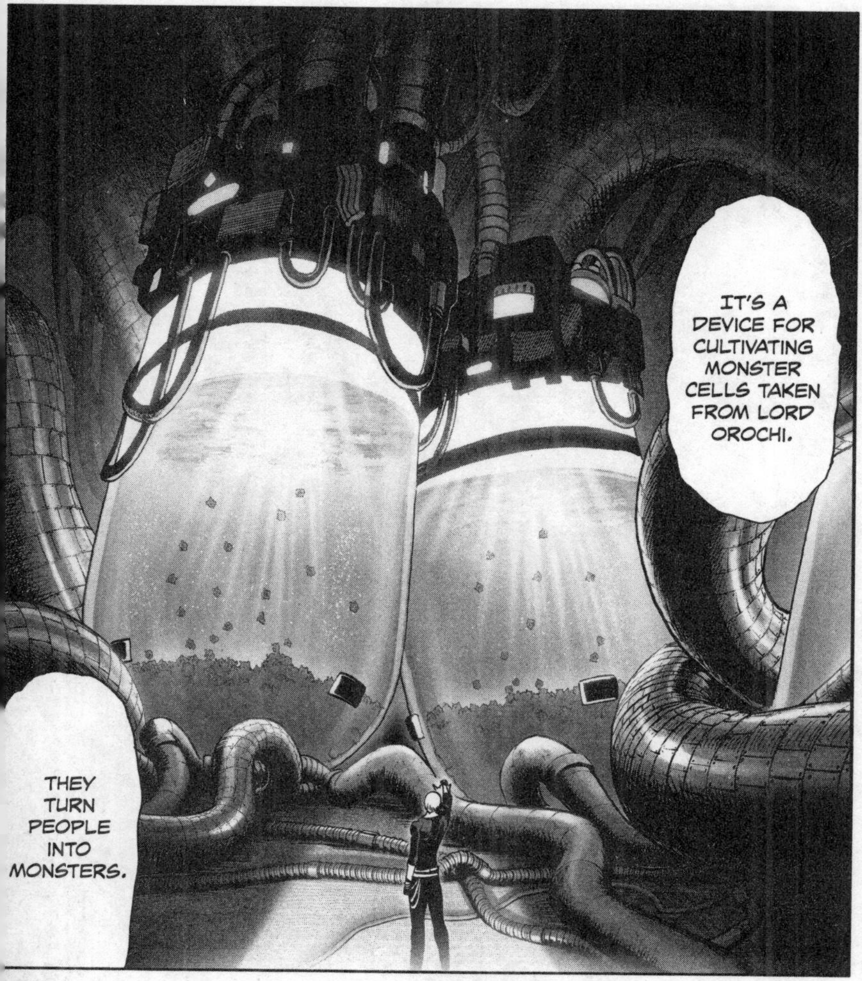
IT'S A DEVICE FOR CULTIVATING MONSTER CELLS TAKEN FROM LORD OROCHI.
THEY TURN PEOPLE INTO MONSTERS.

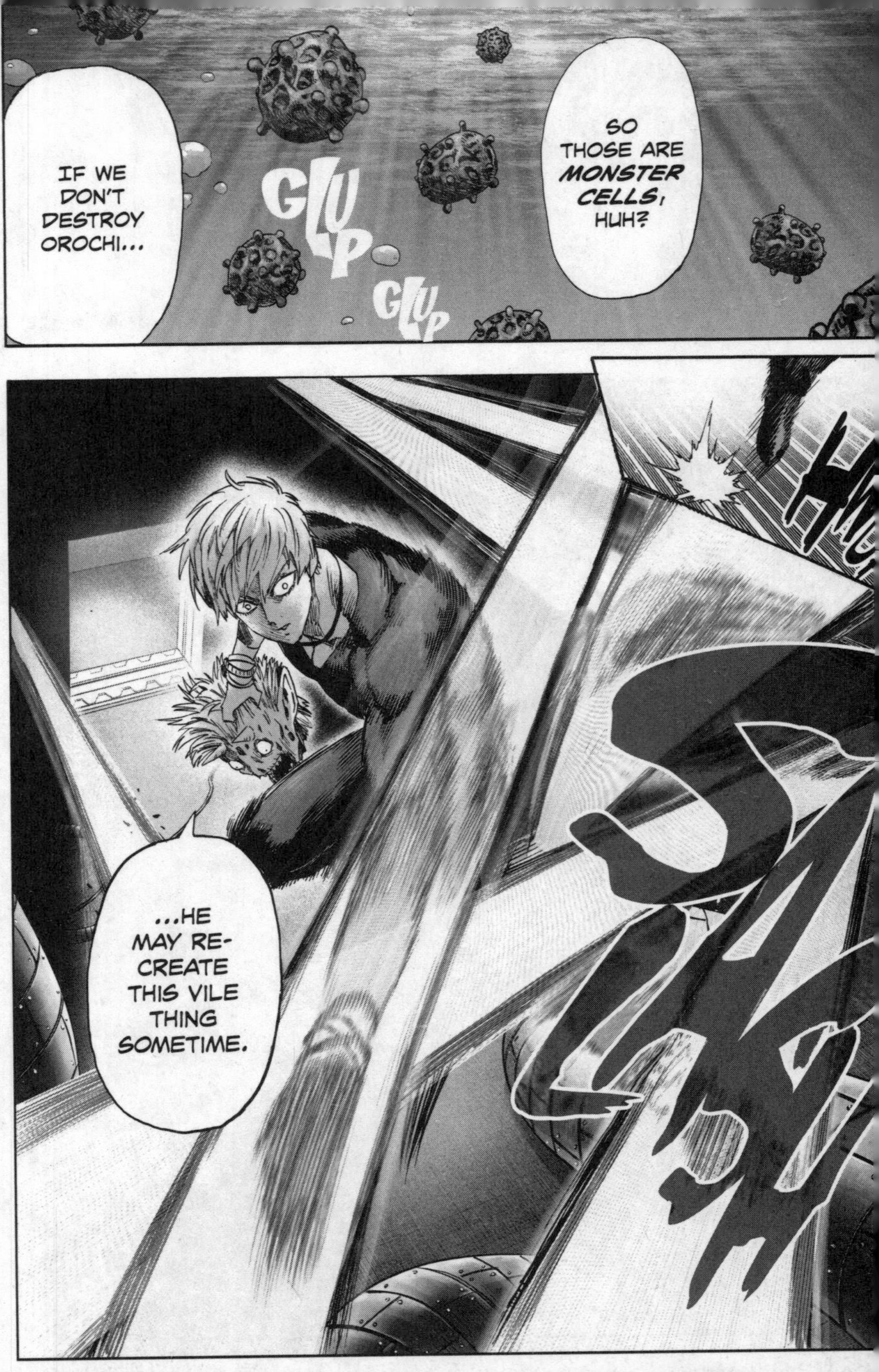
SO THOSE ARE *MONSTER CELLS*, HUH?
GLUP
GLUP
IF WE DON'T DESTROY OROCHI...
...HE MAY RE-CREATE THIS VILE THING SOMETIME.

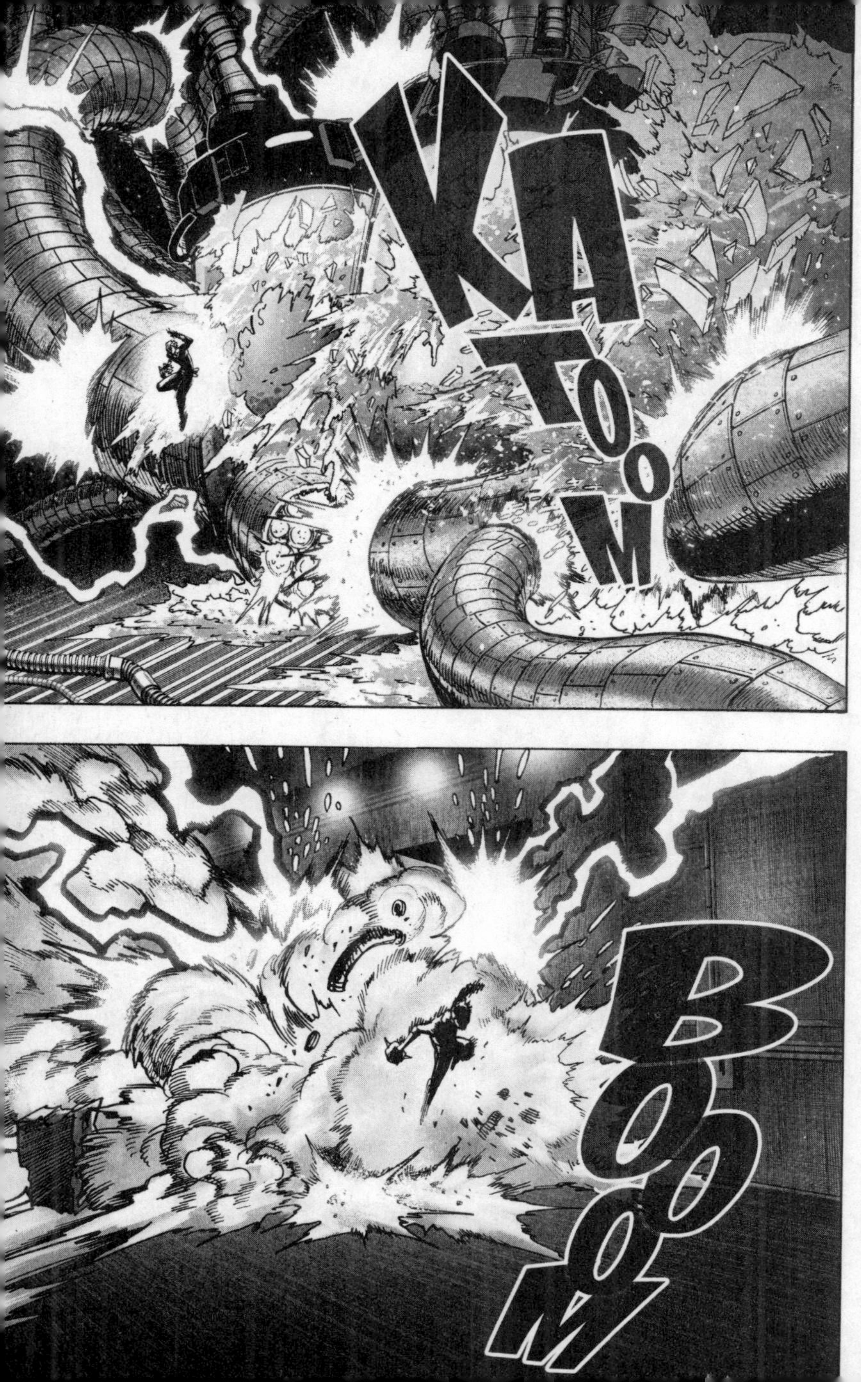
KATOOM
BOOOM

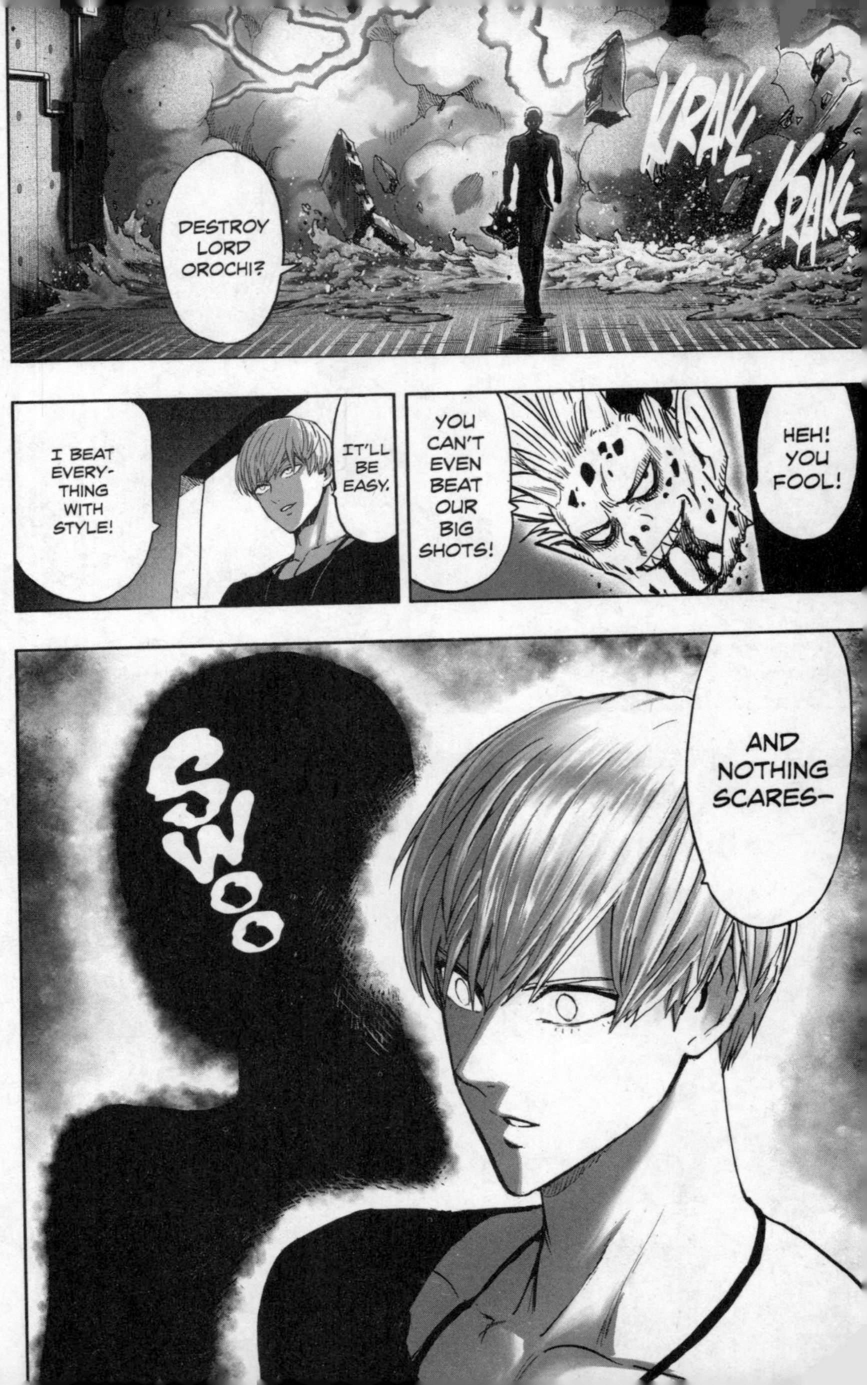
KRAKL
KRAKL
DESTROY LORD OROCHI?
HEH! YOU FOOL!
YOU CAN'T EVEN BEAT OUR BIG SHOTS!
IT'LL BE EASY.
I BEAT EVERY-THING WITH STYLE!
AND NOTHING SCARES—
SWOO

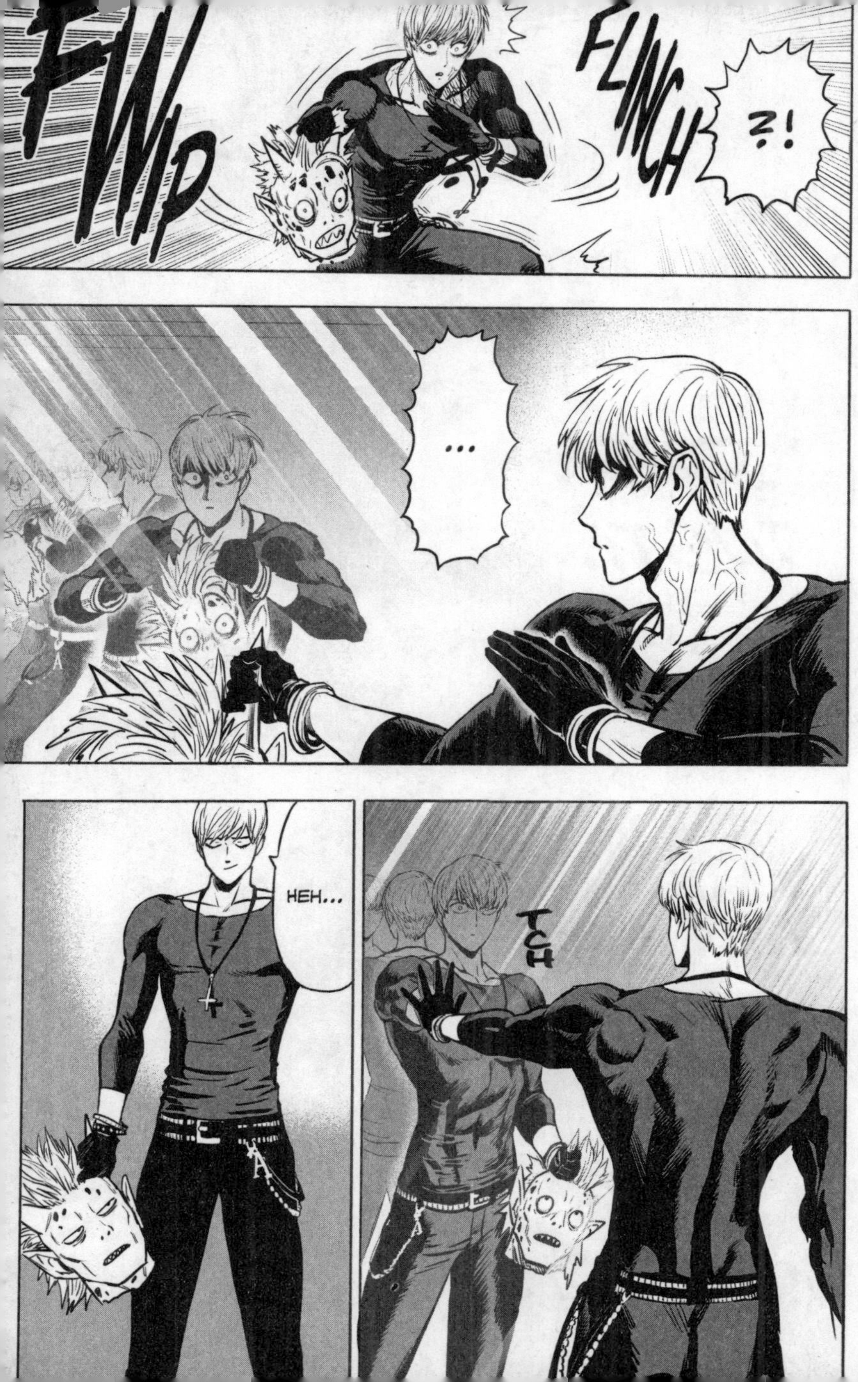
?!
FLINCH
FWIP
...
TCH
HEH...

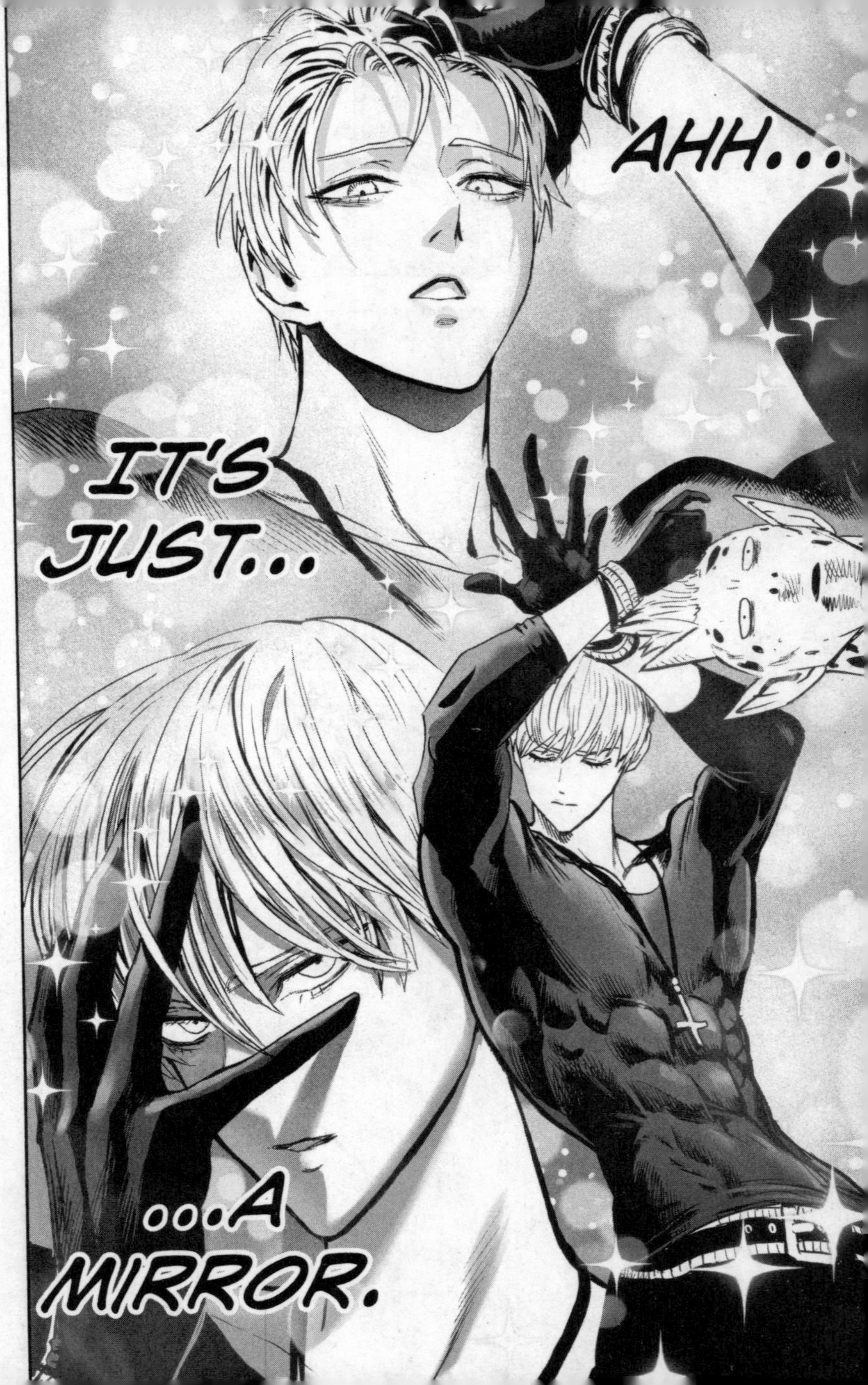
AHH...
IT'S JUST...
...A MIRROR.

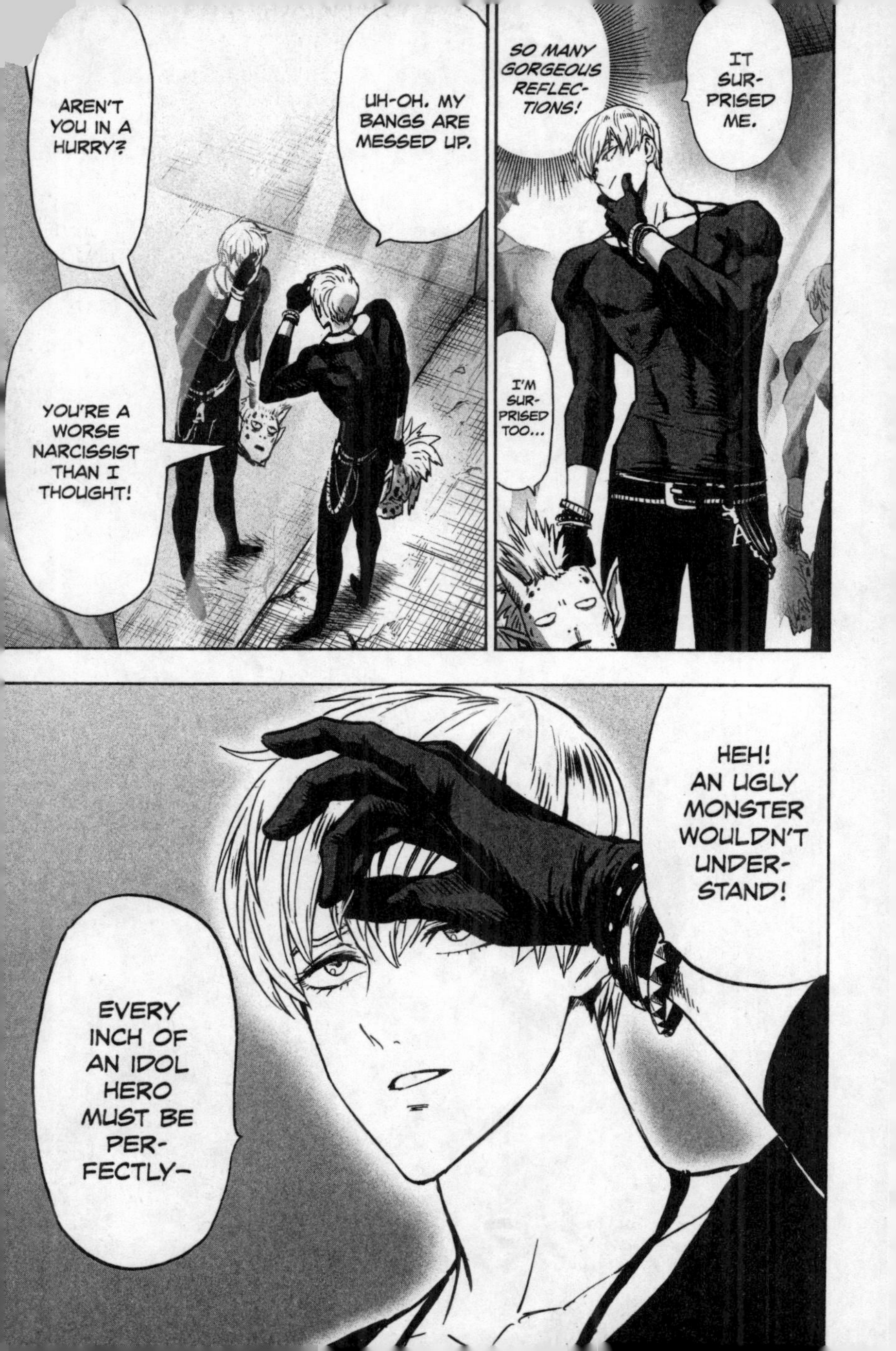
IT SURPRISED ME.
SO MANY GORGEOUS REFLECTIONS!
I'M SURPRISED TOO...
UH-OH. MY BANGS ARE MESSED UP.
AREN'T YOU IN A HURRY?
YOU'RE A WORSE NARCISSIST THAN I THOUGHT!
HEH! AN UGLY MONSTER WOULDN'T UNDERSTAND!
EVERY INCH OF AN IDOL HERO MUST BE PERFECTLY—

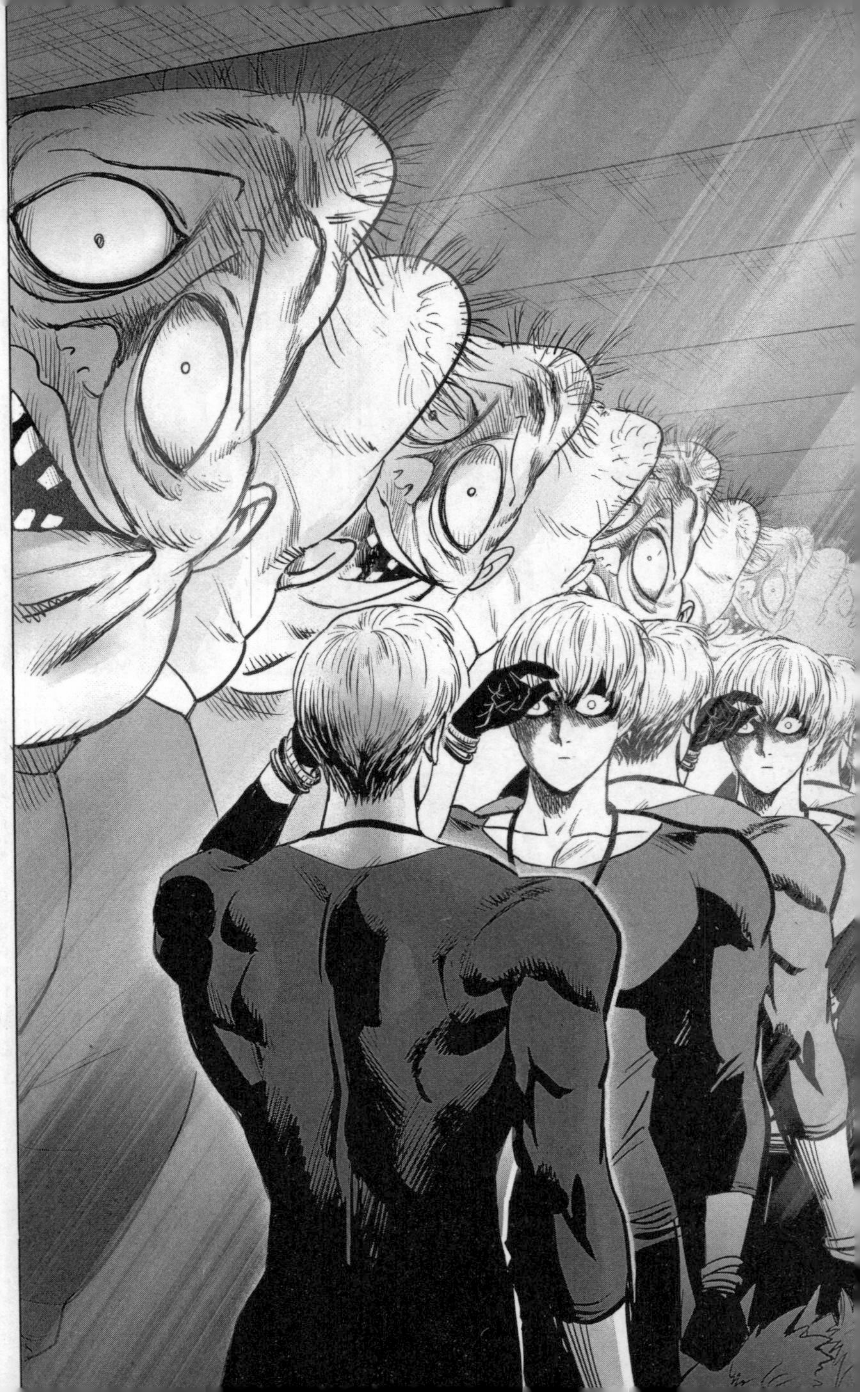

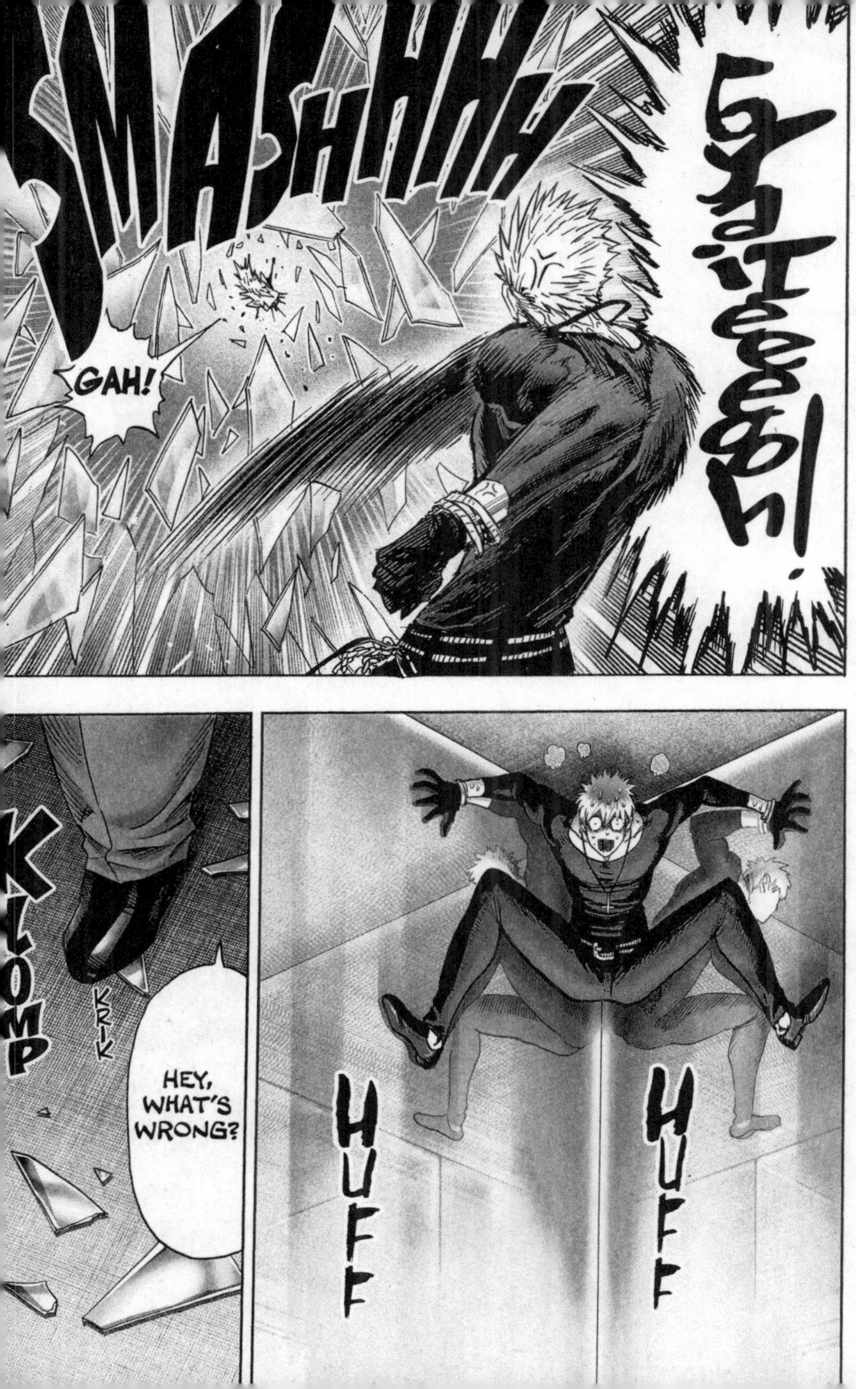
SMASHHH
GAH!
HUFF
HUFF
KLOMP
KRIK
HEY, WHAT'S WRONG?

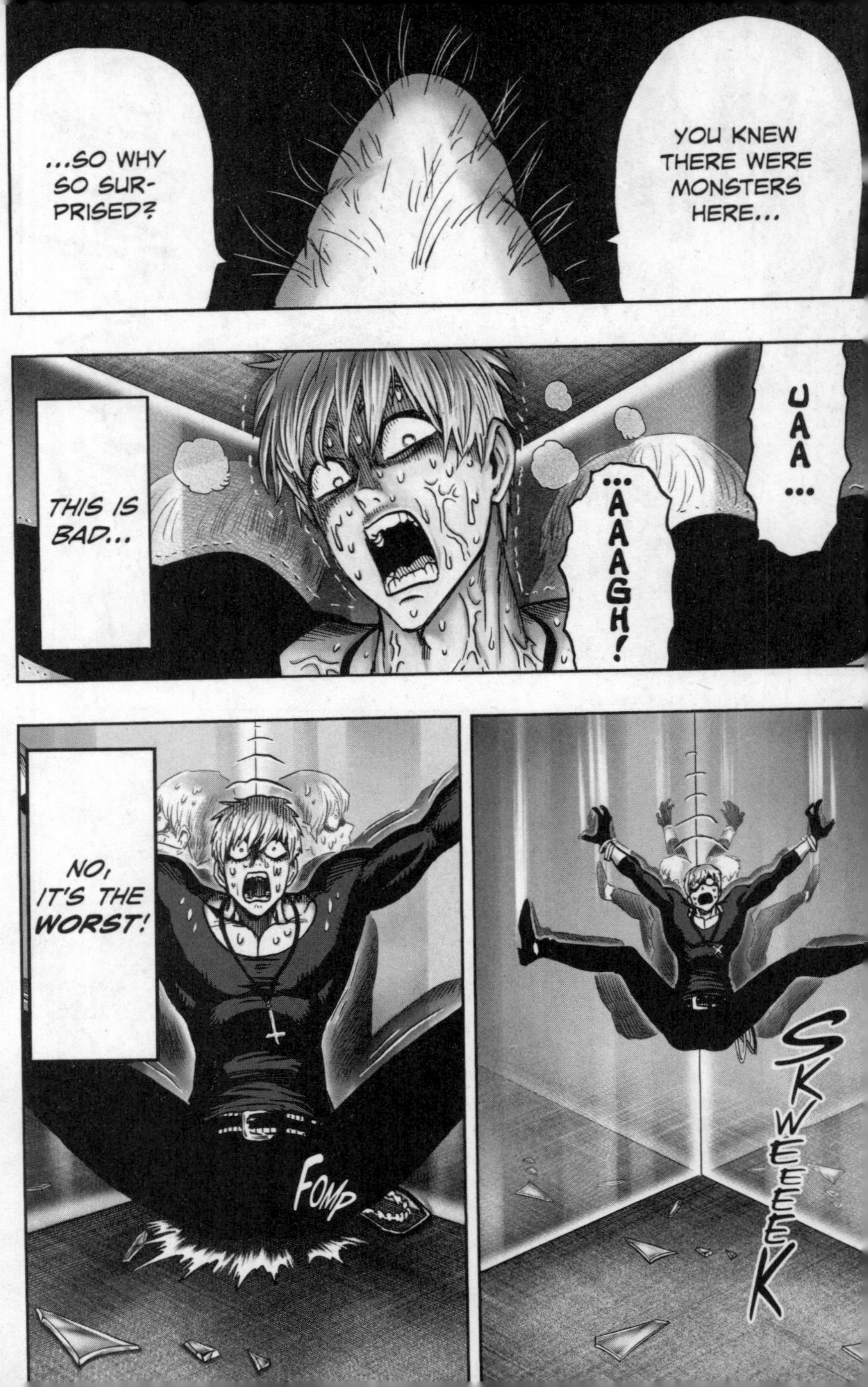
YOU KNEW THERE WERE MONSTERS HERE...
...SO WHY SO SUR-PRISED?
UAA...
...ÄAAAGH!
THIS IS BAD...
SKWEEEEK
NO, IT'S THE **WORST!**
FOMP

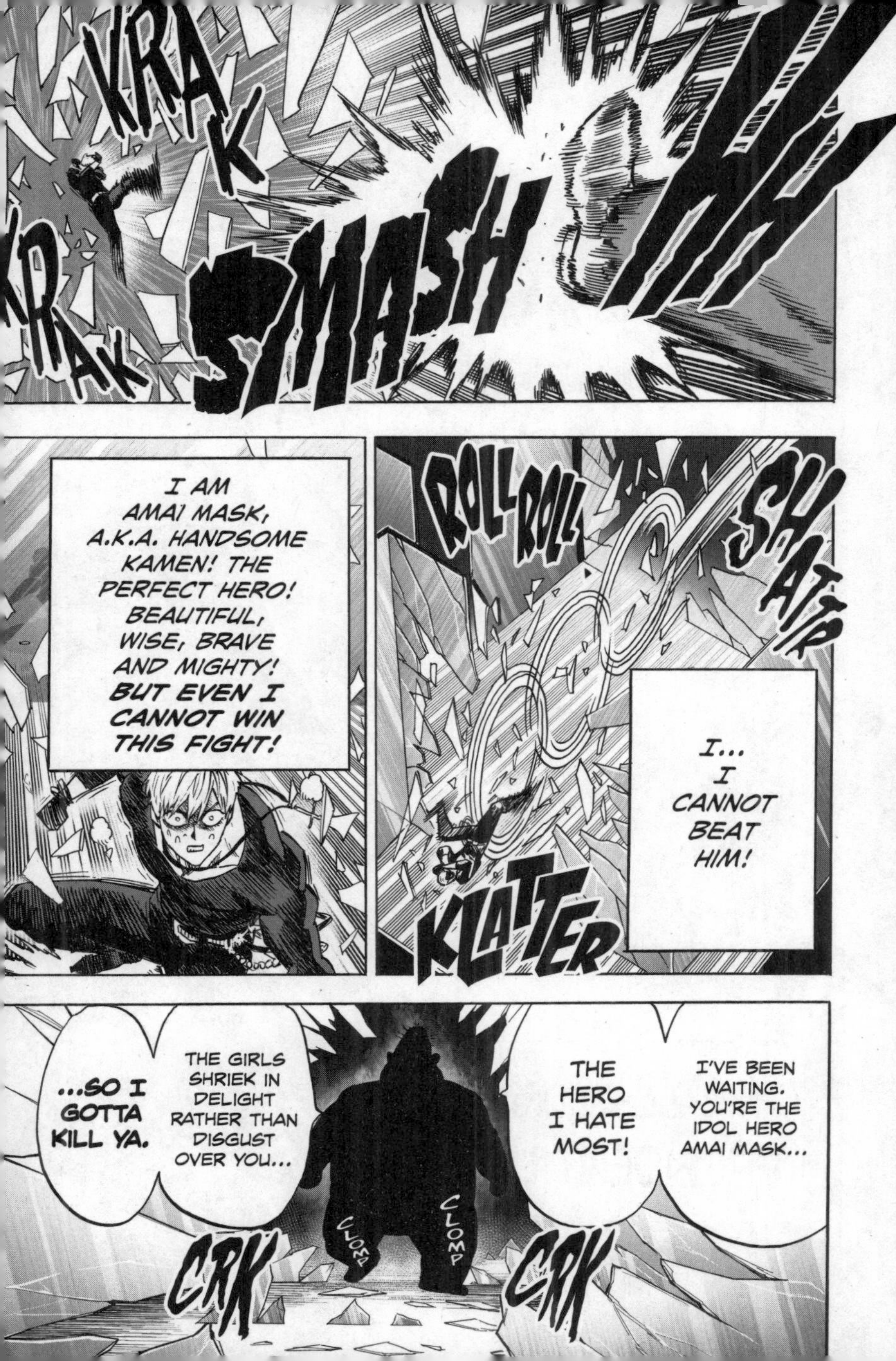
SMASH
KRAK
ROLL ROLL
SHATTR
I... I CANNOT BEAT HIM!
KLATTER
I AM AMAI MASK, A.K.A. HANDSOME KAMEN! THE PERFECT HERO! BEAUTIFUL, WISE, BRAVE AND MIGHTY! BUT EVEN I CANNOT WIN THIS FIGHT!
I'VE BEEN WAITING. YOU'RE THE IDOL HERO AMAI MASK...
THE HERO I HATE MOST!
THE GIRLS SHRIEK IN DELIGHT RATHER THAN DISGUST OVER YOU...
...SO I GOTTA KILL YA.
CLOMP
CLOMP
CRK
CRK

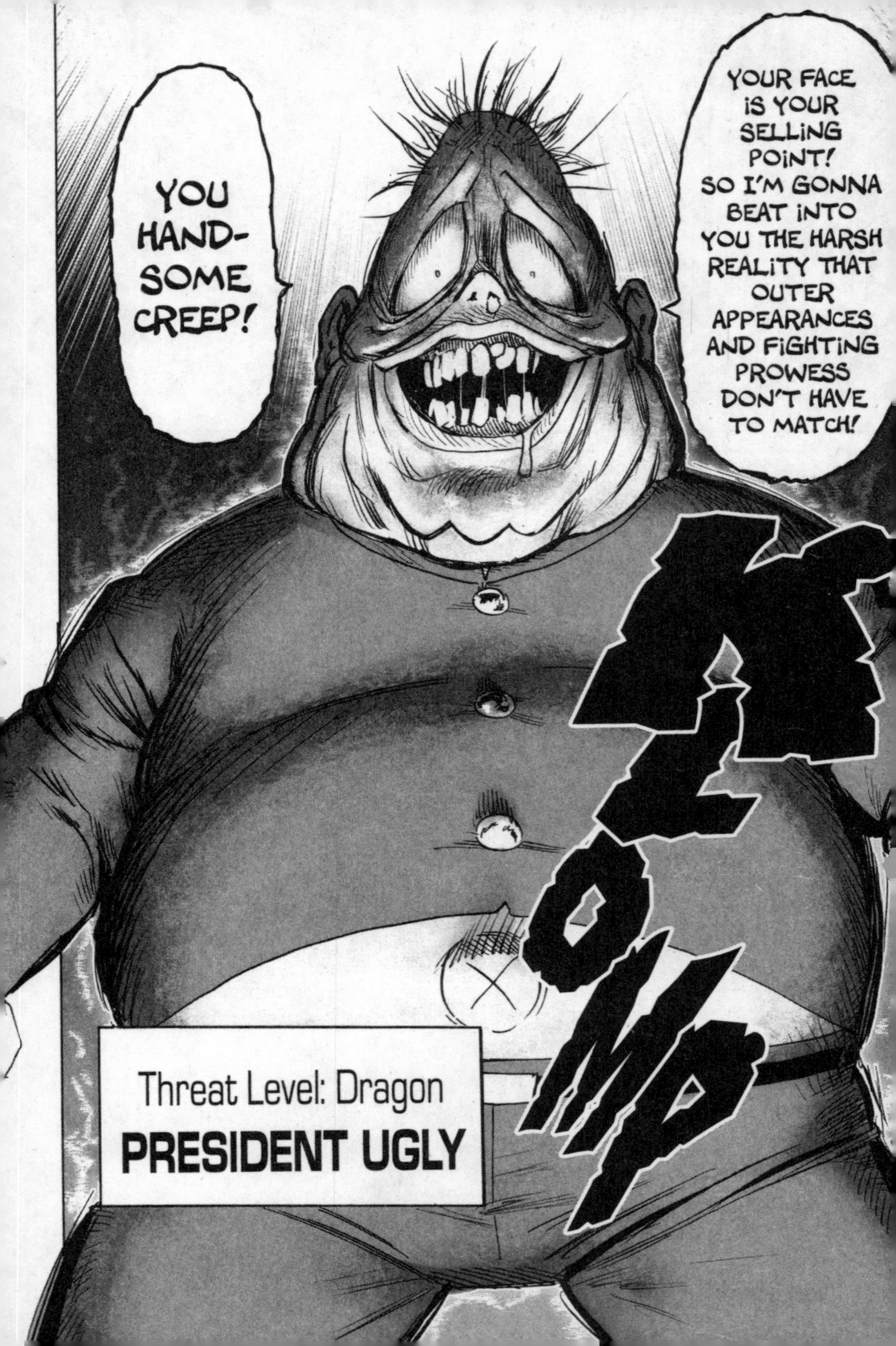
YOUR FACE IS YOUR SELLING POINT! SO I'M GONNA BEAT INTO YOU THE HARSH REALITY THAT OUTER APPEARANCES AND FIGHTING PROWESS DON'T HAVE TO MATCH!
YOU HAND-SOME CREEP!
Threat Level: Dragon
PRESIDENT UGLY

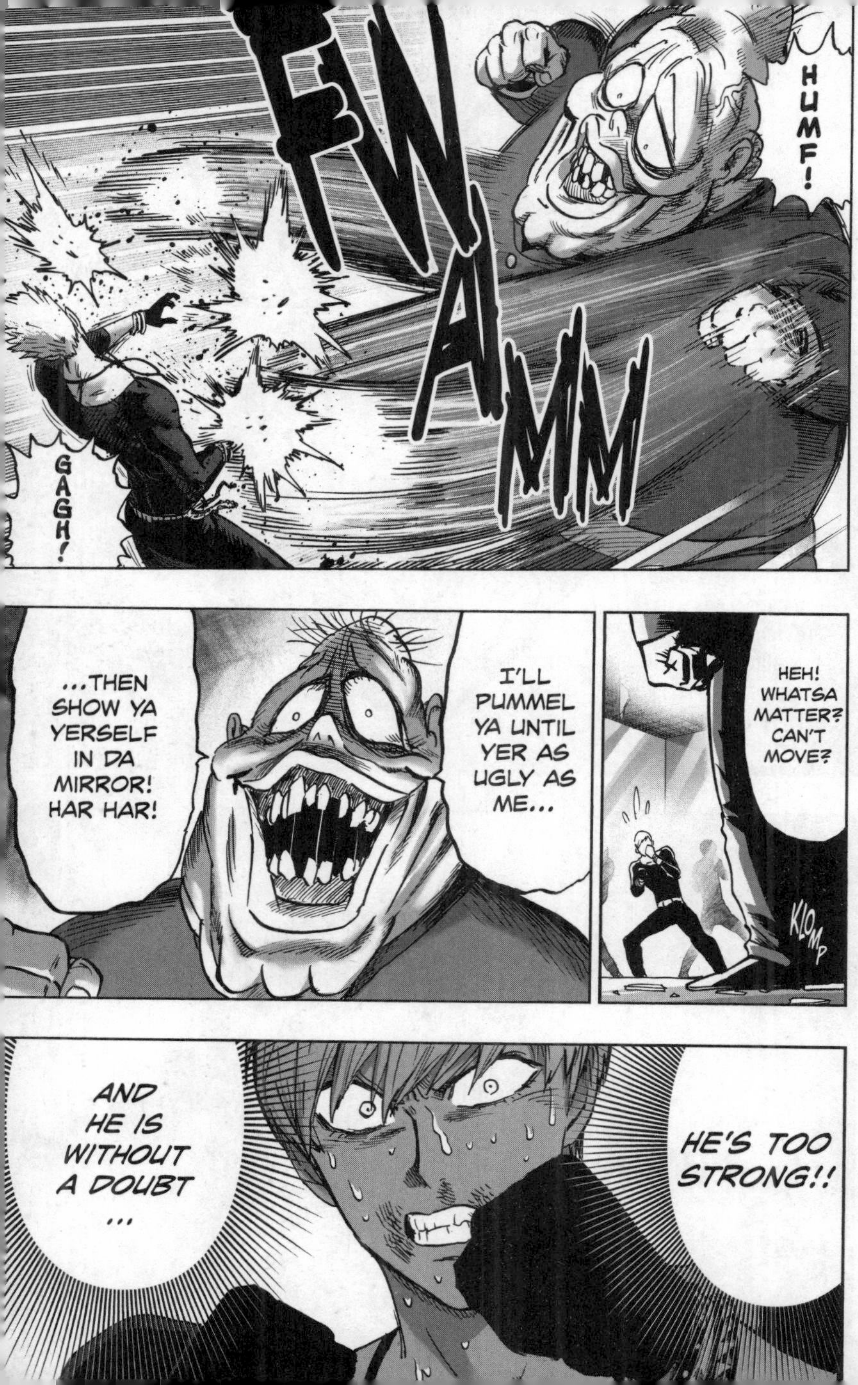
HUMF!
FWAMM
GAGH!
HEH! WHATSA MATTER? CAN'T MOVE?
KLOMP
I'LL PUMMEL YA UNTIL YER AS UGLY AS ME...
...THEN SHOW YA YERSELF IN DA MIRROR! HAR HAR!
HE'S TOO STRONG!!
AND HE IS WITHOUT A DOUBT ...

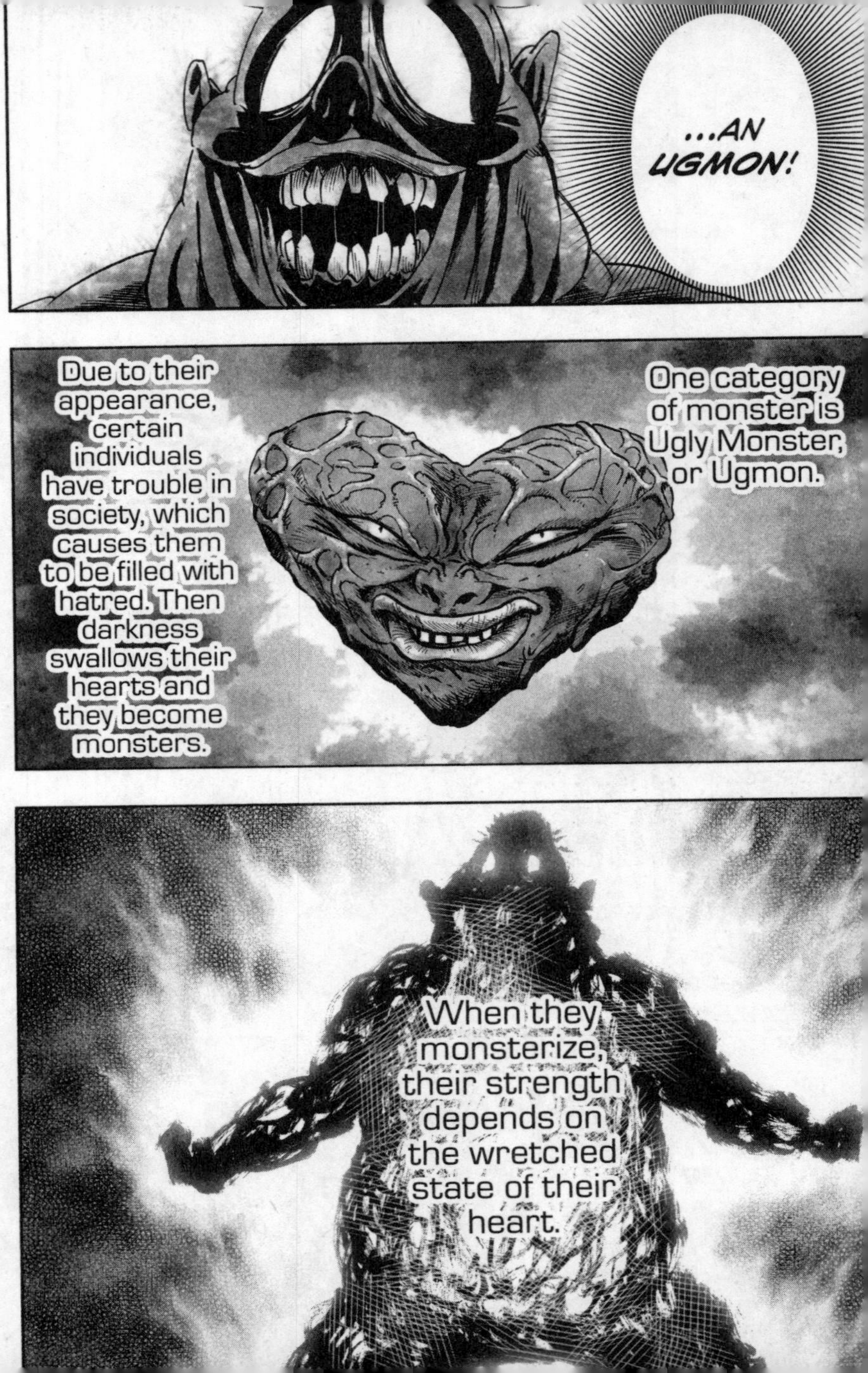
...AN UGMON!
One category of monster is Ugly Monster, or Ugmon.
Due to their appearance, certain individuals have trouble in society, which causes them to be filled with hatred. Then darkness swallows their hearts and they become monsters.
When they monsterize, their strength depends on the wretched state of their heart.

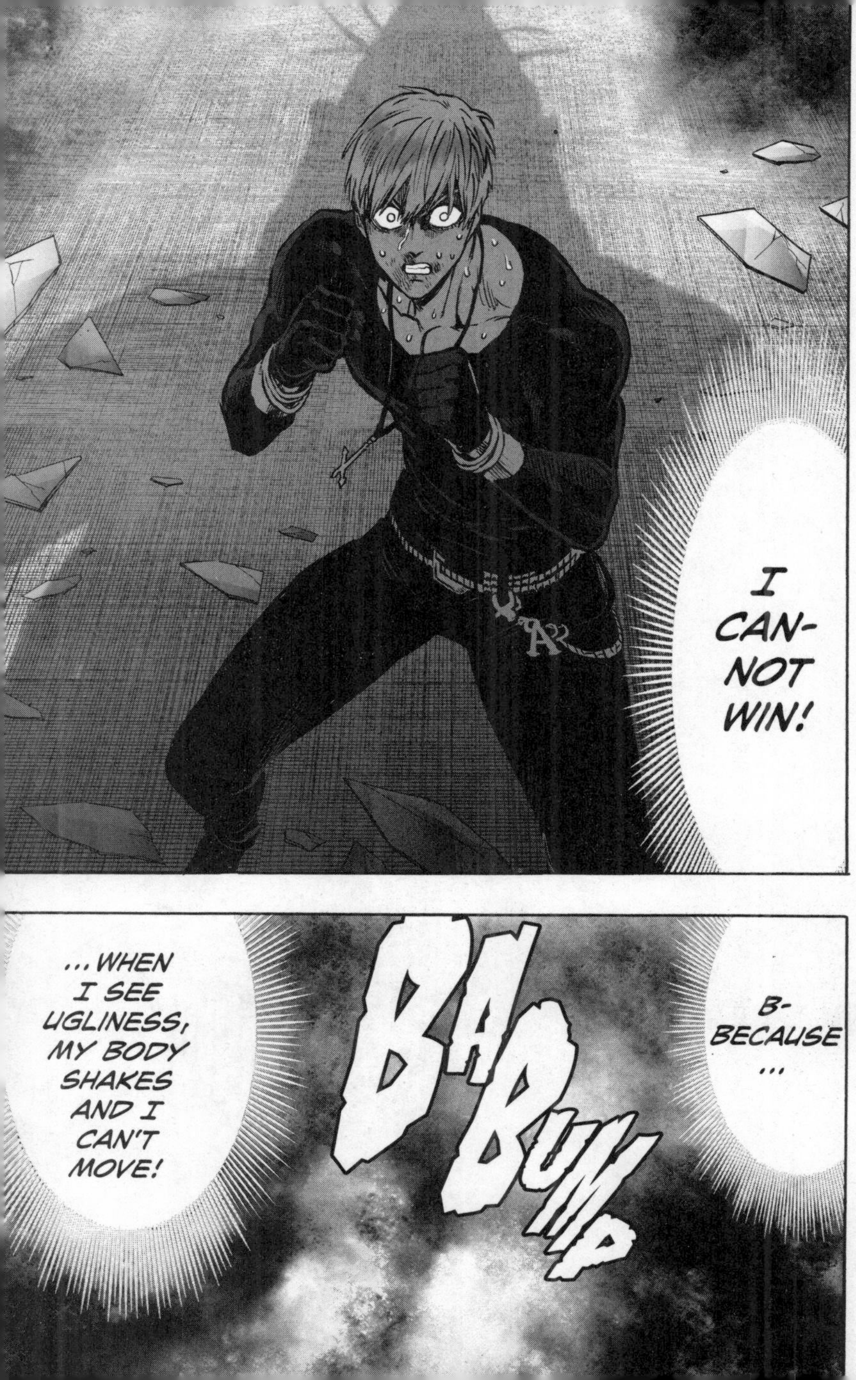
I CAN-NOT WIN!
B-BECAUSE ...
BA-BUMP
...WHEN I SEE UGLINESS, MY BODY SHAKES AND I CAN'T MOVE!

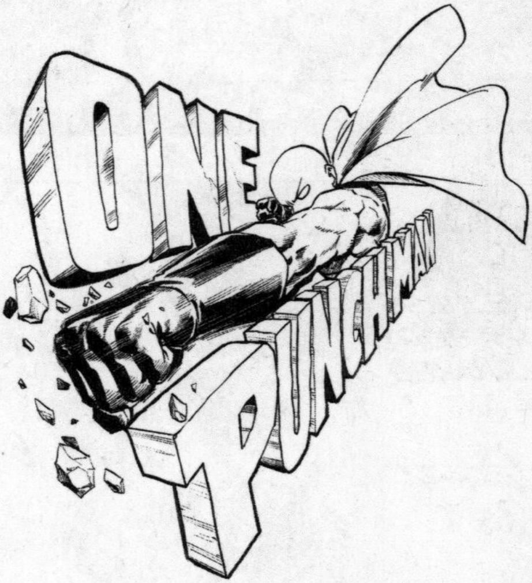
ONE
PUNCHMAN

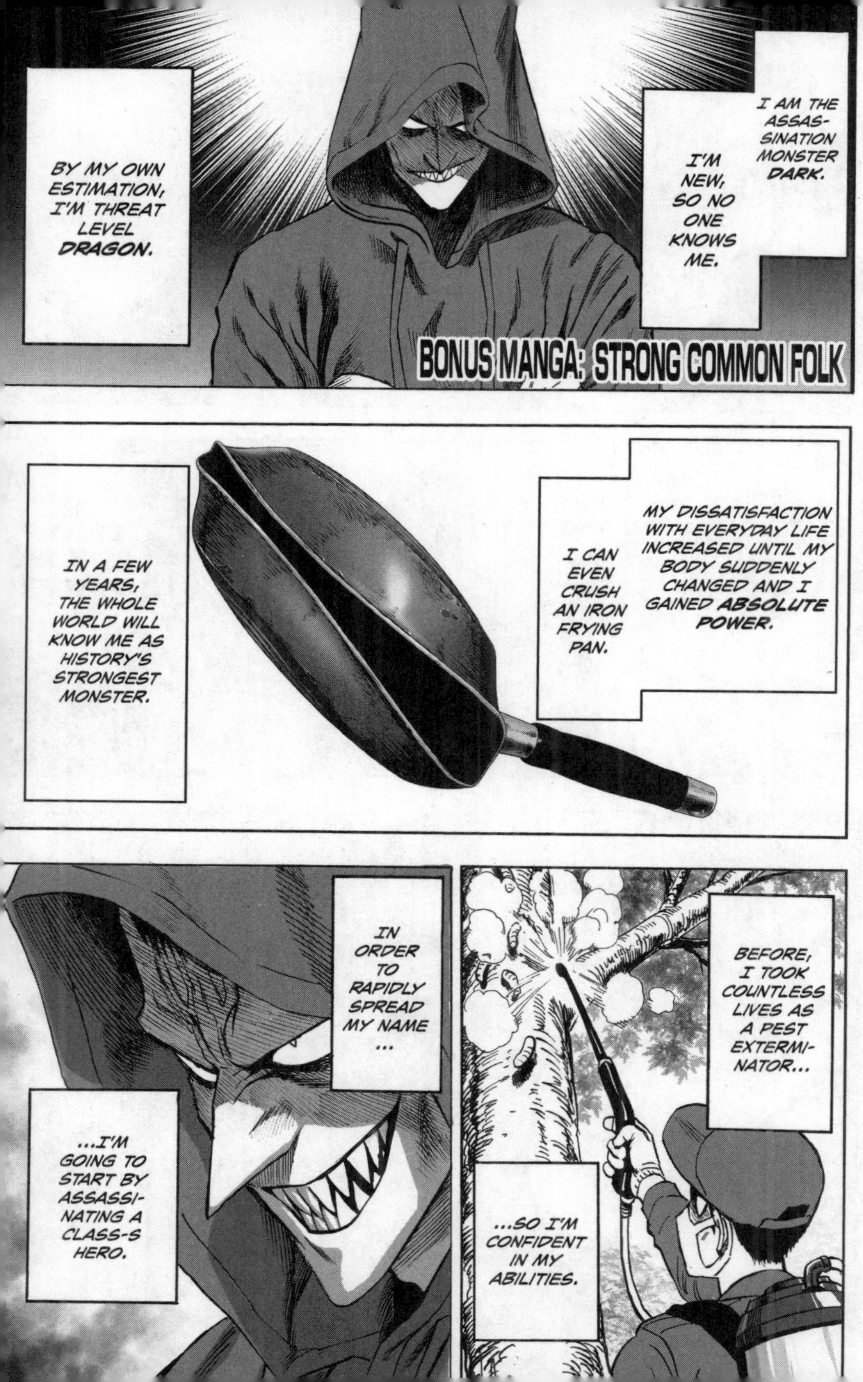
I AM THE ASSASSINATION MONSTER DARK.
I'M NEW, SO NO ONE KNOWS ME.
BY MY OWN ESTIMATION, I'M THREAT LEVEL DRAGON.
BONUS MANGA: STRONG COMMON FOLK
MY DISSATISFACTION WITH EVERYDAY LIFE INCREASED UNTIL MY BODY SUDDENLY CHANGED AND I GAINED ABSOLUTE POWER.
I CAN EVEN CRUSH AN IRON FRYING PAN.
IN A FEW YEARS, THE WHOLE WORLD WILL KNOW ME AS HISTORY'S STRONGEST MONSTER.
BEFORE, I TOOK COUNTLESS LIVES AS A PEST EXTERMINATOR...
...SO I'M CONFIDENT IN MY ABILITIES.
IN ORDER TO RAPIDLY SPREAD MY NAME...
...I'M GOING TO START BY ASSASSINATING A CLASS-S HERO.

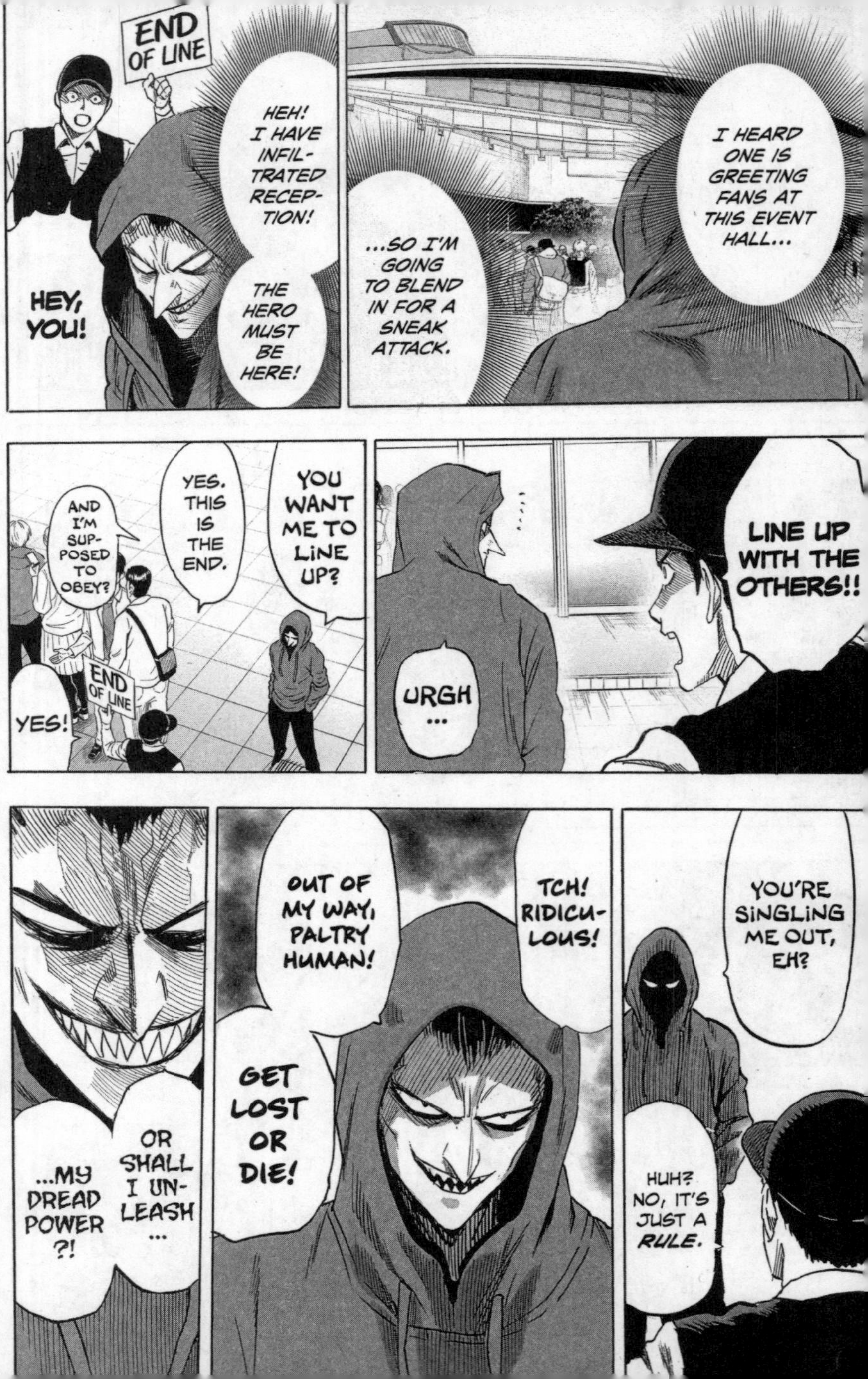
I HEARD ONE IS GREETING FANS AT THIS EVENT HALL...
...SO I'M GOING TO BLEND IN FOR A SNEAK ATTACK.
END OF LINE
HEH! I HAVE INFILTRATED RECEPTION!
THE HERO MUST BE HERE!
HEY, YOU!
LINE UP WITH THE OTHERS!!
...
URGH ...
YOU WANT ME TO LINE UP?
YES. THIS IS THE END.
AND I'M SUPPOSED TO OBEY?
YES!
END OF LINE
YOU'RE SINGLING ME OUT, EH?
HUH? NO, IT'S JUST A *RULE*.
TCH! RIDICULOUS!
OUT OF MY WAY, PALTRY HUMAN!
GET LOST OR DIE!
OR SHALL I UNLEASH ...
...MY DREAD POWER?!

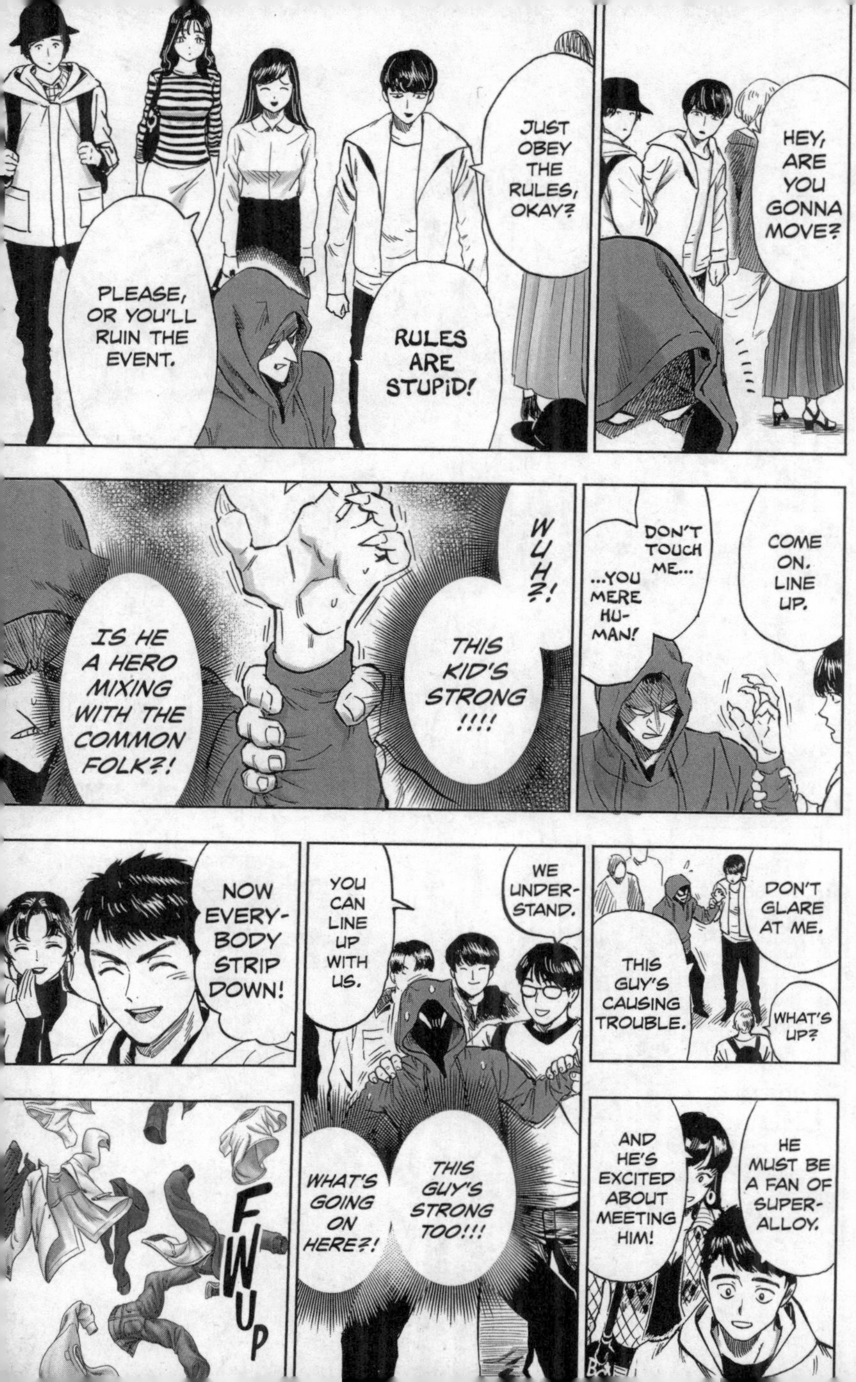
HEY, ARE YOU GONNA MOVE?
JUST OBEY THE RULES, OKAY?
RULES ARE STUPID!
PLEASE, OR YOU'LL RUIN THE EVENT.
COME ON. LINE UP.
DON'T TOUCH ME...
...YOU MERE HU-MAN!
WUH?!
THIS KID'S STRONG!!!!
IS HE A HERO MIXING WITH THE COMMON FOLK?!
DON'T GLARE AT ME.
THIS GUY'S CAUSING TROUBLE.
WHAT'S UP?
HE MUST BE A FAN OF SUPER-ALLOY.
AND HE'S EXCITED ABOUT MEETING HIM!
WE UNDER-STAND.
YOU CAN LINE UP WITH US.
THIS GUY'S STRONG TOO!!!
WHAT'S GOING ON HERE?!
NOW EVERY-BODY STRIP DOWN!
FWUP

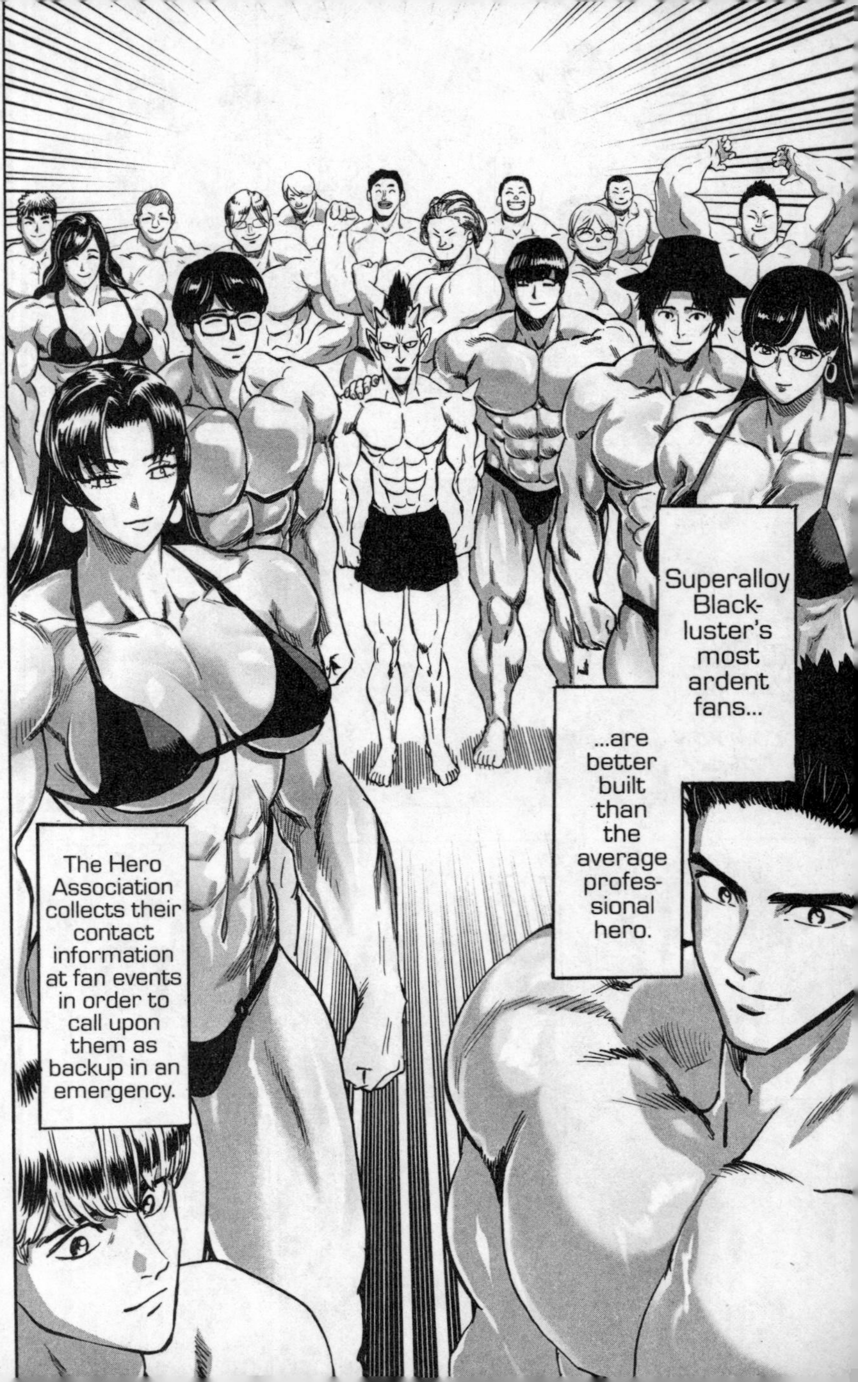
Superalloy Black-luster's most ardent fans...
...are better built than the average profes-sional hero.
The Hero Association collects their contact information at fan events in order to call upon them as backup in an emergency.

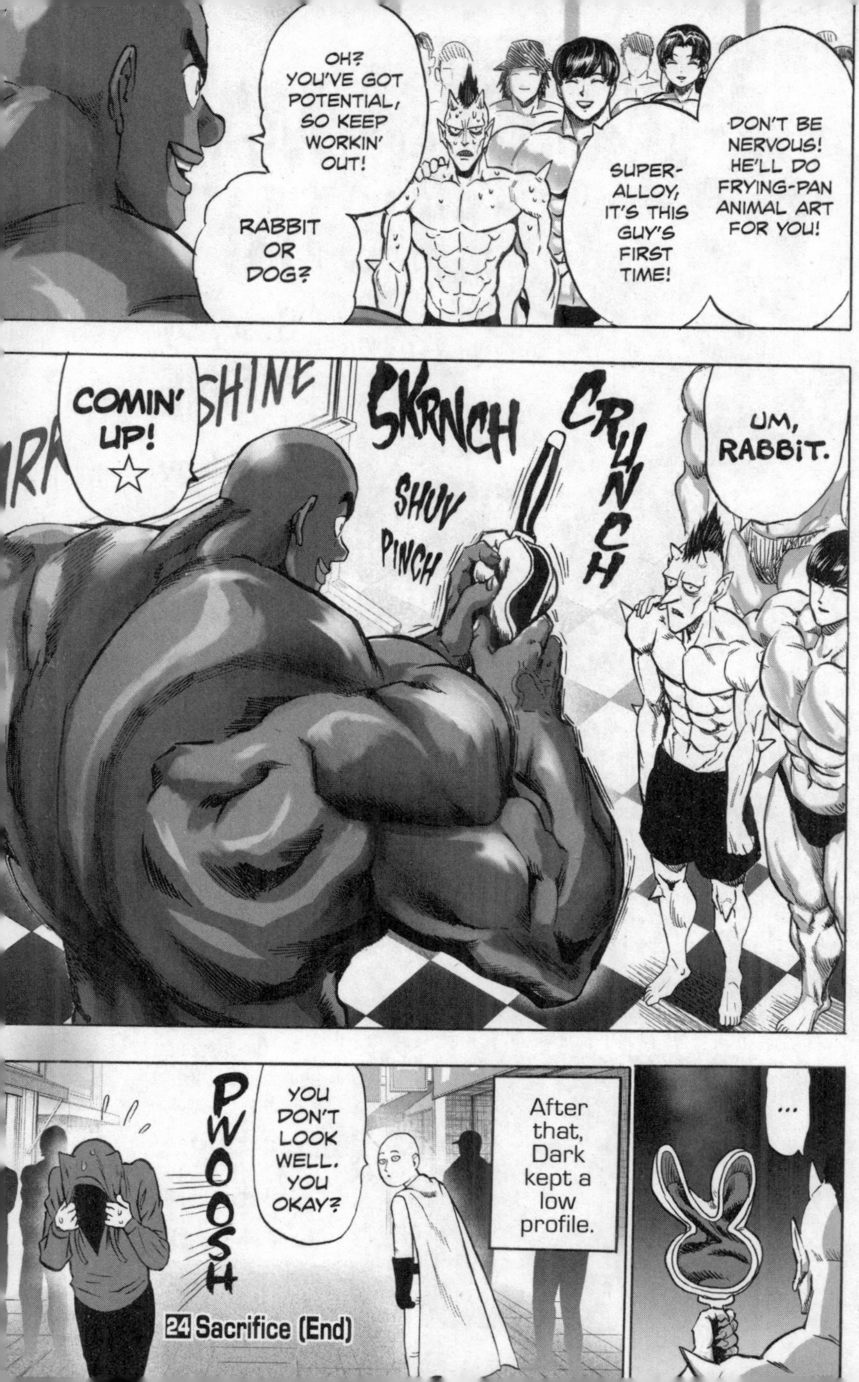
DON'T BE NERVOUS! HE'LL DO FRYING-PAN ANIMAL ART FOR YOU!
SUPER-ALLOY, IT'S THIS GUY'S FIRST TIME!
OH? YOU'VE GOT POTENTIAL, SO KEEP WORKIN' OUT!
RABBIT OR DOG?
UM, RABBIT.
CRUNCH
SKRNCH
SHUV
PINCH
SHINE
COMIN' UP! ☆
...
After that, Dark kept a low profile.
YOU DON'T LOOK WELL. YOU OKAY?
PWOOSH
24 Sacrifice (End)

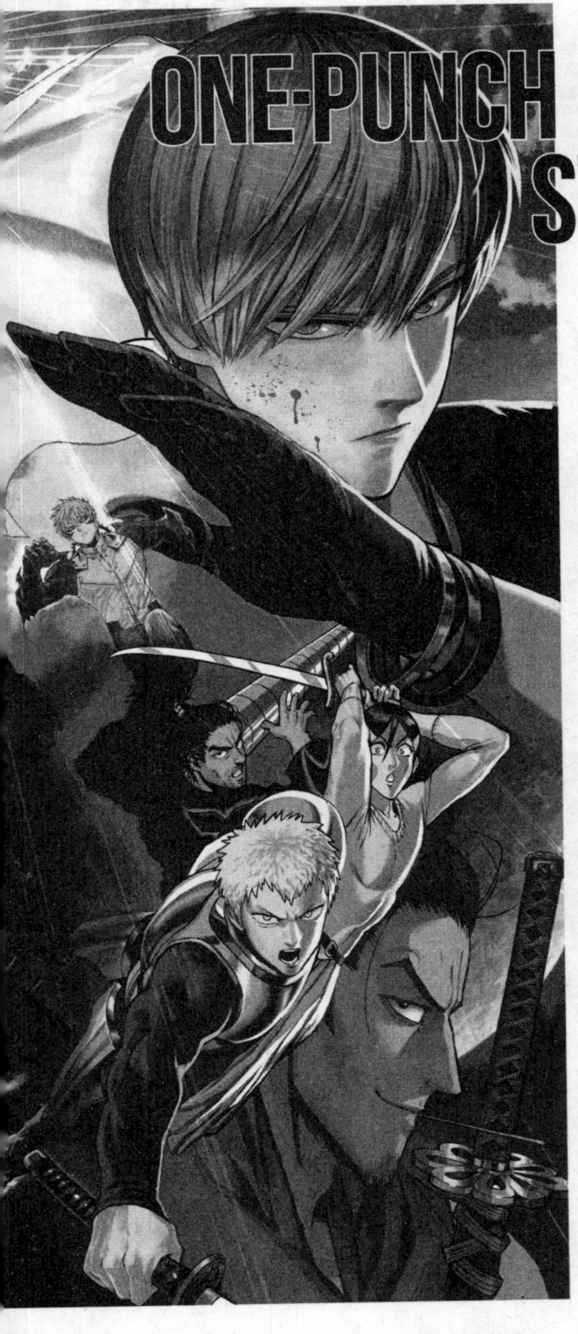

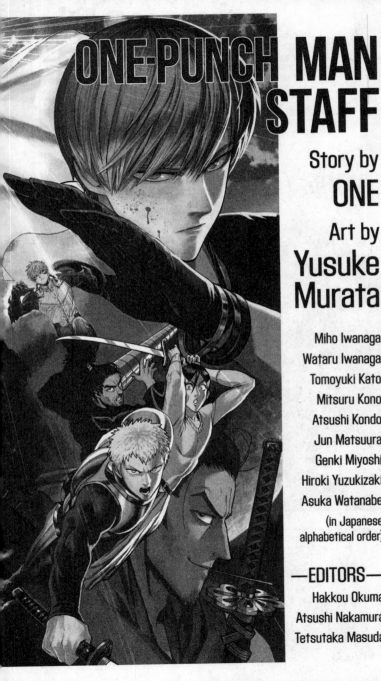

ONE-PUNCH MAN STAFF

Story by
ONE

Art by
Yusuke Murata

Miho Iwanaga
Wataru Iwanaga
Tomoyuki Kato
Mitsuru Kono
Atsushi Kondo
Jun Matsuura
Genki Miyoshi
Hiroki Yuzukizaki
Asuka Watanabe
(in Japanese alphabetical order)

—EDITORS—
Hakkou Okuma
Atsushi Nakamura
Tetsutaka Masuda

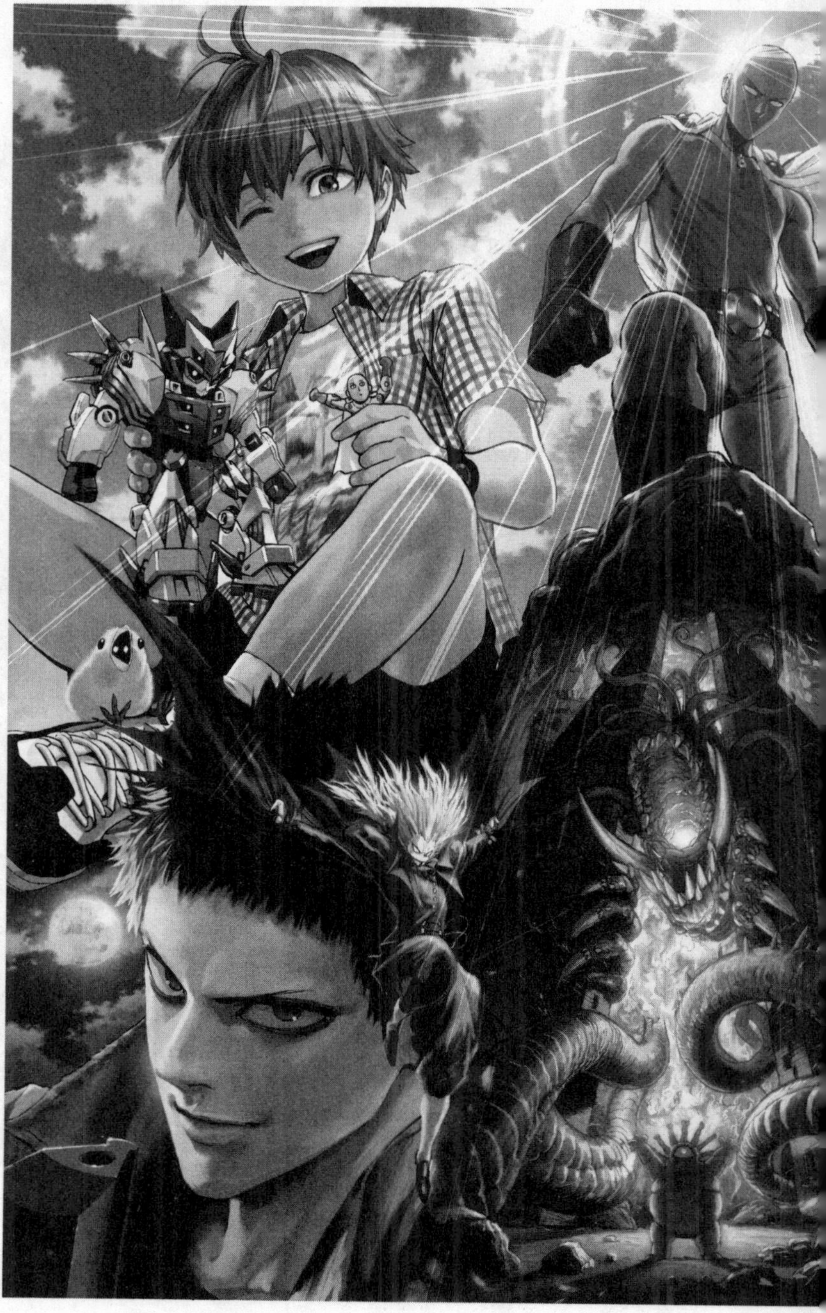

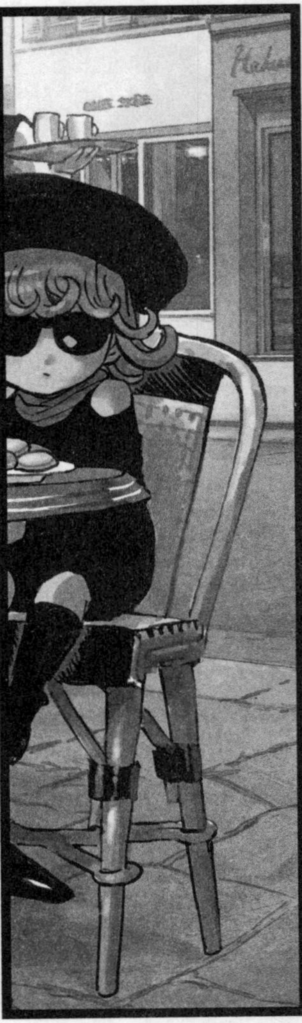

ONE-PUNCH MAN

VOLUME 24

SHONEN JUMP MANGA EDITION

STORY BY | ONE
ART BY | YUSUKE MURATA

TRANSLATION | JOHN WERRY
TOUCH-UP ART AND LETTERING | JAMES GAUBATZ
DESIGN | SHAWN CARRICO
EDITOR | JOHN BAE

First published in Japan in 2012 by SHUEISHA Inc., Tokyo.
English translation rights arranged by SHUEISHA Inc.

Printed in the U.S.A.

Published by VIZ Media, LLC
P.O. Box 77010
San Francisco, CA 94107

10 9 8 7 6 5 4 3 2 1
First printing, November 2022

VIZ MEDIA
viz.com

SHONEN JUMP

RATED T TEEN
ratings.viz.com

PARENTAL ADVISORY
ONE-PUNCH MAN is rated T for Teen and is recommended for ages 13 and up. This volume contains realistic and fantasy violence.

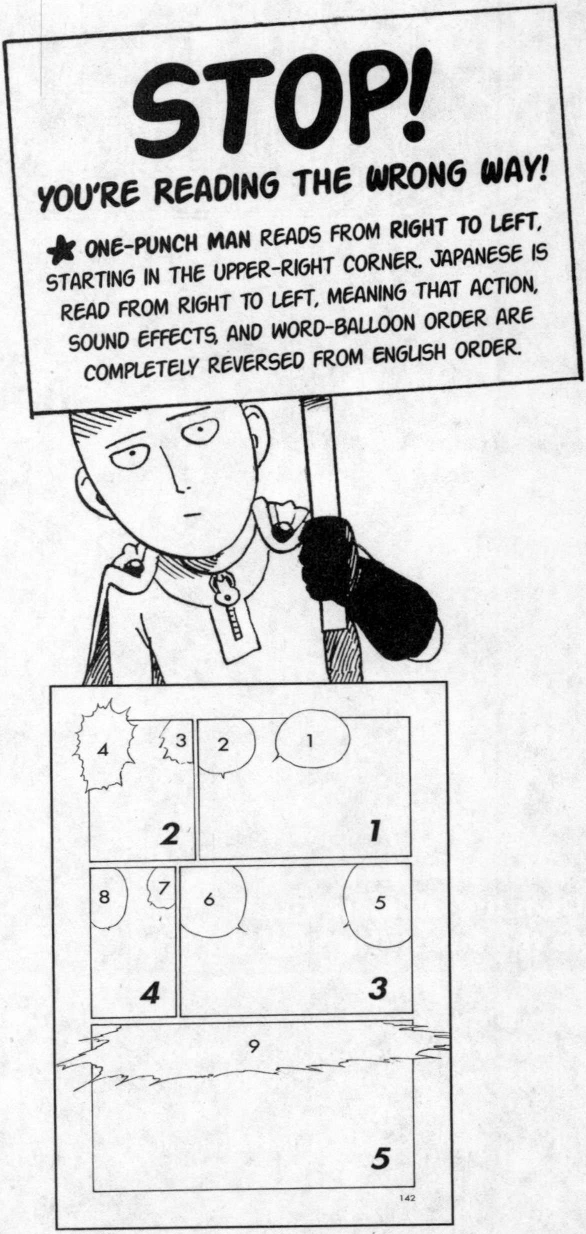
STOP!
YOU'RE READING THE WRONG WAY!
ONE-PUNCH MAN READS FROM RIGHT TO LEFT, STARTING IN THE UPPER-RIGHT CORNER. JAPANESE IS READ FROM RIGHT TO LEFT, MEANING THAT ACTION, SOUND EFFECTS, AND WORD-BALLOON ORDER ARE COMPLETELY REVERSED FROM ENGLISH ORDER.
1
2
3
4
5
6
7
8
9
1
2
3
4
5
142